Handy Household Hints

from

Handy Household Hints

from

Hundreds of Great Ideas at Your Fingertips

RODALE

Icon art © iStock photo
Book design by Christopher Rhoads

Library of Congress Cataloging-in-Publication Data

Heloise.
  Handy household hints from Heloise.
      p.   cm.
  Includes index.
  ISBN-13 978–1–60529–587–9 hardcover
  ISBN-10 1–60529–587–6 hardcover
  1. Home economics. I. Title.
TX158.H433 2009
640—dc22   2009015612

10   9   hardcover

RODALE
LIVE YOUR WHOLE LIFE™

We inspire and enable people to improve their lives and the world around them
For more of our products visit **rodalestore.com** or call 800-848-4735

THIS BOOK IS DEDICATED TO MY MOTHER the original Heloise (1919–1977), who started the newspaper column *Hints from Heloise* in 1959, and to my father, Mike Cruse (1920–2006), who supported her and encouraged her. Like my husband, David, he put up with a lot of travel and work! My mother started out with the sole purpose to help other women get through their day! Housework, taking care of kids and husbands, doing volunteer work, working for pay! So many things and so little time. She knew that others faced the same problems as she did and thought "why don't we help each other"? So in a way, I like to think she started one of the first "social networks" before we even thought of the term.

Today, *Hints from Heloise* and all that it encompasses—from newspaper columns, magazines, books, speeches, television, radio, Web site, podcast, e-mail and more—still stands for the same purpose . . . to provide you with trusted, tested, and safe information.

I am here to help you! I will test the hints, check with experts, and tell you what is and is *not* safe! Also, to everyone who has asked a question or shared a hint, I thank you!

Women, men, young, old, teenagers and oldster, you are all part of *Hints from Heloise*.

Contents

PART 1: HOME MATTERS

Bust That Clutter!

Reuse and Recycle

Storage Tips

Donate What You Can't Use

Toss the Trash

Organize Your Stuff

Shopping

Garage Sales

Kitchen

Bathroom

Floors

Walls, Windows, Blinds, and Drapes

Furniture and Furnishings

Cleaning Products, Materials, and Tools

Vacuuming

Dusting

Getting Rid of Odors

Cleaning Tech Gear

Pants and Jeans

Shirts, Blouses, Sweaters, and Dresses

Shoes and Socks

Hats, Scarves, and Other Accessories

Lingerie and Undies

Jewelry

Storing and Organizing Clothes

De-Lint, De-Static, Repair

Linens and Bedding

Laundry

Organizing and Sorting the Laundry

Laundry How-To

Washing Machines and Their Use

Stain Removal

Drying and Dryers

Ironing

Contents

PART 2: LIFE, SIMPLIFIED

Contents

Acknowledgments

Hints from Heloise has been sharing helpful information for 50 years—this year! When my mother, the original Heloise, started her newspaper column in 1959, in Honolulu, Hawaii, I don't think she could have imagined it lasting this long or in so many forms—from newspapers, magazines, books, pamphlets, and speeches to TV, radio, Internet, e-mail, and text messaging.

Over the 50 years, there have been many people who worked with my mother, and me, since I took over in 1977, when she died. This includes secretaries and assistants, reporters, chemists, plumbers, lawyers, and more.

A special thanks to all of the wonderful folks who sent in their favorite hint; others, who asked questions or needed help with a problem.

Today, my reliable, faithful, and always upbeat editorial director, Merry Clark, is the person who helps keep ME on track and helps me get things done!

My husband, David, who has always been so supportive and put up with all of my deadlines! I don't think he would know what to do if I said, "Oh, there's nothing pressing!"

The team at Rodale IS just the absolute best. They made this book happen, and they deserve a big Heloise Hug and thanks for making the process one of the least stressful I have ever had doing a book!

Thanks also to the editing team, who made my job easy, and to the design team, who just made this so much fun. I love the graphics and the book cover. My contact, Denise, has been wonderful to work with!

Thanks to everyone who had a finger in the pie!

Heloise
2009

Introduction

Making life easier, solving problems, preventing disasters, and sharing hints has been the backbone of *Hints from Heloise* for 50 years! When my mother, the original Heloise, started her newspaper column in 1959, all she wanted to do was help "her housewives." My daddy was in the air force, and as a military wife, she moved around often—as most military families do—and learned to make a home no matter where we were.

Her premise was, "If you have a problem, write me. If I know the answer, I'll print it; if I don't, I'll go to the expert who does! And, if there still isn't a solution, I'll put it in the paper and surely one of the readers has 'been there, done that!'" So, in a way, she started her special kind of social networking—woman to woman!

The old saying—that no matter how much things change, they stay the same—holds true today. We may have microfiber fabrics and high-tech gadgets and electronics to help us do just about everything, but the basic chores of daily life still need attention. Yup, someone still has to feed the dog or cat, take out the garbage, pick up the shoes, load the dishwasher, run the laundry, make the beds, vacuum, dust, and, oh yes, I forgot . . . clean the kitchen! Even with every modern convenience available today, the kitchen counters collect crumbs and someone has to wipe them off!

A Heloise Hint: Think through what you are doing first, rather than just grab a cleaner or spray something on a surface. Find out what your products do and how to use them (read the labels). Many people have not had the advantage to be taught some basic life skills, such as how to clean a toilet or vacuum the carpet. Not sexy I'm sure, but necessary to know! *Handy Household Hints from Heloise* will assist you.

This book offers some tried-and-true hints that have been around for a long time, but are still valid as of the writing of this book. It also has other hints that we have updated. Many earlier hints are no longer safe or don't work! There also are many new, effective products to help in the process. For example, DON'T use window cleaner on your TV screen. Old screens were glass; today there are plasma, LCD flat panels and rear-projection screens, which need different cleaning care.

Here is a hint from me to you. When in doubt, put on your Heloise hat and ask yourself, is this safe, will it work, is there a caution that I should know? Stop, plan the process through, then go on.

You will find icons all through the book to make it easy for you to spot a hint! The five icons are:

Thumb through the pages and you'll start to recognize them. These handy Hints from Heloise will be helpful to you!

A final thought: No matter how small or large a chore, there is a Heloise hint that will make your task easier. When all else fails, it's more important to spend time with your family, friends, and yourself! Dust and dirt can wait until tomorrow! Take a few minutes out of each day to spend on YOU! I think enjoying 5 minutes off is a good mental health break! So sit down and be comfortable, put up your feet, if you can, take a deep breath, and relax! You deserve it.

 Timesaver

 Creative Solutions

 Tech Tip

 Earth-Friendly

 Memory Booster

Home Matters

Welcome home! This first part of the book is all about dealing with your stuff—how to organize it, how to clean it, and how to get rid of clutter and make the most of what you've got. There are chapters dealing with storing your clothes and doing laundry, and caring for your furniture and the things in your home. You'll also find loads of tips on maintaining your home, indoors and out. And since many of us keep an office at home, there are hints on using that space to the best advantage.

Chapter 1

Clutter Busters and Organizers

This chapter is all about getting control of your stuff. The first step is to get rid of clutter—the stuff you don't use and don't need. You will find loads of hints for reusing or recycling the items you don't want anymore. There are also creative ideas for using household items in new

Clutter Busting 101

Here are some ways to stop clutter from controlling your home and life. It seems every closet and room is filled with too much stuff!

First, learn my clutter-busting motto: "A few minutes or a few things." Every day, take just a few minutes to clean up or to pick up just a few items. You'll be surprised how easy it can be to keep on top of things.

Here are seven hints for stopping that clutter from taking over:

1. If you can't locate what you are searching for in several minutes, it's time to rethink where things belong. The more often you use an item, the closer it should be.

2. Enlist the whole family, not just Mom, to climb on the decluttering and organizing bandwagon.

3. If one room or area is beginning to look messy and cluttered, tackle it ASAP!

4. Give the living room, den, or common area a quick pickup before going to bed.

5. Toss out or put papers in the recycle bin every day, including newspapers and magazines.

6. Keep lists or inventories of what you already have. If you don't need it, don't buy it.

7. If something new comes into your home, many people say something old should go out.

and different ways. You'll see tips on donating and selling things, too. Then, you've got to organize the stuff you have left, and you'll find lots of suggestions for organizing all around the house. So dig in!

BUST THAT CLUTTER!

Take little steps to get control of your life. Little steps throughout the week can add up to big changes (and less to do) in the long run.

- Clean one shelf in the refrigerator, freezer, or makeup or medicine cabinet. Throw out dated, old, smelly, or just plain bad items.

- Write one thank-you, hello-how-are-you, or thinking-of-you note or letter a week. I mean a real letter or note that is mailed with a stamp and for which you hand-address the envelope. Not e-mail, but handwritten. It can be just a few lines, but it will be much appreciated and probably kept!

- Take a few minutes each week to clean out and toss trash from a purse, briefcase, or auto glove compartment. I have one friend who cleans out her purse (sitting next to

a trash can if possible) while waiting (and sometimes waiting and waiting) in a doctor's office.

- Have a houseplant that needs a little extra care? Move it to a spot that you will see daily so you can give it the PLC (plant loving care) that it deserves.

- Go through magazines and books and see which ones (even if only a few) can be passed on or recycled.

Pick up as you go. Never carry one item to its place without looking for others needing to be put away in the same spot. Whenever you leave one room to go to another, look around to see if there is anything you can take with you to another room. Always check, on your return, for items needing to go to your next destination. It will make picking up easier, and rooms will stay uncluttered.

Downsize now. Don't wait until you are forced to downsize in older age. Start doing it now. Once a year, go through jewelry boxes and take an inventory. Some pieces may no longer have any use to you (pierced earrings when you use clip-on styles, or other articles no longer appropriate for your age or circumstances).

Bundle up items you no longer like or are able to wear and give them to your favorite charity thrift store.

Some items may no longer be wearable but have great sentimental value. Keep those in a special box. When you are feeling blue, they will comfort you. As for the others, wear them. Wear them while shopping, going to work, or on outings, and they will remind you of happy times—and remind you to slow down and smell the roses.

Once a year, go through those closets. Put aside the pocketbooks and belts that are too small or too large, dresses that no longer fit, and those nearly new shoes that are uncomfortable, as well as all the

---

My Five-Point Plan for Busting Clutter

Are your organizing and cleaning chores overwhelming you? Does clutter control your household? Don't let it! What you need to do is try my five-point plan for clutter control. You either spend only 5 minutes or deal with only five items at a time. You would really be surprised at what you can accomplish in just a few minutes. Here's a room-to-room guide with suggestions of a few things you can do in just 5 minutes!

Bathroom
—Wipe off the counter and sink.
—Clean out one drawer.
—Clean the mirror.
—Toss five outdated medicines or makeup items.
—Clean the toilet.

Bedroom
—Clean under the bed.
—Do a quick dusting.
—Organize one drawer.
—Straighten the top of the dresser.
—Go through magazines and books.

Kitchen
—Give one shelf in the fridge a quick wipe-down.
—Wipe off the top of the refrigerator/cabinets.
—Clean the floor.
—Take out the garbage.
—Toss five things from the utilities drawer.

Living Room
—Do a quick top dusting.
—Clean and straighten coffee tables.
—Pick up and put away shoes, hats, and backpacks.
—Vacuum a chair or the sofa.
—Clean out one stereo or book cabinet.

Another way to get a lot of small things done is to do them during the commercial breaks while watching a favorite TV show. Give it a try, and you will be amazed!

scarves that go with outfits you no longer own.

Clean and bundle up this material and give it to your favorite charity thrift store. Don't replace anything unless you get rid of something first. You will revel in the empty closet space and feel good that someone else can enjoy your nice pieces.

Once a year, also go through your books, jigsaw puzzles, and games. Gather up glasses, plates, and pots and pans you no longer use. Your favorite charity thrift store will recycle them to new users.

Stash appliance cords. Appliance cords can clutter up kitchen counters when the appliances aren't in use. Make a nifty storage container to get each cord out of the way. Take an orange juice can that has been opened on both ends. (Drink the juice first!) Put some pretty adhesive-backed paper around the can that matches your kitchen. Unplug your cord and wind it inside the can.

Get rid of all those plastic bags. You can recycle plastic grocery bags, but the best way to rid your house of them is not to bring them home in the first place! Try to remember to take reusable cloth bags into the store when you go. You might also want to carry a few folded plastic bags in your coat pocket just in case you forget. But you won't have extras to deal with anymore.

Get rid of excess food boxes. Half-empty boxes of cocoa mixes, granola bars, and other packaged foods take up space in the pantry. If you have ample counter space, fill several baskets with the assorted packets and keep them on the counter with the fruit bowl. They look nice, the items are right at hand during the morning rush, and your pantry is now neater. Whenever you open a new box of some item, put all the individual packets right into a basket, and the box into the recycling bin. Who knows? You might just eat more oatmeal!

Declutter cleaning supplies. To get rid of clutter under the sink, hold an annual "spray meeting." Collect all the sprays and cleaning solutions below your kitchen and bathroom sinks in one place. Then sort them, making sure your kitchen and bathrooms have exactly the right sprays or cleaning products they will need. Redistribute a bottle if one bathroom has too much and another one has too little.

Use empty spray bottles bought at a discount store to create two bottles of one item (be sure to label both clearly).

Also, note the sprays you've forgotten you have. Take an inventory, and you might not need to buy new cleaning supplies for a while.

Avoid bathroom clutter. Keep some plastic grocery bags in your bathroom. In the morning, grab one and take a minute or two to walk through the house. Stop in each bathroom and empty trash and grab anything else that needs to be tossed. This daily patrol takes almost no time and prevents the dreaded full-trash-can dilemma.

Reduce bathroom trash. Remove and recycle all packaging on toothpaste, contact-lens cleaner, and other bathroom supplies before placing the items in cabinets. You'll cut down on waste in the bathroom.

Sort out the medicine cabinet. Organize your bathroom's medicine cabinet at least once a year by simply taking a good look at what has been building up behind that closed door. Keep your home medicines up to date and discard those that:

- Have expired

- Have contents, such as capsules, that are discolored, smashed, or cracked

- Are stuck together, or contain tablets that have become soft

- Show signs of deterioration, such as aspirin tablets that smell like vinegar

- Are in liquid form and have become separated

- Have lost their label, or the label has become illegible

Once you've weeded out the discards, arrange the remaining medications so the labels can be read easily, and keep them out of the reach of children. Never place any medications near insect repellent or mothballs—both can emit vapors that could be absorbed by a medication.

And while you're at it, place items used daily on lower shelves, along with first-aid items like bandages, antiseptics, creams, and salves, for easy access. Also, cold and cough supplies and thermometers can be stored on a higher shelf once the cold season has passed.

Declutter your multipurpose bedroom. Have you noticed lately that the bedroom is not just for sleeping anymore? It is now a hub of activity in many homes—reading, exercising, eating, dressing, watching TV, and working on the computer. But this is the room where we're supposed to be the most relaxed . . . and it seems clutter is everywhere! Here are some hints to help you get things in order. And, after the initial sprucing, just 5 minutes each morning should keep all these minor eyesores out of the way:

- Make the bed first thing, and the room immediately looks better!

- Pick up shoes or clothes that are lying around and put them away.

- Quickly straighten the tops of the dresser and nightstand(s)—the less on these surfaces, the cleaner they look.

- Put away reading material that's accumulated next to the bed, and don't overlook paperwork around a computer. A magazine rack or large basket strategically placed in the room would provide an organized home for these items.

- For the closet, organize shoes on a shoe rack to keep them off the floor, and sort and recycle unused hangers that take up space!

Remember, a quick 5-minute walk-through each day will help keep your bedroom in order. Time yourself—you will be amazed how much you can get done in just 5 minutes. Better yet, do the picking up during a TV commercial—why waste time?

Gain space in your closets. Could you use a little more closet space? Take out every hanger that's not holding a garment. Keep all those empty hangers in a laundry basket near your washer and dryer (or hang them on a towel rack mounted near your dryer) so they will be available when you remove your garments from the dryer.

Since even empty hangers take up space, you can gain as much as a foot or more of usable closet space simply by removing them.

Bust clutter with baskets. Baskets are a clutter-saver! You can use them to hold everything from hair accessories, books, and magazines to some of the "junk" that accumulates on your desk.

If you've got baskets that are dirty from neglect and long storage, clean them up first. Wash them in warm water and a little furniture soap, swish them vigorously, and use an old scrub brush or toothbrush to get dirt out of the cracks. Then rinse the baskets and let them air- or sun-dry.

Cut off unwanted catalogs. If you are receiving too many mail-order catalogs and duplicate catalogs, simply call the catalog's customer-service department's toll-free number and request that the catalogs be discontinued (or reduced to only one copy). If you are persistent, the catalogs will stop! Persist, persist, and they will stop one day.

This technique also works for unwanted mail, including donation requests from charities and other non-profit organizations. After donating to a charity, you probably don't want that money spent on additional direct-mail appeals to you. Once a year is enough!

Head off unwanted catalogs and save a tree. Here's another way to stop catalogs: Tear off the back page. Then go to the company's Web site and ask to be removed from the database. You could write something like "In order to save a tree, please remove my name from your database. Thank you." Then give your name and address as they appear on the catalog. You'll have fewer catalogs clogging your mailbox. You can always shop online.

Cut catalog clutter. Here's an easier way to order from a catalog and also get rid of a pile of catalogs sooner. Just tear out the page that has the item you want and the order form. The form usually has the phone number, account number or source code, and any other numbers needed. You might also want to save the front cover, and the back cover if it has the mailing label on it, because often the impor-tant numbers are on these pages. After ordering, just fold one inside the other and put them in a folder labeled "Awaiting Delivery." Recycle the rest of the catalog. No matter how much you order, your catalogs won't be stacking up.

Condense instruction manuals. The manuals for many cell phones and other electronic devices and appliances are as thick as small books. Most contain sections in foreign languages. To make the book smaller and easier to handle, tear out everything except the English section. The book will be easy to use and won't take up much space in your travel bag.

Keep manuals in a binder. What to do with all those owner's manuals you receive with each new purchase? Punch them with a three-hole punch and keep in a three-ring binger. Before filing away, write the model number and serial number on the inside cover of the manual and attach the sales receipt. Now you know exactly when each item was purchased and from where.

Additionally, most owner's manuals have a blank page or two at the back. Use those pages to keep a record of problems, dates, and solutions. You can even create indexes in the binder to separate rooms in the house. Manuals for items in a particular room are filed accordingly.

This also is a good place for keeping warranty information. For manuals or warranties that are too small to punch, most office-supply stores carry a three-hole-punched pouch with a fastener that can be put in the binder. All those small items can be kept in it.

Corral sports gear. Are you tired of picking up footballs, basketballs, and soccer balls from the garage floor? Use a large, spare trashcan to hold kids' sports equipment. They will know where to put and find their gear.

REUSE AND RECYCLE

How to recycle less often. If you find yourself making a lot of trips to the recycling center, here's a way to save space in your bins: Cut out both ends of cans, put the lids inside, and crush the cans by stepping on them. Also crush plastic bottles and containers.

Donate or recycle, don't dump. Recycling is important no matter where you live. If your apartment complex does not have recycling containers or trash bins, talk with the complex manager. Also, maybe the management would consider a "set things out" day once a week or month where others are free to come take a look-see and "adopt" an item.

Anchor piles of papers. Many of us put newspapers in bundles or bags at the curb on garbage day, only to have them blow down the road several times before the truck comes. When you get fed up with running down the road to bring them back, anchor them down: Drive a stick into the ground and put

Unlimited Uses for . . . Shelf Liner

Here are a few hints for using mesh shelf liner:

- Put a piece under throw rugs, especially one in front of the bathtub.
- Cut a piece to fit the console in your car or on the dashboard. No more sliding cell phones, change, pens, tokens, or notepads.

- Use on a dinner tray to keep the plate from sliding.
- Line the vegetable bin drawer in the refrigerator.
- Use under plants on a window ledge.

the ties, or handles of the bags, over the stick.

Make the most of plastic pails.

Here are some great uses for plastic ice cream buckets:

- Invert the lids and shred carrots or cheese onto them.

- Drill small holes in the bottom of the pail; fill with pea gravel and dirt. Pop in a few plants and voilà! Instant patio garden.

- Use them to transport food donations to picnics or school events. No huge loss if they disappear.

- Use them to store food or other "stuff."

- Stash cleaning supplies in them and take them along when you are cleaning a room.

Make a dispenser for straws. Cut a small hole in the plastic lid of a chip canister to dispense one drinking straw at a time.

Stash newspaper bags. Do you save and reuse newspaper bags? Take an old pill bottle (3 inches tall by 6 inches around) and stuff the bags in it—you won't believe how many newspaper sleeves it will hold. Tuck a "bottle of bags" in the glove compartment of each car, where they'll come in handy for many things while taking up almost no room. If you collect too many bags, give a bottle of them to friends.

Another use for newspaper bags. Plastic newspaper bags make excellent disposable gloves for chores around the house. Use them for messy indoor cleanups and in the garden for sap-filled plants. They work really well and can be tossed when done.

If you sprinkle a little baking soda in the bags, it will keep your hands from sticking to them.

Stuff purses with newspaper bags. Plastic newspaper bags make wonderful stuffing to put inside of tote bags and purses when you store them, instead of tissue sheets, which cost money.

Before you reuse a plastic grocery bag, do this. If you turn the bags inside out before storing them for reuse, the printer's ink, logos, and legends will not stain their surroundings.

Another use for plastic shopping bags. Use them for liners for your small bathroom wastebaskets. They fit perfectly and have handles that allow you to whip them out and throw away.

Use plastic bags to stuff cushions. Use plastic store bags for stuffing cushions for plastic outside chairs and for dining-room chair cushions. When the cushions flatten out, open the back and just add more bags. When the covers are dirty, undo the back, remove the bags, launder and dry the covers, restuff with new bags and stitch them up, and they will be like new.

Prevent sink cleanup with plastic bags. One plastic bag may be able to completely cover the bottom of the disposal side of your kitchen sink. Anytime you do anything messy or have material that you don't want down the disposal, grab a bag—for shucking corn, destringing celery, melting ends of candles, gluing, arranging fresh flowers, or repotting plants. When you're finished, just fold the mess up and toss—instant cleanup.

Use those plastic bags for garbage. Plastic grocery bags are perfect for holding small amounts of garbage. If you live where garbage is collected several times a week, use grocery bags instead of wastebasket liners to collect your garbage.

On the other hand, if your garbage is collected once a week, you can use the grocery bags to collect drippy or smelly trash until collection day.

Give your bags a better handle. It doesn't take long for plastic grocery-type bags to become uncomfortable when carrying them if there's anything very heavy inside. One solution is to take a 4-inch piece of old garden hose and cut a thin section out of it lengthwise. Slip the hose onto the handles of the plastic bags and have a reusable "handle" that won't cut into your hand. A bonus is that it will help keep several bags together.

Stash grocery bags in boxes. If you buy the large, economy-size boxes of large kitchen trash bags, when a box is empty you can use it to store plastic grocery bags. If you like, cover the box with pretty wrapping paper and hang it in your kitchen cabinet.

Use bags for litter control. If you go for a walk in the morning, take along a plastic grocery bag to pick up any paper or plastic bottles lying along the street. It will help keep your town neater and recycles the bags.

Use cloth bags instead of plastic. It's great to reuse and recycle plastic bags. Even better, how about bringing your own cloth tote bags to the store? Not just for groceries, but for trips to the mall as well. Hang your empty bags near your purse so you remember to throw them back in the car for next time you need them. And keep a few right in your trunk, too.

Reuse plastic bread bags. Here are some ways to reuse plastic bread bags:

- Use to transport dirty diapers when you're far away from a trash receptacle.

- Put in a gym bag to hold a wet swimsuit.

- Line a coffee can with one and use the can to collect wet garbage.

- Use to cover your hand for a messy job, like picking up after Fido.

How to use plastic zippered bags. For new moms (and babysitters), here are some other uses for the plastic bags (usually with a zipper or snap) that sheets, curtains, and pillowcases come in. The medium-size ones are good for storing clean diapers. Use another bag for used diapers, and another for dirty outfits or other baby items.

More ways to use zippered bags. Use large comforter bags for storing extra blankets, winter hats, and mittens.

Use small zippered bags from pillows to store children's hair ties, or as a travel bag for cosmetics and hair

Unlimited Uses for . . . Newspaper Bags

In some towns, newspaper carriers have to pay for their own plastic sleeves, so do your carrier a favor. Save your newspaper bags until you have enough to fill a plastic grocery bag. Tie the bag full of bags to the outside door for your carrier to take and reuse. The first couple of times, put a note on the bag to let your carrier know the bag is for him or her.

Long-sleeve newspaper bags have all kinds of uses:

- Use to store rolls of holiday gift wrap.
- Use to store balls of yarn.
- Use as a makeshift rubber glove.
- Keep one in the kitchen for food scraps. Then just knot it closed and put it in the trash.
- If you're a golfer, use two of the plastic newspaper sleeves to store your golf shoes. The bags will keep your car trunk free of grass and mud when you travel to and from the golf course.

- If you own a dog, save a few dollars on waste-pickup bags by using the newspaper bags.

- Store decorative outdoor banners in them. Put each banner in a separate sleeve and keep them all together in one box.

- Use as an umbrella cover—keep your car dry when running errands.

- If you do not recycle your coffee grounds as part of a mulch for gardening, place them in a plastic newspaper bag, tie a knot close to the grounds, then turn the ball of grounds into the bag again and re-knot. Dispose of the package in the garbage can, with no leaks!

- Use to stuff handbags and totes when you're not using them.

items. They can also be used for children's markers, crayons, or colored pencils, and for yarn or craft supplies.

Store kids' toys in plastic zippered bags. Plastic zippered bags are wonderful for organizing children's toys. Some toys have many parts and pieces, and this is a great way to keep them all together when put in a toy bin. When you want to hand down or donate toys, all the parts will be included.

The big bags for comforters and quilts hold large sets, such as building blocks.

Travel bags for free. Zippered plastic bags from sheets or pillowcases make perfect traveling bags for toiletries, and they are also good for storing supplies in a bathroom cabinet. You can put necessary medications in one bag, first-aid supplies (bandages, gauze, ointment, and tape) in another, and lipsticks in another.

Also, you can prepare an emergency first-aid bag and a travel bag with miniature toiletries for last-minute trips.

Use zippered bags for shoes. The zippered bags that contain sheet sets are perfect for storing shoes. You can

Unlimited Uses for . . . Plastic Grocery Bags

If you are like most people who save plastic grocery bags, you find that they can quickly multiply out of control. Anything you can do will help. Millions of bags, adding up to literally tons of plastic (that can be recycled), are added to landfills every day! So, reuse and recycle.

Here are some ways to recycle plastic grocery bags:

- Use one as a floor protector for the commode plunger.
- Wrap them around breakable items as a cushion in storage boxes.
- Use as packing and filler material.
- Wrap one around off-season shoes to keep them dust-free, or use to cover shoes when traveling.

- Carry a few rolled up in a baby travel bag to wrap up soiled diapers.
- Carry some in your glove compartment to use as litter bags or makeshift rain hats.
- Put some in your travel luggage for all kinds of emergencies, smelly clothes, damp things, or items that might leak.
- Fold and stack them in one bag or box for using again.
- Use them to bring home wet or dirty clothing.
- Tie one to your lawn mower handle and gather trash as you go.
- And why not take a good supply back to the grocery store to recycle?

place them in your luggage when you travel and not have to worry about getting dirt on your clothes.

Repurpose paper shopping bags. Shopping bags—the large, paper kind with handles—have loads of uses. They have a square bottom and come in handy during the holidays when your family gathers and has stuff to take home. They are easier to carry than plastic bags, hold more, and let your items travel more safely. Save your shopping bags to use again and again.

Reuse dry-cleaner bags. You can use dry-cleaner bags to hold trash (as long as it's not too heavy). Simply tie a knot at the hanger slot at the top of the bag and insert the bag in the trash can.

Cushion bowls with bubble plastic. To stack large serving bowls without chipping or breaking, place a piece of bubble plastic, cut according to size, between each one. You can also use thin, cheap paper plates to put between china plates to protect them.

Mix up the cereal. Here's a way to keep your family from being bored with breakfast and reuse cereal packaging, too. Buy two or three boxes of different kinds of cereal at a time, combine them in a large bowl, and then put the mixture in airtight containers. It makes for a good variety.

Then take the bags from inside the boxes and shake out the crumbs. The bags make excellent packages for some of your refrigerator foods.

Reuse cereal bags. After you've shaken out the crumbs, the waxed-paper liner in cereal boxes can be used as a package for some of your refrigerator foods. You can also use the liner as a bag or opened flat when you are measuring ingredients for cooking and baking or breading meat, fish, or veggies.

Toss the wastebasket, too. After the long boxes that held a 12-pack of pop are empty, they make good disposable wastebaskets for the laundry room, office, and sewing room.

Use muffin tins for more than just muffins. Here are four uses for a muffin tin:

- Carry a meal to a sick child— small portions of peas, mashed potatoes, and other foods.

- Invert the tin to hold taco shells upright while filling.

- Make large ice cubes for a cooler or a punch bowl.

- Use to make individual meatloaves or casseroles.

From bathroom to kitchen. If you have some 12-by-12-inch tiles left over from tiling a bathroom floor, put stick-on felt pads on the corners of two and put them on either side of your stove top. Use them as a place to put hot things rather than burn your countertops.

New uses for egg cartons. Here are some handy ways to reuse a clean, foam egg carton:

- Store small earrings in it, separated by color or size.
- Put it in a desk drawer to hold paper clips, staples, push pins, and other small items.
- Carry deviled eggs to a picnic (cover the bottom with plastic wrap first).
- Store buttons.
- Use as packing material to cushion breakables.
- Put small pieces or parts in one when assembling something.
- Use to store small light bulbs or nuts and bolts.

Other ways to reuse strawberry baskets.

- Keep a plastic strawberry basket near the kitchen sink to hold scouring pads.
- Use one as a small, disposable colander.

- Line one with a small swatch of fabric and use to hold hair barrettes.
- Use to store small packets of dried seasonings, gravy mixes, or drink mixes.

Find a new use for nice mugs. If you don't drink coffee but have lots of pretty mugs in the cupboard, here's a way to use them: Keep paper and pens in the mugs close to your phone (or phones), near the computer, or in your home office to jot down notes and take messages.

Put a spare mouse pad to work. If you have trouble opening a jar, try using a mouse pad. Grasp the lid with the rough bottom side of the mouse pad and give it a firm twist.

Keep little things contained. The plastic liners that hold cookies inside packages are a great help for keeping pins, needles, and sewing notions organized. You can also use them to hold buttons, beads, and just about anything that fits into the slots.

Make a "spicy" toothpick holder. Remove the label and thoroughly wash an empty spice container, such as for garlic powder, that has a plastic shaker top. Fill with toothpicks and screw on the lid. When you need a toothpick, just shake one out. This method of storage keeps the toothpicks clean and easily accessible, and takes only a little space in the cupboard.

Mint containers make a doll boutique. Here's another creative way to reuse the metal tins in which mints are sold. Use them to organize accessories for fashion dolls. Several pairs of shoes, jewelry items, purses, or doll-size hair clips fit in one container. Label them so it's easy to find what you want!

Make your own candy assortment to go. If you like several kinds or flavors of little candies and mints that come in tins, mix a few of each kind in a tin to carry in your purse. You'll have a variety of choices, plus just one tin to deal with.

Stash cords in paper tubes. Don't discard used toilet-paper and paper-towel tubes. They make handy holders for wound-up electrical cords from irons, curling irons, hairdryers, and other appliances.

Make a blade protector for kitchen knives. To keep sharp knives from getting dull or chipped in your utility drawer, make protective sleeves for them out of empty paper-towel rolls. Simply flatten out the rolls and staple them to the correct size.

More ways to use toilet-paper rolls. Cut the cardboard tube in half crosswise, place in a flat container with drainage, fill with potting soil, and plant seeds in them. When it's time to move the little plant outdoors, set the whole tube in the ground along with the plant, and it will gradually deteriorate in the soil.

Make party favors. Use those cardboard tubes to make favors for children's parties—just pop candy in a

Unlimited Uses for . . . Margarine Tubs

Here are a few ways to "recycle" plastic margarine tubs:

- Use to hold small amounts of paint for touch-ups.
- Use to organize beads.
- Can be used as a birdbath for small birds like finches.
- Use to store leftovers.
- Use in the garage for nuts, bolts, and other small items.
- Small tubs are handy for keeping small craft items.
- Hold vegetable scraps in one until they can be composted.
- Use as a travel water bowl or food bowl for pets.

tube and wrap it in pretty paper, then twist each end.

Store hair accessories. The empty tube from a roll of paper towels is perfect for storing hair scrunchies that girls wear. They slip right on the cardboard tube and are neatly lined up.

Put fast-food napkins to good use. When you buy fast-food hamburgers or tacos, there is always a wad of napkins at the bottom of the take-home bag. You probably do not use them all. Take these unused napkins and place them in a plastic grocery bag that hangs on a doorknob in your kitchen (or put them in a drawer instead). The napkins are perfect for wiping up spills or cleaning windows or mirrors.

Reuse squeeze bottles. Have you seen those no-mess ketchup and mustard bottles? They solve the problem of the cap getting all wet and encrusted. When they are empty, you can use them in the shower as a soap dispenser.

Hang the bottle from the shower tap with a shoestring and fill it from that gallon of liquid soap you bought at the warehouse store.

Things to do with paper plates. Paper plates are very useful, and they are cheap, too! Here are some ways to use them:

- As a spoon rest. If soiled, just toss when done.

- In a microwave to catch drips and spills. Replace as needed.

- Under a soup bowl to catch drips and spills.

- Under a pet dish to protect the floor.

Reuse twist ties. Here are some uses for wire bread ties:

- Strip and use the wire to fill in for the screw you lost on your eyeglass frames.

Unlimited Uses for . . . Metal Mint Tins

After eating all the mints in one of those cute metal tins, reuse it to hold:

- A sewing kit
- Beads
- Hair accessories
- Small jewelry

- Cotton balls or swabs
- Coins
- Little packets of sugar or sweetener (Not all restaurants have the packets, so carry your own in your purse.)
- Calling, business, or baseball cards

- Use the ties to hang ornaments, or in floral arrangements.

- Bend a stripped bread tie into a V shape to make a needle threader.

- Twist several paper-coated ties together to bind poultry legs for roasting.

- Use them to bundle appliance cords. This makes storage neat and tidy!

Save plastic lids. Use the plastic lids from coffee cans on the bottom ends of new cans to prevent rust rings on your countertops. You can do the same thing in the bathroom with cans of shaving cream and hair spray.

You can also use the lids as coffee-cup covers to keep the heat in longer.

Uses for plastic bakery containers. Here are some other uses for large, rigid plastic containers that are used for cakes and breads:

- Store your stash of ready-made gift-package bows. Stack the containers in the corner of a closet so you can see at a glance. Bows stay ready and perky.

- Store small interconnecting building blocks or other toys.

- Use to create a terrarium or to start seedlings.

Clean and save deli containers. Keep a variety of plastic deli containers with lids and recycle them whenever you take food to friends. After the party, you don't have to worry about bringing them home.

Reuse snack food tins. Here are some handy ways to reuse snack food tins:

- Use to store small toys.

- Use a small tin to hold extra pocket change.

- Store knitting or crocheting supplies in one.

- Use as a small trash can in a spare bedroom.

Reuse yogurt cups. Yogurt cups have lots of uses. Wash them out, and save the plastic lids, too. You can use the cups to keep extra buttons handy, or use them in the utility room for spare nuts and bolts.

Put sugar bags to work. Don't dispose of those extra-thick bags that sugar comes in. They can be used for many things.

When you go on picnics, instead of

lugging a heavy bag of charcoal, you can fill up an empty sugar bag with charcoal. It's the right size, and the bag won't rip easily.

Another time to use sugar bags is when you are frying chicken. Put flour in one and shake with the chicken pieces to coat them. It's better than using plastic bags.

Don't toss your corks. Here are some additional uses for wine and champagne corks when the bottle is empty:

- Keep some in a fishing tackle box for attaching loose hooks and lures.

- Make the corks into a hotplate holder by gluing them together or gluing them to a piece of wood.

- Attach them around a picture frame to give to a fisherman.

Customize advertising magnets. Paste a picture or even a favorite poem on advertising magnets. You can put them on any metal surface, like a filing cabinet or the fridge. Just type what you want on a label, place on the magnet, and trim the edges to fit. The magnets also work well for labeling keys. Type a label, stick it on the magnet,

punch a hole in the corner and, using strong string, attach the key to the label. Then hang it up.

Use pliers in the kitchen. If you're getting on in years and your grip is not what it used to be, keep a dedicated pair of needle-nose pliers in the kitchen. The kind with rubber-covered handles are easiest to grasp. They come in really handy to pull milk safety strips, tear open bags, open small bottles, and perform other tasks. Use them to open a metal spout on a container of salt or box of dishwasher soap.

Remove the label first. To remove the label from one of those handy spray bottles, fill the bottle with hot water, let stand for 5 to 10 minutes, then just peel off the whole label.

Substitute bottle caps. If you lose the lid to a bottle of isopropyl alcohol or hydrogen peroxide, try substituting a cap from a 20-ounce or 1-liter soft drink bottle. It should fit perfectly!

Make freezer packs from plastic bottles. Reuse clean 16-ounce plastic bottles from soda or tea to keep picnic coolers cold. Fill the bottles about three-quarters of the way with water (leave a bit of room for expansion as the water freezes) and keep them in your freezer until you need them. They are great for keeping medical supplies, baby bottles, milk, and soft drinks cool on car trips.

Don't toss tissue boxes. Here are some ways to reuse square tissue boxes:

- In a bathroom for cotton balls;

- On a makeup table to dispose of used makeup-sponge wedges;

- In the laundry room for stashing dryer lint, loose threads, and other small trash;

- To hold plastic grocery bags;

- To keep near your sewing machine as a trash box to dispose of bits of thread and fabric clippings.

Another way to reuse a tissue box. Take an empty tissue box, cut the top diagonally to each corner, and then fold the four parts down inside the box, stapling each. Apply tape to the staples so the sharp edges don't become a problem. You can use these boxes for storage and as cheap organizers.

Repurpose a toothbrush holder. A cup with four holes on top that's meant to hold toothbrushes makes a great dispenser for cotton-tipped swabs or crayons.

Another way to reuse pantyhose. Cut the whole stocking into ½-inch to 1-inch bands. These make the best elastic-like bands for anything and everything. They stretch, never break, and can be cut and tied together for a longer stretch.

Use versatile paper clips. Large paper clips have lots of uses besides holding papers. Here are some:

- Bend them into an "S" shape and use to hang toys in a bird cage.

Unlimited Uses for . . . Peanut Butter Jars

Save peanut butter jars. They are plastic, unbreakable, and see-through. They come in several sizes, too!

- Use to store pasta, rice, and beans, and other food items—a good way to prevent weevils and pantry moths.

- Use plastic (not glass) jars as freezer containers.

- Use as "to-go" containers when a party is over and there are lots of leftovers.

- Use in the garage for hard-to-find items: nails, screws, small light bulbs.

- Use to store Christmas decorations. They can hold the hooks for decorations and other small items.

- Use one or even two together to extend the length of a necklace.

- Add to a zipper pull for more tugging power.

- Mark movies or programs in a television guide that you want to watch.

- Use as a replacement for a zipper pull on a purse, jacket, or sleeping bag.

Don't toss old business cards. Use outdated business cards as bookmarks for library books. Record the due date on the back. When you start a new book, just cross out the old due date and add the new one.

Put old check boxes to work. Here are some uses for an empty check box (separate the top and bottom and you have two boxes):

- When put in a drawer, it can hold paper clips or push pins.

- It's great for carrying coupons.

- Handy for keeping business cards in one place.

- Can hold packets of seeds for flowers, vegetables, or herbs.

Reuse shipping boxes. Try to save the shipping boxes in which you receive merchandise to reuse for future mailings. The problem is that these boxes often have printing or labels on them that have to be removed or marked out before the shipping companies or the post office will accept them.

An easy way to meet these requirements is to simply turn the box inside out. There is usually a seam that can be carefully opened, and the box can be turned in reverse and either reglued or taped back together along the seam. The result is a clean, unmarked, good-as-new shipping box. And a bonus is that you are recycling boxes you thought you couldn't use.

Recycle foam peanuts. Many package mailing offices will take foam packing "peanuts" and reuse them. The plastic foam must be clean and dry to be reused.

Call the Plastic Loose Fill Council's toll-free phone number, (800) 828-2214, and listen to a recorded message for your area listing the names and addresses of participating businesses. Or simply ask the store nearest you!

Make a quick label from an envelope. Need a label to remember what you put in a container, but can't find out? Try cutting the flap off the back of an envelope, then cut along the sticky edge, and bingo, instant label.

Make a cookbook from a calendar. Save your outdated weekly calendar and engagement books to make cook-books with the recipes you get from friends and the ones you cut and save from newspapers and magazines. You

---

Unlimited Uses for . . . Coffee Cans

Here are some ways to reuse your empty coffee cans:

- Use large cans for pouring off grease from ground beef or other greasy foods. When a can is full, just put the lid on and either throw it in the trash or use for suet in bird feeders.
- Store hair clips, barrettes, and other hair accessories.
- Store paintbrushes, glue sticks, and all sorts of craft items. Use a black permanent marker to mark on the lid what's inside!
- Keep children's small toys together.
- Use for storing macaroni, beans, and other pantry staples (be sure to label the contents).
- Use a large coffee can as a small trash can in the kitchen. Keep it under the cabinet when not in use. The produce bags from the grocery store fit the can perfectly. The lid keeps odors contained.
- Plastic cans make good garbage containers. Lined with a produce bag and with the lid snapped on, they can hold garbage odor-free indoors during cold or inclement weather.
- Cut a hole in the plastic lid and collect your loose change. Before you know it, you will have enough for a dinner or movie!
- Use to hold extra grass seed.
- Store flower fertilizer.
- Use for mixing liquid fertilizer (be sure to label the container if you don't use all the fertilizer at once).
- Use to carry small amounts of potting soil so you don't have to lug the whole bag.
- Use for storing craft supplies.
- Put one in a shed or garage to hold nails, nuts, and bolts.
- Use a small one as a scoop for dog food or birdseed. (The container is easy to grasp when filling a feeder.)
- Store items such as clothespins and dog accessories in a coffee can on a shelf in the garage.
- Use plastic coffee cans to store paint. The built-in grips make them easy to handle while painting. The snap-on lids seal well and are easier to open and close than metal paint cans. Fill them no more than halfway for easier handling.
- Carry a can with a roll of toilet paper in it in case of an emergency on the road when there is no restroom in sight.

will still be able to enjoy the beautiful pictures in the books, and they will still be useful!

Reuse calendar pages. Collect pages from a one-page-per-day calendar and use the blank backside of each page as scrap paper. The pages might be just the right size to fit in a scrap-paper holder. A bonus: You get to reread the funny sayings on the calendar side.

Pack with pages. Recycle old catalogs and magazines by using the pages as packing material. This is better than using newspapers, because it doesn't leave newsprint on your hands or the packed items.

Stash toothbrushes in a flower pot. The newer toothbrushes with extra-large handles don't fit in traditional toothbrush holders. Try putting yours in small flowerpots (with the hole in the bottom). They hold both tooth-brushes and toothpaste. Each family member can have a different color pot.

Keep a flowerpot in your kitchen. Put kitchen brushes, sponges, and scrubbers in a clean flowerpot. The holes at the bottom and the saucer underneath are perfect for drainage. The pretty flowerpot will decorate the area around your kitchen sink and tidy up your dishwashing tools.

Stick other stuff in a flower pot.

Terra-cotta pots can also hold pens and pencils. Or use one to hold a candle.

Save silica gel packets. Handy little silica gel packets (desiccants) are great to help absorb moisture in places like:

- A mailbox
- Camera bag
- Shop drawers where you store nails, screws, or other metal things that can rust
- Plastic storage bins (especially when storing household goods or clothes)

A great use for metal cans. Our service personnel serving in war zones overseas need and appreciate care packages from home, but the right packaging can make all the difference. Food items sent in cardboard boxes may be attacked by rodents, depend-ing on available storage facilities. If that's a problem for your loved one, pack your gifts in metal cans with metal lids. After the goodies are gone, there's a pest-proof storage container for personal belongings.

Reuse can lids. If you have the type of can opener that leaves a smooth side on the lid, try using the lids from larger cans as spoon rests. Just wash the lids in the dishwasher. Keep several so each spoon you use for cooking has its own rest.

Give popcorn tins a new life. Popcorn tins have lots of uses when the popcorn is gone. Wash them out well, and dry them before reusing. You can paint them or decorate them, and they are the perfect size for bathroom trash cans. Plastic bags you get from the grocery store also fit in them as liners.

Recycle your coffee cup. Save a paper coffee cup with the lid after your morning coffee and use it as a trash container. It is perfect to stash candy wrappers, apple cores, tissues, or other small stuff. It stores conveniently in a cup holder by your seat in the car. When it is full, just toss it into the trash.

Rejuvenate an ashtray. If you no longer smoke, you can find new uses for pretty ashtrays. Place a large one on the stove to hold cooking spoons and collect any drips. In the living room, fill a beautiful ashtray with rose petals and fragrance. During Christmastime, fill some with greenery.

Tote an ice cream tub. Large ice cream tubs with handles come in quite handy for storing cleaning supplies around the house. They're also great for toting things around. For example, a college student could use one of the tubs to carry toiletries to the bathroom and back.

Put old marbles to work. Kids often have a bazillion marbles thrown in the bottom of an old toy chest. Instead of throwing them out, use them in the bottom of a clear vase to anchor silk or plastic flowers. The marbles will

Unlimited Uses for . . . Coffee Filters

Round coffee filters aren't just for coffee makers. Here are some other handy uses:

- Hold messy foods like tacos.
- Poke a frozen ice-pop stick through one so all drips will be contained.
- Place between nonstick frying pans when storing them to protect the finish.
- Put in between china plates to keep from scratching.
- Place in a plant pot before filling with soil so that the soil doesn't come out the drainage hole.
- Use to dry windows or clean mirrors and leave them lint-free.
- Use to dry wineglasses.
- Use to apply shoe polish to shoes.

look nice and won't have to be picked up anymore.

STORAGE TIPS

Keep coins in a film can. A 35-mm film canister will hold several dollars' worth of quarters. Tuck one away in your car or your purse so it'll be handy when you need change. You can also put one in a child's backpack for snack money.

Separate stuck glasses. Have you ever had two glasses get stuck together? How do you get them unstuck? Give this a try: Put ice cubes in the top glass and dip the bottom one in warm to hot water. Gently pull the glasses apart. Or pour some baby or mineral oil between the glasses, allow them to sit for a while, and then gently pull them apart. Wash in hot, soapy water and rinse. This should do the trick!

Make silverware snug. If your kitchen silverware tray slides back and forth every time the drawer is opened and closed, try this: Cut the cardboard tubes from paper-towel rolls to fit between the back of the tray and the drawer. Your silverware tray will stay snug.

Put a napkin holder to new use. A metal napkin holder that you are not using makes an excellent holder for several cutting boards. It is attractive, the boards are off the counter, and the holder can be moved quickly to clean around it.

Handy storage for grocery bags. Save large, empty tissue boxes, fold the bags, and stuff them in the boxes.

Unlimited Uses for . . . Milk Jugs

Plastic milk jugs have loads of uses. Here are a few:

- Fill with water three-quarters full and freeze. They're great in a picnic cooler.
- Cut off the top, leaving two-thirds of the jug, and use to sprinkle fertilizer or bug dust on lawns.
- Keep a used milk jug full of water in the trunk of your car.
- Cut a milk jug in half, fill the bottom with sand, and place a candle inside to line walkways or a patio.
- Use to mix up plant food, but always label your containers so you don't forget what's in them.

When you need a bag, just pull one out like you would a tissue!

You can also stash grocery bags in an empty coffee can. Simply cut a round hole in the plastic top to quickly and easily pull out a bag when needed.

Or, get a good-size shoebox, or a box of similar shape. Tape or glue on the top, cover it with pretty gift wrap, cut a large slit in the middle of one end, cut out the opposite end, and tack or tape the box—endwise—on the wall. Tuck the bags in the top and pull them out through the slit at the bottom.

Another option is to buy large, economy-size boxes of large kitchen trash bags and, when a box is empty, use it to store grocery bags. Simply cut the holes a little larger. You could even cover the one in your kitchen with pretty wrapping paper and hang it in a kitchen cabinet.

Roll up your dish towels. Do your dish towels not fit in a small drawer? Roll them up and they'll all fit very nicely. In fact, you may be able to put twice as many rolled towels in the drawer as folded ones.

Multiuse paper clips. Use a 3-inch paper clip to close opened food packages or anything you want to keep fresh around the kitchen.

Make gaskets for canisters. If the gaskets on your clear-glass canister set wear out, it may be impossible to find new ones. So, make your own. Go to an automotive shop and buy a sheet of cork gasket material that is used for car gaskets (these gaskets are usually made from high-grade cork granules and mixed synthetic rubber binders). Lay down an old gasket, trace around it, and cut it out for a perfectly sized replacement.

Split up a big bag of chips. If you buy big bags of chips from a discount membership store, split them up. To save space and keep them fresh, divide the chips and put them in gallon-size, resealable freezer bags, or use the sandwich size and make individual servings for ready-to-go lunch packs.

Extend strawberry life. Here's how to keep strawberries fresh a little longer: Place ripe strawberries (before washing or capping) in a plastic container lined with paper towels. Place paper towels between layers of berries and cover the top layer with a paper towel. Seal the container with a tight-fitting lid and place it in the refrigerator. These berries will keep for a few extra days.

Storing powdered milk. Anyone who buys powdered milk knows that it often comes in large, bulky boxes.

To save cabinet space, fill a quart-size glass milk bottle with the powdered milk. It's easier to handle and is convenient to store on the shelf.

I like to make a "skim cream" for my coffee by adding powdered skim milk to a little water in a small jar with a tight-fitting lid. Sometimes I add powdered skim milk directly to my cup of coffee. Few calories and extra calcium.

Keep the baking soda dry. If you live where the high humidity cakes the baking soda after you open the cardboard container it comes in, here's a solution. Repackage the baking soda in a cleaned, empty container that originally held Parmesan cheese. These containers even provide a shaker top for when you need to use the product.

Store oil without the tall bottle. If you like to place your vegetable-oil bottle near your stove, but the space is not tall enough, find a substitute container for the oil. A large, upside-down ketchup bottle may do the trick for you. Just make sure you have the bottle pointed down into the skillet when you squeeze it.

Get the most from a shelf organizer. You can buy an organizer to more efficiently store your canned food. This organizer acts like risers for a cho-

rus—the cans are lined up in tiers. To avoid having to shuffle cans to see what you have, turn the cans upside down. Then the picture of what was in each can will be in plain view instead of the brand name. Turning cans upside down would probably also help if you are looking through cans on a shelf without an organizer.

Use clothespins to close bags. To reclose a bag, instead of using wire bag ties, which can twist and bend, buy a package of colored plastic clothespins for a dollar or so. They will keep any bag closed—be it soft plastic, as in bread wrapping, or an opened bag of potato chips, where you just fold over the end and clip it shut, making it reopenable anytime you wish. They are also great for twisting and gripping plastic packaging for the freezer.

Rotate in the refrigerator. Use two rotating trays (bottom part only) in your refrigerator. On one put jellies and jams. On the other put olives, pickles, relish, and other condiments. When you need something from the back of the shelf, just spin the turntable. Saves space, and makes it easy to get to any item.

Another option for easy access. On the second shelf of the refrigerator, where the butters, mustards, cottage cheese, and dinner leftovers tend to get shoved to the back, place a cookie sheet that can be slid out for easy access to the contents. It's sanitary, too, for cleanup of spills!

Protect nonstick pans. To prevent scratching and marring of nonstick fry pans while storing them, place a round piece of cut cardboard on the inside bottom of the pan before placing another one on top on it.

Use a pizza cutter creatively. Keep your pizza cutter close at hand for slicing toast, cutting sandwiches, and chopping vegetables.

Kitchen cupboard keepsakes. Here's a hint for readers who have small children and not enough room for all the papers and drawings they bring home from school. Keep pictures, poems, favorite quotations, or special cards on the inside of cupboards. You can turn all your cupboards and cabinets—not just those in the kitchen—into little galleries of keepsakes. Kids can keep their special drawings (and sometimes copies of their report cards) inside lower cupboards that they can see at their height.

Rotate your plates. When you become an empty-nester, you may find yourself using the same two dinner plates every night, and they start to show wear. The same goes for linens, towels, and sheets. Rotate your things by removing what you need to use from the top of the stack and putting clean items away on the bottom of each pile. It will save your things from being used so often.

Eliminate "flying saucers." No matter how carefully you stack plastic containers, the whole kit and caboodle can come flying off the shelf when you reach for a container. To corral them, buy a plastic dishpan that fits your shelf. Whenever you need a plastic container, take the dishpan off the shelf and pick out the container and lid you need. The dishpan goes back on the shelf, and there are no more "flying saucers."

Instant drawer liners. If you get a sudden urge to clean out your kitchen drawers and have nothing on hand to

On the Light Side
Protect Stored Dishes
Do you have nice dinner plates that you want to protect while stored? Which of the following can you place between them?
  a) paper plates
  b) coffee filters
  c) rubber mesh
  d) all of the above
For your information, "d" is the winner!

reline them with, try using terry kitchen towels. They are colorful, and each one is different. No more sliding of silverware holders or utensils. The towels are washable and reusable.

Store tissue rolls handily. Paint the handle white on your bathroom plunger and stack rolls of bathroom tissues on it, making both tissues and plunger handy when needed. This storage method also opens up space in the cupboard or linen closet for something else.

Keep that paper on the roll. Before you put the toilet-paper roll on the holder, slightly flatten the whole roll; then, when you want some paper, a whole lot of it doesn't come rolling off. This is very useful technique when you have young children, too—active toddlers love to unfurl rolls of toilet tissue.

Store blankets right in the bed. Ever wonder what to do with the blankets you take off the bed for the summer months? Fold them longways and put them between the mattress and box spring. They are out of the way, and when you're ready for them again, you know where they are and what bed they go on.

Create storage where there's no space. If you live in a small apartment, storage space is limited at best. So get creative. No place in the closet to store a box of Christmas ornaments? Take out your trusty glue gun and cover the box with some fabric that matches your living room. Then stand the box in a corner of the room and set a plant on top. Problem solved!

Make storage portable. If you have a lot of clothing or other items to gather for donation or storage, here's an easy way to collect them without lugging lots of bags or boxes around. Buy some new 32-gallon trash cans with wheels and some heavy-duty garbage bags. Use one can for things to be donated, and another for things to store. Just roll the cans from one location to the other. When they are full, close the trash bag and roll the can out to your car. Then replace the trash bag and start again.

Leave those items you plan to store in the can and roll it right to your storage area.

Store your stuff in clear plastic bags. Try to store items in clear plastic bags because it's easier to see the contents. Sometimes valuable items stored in dark plastic bags are inadvertently thrown out by family members who think they are garbage and "helpfully" put them on the curb.

Make your yardstick easy to find.

Yardsticks have a way of slipping behind or under obstacles, making them hard to locate. Use a piece of self-gripping fabric tape on the stick and another one on the wall in your broom closet and in the garage, and just hang your yardsticks. They will always be in sight.

Give an old coat rack a new life. If you've got an old coat rack and no place to put it, move it to the laundry room. Put loops on your brooms and mops and hang them from the coat rack.

Store rags in a box. Keep an empty box from large trash bags in your shed to hold small rags. Simply cut the holes in the box a little larger.

DONATE WHAT YOU CAN'T USE

A warm donation. You never know what might be useful when a disaster strikes. When San Antonio welcomed thousands of evacuees from Hurricane Katrina in 2005, donations were being accepted by the Salvation Army. One group had 250 lined, wind-resistant sports jackets. The temperature was 95 degrees, with no relief in sight, and the donors didn't think the jackets would be useful.

But they were—the air conditioning in the giant buildings was so cold, the

Unlimited Uses for . . . Applesauce Cups

You can reuse clean plastic applesauce cups in lots of ways. Here are some:

- For dipping cat or dog food, cereal, rice, oats, flour, cornmeal, macaroni, or sugar from their storage containers.
- To help combat odors in refrigerators by filling with baking soda—use in the microwave, too.
- Use for individual servings of gelatin. Pour right into the cup.
- Use for single servings of salsa or dips.
- Cut off the bottom and use for a biscuit or cookie cutter.

- In the bathroom, fill with baking soda and salt for brushing your teeth.
- Use for holding buttons, change, needles, or tacks.
- Use for soaking small items in cleaning solutions.
- Put detergent in them to clean dirty spots on clothes using a toothbrush.
- Trace around one for a perfect circle.
- Use in children's sandboxes for playtime.
- Start seeds in the spring.

Salvation Army actually had many requests for coats. So always ask if you're not sure items you have to donate are needed—you may be surprised.

Check that date! If you donate food to a charity, be sure to check the expiration dates. Most packaged food, even sodas, have an expiration date or a "best if used by" date imprinted on them. Please, when you are trying to feed those who are in need, make sure the food is still safe to use. A good philosophy for donations is, "If I would not use it, I will not pass it on." It is important to donate food that is edible. Staples such as rice, beans, and canned goods are always welcome.

Have a pajama party for a good cause. Local centers for the abused and homeless often welcome donations of new, unworn clothes and pajamas. In one town in Illinois there's an annual "pajama party," when residents donate pajamas for an abuse prevention center. Many clients—including children—come to these centers with only the clothes on their backs. The new pajamas are a warm, welcome treat for people in crisis.

This is an easy, step-by-step project. All you need to do is some simple advertising, provide a collection area, and deliver the items to the charity. Folks, you can collect much-needed items at your workplace, gym, or place of worship. It is a "user-friendly" project that benefits many. You can make a difference!

Donate plastic grocery bags. Plastic grocery bags can be used at charity thrift shops and inner-city churches that have food pantries and clothing for the needy. You can also take bags to area nursing-home residents. Another possible place to donate plastic grocery bags is your local library. The bags can

---

Unlimited Uses for . . . Plastic Spray Bottles

Here are a few ways to reuse an empty, clean plastic spray bottle:

- Fill with water and a few drops of orange or lemon essential oil to mist stinky trash.
- Fill with water and use as a plant mister.

- Fill with water and give to kids to use as "spray guns" (outdoors, please!).
- Make a solution of half vinegar and half water in the bottle and keep in the car to deal with dirty windows or other cleanups.

come in handy for people to carry home books. Or, take bags to a senior citizen community. Just call before leaving any donation to be sure it will be accepted.

Another take on donating bags. If you want to donate grocery bags to a thrift shop or other institution in your area, in addition to calling to see if they will accept the bags, ask if the bags need to be in any particular form. Some groups prefer that bags be clean and smoothed flat, not crumpled up. Paper or plastic shopping bags with handles also may be preferred if they are flat or folded and clean.

Flattened packing paper, tissue paper, and bubble plastic also are needed for wrapping breakables.

Give magazines a second life. Lots of folks save their old magazines, thinking that there should be something they can do with them. Here are some places where you can donate used magazines:

- Nursing or assisted-living homes
- Veterans hospitals
- Senior citizen centers
- Youth-detention centers
- Prisons or jails

Many schools have recycling bins for newspapers and magazines. You can also drop them there. Before you take the magazines to any of these places, be sure to give them a call first to make sure they will take them. And tear off the label with your name and address.

TOSS THE TRASH

Dispose of cans safely. Tossing sharp can lids into a trash bag can be dangerous. The sharp edges can poke through the plastic and seriously cut the person taking out the trash. To prevent injuries, always put the can lid inside the can and bend it so it cannot fall out!

Be careful with cans. Pull-top cans make it easier for kids to open them, but a hazard comes with these cans. The rim of the can may be quite sharp, and can cut into your finger. When washing out these cans for recycling, do so carefully.

Dispose of fluorescent tubes and bulbs safely. If you break a fluorescent light bulb, do *not* pick up the pieces with your bare hands. Instead, wear protective gloves that are disposable, and open the windows or doors for ventilation at least 15 minutes before starting cleanup. *Do* *not* vacuum up any residue or small pieces of glass. Pick up the small particles with a damp paper towel or piece of duct tape, and put all of the broken pieces in two sealed plastic bags, along with the paper towel or duct tape. Wash your hands well after handling the bag. And do not burn the bulbs!

Fluorescent lamps contain a small amount of mercury. The larger, longer bulbs are more hazardous than the small, compact bulbs, but both should be cleaned up with caution.

All fluorescent bulbs should be taken to the dump (you need to check locally for hazardous waste disposal guidelines), as you would batteries or electronics. The packages containing the bulbs warn that they contain mercury and should be disposed of properly, but they do not mention the precautions for cleaning up broken bulbs.

Call your trash company to see if there is a collection site in your area. If there isn't a hazardous waste center near you, the garbage company should be able to tell you how to prepare the bulbs for proper disposal. You can also call the United States Environmental Recycling Hotline at 877-EARTH-911. Enter your Zip code and you will find information for your state. It takes a while to go through the prompts, but be patient.

Keep garbage-bag ties handy. Keep your garbage-bag ties attached to the garbage-can handle, and you will never have to look for the ties when it's garbage pickup day.

Double-line the can and quit scrubbing. When it is time to put a new trash liner in the trash can, put two bags in the can, one opened on top of the other. The double liner makes emptying trash a little easier, and if you're rushed, there will already be a liner in place—you won't have to put one in. A bonus is that it keeps the can clean. No one likes to scrub out sticky trash containers.

Deodorize the trash can. A little baking soda sprinkled in the kitchen trash can every so often will help control odors until it's time for trash day.

Diaper-disposal system. An airtight diaper-disposal system also works quite well for adult disposable underpads—it holds 14 to 18 pads. What a wonderful container for those with bladder-control issues.

How to dispose of a worn-out flag. After years of service, an American flag will fade and become somewhat frayed. You can't just toss an old flag in the trash: There is a special procedure, and a ceremony, that should be followed for disposal. Contact a local boy or girl scout troop, VFW (Veterans of Foreign Wars), or American Legion Post for information on how to retire your flag. Some of these groups will take your flag and hold it until a ceremony is scheduled.

ORGANIZE YOUR STUFF

Make cleanup a family affair. Keeping the house cleaned and straightened up is a never-ending job when you've got kids and both parents work full-time.

Here's one way to keep things picked up: Make a chart with all the rooms listed—living, dining, bath, utility, and kitchen. Then make a slip of paper for each room, place the papers in a jar, and have each family member grab one. That room then becomes the responsibility of that person for the week.

Start children young. Everyone in the family (after age 5 or 6) should have a cleanup job as simple as emptying wastebaskets, picking up things on the floor, and putting away toys, books, and magazines. Start them young, and it will become a good lifetime habit.

Getting chores done. Getting the family to pitch in and help do chores

Unlimited Uses for . . . Pantyhose

Here are some ideas for reusing pantyhose:

- Cut the tops off the elastic part and use as large rubber bands for boxes.
- Cut off the legs and use them to tie tomato plants to stakes.
- Use a large piece of pantyhose to strain paint.
- Cut hose into small pieces and use to stuff pillows or cushions.
- Use to remove pet hair from furniture.
- Store onions in one leg. Place an onion in and tie, and then place another.

- Store rolls of wrapping paper. The hose keep the rolls rolled up and protected much better than a rubber band or piece of tape can.
- Use for making dolls or stuffed animals.
- Cut out the elastic waistband and put it around the kitchen trash can to keep the trash bag from falling down inside.
- Use the hose as a filter over your vacuum-cleaner attachment if you lost something small on the carpet or floor. The pantyhose will catch the missing item before it's sucked into the vacuum.

can be a battle. Try this approach to motivate your crew. Make a list of chores that need to be done and put a corresponding dice number (1 to 6) alongside each chore. Get the whole family together and tell them they are going to "roll" for their choice of a chore.

This way everyone has the same chance of getting the chores they want or don't want. It may also help to tell kids that if the chores are not done, then no allowance will be given.

Label packages to track prices. When you find products such as canned goods, cleaning supplies, boxed foods, toilet paper, paper towels, and tooth-paste—things you use in your every-day life—that have a better price than you have been paying, use a marker and put the price on the item and where you purchased it. When you

need to replace an item, you will have the information right at hand.

Keep your cupboards current. Keep a permanent marker in a kitchen drawer and use it to inventory pantry supplies. Once a year, take everything out of your cupboards and label each item with the current year. When you find things with the prior year on them, try to use them soon (for food items, make sure they are not past their expiration date).

Organize canned goods. When you buy canned goods, use a felt-tipped marker to write the month and year on each can before storing it. You'll be able to use items before they expire and keep the cans rotated.

Make expiration dates easy to see. Take a fine-point permanent marker and write expiration dates in big let-ters on spice containers, medications,

Unlimited Uses for . . . Binder Clips

Here are some ways to reuse those handy binder clips:

- Hold coupons while shopping.
- Gather your lists of things to do and clip them together to grab and go.
- Take a couple on trips to hold motel/hotel drapes closed.

- Clip bills together until they are paid and sent out.
- Clip important reminders to the sun visor in your car.
- Keep bags of chips, crackers, and cook-ies closed.

and other perishables. Then you won't have to look for your reading glasses when trying to read that fine print. Keeping a magnifying glass around is also helpful.

Get more space with this silverware holder. The limited slots in most average silverware-holder trays can be frustrating. To get more silverware into your kitchen drawer, replace the slotted tray with small plastic baskets. They hold three times as many forks, spoons, knives, and other utensils. Now, the silverware will stay put!

Store knives this way. When storing knives in a knife block, place them in upside down, with the sharp edge facing up. This prolongs the sharpness of the knife as well as keeping your storing block in better condition. Just be careful when removing a knife from the block.

Gain easier access to the fridge. Folks suffering from arthritis often have difficulty bending down to look in the back of the refrigerator. For easier access, buy cookie sheets that are the same width as the shelves, put one sheet on each shelf, and place the shelf's items on the sheet. Then all you've got to do is pull out a cookie sheet to get the things that are in the back.

A pick-and-pack snack holder. Use a tall, hanging shoe holder in the pantry closet to hold kids' snacks and school lunch-bag items. Leave less desirable items in compartments toward the top, where the kids can't reach quite yet, and the healthier stuff below. Packing lunches can even become a group effort as you tell them to get things from different compartments.

Gather up jelly and preserves. If you have many jars of jelly and preserves in your refrigerator, buy a clear plastic shoe box, put it on a refrigerator shelf, and fill it with the jars of jam. Then you can just pull out the plastic box to select the jar you need.

Freeze-ahead sandwiches. Taking your own lunch to work or school is a great way to save money, but packing lunches for the family can make mornings hectic. Here's how to save time.

After grocery shopping on Saturday, make all of the sandwiches for the week, seal them in freezer bags and label them. Then pop them all in the freezer, and they'll be ready to stash in lunch sacks before going to school each morning. The sandwiches will thaw by lunchtime.

Keep in mind, though, that some

things freeze well and others don't. Mayonnaise, lettuce, and cream sauces don't freeze well. But most meats, deli meats, and hard cheeses will. You always can add fresh lettuce and tomatoes to the sandwiches at lunchtime by packing them separately.

Save the small condiment packages of mustard, mayo, or ketchup from fast-food restaurants and add them to the lunch bags. That way, condiments can be added right before you eat your sandwich.

Other items to toss into the sack can be kept on the counter near the door. Fruit, cookies in bags, pretzels, carrot sticks, and other snacks can be put out ahead of time.

A real bonus of working ahead is the elimination of surprises, like being out of peanut butter at the last minute.

Long-handled helpers. Do you hate it when the quart jar of mayonnaise gets low and you get mayo all over your hand when trying to get out the last bit in the bottom of the jar? Use an iced-tea spoon or a long-handled spatula to clear out the jar. You can use iced-tea spoons for all sorts of jobs!

Be ready for baking. If you do a lot of baking for family or school events, it helps to be organized. Place all your baking supplies near the stove, refrigerator, mixer, and outlets. Before you begin baking, read the recipes quickly, gather the needed items on the counter, and put each one away after you use it. This procedure clears the kitchen and reminds you where to pick up if the telephone or a visitor interrupts the procedure. A messy kitchen is the last thing cooks need if they are completing a chore after an exhausting day or late at night!

Hang, don't drape, kitchen towels. Instead of draping your kitchen towels over the sink faucet or around the refrigerator door handle, place them in a ring-type holder commonly found in the bathroom. The stand keeps the cloths neatly folded and allows them to dry thoroughly after use.

Another way to hang kitchen towels. If your kitchen has no place to hang kitchen towels or pot holders, try this easy fix. Purchase two sets of mini magnetic curtain rods. Place one rod on the oven door, one on the refrigerator door, and two on the side of the refrigerator.

Hang your dish towels and matching pot holders from these mini curtain rods. They are handy when needed and look nice; they are also removable, so you can easily clean the surface behind them.

Keep dish towels from sliding. If your dish towels always slide off the oven door handle, clip the sides of the folded dish towel together with a clothespin and they won't slide onto the floor any longer.

Try a new way to store utensils. You may find that putting utensils into a drawer sideways instead of straight seems to let you fit more into the drawer, and you can see what you are looking for more easily. The utensils seem to stay in place better, too.

Keep a freezer inventory. If you have a chest freezer, or another one you use for long-term storage outside the kitchen, it's a good idea to keep track of food stored there. Using a white-board marker, keep a running inventory of what's in the freezer. When you add items, write them on the outside of the freezer doors. When you remove items or partial items, you can easily wipe away the item from the inventory list or modify the amount that's left in the freezer.

Help for snack lovers. Are your cabinets cluttered? If your family loves snack foods, you may find that almost-empty bags of potato chips and other snacks are getting buried under the new bags in your cabinet. You may end up with several almost-empty bags of some varieties of chips.

Here's a fix: Put a row of cup hooks across the top of the cabinet halfway between the back and the doors. Then fold over and clip all the bags with binder clips from an office-supply store and hang the bags on the cup hooks. Small packages can now sit on the bottom of the cabinet under the hanging

Unlimited Uses for . . . Foam Peanuts

Other uses for plastic foam peanuts include:

- Secure them in plastic newspaper bags and use to stuff valances.
- Give a beanbag chair a "lift" by stuffing with some foam peanuts.
- Put in clean, plastic milk jugs, seal, and use on a trotline as buoy markers.
- Put in the bottom of a large planter, then fill the pot with dirt. This reduces the amount of soil needed and lightens the weight of the planter. Note: First put one foam peanut in a glass of water to see if it dissolves; if it does, it won't be much use in a planter.
- Stuff an old pillowcase and sew up the end for a quick bed for a cat or small dog.

bags without getting buried, and all the bags are in a neat row like clothes hanging in a closet.

A new use for plastic lids. Put the plastic lids from large coffee cans between your nonstick skillets and pans to keep them from scratching. They also are useful in RVs and campers to keep items from rattling and making noise while traveling on the road.

Identify your mug. Many families have a set of matching coffee mugs. If your family members use their cups for beverages throughout the day, you're likely to forget whose cup is whose. Put a different colored twist tie on each cup handle to identify them. Use the ties over and over each day until they wear out—they will last a long time.

I.D. drinking glasses. In a houseful of family and friends, drinking glasses can get confused. To solve the ques-tion of "whose glass is whose," and also cut down on glass washing, clip a named clothespin to each glass. Keep the clothespins in the kitchen, in an easy-to-find spot.

Sort spices with chopsticks. Lay chopsticks in your spice cabinet to form front-to-back alleys for "same-type" spices (for example, Italian spices). Keeps them "in line" and organized, and you'll be able to find them easily.

CD racks come in handy. Since MP3 technology made its appear-ance, wire CD racks have been falling by the wayside. But don't toss them out. Placed in a kitchen cabinet, the racks make excellent separators and organiz-ers for plastic container lids.

Make a recipe album. Small photo albums are good for recipes that you accumulate from newspapers or copy down from friends. The recipes are kept clean, are easy to get to, and can

Unlimited Uses for . . . Clothespins

Don't toss those extra clothespins. Here are a few handy uses:

- Use them to close cereal and crackers packages instead of buying "chip clips."
- Clip a stain on clothing to remind you to attend to it.

- Use clothespins to fasten a trash bag to a lawn chair when cleaning up the yard.
- Use to hold or separate papers.
- Keep coupons or receipts together until you use them.

be categorized according to different types of foods.

Customize magnetic cards. If you receive magnetic business cards from local businesses but don't receive them from your favorite establishments, purchase stick-on magnets and make your own refrigerator magnets from the cards of the businesses you deal with regularly. Or, just glue the desired business cards over the magnetic ones you do not plan on using.

Organize bathroom accessories. Most bathrooms are full of stuff— blow-dryers, curling irons, brushes, combs, makeup sponges, and bath loofahs. Most of it is probably just shoved under the sink or lying on countertops in the way. Organize your items in a clear-plastic shoe holder (the kind with pockets) that can be hung on either side of a door. You won't have to deal with all those twisted cords anymore, and things will always be eye level and easy to get to.

Prepackage pills for convenience. It's a good idea to organize vitamins and pills you take every day. Some people use a lot more than what those 7-day pillboxes will hold. Try using the little plastic zipper-top bags that come with your clothes and hold extra buttons. Or pick up a package of a hundred 2-inch-by-3-½-inch bags at a crafts store. They work great. Once a month, load them up, and you're set. Take them while traveling, or use them at home each morning. You can label the outside with a marker for details if you would like. Save the bags and reuse them.

Line up medicine bottles. To keep track of when you take daily medicines, line up all the medicine bottles right-side-up in the medicine chest. Each time you take your medicine, turn the bottle upside down. At the end of the day, upright all the bottles to be ready for the next day.

Contain toothbrushes. Use a small bud vase for toothbrushes that don't fit into old-style holders. Find an inexpensive vase at a discount store, or go for silver or pewter if you like. As cheap as they are, you can change them often and spruce up the décor.

Put a new spin on cosmetics storage. Little bottles and jars of fingernail polishes, perfume, body sprays, and makeup have a way of ending up in a mess all over the bathroom. To organize them, buy a plastic turntable that's usually used for spices. Put all of your bottles on it, and when you want to find something, just give the table a spin and find it quickly!

Untangle those bathroom cords. To keep the cords of your hair dryer and curling iron from tangling when stored in a drawer, purchase some inexpensive hair clips. They come in all different sizes. Just zigzag a cord and clip it together.

Keep soap in place. If you are tired of a soap bar falling off the wall holder into the shower, here is the answer: Take a piece of rubber shelf liner and put it into the holder. Lo and behold, the soap bar stays in place, and the liner can be cleaned easily.

Fix a hanger. When hanging up a pair of pants, often the cardboard roll on an older hanger will bend, and the pants won't hang correctly. Rather than throw away the hanger, just insert a short, old pencil or a golf pencil into the roll to straighten out the bend. Now the pants will always hang straight.

Give an old evening bag new life. If you have a special evening bag that might be soiled or that has lost a bead or two, don't throw it away. Instead, why not use it as an elegant storage container for jewelry, coins, or other small items on your dresser? Now you can continue to enjoy its beauty and elegance.

MAKE THE MOST OF CLOSET SPACE

Closets are never big enough to hold everything we want to put in them. Culling through your stuff is always a way to create more room, and so is better organization. Create extra storage space with these six ideas:

1. Take advantage of storage boxes and color-coded hangers. Use the space in the tops of closets by installing additional shelves or hanging racks. Put boxes on top of shelves for more organization space.

2. Place hooks or over-the-door hangers on the door, and use multilayered storage gadgets to hang pants, suits, and ties.

3. Hang matching outfits (slacks and shirts) on one sturdy hanger. Use multiple pants-and-shirts hangers.

4. Get plastic crates and storage bins from container or department stores. Plastic milk crates can be stacked on their sides to hold sweaters, shoes or handbags, and then stacked on top of each other.

5. Put old bookcases in closets for ready-made shelving.

6. Store out-of-season or infrequently used items in seldom-used suitcases.

Easy I.D. Colored self-adhesive dots easily identify which appliance is plugged into the outlets on a surge-protector strip. You also can use them on water-bottle caps so you know which is yours (especially great when you have children).

Mark the top of plugs. Use a dot of nail polish on the top of an appliance plug so you know which way is up. Many plugs fit only one way, and this saves time. Just put a dot above the right prong so it is easy to see.

Sort cords in the kitchen. Here's another way to use nail polish to organize appliance cords. If you keep various appliances on your kitchen counter, and they all have white cords, here's a timesaver. To find the right one, mark each plug end with a different-colored nail polish.

Ponytail appliance cords. Rather than using twist ties to shorten electrical cords on appliances or bundle them up for storage, you can use ponytail bands—the kind with a ball on either end. Tie one ball on the cord and wrap the other around the folded cord like it's a ponytail. Make the cord just long enough to reach the plug, or if you're putting the appliance away, to fit into the storage space.

Corral those electrical cords. Appliance cords have a habit of coming loose on shelves and in cabinets when you store the iron or blender. Most of us wrap the cord around the iron or iced-tea maker, where it stays for about a second before coming loose.

Here is a way to keep the cords neat and tidy. Wind them around, then put them inside one of the soft-sided bottle or can holders that keep your soft drinks or beer cool. The cord will stay in place because the fabric is nonslip, and then it will slip through the handle of your iron or just lay neatly beside a stored mixer or blender.

Or, use cardboard bathroom tissue rolls to roll up your cords.

Organize those cords. Here's a hint for those surge protectors that are always a rat's nest of black electrical cords and usually are hidden behind a heavy piece of furniture.

Tape a piece of masking tape around the end of each cord, just above the plug. Write the name of the electrical device to which the cord belongs (TV, DVD player, clock). When it comes time to unplug one of them, you won't accidentally unplug the clock and have to reset the time!

Keep your chargers straight. Many families today have lots of battery-operated devices that have chargers.

You may have several portable phones, each with a charger, and also hand-held, battery-operated power tools, such as drills. If you receive several sets of return-address labels in promotional mailings, put them to work to sort all those chargers. Cut off two of the same pictures from the labels and put one on the charger and one on the corresponding appliance. Just use a different set of pictures for each appliance or tool.

Cute cassette storage. If someone in your family still likes to listen to cassette tapes (and many of us do!), you may find them all over the place. Make a handy storage container from an old shoe box that you decorate.

Tackle boxes aren't just for fishing. Even if you don't fish, tackle boxes come in handy. Use them for storing needlework and sewing supplies, beads, jewelry, makeup, and all sorts of small items.

Don't lose tiny parts. When working with small items that have tiny parts, place the object into a clear plastic bag that affords room for your hands and tools as well.

That way, when you remove a tiny screw it falls into the bottom of the bag, and you don't have to hunt for it

or worry about it getting lost. It's also very handy to have everything contained and right at your fingertips when it comes time for reassembly.

Keep track of loyalty club cards at a glance. An easy way to remember all of your "loyalty club" numbers (for hotels, airlines, and other groups) is to print them on a blank business card and have it laminated. You can easily fit 12 to 14 numbers on the card, and it saves so much time rather than searching through a wallet or purse for them. Pull it out whenever you need it, and presto, you have all of the numbers at once!

Make an easy call for home repairs. Knowing where all of the household maintenance receipts are helps when you need repairs, and at the end of the year, too, when tax time rolls around. One way to make it easy: Staple the top of one side of a plastic zipper-top bag inside the cover of your telephone book. When you have work done on the house or car, just put the receipt in the bag. When you need some work done, just head for the phone book to call a repair service and find your receipt for past work. Calling the same company that did previous work for you can save you money—sometimes hundreds of dollars—if something you need replaced is still under warranty.

Put warranties in a binder. Get a binder and put plastic sleeves in it to hold instruction and warranty booklets from appliances and electronics, as well as receipts. Keep the binder in your home office or on a kitchen shelf. If you ever need to check a warranty or purchase date, you will know just where to look.

Or, put those manuals in a drawer. Another option is to keep all the owner's manuals in a large envelope in a kitchen drawer.

What to do if you lose an owner's manual. If you can't find an owner's manual, visit the manufacturer's Web site, or call the company (most have a toll-free number) and order one. Some companies may charge, so be sure to ask about the cost.

Try a family file cabinet. File cabinets can be the perfect way to keep track of papers for family members. Give each family member a file drawer to keep his or her "stuff" filed in. File folders are cheap and can be labeled easily.

All the important papers—the kids' school papers, medical papers, toy information—everything goes into each person's file drawer.

When family members need something, they can look in their file drawer first, before they ask you.

Mark your place in magazines. If multiple members of your family like to read the same magazines, but you have trouble remembering where you left off, here's a trick to try. Instead of using traditional bookmarks, which fall out too easily, take a square sticky note and cut it in as many strips as you have magazine readers. With the sticky part attached to the magazine, write a family member's name on each strip of the sticky note. Use your note to mark the last page you have read. No more confusion. As a bonus, you will know when the magazine has been read completely because the other people's sticky notes have been removed. Then you can recycle the magazine or pass it on to someone else. If you want to save an article, you can rip it out once the other sticky notes are past the article you want.

Keep track of magazine reading. When you have finished reading a magazine, put a small circle in the upper right-hand corner of the cover. Have the next family member to read it put an "x" in the same spot when finished with the material. Give each family member his or her own symbol. When everyone has marked the cover, put the magazine in the recycling bin.

A better way to save magazine pages. If you like to clip recipes and other useful info from magazines, you need a simple way to keep the clippings so you can find them later. You could cut out recipes and glue them to 3-by-5-inch cards to keep in a file box.

Or, try tearing out the entire page, punching holes in the side, and placing the pages in three-ring binders. You might have one for recipes, another for holiday hints, and one for decorating hints. The info will be easy to access whenever you like.

Keep track of magazine renewals. You may be paying for the renewal of a magazine months before it is actually due, so keep track of your subscriptions. Keep a simple list for each year—stating the name of the publication, the amount you paid, when you paid, and for what length subscription. You can also keep track of political and charity donations and membership dues for organizations you belong to. Keep the old lists if you pay for more than one year at a time.

Another way to keep track of subscriptions. To remind yourself to renew your magazine subscriptions (since renewal notices are sent out so far ahead of time), attach the statement with the envelope to that month's page on the calendar. Then, when you turn to that month, it is there, waiting to be renewed.

Make an easy-update phone book. Address books get messy as people move and change phone numbers, and eventually they fall apart. Try this trick for making your address book easy to update.

Buy one or more inexpensive photograph albums and cut plain typing paper into sheets to fit the album pages. Type or neatly write all the names, addresses, and phone numbers for each letter of the alphabet and insert them into the pages. Better yet, make duplicate copies of the album to keep by each phone in the house. Because each page of the album is encased in plastic, it will stay neater, and it is very easy to change a number or name when needed.

Keep a handy message center by the phone. Keep a little ringed binder next to the phone. It comes in handy when you need to write down a number or a message. The binder also allows you to write down messages and then erase them from the machine. Family members will learn to look at the book to see if they have any messages.

Keep a notepad upstairs. Keeping a notepad and pen on the dresser in your bedroom can be invaluable when you are upstairs and want to remember something (chores, groceries, whatever). That way you won't forget by the time you get to your notepad in the kitchen downstairs.

Detergent bottle caps. The plastic caps that come on large laundry-detergent bottles are great for keeping small things in a cabinet drawer—also in the workshop and many other places. They can store small items in one place.

You can even spray-paint them to spruce them up.

Get to your license easily. If your wallet is full, it can be hard to pull out your driver's license when you need it to show identification. Slip a strip of paper into your wallet along with your license. Then you can pull on the strip of paper and the license will come out easily.

How to part with treasures. Sooner or later, many of us have the unpleasant duty of distributing possessions from the homes of older family members, or even our own homes when we need to downsize our living space. It can be very difficult cleaning out a loved one's home. There are so many memories and treasures.

Here is a way to distribute possessions among family members and friends. Take photos of the items that will need new homes and make two sets of prints. Number each item, and make two lists corresponding to the numbers. You can, if needed, also develop two lists, one of relatives and one of friends in priority order. Send a set of prints to the person at the top of each list, along with a copy of the numbered list for that set of prints and a list of people (with addresses) who are to see that set. Ask each person to write his or her name on the list beside the number of the items they want and pass the package to the next person. If there are duplicate requests, resolve them by priority or by trading off pieces.

Pieces left unclaimed can be sent to a thrift shop. The pictures will serve as a permanent reminder of the extent and richness of your loved one's valued possessions.

Have an errand basket. Keep an

errand basket near the back door into which you drop letters to be mailed, shopping lists, shoes to be repaired, a blouse with a lost button to be matched.

This basket can help keep you sane, especially if you have small children, when there is an endless list of errands to run and chores to do.

For commuters, a handy basket. If you have a lengthy commute from home to work each day, you probably also combine after-work errands to save gasoline. Keep a divided basket (similar to the type used for napkins and plastic utensils at a picnic) in your car. In the longer section place coupons, a memo pad, a small makeup pouch, and a calendar. In the three smaller sections keep postage stamps, change (for tolls, drive-through trips, and soda machines), a pen, a small hairbrush, and other items you might need. Also put in a couple of individually wrapped wet towelettes and a small pack of tissues. Take this basket inside with you when you get home, and add whatever you might need for the next day. The basket "filing" system will help you stay organized, and you will always have what you need when you are away from home.

Organize errands by distance. When you have lots of errands to do, make a list of them, beginning with the ones that are farthest away from home, and on to the closest. If you don't have enough time to get them all done, or if you get tired, the remaining errands are those that are closer to home. This way, you can quickly do them later on.

Hang keys on a hook. Always misplacing your keys? Put up a key hook right inside the door you use to go in and out of the house. Get a plaque with enough hooks for every family member, and hang your keys on your hook as soon as you walk in the door.

I.D. your keys. Label or photocopy extra keys you keep around the house. It's all too easy to forget what the keys are used for.

Risk-free key I.D. One way to identify your keys is to swap your last name and address with a friend. If you lose your keys and someone else finds them, they won't be able to steal your car because your friend's key won't fit in your car, and your key won't fit in theirs.

Keep a key handy without pockets. Since women do not have designated pockets as men do for their personal effects, it is easy to exit cars and forget our keys.

Here's a way to keep from getting stranded if you lock your keys in the car: Buy some baby-diaper pins, put an extra house and car key on one, and pin the spare keys to your waistline or inside a pants pocket.

Make yourself a binder for each child. If you have children who are in school, you have a lot of papers to keep for school, sports, church, and other activities. To keep track of all those really important papers for each child, buy a three-ring binder and divider folders. Label each section with a child's name. When they bring home papers that you need to keep for reference for the whole school year, simply use a three-hole punch on the paper and put it in the correct area. You will have easy access to all important numbers and dates.

Keep news clippings. Anytime your kids (or relatives or friends) make it into the newspaper, clip the article for them, and save it. Also cut out the date from the top of the newspaper page, and include the name of the newspaper, too. Tape the date to the back or top of the article.

Put the article in a clear plastic scrapbook page, or have it laminated at a local copy shop to preserve it.

Keep a calendar on the fridge. For easy access, hang a calendar on the side of your fridge with a suction-cup hook. If your refrigerator does not have a smooth finish and the suction cup will not stick, try this: Take a smooth magnet and put the suction cup on it, then hang your calendar.

Make your calendar easy to see. As we get older, we forget things. So, have a large calendar on which you mark important dates that you need to remember. You can even use colored sticky notes.

Also keep a listing of important dates in your address book on some blank pages. You might want to note birth dates and anniversaries, dates of new car battery or tire purchases, appliance purchases, even the death date of friends' spouses. That way, you can always call or write them on that date to let them know that they are not alone.

Color-code your calendar. When you note birthdays, anniversaries, and appointments on your calendar, take a black permanent marker and draw around the square of the date. Then use a highlighter to color the name— blue for doctor appointments, yellow for birthdays, and green for anniversaries. Give each kind of occasion its own color so you will know at a glance what you have coming up. It can save you from forgetting important dates.

Or, color-code this way. Just have each member of your family use a different-colored pen to write his or her activities on a large family calendar.

Hide the calendar. An alternative to hanging a calendar with a magnet on the refrigerator is to put a cup hook on the inside of your pantry door and hang it there. It's handy for daily viewing and out of sight.

Organize your holidays. After the holidays, when you put up your new calendar for the following year, note on the back of the month of December page what you served at holiday parties. Was there too much food or not enough? You can also note whether you need more wrapping paper or boxes, and anything else you'll need to remember when December rolls around again.

Secure a large calendar. Keep a calendar on the side of your refrigerator to track the activities of your family. If you have a large family and need a large wall calendar to keep track of everybody's activities, magnets or suction-cup hooks may not be strong enough to hold it. For better support, buy an inexpensive Christmas stocking holder to place on the top of the refrigerator and hang the calendar from that. It will hold the calendar easily and will not mar the surface.

Keep the calendar from falling. The holes in wall calendars often rip when the entire weight of the calendar hangs from just one hole. It's likely to occur at the beginning of the year, when most of the months hang down. You can try to reinforce the hole in each month's page, or use this solution: Fold up the months not being used behind the month being used, so that the only weight hanging down is the one page for the current month.

Buy greeting cards in advance. To be ready for special occasions, it's a good idea to buy cards when you see them for special people or events. But when you look at the cards later, you'll probably have forgotten whom they were for. So, before you put a card away in your desk, write the intended recipient's name on the envelope where the stamp is placed. That way, when you are ready to send the card, the stamp will cover the name.

Make a greeting card file. To find a greeting card fast when you need one, keep the cards in an accordion file. Categorize them by occasion: birthday, get well, anniversary, graduation, sympathy. Keep each card with its envelope or have a separate file for envelopes. Organize the envelope file by size: Stand all of the envelopes end to end, deck-of-cards style, and pull the shorter ones out, until all are in order, shorter to larger. When you pick a card to send, it will be easy to find an envelope to fit the card.

Make a portable card list. Type a list of the month and date for birthdays and/or anniversaries you need to remember, then make this list small enough to fit in your wallet—the size of a regular credit card. When you buy a card, cross off the person's name, and you'll be ready when it is time to recognize someone else's celebration. If you have access to a color printer, put the birthdays in one color and the anniversaries in another color. Just update the list as your family grows.

Use a greeting card organizer. If you find it cumbersome to transfer birthdays, anniversaries, and other occasions to your new calendar every year, you might like to buy a greeting-card organizer. Write down all the birthdays and other important dates, and add new ones whenever a family member has a wedding or a baby. Keep the organizer where it's easy to find.

Organize important addresses and numbers. On regular 3-by-5-inch cards write the names, addresses, and telephone numbers of family members and friends, and on colored cards write the names and addresses of doctors, medical labs, and other important, quickly needed names. This makes finding numbers much quicker.

Start micro-tasking and quit clock watching. It's amazing how much you can get done in 5-minute "sprints" of time. When you have a few minutes before you have to leave for an appointment, put that time to use and do a couple of small tasks around the house. This is what I call micro- or mini-tasking. To avoid clock watching to stay on time, set the timer on your oven for a few minutes before you need to walk out the door. When the timer goes off, stop what you're doing and leave. Small missions will be accomplished without the worrisome clock watching!

Minimize your schedule. If you work a part-time job and get a new work schedule each week, it helps to print out each weekly schedule. But instead of making a full-page copy that will get wrinkled and torn, try reducing the schedule so that it fits in your wallet. It's easily accessible, and you'll always know where it is.

Put appointment reminders where

you'll be sure to look. Here's a novel idea for keeping tabs on your appointments: Put appointment cards in your flip-open eyeglass case (by date). If you use reading glasses, you won't miss an appointment.

Another appointment minder. Put a reminder note (in large, black, printed letters on a large piece of paper) on a floor or bathroom mirror with the time and place of important things you need to do the next day, so that you'll see it first thing in the morning. It can keep you from forgetting an appointment.

Leave a reminder on a mirror. Or, write a reminder note (in large letters) with soap or a lip-liner pencil right on the bathroom mirror with your next day's appointments. When you've read it, just wipe it away.

Don't miss activities. When you see a newspaper article or flier about events or activities of interest to you, cut out the info and put it in a folder. Each Friday night, review this folder so that you can plan your weekend accordingly.

Another option is to post possible things to do on the refrigerator door.

Thank-you cards made easier. Sending thank-you notes after the death of a loved one or after a happy occasion like a wedding or birth is time-consuming. It takes hours of time to try to find addresses, especially out-of-town ones.

The next time you need to send a card or gift that will get a response, attach an address label of yours to the card to make it easier for the recipients to send a thank-you note or reply.

Did I turn that off? Many of us wonder after we've left the house if we remembered to shut off the electrical appliances that we used that morning. Here's a system to help. Right before pouring the last cup of coffee, turn off the coffee maker; before pressing the last seam, unplug the iron; before curling the last strand of hair, unplug the curling iron or hot rollers.

When you back the car out of the garage, press the button on the remote to shut the garage door and then wait while you fasten your seat belt and tune the car radio. Watch the door go down and then wait a few seconds before leaving. That way, you will be sure that you haven't left the garage door open or that the door hasn't gone down and right back up again, which can happen occasionally.

Make a monthly checklist. You

know all those things you're supposed to do once a month? To keep track of them, create a first-of-the-month checklist on your computer. On the first of each month you won't forget to do things like give the dogs their heartworm pills and put on flea and tick medicine, update the family calendar, check the smoke alarm and carbon-monoxide detector, flip the mattress, check all the fluid levels and tire pressure on the vehicles, run vinegar through the coffeepot, defrag the hard drives on the computers, and change the air-conditioning/heating filter.

Clean up as you go. If you like to walk around the neighborhood, you can do some good at the same time. Don a plastic glove, carry a couple of plastic bags and pick up litter to help keep your little corner of the world neat and tidy.

Prevent fires with a clay pot. With indoor smoking becoming more and more taboo, consider this tip to reduce smoking-related fires outdoors. If you are hosting an outdoor party, set a clay pot with a hole in the bottom upside down in a clay saucer as a receptacle for ashes and cigarette butts. It keeps the stench to a minimum and prevents ashes from flying around in the breeze.

It also can stop a fire caused by people putting not-quite-dead cigarettes into containers that might have paper or other combustibles inside.

Get help changing the sheets. Make your life easier when guests visit at your vacation home. Establish a house rule: "When you leave, you take the sheets off the bed you used and put on a clean set of sheets." The beds will be ready for the next guests, with less work for you.

Save water. Whether or not we live in a dry climate, we should all do our part to conserve water. Here is one way to do it. Did you know that you waste a lot of water running the tap while waiting for the water to get hot? It can add up to a gallon or more each time. Capture that water in a pail or jug, and use the "saved" water for houseplants.

Use extra mouse pads. An extra rubber computer mouse pad can make a helpful coaster on a nightstand. When you place cups or glasses on it, any splashed water will not reach the wooden surface underneath, and you won't have to worry about spots or stains. The same idea will work on tables in other rooms, too.

Separate coffee filters. If you wet

your fingers slightly, you can separate coffee filters with ease.

SHOPPING

Make your shopping list easy to read. Use a different-colored ink to cross out the items on your shopping list. It's such a simple thing, but it really makes it easier to see what you have and have not bought as you shop.

Make a master shopping list. Type up a list of the items you buy each week at the grocery store, and put them in the order they are found in the store where you shop. Print about 20 copies on your computer or at a local copy shop. Then you can just check off what you need, rather than having to write out the item each week.

Use a store directory. Large stores and shopping malls often have a store directory available. Take one home and use it to plan your shopping. When writing out a shopping list, the directory shows the aisle number where items you need can be located. You will save time and a lot of extra walking.

Make grocery notes instead of a list. Keep about 20 sheets of a sticky-backed notepad inside your wallet or purse and use them to jot down notes or grocery lists as needed. When you go to the grocery store, stick them on the handle of the grocery cart. This method could eliminate hunting for lists.

Make a visual shopping list. If you send a spouse or teenager to pick up some items at the store, why not show them exactly what you need? Take a photo with your shopper's cell phone so they'll know exactly what you want. Take a picture of what you want to purchase, and you will have it with you when you go shopping.

Make your grocery list easy to see. Keep your grocery list in plain sight while you shop. Take a clothespin to the grocery store and pin the grocery list to the top rail of the shopping cart.

Don't forget to use your coupons. To keep yourself from forgetting to use a coupon at the store or restaurant or wherever you are going, fold it up and put it in your wallet right next to your debit card.

Conquer coupon craziness. Using coupons can help you save grocery dollars, and here's a way to save time, too. Sometimes, at the end of scanning coupons when you shop, for whatever reason a coupon will not scan. Then you have to search every bag for that item(s) to make sure of the correct item, size, weight, and brand name. If you use more than one coupon, the search for these items in already-packed bags stuffed in the cart is very aggravating.

Is there an easier way? You bet. Leave all the items for which you have coupons until the end, and make a point of showing the cashier each coupon with the corresponding product.

Make coupons easy to see. When you file money-saving coupons that you want to use, mark the expiration date in bold writing somewhere on the coupon. You will be able to easily see the date when you go through your folder or purse, instead of squinting at fine print.

Organize those coupons. What is the best way to keep coupons organized? Here are a few suggestions:

- File by expiration date.

- File by store aisles.

- File by categories, like canned goods, dairy, and cereal.

Abide by the Code of Consumer Ethics

The Better Business Bureau has a Code of Consumer Ethics that spells out guidelines for ethical shopping. It's well worth reading and following.

"The Better Business Bureau's mission is to promote, develop, and encourage an ethical marketplace. The public shares the responsibility for maintaining an ethical marketplace. Therefore, the following Code of Ethics has been established to guide the public in this role.

EDUCATION—Know your rights and responsibilities, comparison shop, read contracts and ask questions before buying. Investigate offers that sound too good to be true.

TRUTHFULNESS—Don't return used goods under the pretense that they are damaged if they are not. This practice, as well as price-tag switching and shoplifting (or failure to report shoplifters), costs all consumers in terms of time and money.

HONESTY—Exhibit the same kind of honesty you expect to receive from business firms. If a sales clerk makes a mistake in your favor, point it out as quickly as you would a mistake in the company's favor.

INTEGRITY—Live up to your obligations. Enter agreements in good faith, and pay your bills when they are due. If you can't, inform the merchant and explain why.

COURTESY—Recognize that store employees are individuals. Treat them as you wish to be treated.

SENSIBILITY—Don't make unreasonable demands. Respect the firm's right to limit services and products offered. Don't expect to get something for nothing. Remember, always turn to our BBB for assistance with any marketplace decision or dispute."

Source: Better Business Bureau Consumer Code of Ethics

Organize coupons in an album. Instead of using messy coupon wallets that store loose coupons, buy a small, pocket-size photo album. After attaching some adhesive index tabs every few pages and marking them with different categories (e.g., "frozen foods," "dairy"), slide your coupons into the photo pockets in their respective sections. It's fast and easy to flip through while at the store and see which coupons you have and which ones are past their expiration dates.

Go green with shopping bags. For a healthier planet, try to cut down on the number of plastic bags you use. Paper bags can be reused lots of times. Some stores give a rebate for using paper or cloth bags.

You can take several large cloth or heavy-mesh tote bags to the grocery or discount store, and use them instead of paper or plastic at the checkout. The tote bags hold more items, stand up when full, and last for many years. At other stores, such as department or home-improvement stores, you can take a small mesh bag or a large mesh tote.

Over the course of several years, you will be able to avoid using hundreds of plastic bags, even if you're not a big shopper. Keep the cloth and mesh bags in the trunk of your car at all times. It's a matter of replacing a wasteful habit with an environmentally good habit.

Remember that special item. When you are shopping for a certain item and find it, you can use your digital camera or cell phone to take a picture, and then write down the price and the store where you found it. When you go from store to store, you won't forget what you saw earlier. That makes it easier to decide.

Easier opening bags. When opening those plastic vegetable bags in the produce section of the grocery store, first wet your fingers from the vegetable bins that are misted to keep veggies fresh. The bags open like magic.

Bag the meat. Many supermarket meat departments offer plastic bags to contain leaky packages of meat. To keep your hands clean, invert the bag and use it like a glove to look for the package you need. When you find the meat you want, grab it with the gloved hand and wrap the bag around it. Then you can shop for veggies without worrying that you have some residue of blood on your hands.

Keep your purse safe. Never leave your purse unattended in a cart while shopping. Even if you strap the purse into the child restraint on the shopping cart, someone can just walk by, reach in, and grab something from it.

Save time in the checkout line. Do you hate standing in the checkout lines at the store? To make it faster and more efficient when purchasing greeting cards, always put each card facedown under the flap of each envelope. The bar code is visible to the checker, and he or she doesn't have to turn over every card to find it.

Make bar codes work for you. These days, almost all retail operations use a bar-coded inventory and retail sales system. An item cannot be entered into a cash register without a bar code or its accompanying number. Knowing the price just isn't good enough anymore.

To make shopping go faster, as you approach the checkout stand at a department store, try to arrange all the merchandise on the counter so the tags and bar codes are in sight, and the salesperson is able to quickly scan the bar code. Place the garment or package with the tag facing up and visible. Don't make the clerk go on a hunting expedition.

Control grocery bags in transit. Stopping at the grocery store can be awkward when you drive a pickup truck. You probably have to climb into

the bed of the truck or find a rake or hoe to retrieve the cans and other goods that slide out of the plastic bags.

To save your back, purchase an inexpensive tension shower-curtain rod, tighten it up under the lip of the truck bed near the tailgate, and hang shower curtain hooks on it. When you shop, take each plastic bag and hang the handles on the hooks to keep all the bags in place.

Put grocery bags in boxes. Here's another hint for those of you who go grocery shopping in a pickup truck. Put three or four large, sturdy boxes in the truck (with the flaps folded down). Put your grocery bags into the open boxes, and the bags won't go sliding around and dumping stuff all over the truck bed.

Also, separate the bags containing crushables (bread, chips, cookies, or pretzels) from bags containing heavy items such as bottles of soda or juice.

Contain purchases in the car. Keep a rectangular laundry basket in the back of your car. When you go shopping, put your packages in it. No more shopping bags all over the trunk and out of reach.

Keep a cooler in your car trunk. It's a good idea to keep a cooler in the car trunk when you go food shopping, so you can run errands afterward without perishable foods spoiling. Frozen foods won't thaw (unless they are in the cooler for a long time) and refrigerated foods will stay cool. Keep a few of those extra plastic sacks in there also. You can use them to double-wrap any meats and keep them, especially chicken, from possibly dripping onto your other purchases. And of course, because you are recycling the bags, you are also helping the environment.

Use mesh in the trunk. To prevent groceries from sliding to the back of the car trunk, put a piece of mesh shelf liner across the trunk of the car, and add a laundry basket. Set bags of groceries in the basket. When the basket is full, if you have more groceries, set them on the mesh and the bags won't slide.

Keep paper bags in your car to reuse. After you go to the grocery store, fold the paper bags and put them in the trunk of your car. The next time you shop, take them with you and reuse them. You will be surprised to find out how many times they can be reused. When the bags begin to wear out, use them to hold papers to be recycled.

Label your favorite products. When buying favorite household products that are not carried in most stores, save time and gasoline looking around for replacements by marking on the package where you bought them. You'll know right where to go.

GARAGE SALES

Save on your garage sale. To cut the costs of hosting a garage sale, ask your neighbors to join in for a weekend sale. That way, you can share the cost of the classified advertising and refreshments. You also will make more money because customers love big block/neighborhood sales. There are more opportunities for buying.

Save time on tagging. Most garage-sale experts say you should put a price tag on every item you will sell because it will make your sale run more smoothly. People won't constantly be asking how much an item costs. However, you can group like items on a table or in a box and put up one sign: "Each item 25 cents." Less prep work for you!

Make a great garage sale sign. Good signs are important for a successful sale. Put the address at the top of your sign in big enough letters and numbers so that it can be read from a passing car. Use a black marker and print large!

Next, you need the date, so that people can know that it is a current sign, and last, the words "garage sale." Some people cut a poster board in quarters and then try to write too

Garage Sale Basics

Summer is one of the best times to have garage sales. They can be fun and give you some extra money for a special day out! Get together with family or neighbors—the bigger the better. Here are a few hints to make your sale successful:

- First and foremost, some cities or counties require you to get a garage-sale permit. Check with your local government before having a sale. Some areas also limit how many times you can have sales during the year, so plan accordingly.

- Prepare for your sale. Go through items carefully so you don't sell something that is valuable or an heirloom.

- Advertise in your newspaper or put up posters in your area with the address, time, and date of your sale. Do not place signs on telephone or other utility poles. You may want to put signs in local stores and laundromats. (Be sure to take the signs down when the sale is over.)

- If more than one person is selling items, buy different-colored paper dots to put on items. When you sell the item, take off the dot and place it on a piece of paper. This way at the end of the sale, you will be able to easily add the sales.

- Place large, attractive items near the curb to lure people to your sale.

- Display items so that they can be easily seen. Don't make buyers dig through clothing. Put some of the large, brightly colored or one-of-a-kind items near the street to attract buyers.

- Have boxes, plastic bags, and newspaper on hand.

- Be sure to price every item. Be prepared for some haggling—if you want to sell stuff, you may have to lower the price.

- Have plenty of change on hand. If you have a lot of things marked under a dollar, make sure you have enough to change paper bills.

- Keep a close eye on the cash register; a "cash-only" policy is probably best.

- If you have a ton of children's toys that aren't selling, as the day progresses start giving toys away to children who come to the sale with adults.

- Have extension cords ready so that electronic items can be plugged in and tested.

- As a safety precaution, lock all doors to your home, and don't let anyone in to use the restroom.

- Donate any leftover items to local charities.

much information on it. You don't need that much information! If people can just find you, they will see what you have for sale. Be sure to check local regulations governing garage sales before posting signs.

And finally, be a good citizen and remove the sign as soon as the sale is over so it doesn't become clutter and trash on the roadway. It is very annoying for shoppers to go several blocks out of their way only to find that a sign was left from last week and the person holding the sale just didn't bother to take it down.

Shop smart at garage sales. Usually when you go garage-sale shopping, you'll find some things you will be bringing back home with you. Here are a few helpful items to take with you that will make life a lot easier if you buy that "find":

- Keep a cardboard box or a tote bag in your car to hold your purchases, so things don't roll around while you're driving. It'll make carrying items into your home easier, too.

- Keep some newspaper in the car so that if you need to wrap up anything breakable before you leave the garage sale, you'll be ready. There's nothing worse than arriving home to find your new treasure in pieces.

- Keep a container of diaper wipes or a roll of paper towels and a bottle of hand sanitizer handy. Garage sales have lots of terrific finds, but often a lot of dust and dirt come with them.

- Also, take a few business cards or handwritten cards with your name and cell-phone number. If you see something you really want, but only if the price comes down, you can ask the seller to call you if it is marked down.

Chapter 2

Cleaning Up

This chapter is all about keeping your home clean, from the kitchen to the bathroom and all around the house. There are hints on using different kinds of cleaning products and tools, and tips on vacuuming, dusting, and deodorizing, too. I've always believed that it's best to start with safe and easy cleaning aids that you have at home, then go on to stronger cleaners or commercial preparations if necessary.

Sit down to clean up. When you're getting on in years and do all your own housework, some of the bending and stooping can stir up arthritis or back problems. Keep a folding camp-stool, or a rolling stool, in the house and use it to sit on as you dust or polish furniture and cabinets. Just scoot around, using your feet until all the lower work is done. Your joints—and your back—will be happier.

KITCHEN

Clean refrigerator coils. When cleaning the coils on the bottom of your refrigerator, use the attachments hose of your vacuum cleaner. If there's some dust you can't reach, blow it away with the can of compressed air that you use to clean your computer.

Make refrigerator cleaning easier. Cleaning an older refrigerator with wire-rack-style shelves is difficult and time-consuming. To speed the job, buy an extra pair of rough, skin-exfoliating gloves meant for use in the shower. Just put on the shower gloves, dip your hands in the cleaning solution, and systematically rub your fingers over the wire racks.

Deodorize a freezer. If you buy a used freezer that has a nasty odor inside, here's a way to get rid of the smell: Place an open can of coffee inside the freezer for a few days (keep the freezer running). The odor will disappear, and the coffee should still be usable, with no unpleasant smell.

Make the most of baking soda.

Take two ½-pound, empty, clean, soft-margarine tubs. Fill each one half-full of baking soda. Save the lids. Place one tub in the freezer and one tub in the refrigerator. Change frequently. Each time you replace the old with the new,

Then & Now: Updates for Hints

Over time, many hints need to be updated because fabrics, cleaning products, and surfaces change. So, here are some "Heloise Updates" that you might find interesting:

For a ballpoint ink stain:

Then, we recommended using hair spray.

Now, use rubbing alcohol.

Why? Fabrics, ink formulation, and hair-spray ingredients are different today.

To remove ballpoint ink from washable clothing, lay the garment on a towel, stain side down. Dampen a cloth with rubbing alcohol and lightly dab (don't rub) the stain from the back side. When the stain is removed, launder as usual.

For candle wax on carpet:

Then, we suggested paper towels and an iron.

Now, it's ice and a metal pan.

Why? Updated information from the Carpet and Rug Institute.

To remove candle wax from a carpet, fill a metal pan with ice. Put it on top of the candle wax until the wax is frozen solid. Then, hit it with a small hammer to break up the hardened wax. Pick up the pieces and vacuum. Follow by using a dry-cleaning solvent or carpet stain remover.

For treating jeans so they don't fade:

Then, soak jeans in salt and water or vinegar and water.

Now, use specialized laundry products that help retain color.

Why? Today's denim is manufactured with modern dyes, and salt or vinegar does *not* set colors.

There are many variables to keep in mind when you are trying to remove stains from clothing or countertops, marks on wallpaper, or a spill on a carpet. Each is unique, and all factors need to be considered before you begin to tackle a stain. Most important, *always* check the manufacturer's recommendations before beginning any type of cleaning.

put the lid on the old tub and keep it under your kitchen sink. When you want to scrub out your sink, use the old baking soda. It is nonabrasive, and when it is washed down the drain it will freshen the pipes and the garbage disposal.

Clean up hard-water stains and deposits. Clean hard-water stains on the plastic tray for the water and ice dispenser on your refrigerator door with vinegar, if you can remove the drip tray. Heat some household vinegar until warm—*not* boiling—and soak the tray. Scrub with a soft brush, rinse, and that's it!

Warming the vinegar will help speed the process, and you'll even notice it bubbling while working.

Vinegar is also great for the aerator on the sink faucet. Stubborn hard-water deposits can make cleaning the shower doors, tub, faucets, and anything that comes in contact with the minerals found in tap water difficult to clean. Vinegar works wonders on such surfaces, even your pet's water bowl.

One gallon of plain old white vinegar can eliminate harsh, expensive commercial products, and it's safe for the environment, too.

Get burned-on food off pots. To clean pots and pans that have burnt-on food, just put enough water in the pot or pan to cover the burnt-on food and put in a dishwasher detergent packet. These packets usually are solid on one

STEP-BY-STEP CLEANING

When an area or space needs cleaning, have you wondered what basic steps must be taken to get the best results? Well, here they are:

- Before you decide to use a commercial cleaning product, read the label first. Because cleaners differ, you should check that the one you are using is safe for the surface you are cleaning.

- Prepare the area for cleaning by removing food, dirt, and loose substances. My favorite way is to use the vacuum, even on furniture (use the upholstery attachment).

- Apply enough cleaner to cover the surface, and allow it enough time to work. Don't wipe it off too fast, or you'll have to repeat the process.

- Remove the cleaner properly. Use a squeegee, sponge, or cloth to soak up the mixture and the dirt. Rub stubborn areas. Rinse, if needed, and wipe up all the liquid. Dry with an absorbent cloth or air-dry as instructions indicate.

side and liquid on the other. Let the packet dissolve in the water overnight. The next morning, dump the water and rinse. The pot or pan should be spotless.

Soak away burned-on food. If you forget about a pan on the stove and burn food onto it so badly that it sets off the smoke detector, don't throw out the pan. Instead, add some dishwasher detergent to the pan, stir to dissolve, fill it with hot water, then let it soak overnight. The next day, the pan should be easy to clean.

Loosen stuck-on food another way. After you dish up a meal, put some

CLEANING YOUR HOME AWAY FROM HOME

When you're at your getaway home, cabin in the woods, place at the beach, river, or lake, or in your camper, you want to enjoy your downtime as much as possible. However, household cleaning still needs to be done. Darn it! Here are a few hints to help keep things tidy without taking too much time:

- Start with choosing one thing a day in the kitchen area, which is usually the center of activity. Clean a stove top, straighten one cabinet or refrigerator shelf (be sure to check food expiration dates), or clean out just five things from any drawer.

- Vacuum, mop, or sweep only the high-traffic areas. Put on an attachment and vacuum a bookcase, lampshade, tabletop, or even picture frames.

- Keep a roll of paper towels in bathrooms for quick cleanups. Line the garbage can with a plastic bag, newspaper, or brown grocery bag to keep it clean. Use your bath towel or a squeegee to wipe down the shower walls and door after each shower.

- Don't fret about the rooms people don't see! Just try to keep the "public" areas picked up in case of drop-in guests.

- If something is out of place, pick it up and put it away when you walk by. To make things a bit easier to keep up, designate at least one chore to everyone in the house that he or she is consistently responsible for.

- Buy extra cleaning products when they are on sale to have on hand. If you are out of a cleaning product and the store is too far away, think "substitutes." A great substitute for window and mirror cleaning is alcohol or vinegar and a page of newspaper. Or, if you're out of automatic dishwasher detergent, hand-wash the dishes and put them in the dishwasher to dry—they'll also be out of sight. For a quick sink or tub cleaner, use baking soda and liquid soap.

- If you do these little things along the way, your weekend or vacation time can be relaxing, and your second home will stay clean, too.

water and baking soda in the pan. When it's time to clean the pan, the baking soda will have loosened anything that is stuck to the bottom, and almost all of it will come right off with a gentle swish of the dishcloth.

Unstick stubborn burnt-on food. Try this method for removing burnt-on food you can't scrape off the bottom of a pot: Add enough water to cover the bottom of the pot, then liberally sprinkle the pot with baking soda. Put back on the stove and bring to a boil, then turn off the heat and let sit for a few hours. With a little scrubbing, the pot should be as good as new.

Remove hardened sugar. For really stubborn food, like hardened caramel or sugar, cover the bottom of the pan with about an inch of water and a generous sprinkle of baking soda and set it to boil. After a few minutes, the sugar will dissolve, and you can clean the pan with a quick scrub of your kitchen brush.

Put credit cards to a new use. Here is a useful job for those unsolicited fake credit cards that arrive by mail: Use them as pot scrapers. They are great at removing cooked-on food, especially after the pan is soaked in water.

Clean the coffee-pot filter basket.

Baskets in coffee pots can get pretty cruddy-looking. If your basket is removable, the easiest way to clean it is to put it in the dishwasher every so often. If it's not removable, try using good old vinegar and baking soda. Put in enough baking soda to cover the bottom of the basket, followed by about 2 tablespoons of vinegar to make it fizz. When the fizzing stops, add a little more vinegar to make it fizz again. When the basket is clean, rinse it well with water.

Or try this method: Take a bowl that is just big enough for the basket to fit into, add about a tablespoon of dishwasher detergent, and fill the bowl with hot water. Add the coffee-filter basket and watch the cleaning action begin instantly. It might need to be done a couple of times, depending on how stained the basket is. Use an old toothbrush to finish the crevices that might still be stained.

Here's another method for cleaning those corners and crannies: Let the basket sit in your dishwater for a couple of minutes, then use a kid's clean watercolor brush to clean out all the crevices.

Clean the coffee-pot reservoir. The coffee-pot reservoir harbors moisture and warmth after the coffee brews, so simply keep the lid open for a few hours and let it dry.

No-mess coffee making. After putting a new coffee filter into your coffee pot, rinse it with water to make the filter adhere to the basket instead of collapsing when you pour in the coffee.

Use vinegar to clean an auto-drip coffee maker. Let the vinegar run through one cycle of the coffee pot, and then pour the hot vinegar back into the reservoir. Turn the coffee maker off and let sit for 30 minutes or so. This allows the vinegar to really break up the lime deposits. Then turn on the coffee maker and let it run through. Follow with several carafes of fresh water.

Before you dump that hot vinegar down the drain, pour in some baking soda. You'll clean the drain *and* the coffee pot.

Clean up a teacup. After years of use, teapots and teacups may look like they haven't been cleaned, even though you scrub them. Delicate china teacups can't go into the dishwasher. To get them clean, put dishwasher powder and water in the teapot and let it soak. Then put the solution in a small bowl and turn your cup top-side-down and let it soak. Rinse well with clear water.

Here's another approach: Use baking soda to remove tea stains from cups. Keep baking soda at hand by putting some in a glass cheese shaker. Keep the shaker under the sink and just pull it out and shake when you want to clean stains from a cup. It's faster and easier than getting out the whole box and putting it on the counter each time you want to use it.

More cup cleanup. To remove stubborn tea and coffee stains from cups, simply use full-strength lemon juice and scrub.

De-crumb the toaster. Periodically use a clean, 3-inch paintbrush to clean out all the crumbs from your toaster.

You can also use a can of pressurized air (used for computer keyboards) for errant bread crumbs that cling to the wires and side crevices of the toaster. A few quick puffs blow them into the removable tray. Just empty the tray first to avoid stirring up the crumbs that have already obeyed the law of gravity.

Get rid of melted plastic. If you leave a plastic bag of rolls on top of your toaster, the plastic will, of course, melt onto the surface if the toaster gets hot. Here's how to get it off. First, unplug the toaster. Then pour a bit of acetone-based nail polish remover on an old washcloth, and rub over the area until the plastic peels away from the metal. Wipe over the area with a damp cloth.

De-grease the stove. After you cook hamburgers, get rid of splattered grease easily. Spray the stove top with vinegar and wipe it down for squeaky, shiny results.

Keep the oven clean. Wipe out the oven every time you use it. It will stay clean for years, with very little work.

Clean up when a pie drips in the oven. If a pie cooks over and drips onto the bottom of your oven, lay two paper towels over the burn and pour water on it until the towels are saturated, to soften the burned syrup. Let the wet towels sit in the oven for sev-

eral hours and the spill will be easier to clean.

The next time you bake a pie, place it on a cookie sheet. This way, the sheet will collect any spills, and cleanup will be that much easier.

Deodorize a microwave oven. Have you ever burned micro-wave popcorn or other food in your microwave? Yuck! Overpowering odors can linger long after certain strong-smelling foods are microwaved, so here are some hints to try:

Lemon, lime, and orange juices are natural odor-busters. They will not only eliminate the burned smell but also fill the kitchen with a clean, citrus scent. Just combine a ½ cup of juice (or chop up a half of any of the above

---

GET RID OF RING AROUND THE BURNER

Are your stove top's burners encircled by ugly rings of baked-on grease or black marks? If so, here's a hint for easy cleanup. All you need to get started is sudsy ammonia (it has a little detergent in it) and an old towel you don't mind cutting up.

First, remove the drip pans, burner rings, and heating elements, if there are any.

Then, cut a circle out of the towel just a little bit larger than the largest burner.

Next, with rubber gloves on, saturate the circle with ammonia, place it on the burner, and cover with aluminum foil so that the ammonia won't evaporate too quickly. Be careful—the fumes can be powerful. You'll want the exhaust fan on and door open, and you should do only one burner at a time.

Let the circle sit there overnight, if possible. Then, wipe off the residue with some mild soap and water and a clean cloth—the baked-on grease should come right off.

citrus fruits) with a ½ cup of water in a 4-cup or larger microwave-safe container. You can add four or five whole cloves, too. Put in the microwave and heat on high until the water boils and creates steam. It's the steam that really accelerates the deodorizing. *Caution:* The water and steam will be extremely hot! Be sure to let the mixture cool completely (at least 15 minutes) before opening the door. Leaving the door open for a while afterward will help circulate the air.

You can also try baking soda to clean as well as deodorize the microwave. Just fill a large bowl with 1 cup of water, 2 tablespoons of baking soda, and a drop of vanilla or lemon extract. Place in the microwave and heat on high for 2 to 3 minutes. Leave the microwave door closed for another 15 minutes. The steam will soften spills so you can wipe them up, and the smell will be gone, too.

Clean cast iron. Cast-iron skillets last for years, but scrubbing them with soap and water ruins the surface. So how should you clean them? When faced with cleaning a cast-iron skillet (with years of baked-on grease and grime) that you've inherited from a relative, put the pan through a cleaning cycle in your self-cleaning oven. The baked-on food and grease will be reduced to ash. Wipe out the skillet and reseason it with oil, and it will be ready to serve more generations of cooks.

Clean a pan with cold water. When cleaning a pan used to cook rice, use cold water instead of hot. The hot water just makes the rice harder to remove; cold water loosens it and makes cleaning so much easier. This tip works for pasta and potatoes, too.

Clean and deodorize plastic containers. Plasticware can get an off smell if you store it with the lid on. To say adios to that funky aroma, apply a thick paste of baking soda and water over the surface (or fill with a half-vinegar, half-water solution). Let sit overnight, rinse, and air-dry near a sunny window. Plastic food containers that smell really bad, or have a sticky feel, should be replaced.

Clean a baking dish with foil. If you make a vegetable dish that doesn't form a hard crust as it bakes and that you cover with foil to bake, you can use the foil to clean the dish. After the casserole is done, remove it from the oven. When it cools off, crumple up the foil and use it to clean the glass dish.

Remove stubborn labels. To remove stubborn, sticky labels from new glassware, all you need is some aerosol oven cleaner. In a well-ventilated room (or outside), spray a layer of oven cleaner over the sticker and gunk. Let sit for 15 minutes or so. You can also rub some vegetable or baby oil on the stickers and let the glass sit for at least 30 minutes. With either approach, grab a nylon-net scrubbie or sponge with a scrubber and scrub the sticker and gunk right off. Then wash and dry the glass.

Get those jar labels off. Most of us love saving jars to reuse, but some labels are very hard to remove. To avoid wasting water by filling a sink or bowl to soak the labels off jars, just wrap the jar with a folded dishcloth that you have soaked with water. Even

the most stubborn labels slide right off. Leave the jars wrapped in the wet cloth overnight so you won't be tempted to keep checking on the progress every hour. If after soaking you have to scrape off any part of the label, leave the wet cloth on longer.

Clean crystal glasses. Old toothbrushes come in handy for cleaning all the little notches in crystal and the indentations in the tops of glass canisters.

Refill soap inexpensively. Dish detergent in a foam dispenser works well, but refills are pricey. When your dispenser is empty, add equal amounts of regular dish soap and water to the empty container and you will have a much cheaper and equally effective

CLEAN YOUR STERLING SILVER

If you're planning on bringing out your sterling silver for the holidays, use the following hints when washing to keep it in beautiful condition for years to come:

Clean silverware in hot, soapy water. Rinse well and dry with a soft cloth. If your sterling silver is old or valuable, don't put it in the dishwasher, because dishwasher detergent could discolor it after long-term use. The heat from the drying cycle also can loosen knife handles. And never place hollow-handled pieces in the dishwasher.

Also note that placing sterling-silver pieces next to stainless-steel flatware in the same basket in the dishwasher can cause electrolysis that over time will remove the silver.

If you have silver-plated or less valuable silver, you can put it in the dishwasher. However, remove it before the drying cycle begins. Instead, dry with a soft towel to prevent spotting.

If the silverware needs polishing, use a polish created for silver, and read all directions before using the product. There are also silver-polishing cloths or mitts.

refill. You might need to shake it up occasionally to mix.

Clean up a stainless-steel sink. To clean paints, varnish, glue, and other gunk from a stainless-steel sink in an art studio or workshop, scrub the sink with rubbing alcohol. It will look like new!

Load the dishwasher. Opinions vary on the best way to load a dishwasher. Some folks like to sort silverware in the basket, placing all the knives in one section, all the forks in another, and all the spoons in yet another. This can save time when you unload the clean dishes, but detergent and appliance manufacturers recommend mixing up the silverware and placing some utensils upside down to prevent this "nesting." That's why it's always a good idea to read the instruction manual for your dishwasher and the package directions for the detergent you use.

Power off dishwasher residues. A white, powdery residue in the dishwasher is probably a hard-water buildup, which means the minerals in the water build up layer after layer inside the dishwasher. Believe it or not, powdered orange or lemon drink crystals will clean them up. It's the powdered citric acid in the drink that does the job.

All you need to do is put 3 to 4 ounces of the crystals in the soap dispenser of the dishwasher. Do *not* add any soap or anything else, and run the dishwasher through a regular wash cycle. Stubborn stains might require a couple of applications.

Or, consider vinegar. Vinegar can help remove hard-water mineral buildup from your dishwasher, but first check your owner's manual to make sure using vinegar is okay for your dishwasher before following these steps:

GET THE BEST FROM YOUR DISHWASHER

Dishwashers are sure a timesaver! Here are some hints to help you get the most from your washer and save energy to boot:

- To save money, choose the air-dry cycle instead of the heated cycle to dry the dishes.
- Don't overload the machine. Doing that will keep the water from circulating, and dishes won't get clean.
- Don't run the washer until it is full. Remember that the same amount of water is used no matter how many dishes are inside.

Begin by starting the empty dishwasher on a regular cycle—do not use dishwasher detergent. Let the cycle run for a couple of minutes, until the bottom of the dishwasher has begun filling with water (just open the door carefully and take a peek). Then add 2 to 3 cups of white vinegar to the water, close the door, and let the dishwasher complete the full cycle. Note: You can repeat this process if necessary.

When done, the hard-water deposits should be a thing of the past. To keep them from accumulating again, run vinegar through a complete cycle periodically.

De-gunk the dishwasher. Yes, the dishwasher *does* need to be cleaned from time to time. Check the drain for bits of food; use paper towels to absorb debris. Start the empty washer, then stop the cycle when the bottom is full of water. Add 2 cups of vinegar (to remove hard-water buildup) and let sit for 30 minutes. Scrub walls with a sturdy brush and finish the cycle.

Clean your dish brush. Toss that dirty dish brush into the dishwasher every time you wash a load to keep the brush clean and long-lasting. Don't literally "toss" the brush, though—put it securely on the top rack or in the silverware basket.

Designate clean or dirty dishwasher. You're going to have to add detergent to the dishwasher cup anyway, so why not have a closed cup indicate dirty dishes and an open cup signal clean

TO RINSE OR NOT TO RINSE

The "rinse or not to rinse" debate—whether to rinse dishes before putting them in the dishwasher—goes on. In general, if you are going to run the dishwasher soon, it's only necessary to scrape off big chunks of food. It is not necessary to "wash" dishes before putting them in, especially if you have a newer machine. However, if the dishes are going to sit for a while, you might want to give them a quick rinse (or run the rinse-and-hold cycle, if the machine has one), especially if the plates have egg or sticky stuff on them.

Also, load the machine correctly. Don't block water jets with big bowls or pans, and when loading silverware, put some with handles up and some with handles down so that they don't nest inside each other. Most dishwashers have specific loading instructions, so check the manual or company Web site.

Also, to save energy and money, wash *only* full loads of dishes. Use only dishwasher detergent—never use laundry detergent or dish soap.

dishes? The person who unloads the dishwasher simply fills the cup with detergent and closes it once the dishwasher has been emptied. Even young children have no problem understanding the "closed cup equals dirty dishes" concept.

It's important to note, however, that if you live in a high-humidity area, the powdered detergent might cake or clump inside the dispenser. When the washer is run, the detergent might stay inside or not dissolve completely.

Clean or dirty, take 2. Here's another way to know whether the dishes in the dishwasher are clean or dirty. Keep a small drinking glass or uncapped jar in the corner of the upper shelf of the dishwasher. When the glass or jar is full of water, you'll know the dishes have been washed. Empty the glass when you empty the dishwasher.

A simple fix for dishwasher odor. Chemicals are not always necessary to deodorize a smelly dishwasher—air often gets rid of smells. If you keep the dishwasher door locked at all times, it can't dry out, which creates odors from the stale moisture. Leaving the door ajar so the dishwasher can dry out after use usually eliminates most of these odors.

Cushion while dishwashing. When stacking small items in the dishwasher that might knock against each other and chip or break, place plastic lids from coffee cans between them. Make sure that the plastic lids are secured so they won't come loose and make their way to the bottom of the washer, where they could melt and cause some damage.

Stove meets dishwasher. When your dishwasher is not quite full, add the grates and drip trays from your stove and the burner tray underneath. This gets almost all of the burned-on and greasy stuff off quite easily.

Keep plastics in place. When you put plastic items in the dishwasher, put a cake cooling rack over them, so they don't fly around.

Get rid of candle wax. Here's how to remove candle wax from the inside of a dishwasher. Soften up waxy areas on the walls of the dishwasher with a hair-dryer on the low to medium setting. Then rub off the wax with a plastic scrubbie, wiping up any crumbs of wax with a damp paper towel. For the dishes, put on rubber gloves and submerge each item in very hot water for a minute or two before using a scrubbing sponge or sturdy paper towel to remove the wax.

Shortcut to a clean feeling. Pour a

couple of glugs or capfuls of pine or your favorite scented cleaner into the kitchen (and bathroom) sink drain when you don't have time to mop. The room will at least smell clean.

Clean the drainer. If you don't have a dishwasher, and your dish drainer gets crusty with mineral deposits, about once every two weeks scrub it with a brush and use lots of vinegar. It'll clean up in a jiffy.

Use a sink strainer. Put a strainer in the kitchen sink to collect the tiny particles that could clog the drain. It sure beats having to call a plumber. You can buy replacement strainers for just a few dollars at most grocery or hardware stores.

Clean the garbage disposal. Take several paper towels and moisten them with a liquid cleaner. Then wipe underneath the rubber flaps at the top of the disposal (make sure the disposal is off). You would be surprised at the gunk that accumulates under there!

Deodorize the garbage disposal. Do you have a problem with odors emanating from your garbage disposal? If you've got an old long-handled kitchen (dish) brush that you are about to toss, let it come in handy one more time. Put a good amount of liquid soap on it and carefully scrub away at the inside

of the disposal unit, even under the rubber gasket. When you pull the brush out, you may be surprised at how much gunk is on it. If you like, repeat the process using bleach to remove any lingering odors.

Scent with citrus. Every time you use citrus products in the kitchen, save the peels. Then cut them into tiny pieces with your kitchen scissors and drop some into the soapy water you use to wash the dishes. Afterward, pour the peels into the garbage-disposal unit, and like magic you will deodorize not only your sink but also the kitchen area with a pleasant scent.

Clean the sink strainer, too. For a cleaner kitchen sink, include the sink strainer and stopper in the dishwasher load once a week.

Freshen drains the best way. This all-natural, homestyle mixture of vinegar and baking soda is a great drain-freshening method that costs only pennies. Just pour ½ cup or so of baking soda down the drain and follow with 1 to 2 cups of cheap household vinegar. Wait a few minutes; meanwhile, put in the stopper and fill up the sink. Pull the plug and let the "whoosh" push everything through.

When using the vinegar-and-baking-soda combination to clean drains, don't use the baking soda you've got for baking. Instead, save the box that you use in your fridge or freezer. After it's been in the fridge for approximately 3 months, use it with vinegar to clean your drains.

Stretch money on scouring pads. When you purchase scouring pads, cut them in half and get twice as many. Many times, half a pad will work for the job.

Scrub with nylon net. A nylon net is a good scrubber, but try the plastic mesh bag that holds onions from the grocery—it's a super scrubber. You can sew the bags together to make a bigger one, but best of all, every time you use a 3-pound bag of onions, you have a new, free scrubber.

Clean surfaces with baking soda. Did you know that baking soda sprinkled on a damp sponge will clean glass and ceramic surfaces without scratching? The next time you have a stubborn stain, give baking soda a try.

Remove marker from a countertop.

DON'T CLOG THE DRAIN

We don't pay much attention to household drains until there's a problem—and it's usually a big one! Keep my list handy; you'll avoid unnecessary blockages and help the environment, too.

NOT OKAY

Garbage disposal: bones; asparagus, artichokes, corn husks, or stringy vegetables (like celery); shells from oysters, clams, or shrimp; large fruit pits; glass, metal, china, or plastic objects; grease, drain cleaners.

Kitchen sink: cooking grease, fats, vegetable oils.

Bathroom sink: lotion, sunscreen, cosmetics, medications, hair.

Toilet: cigarettes, paper towels, sanitary napkins, diapers, condoms, dental floss, adhesive bandage wrappers, cotton balls or swabs, facial tissues (which, unlike toilet paper, do not decompose in septic tanks).

Outdoor drains or sewers: motor oil or auto chemicals, antifreeze, fertilizer, pesticides or poisons, paint, solvents, sealants, pool chemicals, food waste, sand, rags, gravel, trash.

OKAY

Kitchen sink: water used to rinse food or cook pasta or similar foods, bits of food debris, water containing normal-strength household cleaning fluids.

Bathroom drains: soapy rinse water from bathing, showering, and cleaning hand-washables.

Permanent marker that gets onto a plastic laminate countertop can be difficult to remove. Orange-based ink remover may not do the trick. Try this: Use the nylon pad you use to clean your flat-top range (if you have that type), along with the special cleaner that came with the range. Test the range cleaner—or any other cleaning solution—on a small spot before treating the entire countertop. If the ink comes off, finish the job with warm, soapy water to make the countertop look like new.

Get rid of tomato stains. Every household probably has at least one piece of red-stained plasticware, usually from a tomato-based product. To remove the tinge, apply some baking soda with a damp sponge or cloth and let it sit several hours. Then wash as usual. If the stains are persistent, you may have to try this a couple of times.

On the Light Side ~~~~~~

The Amazing Cleaner and Deodorizer

What product can be used to clean and deodorize the refrigerator and freezer, to clean countertops, and as a nonabrasive cleanser (sprinkled on a damp sponge)? What is your guess? The answer is baking soda! Don't you just love this cheap cleaner and deodorizer?

Clean dehydrator trays quicker. While you are washing the trays in a home food dehydrator, turn on the base and let it heat up a bit. Then unplug it, and the warm, sticky residue wipes right up.

Protect stainless-steel appliances. Use a few drops of light machine oil (like the kind used for sewing machines) on a cloth to clean stainless-steel appliances, keep them shiny, and wipe away dirt and smudges. Your appliances will stay smudge-free for months! Keep the cloth in a plastic bag and bring it out for a quick touch-up whenever needed.

Clean the can opener. To keep a hand-operated can opener clean, put it in the dishwasher unless the opener is made from material that's not suitable for the dishwasher. If you can't use the dishwasher, then a bristle brush should do the trick. Find the right brush for the job at a local hardware store or housewares department.

Another way to clean a manual can opener is to simply run a double-folded paper towel through the can opener, then turn the handle back and forth several times. The blade and the gear can be cleaned in this easy way.

Clean up salt and pepper shakers. To clean the tiny holes in salt and pepper shakers, try using a water-fed dental-hygiene appliance. It's like a mini power wash. Just make sure the shakers are empty when you clean them.

Get rid of fingerprints. Did you know that you can easily clean fingerprints and smears from shiny appliances by making a mixture of half vinegar and half water? Use a clean, soft terry cloth to wipe on and then wipe off. The surface will be shiny!

Easy-clean the grill. After cooking on the barbecue grill, when it has cooled off a little, thoroughly moisten a double sheet of paper toweling and place it directly on the surface of the grill and close the lid. Then, after a half hour or so, you'll find that there is no need to scrape the grill—the food residues just roll off.

Clean a small electric grill. The paper towel method is also an easy solution for cleaning an electric countertop grill. Put (usually two) wet paper towels on the unplugged, dirty grill and shut the lid. When you get back to it, all of the "gunk" will be softened. If you forget to clean the grill right after you've used it, it can be cleaned when you have the time.

De-gunk with salt. To scrub gunk off wooden cutting boards, glass baking dishes, and pet bowls, sprinkle a liberal amount of salt on a damp sponge and wipe.

Soak away salt. In a humid climate, salt shakers can become encrusted with hardened salt deposits that clog the holes and make it difficult to remove the tops for cleaning. Soap and water may be no help, but vinegar will come to the rescue.

Put about 2 to 3 tablespoons of vinegar in a cup of water and soak the top of the salt shaker overnight. Then wash, rinse, and dry before using. This method is not recommended for sterling-silver tops.

Easy-clean thermos. To clean out a thermos, put about 1 teaspoon of dishwasher detergent inside it. Add a little water, put the lid on, and shake several times. Rinse well and look inside the bottle. Shine, shine, shine!

Keep sponges mold-free. To prevent mold in kitchen sponges, wring them dry and place them on an edge of the sink so that one corner is hanging off the edge. The corner hanging down allows the sponge to continue draining and to dry without mildew forming.

Rotate kitchen sponges to make sure that they are always fresh and clean. Purchase seven sponges and use a new one each day. At the end of the day, toss the sponge of the day into the washing machine to be washed with the rest of your weekly laundry and start the rotation over again.

Rinsing a sponge in cold water helps it stay fresher, as does placing it vertically against the faucet or on top of a cup so there is good air circulation. And do change the sponge every few days with a clean one from the dishwasher (see following tip).

A kitchen sponge's life span is only 4 to 6 weeks, depending on use—the sponges aren't manufactured to last a lifetime!

Destroy sponge grunge. Sponges that are damp and smell are more than likely harboring bacteria. Rinsing a sponge after each use is not enough to remove the bacteria. Sponge manufacturers suggest either putting the sponge in the dishwasher, being sure to use the heated dry cycle (you must secure the sponge on the top rack; don't allow it to float around, because if it gets down to the bottom, it could damage the dishwasher mechanism), or boiling the sponge in water for about 5 minutes. You could also throw sponges into the washing machine with your dish towels. These methods work on cellulose sponges only. Some sponges have been treated so that they resist odors. So, check for this the next time you need a new sponge.

In addition, wipe down your counters (as long as they are not marble, granite, or other natural stone) with vinegar; the vinegar helps keep the sponge and the counter in tiptop shape.

If none of these methods solves your stinky sponge problem, consider other possible culprits: Is enough fresh air getting into the kitchen? Is moisture being taken out (maybe you need a dehumidifier)? Could it be well water? Did you move from a dry climate to a high-humidity one? These are all possibilities.

Recycle dishwashing sponges. Once a sponge is no longer fit to be used to wash dishes and wipe the counter, cut off one corner to mark it, and use it for spills on the floor, wiping down cabinet fronts, and other cleaning chores.

Avoid sponges altogether. If you have trouble with "grungy" sponges or don't like their expense, use dishcloths instead. Many folks find them easier to keep clean, not smelly, and long lasting.

Use washcloths. Discount and hardware stores often sell bundles of very lightweight washcloths for just a few dollars a dozen. These cloths might not be heavy enough for you to use as washcloths, but they make wonderful dishcloths. Buy a bundle of white ones when they go on sale. Toss in the washer when dirty, and bleach them regularly. One bundle will last you for months.

Wipe up fast with napkins. Buy a large package of inexpensive paper napkins and keep a pile on the kitchen counter. They're usually cheaper than paper towels, and it's much more convenient to grab one for small spills and wipe-ups.

Remove adhesive shelf liner. When it comes time to redo your kitchen shelves, you may be dismayed to discover that the old adhesive-backed plastic liner is so brittle that it comes off in your hands in small pieces, leaving much of the paper stuck on the shelf with no edge or corner to pull off. Adhesive-backed paper is almost impossible to get off shelving.

To remove it you need to heat it up. Use your iron on a low setting, cover the shelf with aluminum foil, and iron the foil. The heat will loosen the glue beneath, and the paper will come off easily.

Clean behind a cabinet. If you have a small space between a cabinet and the wall that's not large enough to get in a mop, take a piece of tape, push it down into the space with a broom handle or yardstick, pull up, and the dirt is gone!

Keep cabinet tops dust-free. This tip is for folks with cabinets in their kitchen that do not reach the ceiling. Have you ever got on a ladder and looked on top of your cabinets only to find a horrifying buildup of grease and dust? The greasy dirt can be hard to clean and can damage the wood. Avoid the mess by placing sheets of newspaper on top of the cabinets to collect the grime. As long as the newspaper can't be seen, this is a good way to collect the dust. When it's time to clean, just roll up the newspapers and toss! It's tidy and easy.

Clean with old socks. If you have some socks you don't need or on which the elastic is worn, put one over a fly swatter and use it to clean under the stove, refrigerator, or dishwasher. Socks work wonders and get out things you can't get to with the vacuum cleaner.

Line shelves with tiles. Try using

inexpensive, self-sticking, vinyl floor tiles to line cabinet shelves. They clean like a breeze and do not stain or scuff.

Deter ants with peppermint. Crush peppermint leaves and place them on thresholds where ants tend to travel. You can also hang a small bundle of fresh sage wherever you store food to deter ants.

Freshen and deodorize the kitchen garbage can. Use a car deodorizer to freshen the kitchen garbage can. Place it in the bottom of the can and then put the garbage bag in. Every time you open the can, freshness is all you will smell.

Also try hanging an over-the-rim toilet deodorizer on the can to get rid of the odor. Deodorizers with metal hangers can be bent to the contour of your trash-can rim.

Deodorize a trash compactor. A trash compactor is a terrific appliance, but compacted trash tends to smell awful after several compressions. To avoid odors emanating from the compactor, place several sections of newspaper on top of the garbage and then compact it. Also sprinkle a little baking soda in every so often to keep some of those odors away.

The added benefit is that the newspapers also prevent food and garbage buildup on the compressor plate, thus keeping it clean and free from buildup and odor. You will get more out of one garbage sack.

Use a trash compactor the right way. Generally speaking, trash compactors are for trash; in-sink disposals are for getting rid of food waste. However, if the disposal is on a septic system, the less "bulk" and large quantities of fat or grease that go down the drain, the fewer problems you might have. In this situation, some food waste may be better placed in the trash compactor.

If you do put bones, fats, and other scraps in the compactor, place them in plastic bags before putting them into the compactor, to prevent odors. Also rinse out cans and plastic milk cartons before placing them in the compactor. Cereal, cracker, and cookie boxes and other paper goods can all go into the compactor. Many folks like to place a newspaper in the bottom of a new bag that they place in the trash compactor. Some also spray it with a room deodorant.

Get rid of rotten potato odor. If you return from a trip to discover that potatoes stored in a cabinet have rotted while you were away, here are a few things you can try to get rid of the smell:

Wipe down the area with vinegar and let air-dry by leaving the doors open. You might have to do this three times or more. If it doesn't work, you will need to visit a home-improvement store where paint that seals odors is sold. Follow the directions exactly, and this should solve your problem.

BATHROOM

Be cautious with cleaners. There are a lot of new household cleaners on the market. Please be sure to read the directions and disclaimers before using any product.

If in doubt, call the 800 phone number on the container. Some of these new products are not to be used on plastic, metals, or older fixtures. Others may damage marble, natural stone, colored aluminum, or even a glazed sink or tub.

Many new products work wonderfully, but you must be extremely careful when using them on some surfaces. It is very important to read product labels completely before starting a cleaning process. Remember, never mix products that contain bleach and ammonia.

This mixture could actually be fatal—so take this caution seriously!

Clean the shower curtain with vinegar. Vinegar will also clean the hard-water buildup and gunk from plastic shower curtains. Just wash the curtain in the washing machine with a towel for scrubbing action, and add a cup or two of vinegar (white or apple cider) to the rinse cycle.

Unclog the shower head. Do you have wimpy water pressure in your shower? Before you call a plumber, check the shower head for mineral buildup. This could be the cause, and you can fix it with a favorite of mine—good ol' household vinegar.

Fill a small bucket or bowl with warm to hot vinegar, remover the shower head, and let it soak in the vinegar for several hours—overnight for best results. To help scrub and remove any softened deposits, use an old toothbrush. Also, unclog holes with a toothpick, sewing needle, straight pin, or piece of wire.

If you can't remove the shower head, pour 2 to 3 inches of vinegar into a sturdy plastic sandwich bag, then tape, twist-tie, or rubber-band the bag so that the shower head is submerged in the vinegar. Again, let this soak overnight, then remove the bag and scrub the holes with an old toothbrush.

After cleaning, turn on the water to the shower head full force to help force out any loosened deposits left inside. If all has gone well, the shower power should be up to par again.

Baking soda in the bathroom. Use baking soda as a natural deodorant, homemade toothpaste, foot deodorant, and even mouthwash. Sprinkle it directly on a damp toothbrush instead of using expensive toothpastes that contain baking soda as one of the ingredients. For a mouthwash, just gargle with 1 teaspoon dissolved in half a glass of warm water.

You can also use baking soda for a soothing bath or as a mild facial scrub that will leave you with a healthy glow.

No more bubbles. If you have trouble getting your bubbles out of the bathtub after a bubble bath, get a dry washcloth, press it on the bubbles, and the bubbles will be gone!

Remove sticky residues. Non-skid appliqués applied to a bathtub don't last forever. When they start to come off, and you'd like to remove the rest of them and apply some different ones, use ordinary white vinegar to do the job. Just saturate a sponge in some hot white vinegar and place it over the decals. Wait a few minutes to give the vinegar time to penetrate and soak in, and you'll have them off, along with any adhesive.

CONQUER THE BATHROOM WITH VINEGAR

Do you have a ton of cleaners in your bathroom cabinet right now? One to clean the glass shower door, one to remove soap scum, something to clean mirrors, maybe even a special tile cleaner? I'm here to tell you that there's one product that can do all these and much more.

Have you guessed it yet? What if I said that it's environmentally safe, it has been around for thousands of years, and it's inexpensive? Yes, it's vinegar, my all-time favorite cleaner and deodorizer.

It can be used at full strength, or you can make a good vinegar-based multipurpose cleaner by mixing ½ cup white vinegar, 1 pint rubbing alcohol, 1 teaspoon dishwashing liquid, and enough water to make a gallon. Fill a labeled squirt bottle, and store the remaining solution until you need it. Use this one cleaner instead of having a collection of not-so-cheap commercial brands for tub/shower, tile, and counters (do *not* use vinegar on real marble, granite, or crystalline surfaces).

Vinegar also works well for removing stick-on hooks from painted surfaces—just squeeze a little vinegar behind the hook.

Squeegee shower doors. Don't you just hate the way the shower doors look after a shower? Even shower cleaners don't work that well. But if you use a squeegee on the doors after every shower, you can keep the buildup contained and will have less scrubbing to do.

Keep shower doors spot-free. If your hard water leaves spots in the shower stall or on the doors (even with a water conditioner), use a squeegee/towel combo to wipe down the stall. Even so, the glass doors may still be difficult to keep clear. Here's a way to save yourself some work.

Hang a shower-curtain liner on a suspension rod just inside the glass doors, and draw the curtain when showering. It will prevent water spots on glass. When visitors come, take down the liner and rod, and show off your crystal-clear shower doors.

You can also try this for hard-water stains (and soap scum): Fill a spray bottle with white vinegar and keep it handy. When you see that familiar haze start to form, spray and scrub with a soft-bristled brush or plastic scrubbie. Rinse with water, and your doors will shine.

While you're at it, pour some full-strength vinegar into the shower-door tracks. Let it soak for a while and then rinse with water. This will keep them from clogging up, too.

Clean the shower door with a puff. An old, plastic body puff can work wonders for keeping a shower door clean. After showering, put soap or body wash on the puff and give the door a quick scrub, followed by a rinse. This prevents scum buildup and keeps the door nice and shiny.

Shampoo the bathtub. A lot of times, regular hair shampoo will work wonders on soap film and dirt. Give it a try, and you might be shocked at how well shampoo cleans tubs and shower walls. Also, try using a little baking soda with the shampoo for some extra "scrubbing" action.

Get mildew off the mat. Has mildew invaded your rubberized bathmat? I'll tell you an easy way to get rid of it and keep it from coming back.

Have you taken a look at the underside of your bathmat lately? If it looks slimy or has patches of black or brown mystery grime, welcome to the world of mildew. To get rid of it, toss the bathmat in the washing machine with hot, soapy water and some bleach. Toss in a couple of bleach-safe towels to add some scrubbing action. Run the washer through its normal cycles, then pull out the bathmat and let it drip-dry.

To keep mildew from coming back, pull up the bathmat after every bath and let it drip-dry. Hang it over a towel rod, or let it drip-dry on the wall. Gently press the mat onto the wall so the suction cups grab hold. The water will drip down into the tub, and your bathmat will stay mildew-free.

Let the shower mat dry. After showering, clip your shower mat to a plastic pants hanger, shake it, and hang it on the shower head. The shower mat stays clean and dry.

Soak up soap residue. Take an ordinary kitchen sponge, cut it in half, and place it in a soap dish. When you place the soap on top of the sponge, the sponge catches the soap residue and can easily be rinsed out.

Save the soap. Some hand soaps are messy in the soap dish. Years ago you could purchase an oval plastic "soap saver" disk to put under the soap. These aren't readily available anymore, but you can make your own. Purchase a plastic craft screen and cut a piece to the exact shape and size you need to fit under your bar of soap. You can get several out of each 12-inch-square screen. Craft screens are very inexpensive.

Easy-clean tub. For senior citizens, bending over to clean the bathtub can be difficult. Here's a way to clean the tub with less bending.

When you shower, put the stopper in the tub, and when you finish with the shower, pour some cleaner in the tub, swish it around the sides with a new toilet brush and let it sit a while, then come back, drain, and rinse.

Keep drains clog-free. Here's how to keep the drain in the bathroom sink from clogging up when you're shaving—just place an old, used

Use Bits of Soap

One way to use those bits of bath soap that are left when the bar is used up is to make a slash (the length of the soap) in the side of a sponge, not cutting it *all* the way through. The sponge will look like an envelope. Insert the soap pieces in the pocket, and when the sponge is dampened, it'll be handy for many purposes.

fabric-softener sheet over the drain. The hair will stick to the sheet, allowing the water to flow smoothly down the drain. When you're done, just toss the sheet into the wastebasket.

Clean a faucet fast. Company on its way and you notice water spots on your chrome bathroom fixtures? Rub the chrome with a used fabric-softener sheet to shine it beautifully. The dryer sheet also does a great cleanup on the basin and countertop. Just be careful that the sheets are not too abrasive for your faucets.

Keep a few used dryer sheets in your bathroom drawer at all times.

Cleaning detail for the bathroom sink. When cleaning the bathroom sink, use a cotton swab to clean the small space behind the tap.

Keep mirrors clean. The moist wipes sold for cleaning windows, toilets, or wood are great, but they can be hard to hold onto. To get a better hold, open the moist towel, place it on a paper towel, and use the double layer. The wipe won't fold up or fall out of your hand. Another way to clean mirrors is to use a dry microfiber towel.

Loosen latex gloves. To fix latex gloves that are stuck together, sprinkle a little talcum powder inside the fingers. Then you will be able to slip them on easily.

Use disposable gloves. Invariably, you'll get a hole in your right rubber glove (if you're right-handed), so rather than accumulating a drawer full of lefties, buy disposable ones to use on your right hand. This way, you will get at least two uses out of each one.

Hold more toilet paper. This may be the cure to the dilemma of the "empty toilet-paper roll" syndrome. Instead of a single-roll holder, we use a paper-towel holder. The bar holds two rolls of toilet paper beautifully, and styles can be found to match any décor.

Bowl brush. A back scrubber with a nylon-net puff makes an excellent toilet brush. It is very inexpensive (use one you were planning to discard) and dries quickly.

Make a toilet-brush holder. Cut the

On the Light Side ~~~~~
Leave a Message on the Bathroom Mirror
A fun way to leave a message for someone or a reminder for you is to write on the mirror with a lip pencil or a bar of soap. The writing will easily wipe off with a tissue. It's cheap, easy to remove, and always at hand.

top half off a plastic juice bottle and use the bottom half for a toilet-brush holder. The brush fits in just snugly enough that you can carry it to another bathroom without dripping water on the floor. Also, the brush won't fall over as it does with some holders.

Freshen the air. Purchase car deodorizers, such as the ones shaped like little trees, and hang one on the pipes in the back of the toilet in each bathroom. The scent it gives off lasts for many weeks. Put one under the kitchen sink, too.

Quick cleanups. Anyone who uses disposable wipes usually will end up with a container of them that begins to dry up. When that happens, add some water and antibacterial dish soap to the container and place the wipes in the bathroom for quick cleanups around the sink and commode between weekly cleanings.

Clean with paper towels. Whenever the three-roll packages of paper towels go on sale for $1, stock up on them. You can use these inexpensive paper towels to clean the bathroom for pennies without worrying about spreading germs, which can be a concern with rags or sponges.

Wash hands with bubble bath. Try using moisturizing bubble bath in your soap dispensers. It won't dry out your hands like regular liquid soap, and it is not antibacterial, which is better for the septic system (if you have one).

Clean a curling iron. To remove hair spray that's baked onto a curling iron, pour rubbing alcohol on a terrycloth towel or make a paste of baking soda and water. Rub over the cool surface of an unplugged iron. Wipe with a damp cloth; let dry.

Clean an electric shaver. If you lose the little cleaning brush for your electric shaver, use an old toothbrush instead. It works just as well, and probably even better.

A better way to clean electric

 Pick Up Broken Glass Safely

When you break a glass in the sink or bathroom, wet a tissue or paper napkin and mop up all of those little slivers. Each little unseen sliver will stick to the wet tissue. This saves many a cut finger!

shavers. The usual way to blow the hair clippings out of my electric shavers is to hold the shaver head up to your lips and blow. But this method lets the bits of hair clipping fly all over the bathroom basin.

Here's a better way: Use a baby's ear syringe as a small bellows to direct high-pressure airflow onto the shaver and its heads. This directs the clippings right into the sink. It is easier to rinse the bowl afterward, and lets you be sure you've gotten clippings out of the corners of the cutters and the shaver heads.

Reuse perfume inserts. Here's a place for those squares of highly perfumed paper that come in department store ads in the Sunday paper. Put them in the bathroom wastebasket, where they give off just a pleasant aroma instead of an intense smell.

Or, cut the ones you like in half and put half in a new kitchen garbage bag, to keep it smelling fresher.

Scent the linen closet. Use opened bath-soap containers for the linen closet and lingerie drawers. The good smell lasts for a couple of weeks, then

ZAP STATIC CLING

Here are some hints to help eliminate pesky static cling in your home. When the weather is cold, heaters on, fires burning in the fireplace, and static cling in full swing, here's how you can enjoy the warmth without all that cling:

- Keep a large pot of water simmering on your stove. The escaping steam will add moisture to the air—and why not add a drop of cinnamon oil or a few orange or lemon peels to the pot? The fragrance is homey and inviting. Just keep an eye on it so that it doesn't boil dry.
- Place cups, bowls, or vases of water throughout the home. As the water evaporates, it will put some of that much-needed moisture back into the air—just refill as needed. For a decorative touch, put flower buds in a bowl of water, with stones or marbles lining the bottom.
- A great clingbuster is a tabletop water fountain. Not only are you keeping the air moist, but also the soothing bubbling sound is very relaxing.
- A fine-mist spray bottle filled with water can be used to "spritz out" static—especially clinging clothes—in a pinch. Just don't spritz silk or other fine fabrics.
- Invest in a cool-mist vaporizer or humidifier.

    Hope these help keep your home static-free!

you can dispose of the paper wrappers or boxes.

FLOORS

Get rid of scuff marks. To remove black marks from floors made by shoes, cut a hole in a new tennis ball and insert a broom handle in the hole. Gently rub the tennis ball over the scuff mark, and it disappears like magic. The nap on the tennis ball takes those scuff marks right off. You can use the ball without the handle, but it's harder on your back.

You can also use plain, dry white paper to remove scuff marks. Give it a try—you won't believe how easily this works.

Another tip is to simply rub tile or laminate floors with a pencil eraser, dry paper towel, or used dryer sheet dampened with water. Doesn't sound like this will work, but it removes them like magic!

Secure a floor-cleaner pad. When you are applying a disposable pad to one of those new floor sweepers, use a plastic tab from a package of bread to push it into the slot.

Quick-clean a vinyl floor. To clean a vinyl floor with light stains, first vacuum or sweep up any loose dirt. Then dampen a mop with just warm water and mop over small areas. Rinse the mop frequently so the dirt is not smeared around.

Be kind to your knees. Sooner or later, there is a time when you must end up on your knees around the house—scrubbing, dusting, or repairing. As your knees age along with you, kneeling gets more difficult. Use a new or partly new roll of paper towels to kneel on. It is soft, and if you need a sheet of paper towel, all you have to do is rip it off.

Another way to give your knees a break is to kneel on a gardener's kneeling pad. Even better, if you've got athletic kids, use a set of old volleyball or roller blade kneepads. They give great knee support, and you won't have to keep moving a pad.

Clean up with cat litter. If a pet (or child) vomits on a linoleum floor, here's an easy way to clean up. Sprinkle clumping cat litter liberally over the mess and wait a few minutes (open a door or window to let in fresh air if you need to). The litter will absorb the mess and also help with the odor. You will see it start to harden in just 2 to 3 minutes. Wipe it up with paper towels and sweep up the dry litter that's left.

If there is no cat litter handy, grab a box of baking soda or cornstarch—both absorb and deodorize.

Clean hardwood floors. Use these tips to keep wooden floors in top shape.

- Never use anything but the correct products for hardwood-floor care on your floor. Other flooring products can cause the floors to become dull and slippery.

- Because water can dull the finish, damage the wood, and leave a discoloring residue, most manufacturers recommend that you not overly wet-mop your hardwood floor. Damp-mopping might be okay.

- Wipe up food and other spills quickly. Use a lightly dampened towel. Then wipe over the area immediately with a dry towel.

Substitute a washcloth. If you clean your floor with the type of mop that has a floor-cleaner bottle attached, sooner or later you will probably forget to buy the wipes that attach to the mop. Substitute an old washcloth—it will cling perfectly to the sticky-sided fabric tape on the pad. Remove the washcloth when it gets dirty, wash it, and reuse it over and over.

Clean—and scent—the floor. Some types of floor-cleaner mops have water bottles that spray water on the floor before the mop passes over it. Scent the room by adding a few drops of perfume or essential oil to the water. (I use lemon, orange, or my favorite—lavender.) After you mop the floor, the room will smell great.

Essential oils can be found in some food stores, drugstores, and health-food stores. *Caution:* Don't use the scented water on a marble floor because it might cause a stain.

Pick up glass safely. Use a dry cotton ball to pick up little broken pieces of glass. The fibers catch shards that you can't see.

Freshen carpeting. Need to freshen those carpets in your home or auto? Simply put some baking soda in a clean, shaker-type spice container and liberally sprinkle all over carpeted areas. Let it sit for 30 minutes or so to help absorb odors, then vacuum it up. It will leave the room—or your car—with a clean, fresh scent. For a jazzy carpet deodorizer, you can add a little cinnamon or apple-pie spice to a shaker filled three-quarters full with baking soda. Mix well, shake onto the carpet, let sit, then vacuum. *Caution:*

Dark-colored spices can stain, so don't use on light-colored carpeting.

 Deodorize a carpet. Make your own carpet deodorizer using a shaker filled with baking soda, to which you add a few drops of your favorite essential oil. Mix well! Use this on your carpet and in your car,

---

Vintage Heloise

Make a Heloise Mat

Have you ever been preparing a meal in the kitchen and spilled something on the floor? You have to stop what you're doing and clean it up. Well, my mother, the late Heloise (1919–1977), came up with the idea of a Heloise Mat for the kitchen. She originally printed her mat directions in December 1963. Here are the directions for the mat in my mother's "voice":

"Take an old chenille bathmat and double it over so that the chenille will be on both sides (bottom and top).

"Lay a large dinner plate or a turkey platter on top. Take a crayon and trace around the edges of the plate for a pattern. Use your scissors and cut out your two circles. Sew these two pieces together (back-to-back) on your sewing machine or by hand. Double-stitch twice around the edges to give it body. Fringe from chenille rugs may be stitched around the outside of the mats for added attractiveness. They make lovely gifts.

"Be SURE not to make the mats any larger than 12 or 14 inches. If you do, you will defeat the purpose. Throw this mat on your kitchen floor and leave it there. You will find it a dandy thing for spills on the floor. Just take your foot and push the Heloise Mat across the spills and save that stooping over. The mat is so small that it takes practically no room in your washing machine each week.

"Why not make two while you're doing it? One to keep in front of your refrigerator and the other in front of the sink. Kick one or the other in front of your stove when frying bacon or meats. Sure saves mopping later. Grease spatters in such a fine spray when we fry that we can't even see it.

"And, gals, you are wrong . . . if you are thinking you can get by with only one side chenille. It's the bottom layer of chenille that wipes up the spills and shines the wax on the floor each time this mat is scooted across the floor with your foot! These mats are also wonderful in the bathroom. When one side gets soiled, just turn over and use the other side."

Update: I use bath towels and double them, doing pretty much the same. Make a few and you'll never want to be without one in the kitchen again!

and sprinkle some on mattresses when you remake the beds.

Get rid of gum. Not only do we track chewing gum into our homes, but more often than not, it winds up on the carpet in our cars, too. If it isn't removed quickly, it can become a yucky stain. So, the best thing to do is put ice in a metal pan and set this on top of the gummed area to harden it. Then carefully scrape off as much as possible with a dull knife. To remove any remaining residue, put a little dry-cleaning solvent on a clean cloth and lightly rub the stain. This should do the trick.

Remove candle wax from carpet. Here's a tacky problem: How do you get melted candle wax out of carpet? This is a common question that I'm asked every winter.

Don't use a steam iron, according to the Carpet and Rug Institute, which instead recommends a cold treatment for wax removal. Here's how to do it:

Put ice in a metal pan and set the pan on the wax until the wax is frozen solid. Remove the pan and hit the candle wax with a blunt object to break up the hardened wax.

Gently remove as much wax as you can—by hand—then vacuum up as much leftover wax as possible.

If some of the wax has gotten into the fibers, put rubbing alcohol on a white cloth. Blot and press until all the wax is removed.

If a color stain remains, try dry-cleaning solvent. Just be sure to test the solvent first on a hidden area of carpet, then follow with a sponge bath of warm water and a drop of liquid detergent.

Remove Silly Putty from carpet. Here's how to do it: First, pick off as much as you can. Then apply a small amount of household spray lubricant. Let it sit for a couple of minutes, and use a terry washcloth to lift any remaining gunk. Dampen a clean cloth with isopropyl (rubbing) alcohol and blot the area; sponge on a solution of dish soap and warm water. Rinse, then let air-dry.

Comb your carpet. A metal flea comb meant for a dog can be a handy tool in the house. The rounded tips and wide spacing of the tines can be used to straighten out the fringe on Oriental carpets without scratching the floor. It takes only take a few seconds to untangle the mess a vacuum cleaner seems to make of these fringes. Don't use your dog's comb; get a separate one for the carpet.

Keep pet stains off the carpet. It's inevitable that an adorable new puppy-in-training or an older dog might have an accident or two on the carpet, but it's not the end of the world. Vinegar can help save the situation.

But, you'll need to get to the stain ASAP. First, soak up as much of the urine as you can with absorbent, white paper towels or an old white bath towel until no more moisture comes from the carpeting. Stand on the towel to really get all of the liquid up.

Now, add ¼ teaspoon of a mild, white liquid hand-dishwashing detergent (nonbleach and nonlanolin) to 1 cup of lukewarm water. Apply to the stain by dabbing on the area, then absorb the moisture with paper towels and rinse with warm water. Repeat several times.

Now for the vinegar. Make a solution of ⅓ cup white vinegar to ⅔ cup water and, with a sponge, apply to the stain, but don't overwet—just dab. Blot with paper towels until completely dry. Problem solved—puppy saved.

Soak up a spill. Got a big spill on carpet or furniture? Use a puppy potty pad to soak it up. Works like a charm.

Clean spots easily. When cleaning spots from a carpet, instead of getting down on your knees, put a thick white sock on your foot, spray the spot, and clean it up by rubbing your foot on it.

Keep baseboards clean. When you sweep or vacuum the floor, clean the baseboards at the same time—no dust builds up.

Clean baseboards with ease. Recycle those expensive, pretreated floor-cleaning pads that attach to a mop by using them to clean the baseboards. After you've used one on the floor, turn it inside out, and it's ready for its next job. Also, cleaning the baseboards while sitting on a plant stand with wheels makes the job much easier on your back. For more comfort, put a small pillow on top of it.

Don't vacuum throw rugs. Vacuum cleaners tend to suck up throw rugs along with the dirt and dust. Rugs

On the Light Side ～～
Which Cleaner Doesn't Last?

It's time to check your cleaning-hint IQ. Which of the following cleaning agents loses its strength after about an hour?
   a) hydrogen peroxide
   b) ammonia
   c) soap and water
   Well, what is your guess? If you guessed, "a," then you are the winner! Hydrogen peroxide, especially when exposed to light and heat, loses its strength after an hour or less. So, if you are using it in a cleaning solution, remember that it will have the "cleaning" action for only an hour at most.

with longer fibers are really a problem. Here's a better way to get out the loose dirt: Before you start vacuuming, toss all of your throw rugs into the dryer on the air-dry or no-heat setting.

It really pounds out the dirt and fluffs up the rugs! Put a dryer sheet in to "sweeten" them, too!

By the time you're finished with the vacuuming, you'll have clean, fluffy rugs. The air setting does not ruin the rubber backings.

Once finished, be sure and clean out your dryer's lint filter.

Hide bleach spots. If you clean your bathroom (or any other part of your house) with bleach, remove the rugs so you don't splash bleach on them. If you do end up with white spots on an off-white or beige carpet, try this temporary remedy. Brew some tea, then take a cotton swab and dab all the spots. This can help until the carpet is cleaned. For bleach spots on other carpet colors, try lightly dabbling the spot with a similar-colored permanent marker as a last resort.

Protect a clean rug. To save a rug from getting rust marks under table and chair legs after you have shampooed it, place a plastic lid from a margarine tub or coffee can under each leg of the furniture.

Clean a concrete floor. If your children drew pictures on a concrete garage floor or sidewalk, don't panic. Here's a way to remove the "art." First step: Wet the stain, then apply enough powdered or liquid dishwasher detergent (both of which contain bleach, as well as deep-cleaning agents) to cover. Scrub with a utility brush; let sit for 20 minutes or so; rinse or hose off. You may need to repeat. While cleaning, keep pets and kids away from the area.

WALLS, WINDOWS, BLINDS, AND DRAPES

Make your windows sparkle. Because cleaning solution dries too quickly on bright, sunny days, save this chore for spring and fall. When it comes to cleaning really dirty windows, nothing beats ammonia and water. Mix a tablespoon of nonsudsing ammonia with a quart of water in a spray bottle, spritz, and wipe with a small towel or cloth. And here's an old hint that still works well: Wad up a bunch of newspapers to dry the glass—there's something in printer's ink that really makes a window shine. Yes, your hands may get smudgy, but just think of all the money you'll save on paper towels!

If the outside windows are grimy, first brush them off with a broom or hose them down. Although a squeegee is a wonderful tool to get the job done like a professional, I usually use a long-handled mop and the ammonia-and-water formula (¼ cup ammonia per gallon of water). Keep in mind, too, that if you wipe right to left on one side of the glass, and up and down on the other side, you'll be able to spot streaks and get rid of them all.

Updated window cleaner. Here's a recipe for an updated window cleaner that is cheap to make and works just like expensive commercial products. Just mix 12 to 16 ounces of water, ½ cup white or apple-cider vinegar, ¼ cup (70 percent) rubbing alcohol, 1 to 2 drops of blue or green food coloring (if desired), and 1 to 2 drops of lavender, orange, or your favorite essential oil.

You can spray the cleaner on sturdy paper towels and attach them to mops that use pads for cleaning in order to clean hard-to-reach windows.

Make window washing easy. Use your floor cleaner with disposable pads along with a bucket containing a light amount of ammonia mixed with water to clean the outside window surfaces. The long handle makes it easy to reach all the way to the top of the window, as well as high windows (if the handle isn't long enough, attach it to a painter's extending pole to reach high windows). Rinse with the hose after cleaning the glass.

For inside windows, use a light spritz of this homemade cleaner, and the wonderful flat surface of the floor pad will make the inside window cleaning almost no work at all. The disposable cloths can be reused time after time.

A cleaner door. After you use an eyeglass-cleaner sheet to clean your eyeglasses, use it to clean the glass panes in your door.

Clean the blinds. Used fabric-softener sheets make great dust cloths for cleaning blinds. The leftover fragrance also leaves a pleasant scent while the cloth pulls away the dust and dirt!

Easy-clean blinds. If you've got mini-blinds on windows in your home or RV, you know how long it can take to clean them. Twice a year, speed-clean blinds with premoistened wipes. Just keep in mind that if the wipes have oil or other additives, they might leave a residue that causes dirt and dust to stick to the blinds even more. You might want to try some wipes that have alcohol only.

Clean blinds faster. Dusting and washing mini-blinds slat by slat is time-consuming but necessary. Use an old sock, or one that has lost its mate, as your wiping tool. Simply slide the sock over your hand, and you can wipe the slats with ease. Footlets or golf socks work best.

Freshen drapes in the dryer. To quickly freshen drapes in the dryer (on the cool or air-dry setting), add a dry fabric-softener sheet. It really freshens the drapes and leaves a pleasant (although not long-lasting) fragrance to the room.

Quick-clean window screens. Before company arrives, do a quick window cleaning, even on the screens. Dirt and pollen make screens look terrible, so take a masking-tape lint roller and roll it over the screens. They'll get clean, with no bent frames in the process.

Get rid of crayon. If a budding artist in your house has decided to try decorating your kitchen or office chalkboard with a crayon, don't stress out! It can be fixed. Put a brown grocery bag over the crayon marks and carefully iron them with a warm iron (but don't get the iron too hot).

You can also try sprinkling baking soda on a damp sponge or cloth and scrubbing until the marks are gone. If a stain remains, you can buy chalkboard paint to make the surface new again. Call a few paint stores to find one that carries it.

Clean crayon marks from a painted wall. If you have young children, chances are they've made marks on your walls with crayon. Don't panic; I'll tell you how to get it off.

- To get crayon marks off a painted wall, gently scrape off as much as possible with a spatula wrapped with a towel. Don't rub high-gloss paints; the sheen dulls easily.

- Next, pour a little dry-cleaning solvent or lubricating oil on a soft cloth and gently dab the marks. It may take some patience.

- If the marks don't come off, try liquid dishwashing detergent and water, and gently rub at the mark. You can then wipe with a damp cloth to clean. This method also can be used on washable wallpaper, but test a small spot first and let it dry to make sure this process is safe.

- Gently rub in a circular motion with a sponge or soft cloth, and rinse. You may need several applications to remove the color and wax.

- To improve your chances, get crayons labeled as washable when you can!

- Let the little artist help clean up the masterpiece—the next time your child might think twice before marking a wall.

Remove wallpaper art. Young artists sometimes like to decorate walls. Here's how to clean up. To remove ballpoint-ink inscriptions from vinyl wallpaper, apply some denatured alcohol by using a paper towel. Let sit for 10 to 15 seconds. Next, gently wipe with a clean paper towel. Stubborn stains might require more than one application.

Crayon marks are waxy and might be a bit more difficult to remove. To send them on their way, you will need some prewash spray or dry-cleaning solvent. Test a small spot first to make sure the cleaning solvent doesn't stain the wallpaper. Use a clean, white cloth, sponge, or cotton swab to apply the solution to the stain. You might need a couple of treatments.

And lastly, let's get rid of pesky grease stains. Dampen a clean cloth with a solution of water and a drop of mild dishwashing detergent. If the stain is stubborn, mix together equal

CARE FOR DRAPES AND CURTAINS

As we all know, drapes and curtains get dusty and dirty. They should be dusted and cleaned on a regular basis to prevent permanent staining. But draperies that have been exposed to the sun for a long time, or are really old, might need to be replaced.

To keep them looking good, take these steps:

- For a quick fix, freshen curtains in the dryer. Set it to the "air only" cycle and run for several minutes.

- For dealing with sheers (and to avoid ironing), wash them (as the label indicates) and then dissolve a cup of Epsom salts in hot water. Dip the sheers into the mixture and hang them in the shower to dry.

- For washable curtains and drapes, vacuum or shake off dust and loose dirt. Soak badly soiled curtains in warm water and fabric-safe bleach—if the label says it's okay for the fabric. Then wash in warm or cold water, whichever the label allows, along with regular detergent. Select a high water level so the drapes can move freely in the washing machine.

parts of baking soda and water to make a paste. Apply to the spot and let it sit until it dries. Brush it off with a cloth.

FURNITURE AND FURNISHINGS

Remove heat marks from a table. White spots on a wood table caused by heat, when they are fresh, may be removed using this old-fashioned method: Mix equal parts baking soda and white toothpaste and apply to the area in a circular motion using a cloth, sponge, or even your finger.

You may have to rub quite a bit before you notice that the stain is slowly fading. Continue until the mark

is gone, then wipe off the mixture with a slightly damp cloth. Buff the area dry. Afterward, use furniture polish to restore the shine.

Hide scratches on wood. You can make shallow scratches on wood less noticeable by rubbing in a bit of shoe polish paste or crayon in a compatible color. Or crack open a walnut or pecan, and warm it in the palm of your hand to release the oil; rub the nut meat over the scratches. Wipe with a clean cloth and buff.

Last-minute lightning cleanup. When company is coming and I need to clean in a hurry, I follow Mother's rule: Pay attention only to the surfaces guests will see, such as the wooden dining room set, the buffet, the coffee table, and the end tables—

Getting Rid of Spider Webs

A creative church group in 1977 came up with this way to clean spider webs from the very high, peaked ceiling in their church. The spider webs were well out of reach of mops or brooms with telescoping handles.

Purchase a large, helium-filled balloon and a spool of thin, strong, nylon fishing line. Turn off the lights (they are likely to become hot), and attach the nylon line to the balloon. After the balloon ascends to the ceiling apex, maneuver it around by means of the spool end of the line to remove the spider webs.

Thirty years later, this hint is still great! I have beamed ceilings in my home, and this method works great on them: Tie a swatch or two of nylon net around the balloon. Leave the cutoff ends of the net at the top of the balloon. The webs will stick to the net! This net can be removed and washed many times.

no one will notice those dust bunnies underneath the sideboard. And my best cleaning friend is the upholstery attachment on the vacuum cleaner, because it quickly sucks up all visible dust. For surfaces that need a little more TLC, I put an old, clean cotton sock dampened with a bit of cleaning polish on each hand, and I do what I call a Texas two-step—with both hands wiping swiftly, the job goes twice as fast.

Unstick paper coasters. The paper coasters put out in some restaurants stick to wet glasses every time. But sprinkle just a little salt on the coaster or napkin and it will prevent your glass from sticking.

Get rid of cat hair. Use a plastic glove to remove cat hair from furniture—it's a fantastic solution to a vexing problem.

Remove a water ring from a vase. Tap water full of minerals is the likely culprit if there's a crusty calcium ring inside your vase. Fill your vase with enough warm, full-strength household vinegar to cover the deposits. Shake the vase, with your hand over the opening, and then let the vinegar work its magic overnight. The next morning, use a nonabrasive scrub pad to get at any bits that haven't dissolved. If you can't reach your hand inside, pour a little vinegar into the vase and a handful of rice for scrubbing action;

KEEP VASES SPARKLING

Over time, vases can become stained with hard-water deposits and just plain gunk. Here are a few easy solutions you can try to make them sparkling and crystal-clear once again:

- For a vase with a large opening—one you can easily put your hand into—mix 1/3 cup of salt and 2 tablespoons or more of vinegar to form a paste. Apply this to the inside of the vase with a damp rag and let stand for about 20 minutes, then rinse and dry.

- For those stubborn areas that don't want to budge, try using a gentle paste of baking soda and water. Follow by rinsing and drying.

- For delicate vases that are easily scratched, use plain vinegar by itself. Fill the vase up to the rim with (warm to hot) vinegar. Let this sit overnight, scrub, then rinse and dry.

- To clean inside vases with narrow necks, use a straightened coat hanger. Just wrap a soft rag around the end and secure it with a rubber band. Then insert it into the vase and gently use it to scrub away any stains.

shake or swirl the vase vigorously until the deposits disappear.

Clean glass bottles. An age-old method for cleaning gunk out of glass bottles is to put some sand (from a beach or playground) and water in the bottle and swirl and shake the bottle (cover the top with your hand). The sand will scrub the inside of the bottle. This method also works for narrow vases that are too small to get your hand into.

Clean a narrow vase. Here is a great way to clean the bottom of a long, narrow crystal vase. Poke a strong chopstick into a soft cloth such as an old T-shirt. Fill the vase halfway with soapy, warm water and use the cloth-covered chopstick to scrub the bottom. It's always surprising how much grime comes off on the cloth.

Keep good silver untarnished. Keeping a silver tea service or other family silver heirloom polished is a nuisance. Probably the best way to keep silver untarnished is to keep it covered when you aren't using it and uncover it when you have guests. If the silver is in your dining room instead of in a closet or cabinet, make a cover of pretty drapery fabric to complement your dining room, and line the fabric with heavyweight flannel. Your silver will be protected and ready for display on special occasions.

Reuse those dryer sheets. Save used dryer sheets for dusting. They grab up dust particles from furniture and lampshades. If you run out of cloths for your floor sweeper, try a dryer sheet. Use two recycled dryer sheets to get enough thickness.

Clean up a dusty centerpiece. There are a few methods to try when cleaning silk flowers. The first is to remove dust by using a blow-dryer. Set it on the lowest air speed and coolest temperature. Hold the dryer about 10 inches away from the arrangement and work from the top to the bottom. You will want to do this cleaning project outside so the dust can blow away. You could also try using a clean brush (for makeup or paint).

Next, put ¼ cup to ½ cup of table salt in a plastic or brown paper bag. Put the flowers in, stem up, hold the bag closed, and give it several shakes.

You might also try giving the flowers a bath. Because most silk-type flower fabric is usually made of nylon or polyester and the stems are made of plastic, water shouldn't damage them. Fill up a sink with cool water and add a few drops of mild dishwashing detergent. Dip the flowers (just the heads) into the water and gently move them around for a little while, rinse, and let air-dry.

Some do well, but others look a little droopy, so test just one flower first, then do the rest.

Roll flowers clean. Silk flowers are easy to dust with a lint roller. Because silk flowers are flexible, you can gently open up the petals and swipe with the roller.

🕐 **Clean up flowers fast.** If you need to spruce up a dried-flower arrangement, simply take it outside, turn it upside down, and give it a good shake. You can also gently dust it with a clean paintbrush or makeup brush.

Clean a planter. Terra-cotta pots can get quite yucky-looking, especially if you live in an area with lots of minerals in the water supply, which causes an ugly white residue on the outside.

To clean the pot, it must be empty. First, wash the pot with some good-quality dish soap and a plastic scrub brush, then rinse well. Wearing rubber gloves (if your hands are sensitive), use full-strength white vinegar and wipe down the whole pot, inside and outside, with a scrubbie sponge. Once the mineral deposits (usually white stains) are gone, let the pot dry completely. Then, to keep the pot stain-free, apply some acrylic sealer to the inside and the outside of the pot. Once the sealer is completely dry, the planter is ready for a plant.

Get baskets clean. Baskets are a clutter-saver! I use them to hold everything from hair accessories, books, and magazines to some of the "junk" that accumulates on my desk. They can get dusty and dirty over time, so here's a way to clean them.

Wash dirty baskets in warm water and a little furniture soap; swish them vigorously and use an old scrub or toothbrush to get dirt out of the crevices. Then rinse the baskets and let them air- or sun-dry.

Clean Plastic Flowers

Plastic flowers get dirty over time in a container. Dusting and cleaning them with a small cloth can still leave them looking dull. Put a drop or so of liquid detergent in the center of each flower and set them, container and all, in the bathtub and turn on the shower. They wash and rinse themselves.

Clean up leaky old batteries. Have you ever needed a flashlight but it wouldn't work, so you opened it up and found that the batteries had leaked everywhere? When a leaky battery has corroded the inside of your flashlight (or your camera), here's a safe way to clean up the mess.

- First, be sure to wear rubber gloves to protect your hands.

- Wipe away any battery leaks with a dry paper towel. If the leaked material has hardened, scrape it off with a plastic or wooden stick. Then use a damp paper towel to wipe up as much residue as possible, and toss out the stick and used paper towels.

- Next, use fine sandpaper or an emery board to remove any remaining corrosion on the contacts of the flashlight.

- To avoid the problem, always remove batteries when you don't plan to use the flashlight (or other battery-powered equipment) for several months, or when you store the item.

Clean a flashlight. If you have flashlights that do not work properly, even if the batteries have not leaked, try cleaning the contacting areas of the flashlight. Use sandpaper to clean the bottom of the bulb, both ends of the batteries, and the top of the spring

---

Battery Smarts

Here are tips on the care and handling of batteries. Hope you get a "charge" out of these helpful hints!

- High temperatures and batteries don't mix. Whether you keep batteries in or out of appliances in areas of high heat, the batteries will not last as long.

- Don't leave batteries in appliances that you are not using.

- Don't mix loose batteries with other metal items like paper clips and coins. And for us ladies, don't put loose batteries in the bottom of your purse.

- Use caution when recharging batteries—follow directions exactly. Don't try to recharge batteries that are not labeled "rechargeable."

- The old, old advice was to keep batteries in the fridge to help them last longer. This is no longer true. Storing batteries in the refrigerator will *not* keep them from going bad, and, in fact, major manufacturers state not to put them in the fridge.

in the bottom of the flashlight. Then apply a light coating of dielectric grease (used for better contact on batteries or other electrical components). Small tubes are available at auto-parts stores. Formerly dim flashlights will work, nice and bright!

CLEANING PRODUCTS, MATERIALS, AND TOOLS

Take a breath of cleaner air. People with allergies and asthma can become the unintended targets of window cleaners, air fresheners, table cleaners, and even construction and lawn chemicals in public places. People often spray these chemicals with abandon, as if they are totally harmless. They are not, and they are a particular problem for folks with respiratory problems, who might suffer asthma attacks from breathing them. If you absolutely must use an aerosol or a pump spray (both of which put tiny chemical droplets into the air), do it in such a way that no one can be harmed.

There are some alternative, natural items, such as vinegar and baking soda, that can be used to clean and freshen around the house. You'll find lots of tips for using these products in this section and throughout this book.

About vinegar. There are many types of vinegar, made from different ingredients, but the process is basically the same as it was thousands of years ago. And each type has its own particular use. But for cleaning, usually white vinegar is best, because it is clear, it won't stain, and it's cheap. You should always have a gallon or two on hand.

If you're looking for a healthy, low-calorie salad dressing, then wine or balsamic vinegar is the way to go. Malt vinegar is a favorite in England, where the British sprinkle it on their fish and chips! It's made from malt syrup and is slightly sweet compared with white or apple-cider vinegar. Apple-cider vinegar is made from fermented apple juice and is great for cooking and pickling.

Get rid of odors with vinegar. Vinegar has amazing odor-busting qualities. It's the first thing you should reach for, especially because it's all natural, safe to use around children and pets, and cheap!

Deodorize with vinegar. Did you know that vinegar can actually absorb room odors? All you need to do is place some shallow containers of vinegar around, and most odors will be gone.

Keep a spray bottle of vinegar on hand. I keep a spray bottle full of vinegar in my kitchen for cleaning appliances and windows, and one in each bathroom for the mirrors, sink, faucet, and toilet bowl. It's a quick cleanup! When the vinegar dries, the smell goes away—promise!

Don't use vinegar on marble. Remember that vinegar, lemon, or any cleaning product containing citric acid should not be used on real marble. The acid in the vinegar will cause the marble to crack and scale.

Rely on baking soda. When you're trying to save money *and* the environment, but your home needs a major cleaning, then the best solution is baking soda. Commercial cleaners can be costly and might contain chemicals that come with warnings, while a box of inexpensive, planet-friendly baking soda could be all you need to tackle many cleaning jobs around the house. You can use baking soda in every room.

Good ol' baking soda is great to have around the house. It comes in handy as a cleaner and a deodorizer! It's a great cleaner when sprinkled on a damp sponge, and you can also use it to freshen up around the home.

Deodorize with baking soda. To banish odors, sprinkle a few tablespoons of baking soda in the bottom of an empty gym bag and leave overnight.

Pour a liberal amount of baking soda into a kitchen trash can before putting in a new bag.

More ways to use baking soda.

Unlimited Uses for . . . Vinegar

For everything from cleaning windows to removing salt deposits on clay pots, vinegar is the product to use. And all you'll need to get going is a gallon of white vinegar and a few cleaning supplies.

- For sparkling windows, add ½ to 1 cup of vinegar to ½ gallon of water. Spray on a window, then dry with crumpled newspaper.

- To make your clay pots look like new, just wipe with a cloth soaked in undiluted white vinegar.

- If your porch or patio has exposed brick that could use a little freshening, scrub with a brush dipped in full-strength white vinegar.

Baking soda, unlike many commercial cleaners, is so versatile that it can be used in cleaning, deodorizing, and baking! What else can it be used for? In this day and age, when we're all concerned about the environment, you can help out. For example, instead of using harsh chemicals to remove burned-on food in a pot, all you have to do is put 3 tablespoons of baking soda in enough water to cover the bottom of the pan. Simmer on the stove until the gunk starts to lift, and, with a little scrubbing, the pot will sparkle again. All for pennies, too.

Scrub with baking soda. Baking soda is a fantastic cleaner for kitchen appliances, counters, the sink, drain, refrigerator, and a zillion other things! Simply sprinkle some on a damp sponge and scrub away dirt and grime. It's nontoxic and is abrasive on most hard surfaces (when dampened with water). To keep baking soda handy around the kitchen, pour some into a clean shaker bottle and keep by the sink. When you need some, a quick shake or two is right at your fingertips. You may never have to buy scouring powder again!

Busting Some Vinegar Myths

Vinegar is a favorite of mine. It has a multitude of uses, and best of all, it is cheap. You don't need to buy expensive cleaners, because vinegar usually will do the trick. But here are some things vinegar *won't* do:

- Adding vinegar to the water when hard-cooking eggs does not make them easier to peel. The older the eggs, the easier they are to peel. So, if you are planning on hard-cooking some, buy them a week or so early.

- Adding vinegar to the water when poaching eggs will not help keep the whites from running. And when you are poaching eggs, the fresher the egg, the more it will hold its shape rather than spread out in the pan.

- Adding vinegar to the washer to "set" colors does not work. Years ago, some of the clothing dyes could be set this way, but new dyes don't react the same way. And only 1 or 2 cups of vinegar added to a load in the washer is diluted so much that it might as well not be there.

- Sponging vinegar on a sunburn will only make you smell like a salad. It has been shown to have no effect in helping heal a sunburn. Use sunblock, and if some rays get through, there are ointments that "cool" and numb the burn. Check your local drugstore.

Clean and deodorize wood. Use baking soda to clean and deodorize a butcher block or wooden cutting board. Dampen a sponge, sprinkle on baking soda, and scrub until clean. Then rinse well and dry.

Soak up grease with cornstarch. To absorb oil and grease spills on clothing, upholstery, and leather, pat on enough cornstarch to cover stains (try to get to them before they set); let it sit a while, then remove with a toothbrush or vacuum.

Clean with isopropyl alcohol. Rubbing alcohol has many uses, it's inexpensive, and a bottle will last a long time. Keep a clearly marked spray bottle of alcohol in each bathroom and the kitchen, too. Try adding a touch of vanilla or your favorite essential oil (I like lavender) for a hint of fragrance. Use it to clean eyeglasses and to remove lipstick and makeup residue from cosmetic bags and compacts. You can also use alcohol to sanitize your phones (including your cell phone)—it removes smudges from makeup and hair products.

Get rid of fingerprints. You can use alcohol to erase fingerprints from chrome and stainless steel, and for cleaning cell phones (but not the screens). Wipe the surface with an alcohol-dampened microfiber cloth or paper towel.

Fade away stains. If you have stains

Unlimited Uses for . . . Baking Soda

Baking soda has a multitude of uses. Here are a few:

- Keep shoes fresh by sprinkling some baking soda inside (do not use on leather shoes).
- Dog toys in need of a cleaning? Baking soda to the rescue! Make a solution of baking soda and water and give the toys a good scrubbing.
- Stinky trash compactor? Sprinkle some baking soda in the bag every once in a while to keep odors at bay.
- To freshen a musty-smelling book, first make sure the pages of the book aren't damp or wet, then generously sprinkle the baking soda throughout the pages and give it a day or two to absorb the odor. Now shake out the baking soda, and the odor should be gone. Strong smells might need a couple of applications. Do not use baking soda on heirloom books!

on unfinished wood, such as butcher block, apply fresh lemon juice with a cotton swab, then let air-dry.

Sanitize with peroxide. Use 3 percent hydrogen peroxide for killing mildew on bath tiles or sanitizing plastic cutting boards. Sponge over the area; let dry, then rinse well. Mop up any spills quickly (hydrogen peroxide can cause fading).

Banish rust with cream of tartar. To remove rust from white porcelain fixtures, mix 2 tablespoons of cream of tartar with a few drops of 3 percent hydrogen peroxide to make a paste. Apply the paste to the stain and let sit. After the paste dries, rinse it off.

Pour bleach easily. The seal on a new bleach bottle can be hard to remove. Try this: Grab a pencil or other sharp instrument, and punch a hole in the center of the seal. You will have better control of the flow. A gentler flow of bleach will not splatter on and ruin some fabrics.

Disinfect toys safely. To disinfect toys shared by children, make a very diluted solution of household chlorine bleach—2 teaspoons bleach to 1 quart water—and pour into an opaque plastic spray bottle (bleach degrades when exposed to light). Spritz over dirty areas; let sit for 5 minutes, then wipe with a damp cloth. Rinse in clear water. Even watered-down bleach can stain, so take care not to spill any of the solution on clothes or carpets.

Put recipes on bottles. If you make up your own cleaning products from my recipes, write the ingredients and instructions on a piece of paper and tape it to a spray bottle right after you make the cleaner. You will always know what is in the bottle, and also what it is to be used for.

Mark bottles. The on/off and stream/spray markings on bottles of household cleaning products can be tough to see. To make them easier to see, use a permanent marker to draw an arrow on the side of the square marked "stream" and to draw outspread rays on the side marked "spray."

Use a toothbrush for fine cleaning. Combine the time-honored trick of

Baking Soda Cleaned Miss Liberty!

Just to show you how versatile and useful baking soda is, 2000 tons of it was used to clean 99 years of paint and coal tar from the copper interior of the Statue of Liberty. How's that for history?

using an old toothbrush to clean in tight spots with the modern technology of the rechargeable, rotary scrubbing appliance. Use an electric toothbrush fitted with a worn-out brush head to clean around sinks, toilets, faucets, and bathtub glass doors; along gaskets; and in other tight spots (like narrow spaces in the refrigerator). The rapid rotary motion does a better job than you could accomplish by hand. Once you start using a toothbrush to clean you will think of many more ideas.

Make rubber gloves last longer. If you always seem to wear out one of a pair of rubber gloves, put a small wad of cotton down in each finger of the glove. The glove will last much longer. If your nails are especially long, put a larger wad in the glove of the hand you use most.

VACUUMING

Freshen the vacuum cleaner bag. When you change the bag in your upright vacuum cleaner, try putting an unused fabric-softener sheet inside the new bag before attaching it to the cleaner. You'll have a fresh scent (instead of an old, dusty smell) to enjoy as you clean the house.

Keep the vacuum cleaner fresh. To keep your vacuum cleaner smelling fresh, add a drop or two of an essential oil (lavender is my favorite, but you could also use peppermint, bergamot, clove, or whatever scent you like) on a cotton ball and drop into the vacuum bag. Or, put a few drops of your favorite perfume on the cotton ball instead.

Revamp a vac. When your vacuum cleaner gives out, save the hose and tools. You can purchase an inexpensive wet-dry vac on sale and use your tools with it. Duct-tape the old and new hoses together and use the old tools with the new shop vacuum. Most wet-dry vacs are very lightweight and convenient and do not require bags; the two hoses will give you a long reach from one plug-in spot.

Replacement vacuum filters. Handheld vacuums have filters that should be replaced from time to time. Unfortunately, these filters are not standardized, and sometimes finding one is impossible. Since most of the filters are attached to a plastic frame, you can tear off the old filter, place a coffee filter on the frame, and secure it with a rubber band. Trim off the excess filter paper. This is fast, simple, easy to do, and cheap.

Comb the vacuum cleaner brush. Try using a cheap, plastic comb to remove lint and fibers from the roller brush on the vacuum. You can use either end as needed, and the combs are inexpensive to replace.

Vacuum up pests. Pesky mosquito indoors? Reach for the vacuum hose!

Vacuum under chairs. When vacuuming around and under heavy chairs, just tip them forward—it's a lot easier than pushing them out of the way. Then it is a snap to vacuum and dust.

DUSTING

The best way to dust. Dust in our homes is a never-ending problem. It seems that we've just dusted and it's back! Here are some hints to help control dust:

- When you dust, don't just move it around. Instead, remove it! Using a dry cloth or feather duster only rearranges dust and pushes it into the air. So, depending on the surface to be cleaned, you need to use a furniture polish, multipurpose spray cleaner, or slightly damp cloth to pick up and hold the dust. I like to put clean, old socks over my hands and spray them with furniture polish, then dust, dust, dust. The new dust wands with replaceable dusting cloths work well, too.

- Microfiber cloths do a super job of removing dust from furniture, computer screens, and even pets! I keep one handy in the glove compartment of my car. And once they've put in a good day's work, you can throw them in the wash (alone, not with anything that gives off lint) and they're ready for the next cleaning chore. (Visit www.Heloise.com for more hints using microfiber cloths.)

Do a 5-minute dusting. Stand in the middle of the room and look at all surfaces—dining room, coffee, or side tables and nightstands. During the week, do a 5-minute quick dust. My mother called this "top cleaning." It will help control the dust until you have time for a more thorough cleaning.

Dust with shoulder pads. If you dislike shoulder pads and remove them from dresses and blouses, use them to make a "mitt" to dust your blinds. Cotton shoulder pads work best.

Clean with canned air. If you have lots of knickknacks, try dusting them with the canned air sold for cleaning computers and electronic devices. You'll be able to get into little nooks and crannies.

Dust with a lint roller. It can be somewhat difficult to dust lampshades with all the grooves. The dust seems to go everywhere. Try running a sticky lint roller over the lampshade instead of using a cloth. Just roll up and down a few times and the lampshade will look as good as new.

"Baste" lampshades clean. Try using a silicone basting brush to clean pleated lampshades. You may find that the slight tackiness of the bristles allows the brush to grab the dust better than other natural-bristle brushes. These brushes are readily available, even at discount stores.

Keep dust rags handy. Cut up old, white cotton T-shirts and keep them in the laundry room. When you need to dust, you can just pick up a rag and you're ready to go.

Keep dust out of the house. Placing mats at each door will help keep dust from coming into your home.

Keep Down Dust

Here are some easy spring-cleaning hints to help you lower the amount of dust in your home. Most people who sneeze around dust are actually allergic to microscopic organisms that live in the dust—dust mites. It's important to keep the amount of dust in the home—especially the bedroom—to a minimum. Here are some ways to do that:

- Wash bedding in the hottest water possible at least once a week.
- Regularly dust off your bedroom furniture, especially the bed frame, with a wet cloth. Also pay attention to dust on ceiling-fan blades, windowsills, and the tops of doors. You might want to wear a dust mask when cleaning.

- Remove carpet if possible. If not, vacuum often, making frequent bag changes, too.

- Keep windows and doors closed as much as possible to prevent dust from coming inside.

- If you're a pet lover, dogs and cats really should not sleep with you. Even the cleanest pets carry around all sorts of dust, lint, pet dander, and hair that can really aggravate your allergies at night. At a minimum, if Fido or Fluffy shares the bed (confession: our Cabbie, a mini schnauzer, does), try to use a damp cloth to wipe off the coat and paws before bedtime.

Dust in high places. Attach a dustcloth to a mop or a painter's extending pole to dust ceiling fans and high corners.

Keep a cleaner house. Use dryer sheets to do other cleaning chores. Whenever you take the laundry out of the dryer, collect all the dryer sheets on one side. When done with laundry, grab the used sheets and use them for a quick dusting, especially in the corners of rooms where dust bunnies and pet hair accumulate. Their ability to grab dust and hair makes the sheets perfect for reuse. It only takes a couple of minutes to hit problem areas between your regular cleanings.

Dust easily. If you are unable to bend over while cleaning, you can use a can of pressurized air (if you keep one on hand for cleaning your computer) and use it to blow the dust off the edges of baseboards, pleated lampshades, and silk flowers. Canned air is expensive, but wonderfully useful. Please be mindful that all inhalants can be misused and abused, so store them safely.

Dust with a pastry brush. Here's a really simple dusting tip: Pull out your pastry brush and dust off your telephone.

Dust your houseplants. If you notice a houseplant with dusty leaves, grab a microfiber cloth and dust the leaves. It works wonderfully, and the leaves will be shiny and dust-free. These cloths are fantastic for dusting just about anything, from plants to pets.

GETTING RID OF ODORS

Freshen breath *and* air. Make your home smell fresh by placing ⅓ cup of mouthwash in an inconspicuous place in the bathroom. With ceiling fans and air conditioning, the mouthwash evaporates and distributes into the air. When you come home or when you have visitors, there will be a fresh, minty scent in the air. All you have to do is freshen the cup every 3 or 4 days.

Make your own air freshener. Felt holds the scent of room sprays a long time. Just take a piece of felt, cut out hearts, stars, or any other shapes, and sew a string through the top. Spray with room spray or your favorite cologne and hang in your car, bathroom, or anyplace you want to smell fresh. When the odor dissipates, just spray the felt again.

Keep closets fresh. First, make sure all the clothes are clean and that shoes have been aired out before storing them in the closet. Now, you can try one or all of the following:

- Make an air freshener, using a small jar with holes punched in the lid. Inside, place a cotton ball and add a few drops of a favorite essential oil, like lemon, lavender, or orange.

- Apply a perfume or cologne to a washcloth or small piece of fabric and put it in the closet. Don't let it touch any of the clothes.

- Place dishes of baking soda around the closet, or you can add 3 to 4 teaspoons of a spice (cinnamon or nutmeg) to a box of baking soda.

- Also, keep the door open as much as possible to let in some fresh air.

- Sprinkle baking soda or a carpet deodorizer on the floor of a closet, let sit overnight, and then vacuum. Baking soda is a great, cheap cleaner and deodorizer.

Get rid of fireplace odor. Sometimes a fireplace can smell like wet ashes. Creosote—a byproduct of steam and soot from burning logs—could be the source of the odor. Over time, it can build up inside the chimney. After sweeping the floor and walls of the inner hearth, pour household vinegar on an old cloth and wipe down the inside surface to help neutralize odor. If the smell returns, a leak in the flue may be letting in moisture, in which case you should call a chimney sweep to provide a thorough inspection and cleaning.

Use perfume inserts. Save the perfumed advertisements that come in department store statements. Open the perfumed flap and place the entire advertisement in "smelly" places—the shoe rack in the closet, the new wood bookcase that smells of factory glue, closets that you don't open very often, between your garbage can and the liner. But never put them in food pantries!

Cancel milk with vinegar. If you get a leaky carton of milk at the store and it gets onto your car upholstery, the best remedy is to clean your car as soon as you get home. If you can't, and the car smells bad the next day, try sponging the area with a diluted solution of vinegar. If that does not get rid of the odor, pour straight vinegar on the spot, wait about 10 minutes, and blot it up with clean, white rags. Repeat the next day if necessary. And return that defective milk carton to the store where you bought it.

Deodorize a T-shirt. To deodorize T-shirts that have been stored and smell musty, simply soak in 1 part vinegar and 2 parts water for 20 to 30 minutes, then wash and dry.

Keep an outdoor garbage can odor-free. Here's a way to keep your outdoor garbage can from smelling bad: After the trash is picked up, leave the can out in the sun for several hours with the lid off. Then, before you put in any new trash, place some newspaper (if you don't recycle) in the bottom of the can. This will ensure that all the garbage comes out when the can is emptied.

Deodorize kitchen trash. To freshen the kitchen trash container, use it as a mop bucket every once in a while. That way, you get two jobs done at once.

Scent the air with old perfume. Have old perfume lying around? Use it as a room deodorizer, especially in the bathroom!

Penny-wise air freshening. If you live on a tight budget and like to keep your home clean and fresh-smelling, instead of buying an electric room deodorizer, buy car air fresheners. They cost less than a dollar and come with a string to hang anywhere. They come in all shapes and fragrances, and they last a long time.

CLEANING TECH GEAR

Keep the computer clean. Because many of us spend a lot of time at computers, they do get dirty from all that use. We also need to take care of our computers. If you clean it frequently, your computer will stay in better running condition. Try these cleaning hints to keep your computer in tiptop shape:

What Gets Cooking Odors Off Your Hands?

What else besides vinegar can be used to clean smelly hands of onion, fish, or other odors?

a) Lemon
b) Sugar and a drop of detergent
c) Baking soda
d) All of the above

Well, what do you think? If you said "all of the above," then you know your scents. Cut a lemon in half and rub it on your hands, followed by soap and water. Or pour some sugar in the palm of your hand, add a drop or two of liquid detergent, and wash those odors away. You can also put a sprinkle of baking soda in your wet hands, scrub vigorously, and rinse. Clean and fresh!

- First, turn the computer off, tip the keyboard upside down, and gently tap the back of it with your hand. You'll be amazed at what comes out! Then use a soft-brush attachment to your vacuum cleaner to gently vacuum the keyboard.

- Recycle a used dryer sheet (don't use new ones) to wipe off the keyboard. It will lift off dust and might eliminate static electricity. Then you can toss the sheet.

- Electronics stores carry products specifically for cleaning computers, such as cans of compressed air and wipes for keyboards. Check with a salesperson for the right product. Alcohol-based wipes are perfect to keep handy for a quick swipe to remove fingerprints.

Clean your keyboard. To clean debris out of a computer keyboard, unfold a paper clip and run it between the keys. It quickly picks up hair and dust bunnies that get caught in those tight spaces.

Clean your keyboard, take 2. To help remove the buildup of dirt and germs from a computer keyboard, use a cotton swab dipped in isopropyl alcohol to clean in between the keys

and the buttons. The alcohol evaporates quickly and will not harm the keyboard.

Clean CDs and DVDs. If you own CDs or DVDs that are grimy or skipping, it's time to clean them! Here is the best way to clean them without scratching them—doing this the wrong way can cause damage:

- Pick up the disc and hold it by the edges.

- Use a soft, lint-free cloth to wipe the surface, starting at the center and moving outward to the edge. Wipe across the disc in a straight line, rather than in a circular motion; following the grooves can cause micro-scratches that will damage the disc.

- If simply wiping the disc does not help, dampen the cloth with a gentle soap-and-water solution and wipe again from the center out, not in a circle.

- *Never* use household cleaners, abrasives, or solvents on CDs or DVDs.

- Keep your discs in the best shape possible by storing them in their protective covers when not in use.

Chapter 3

Wardrobe and Laundry

In this chapter we'll take a look in your closet to find better ways to organize and store your clothes and linens. There are tips on the clothes you wear, from head to toe, and jewelry, too. The second part of the chapter is all about keeping your clothes and linens clean, from washing and drying to removing stains, ironing, and getting rid of lint.

Watch the weather. It's a good idea to watch the news at night to see what the weather is going to be the next day so that you can dress accordingly. However, sometimes the weather person is not on the mark. So, before you change out of your pajamas in the morning, step outside to quickly check the weather.

PANTS AND JEANS

Keep slacks wrinkle-free. When you hang up your slacks, fit a wire coat hanger in the waistband so the slacks hang straight down to avoid having a crease at the knees.

Keep drawstrings from slipping. To keep the drawstring on kids' fleece exercise pants from sliding into the waistband, sew a small button on each end of the string. This will also work for jackets and other clothes with drawstrings.

Find comfy pants. Some elderly women's stomachs can become large as they age. Instead of buying pants with elastic all around the top that are not very stylish, these ladies can shop for pants in the maternity department of a clothing store. These jeans fit better around the bottom and are comfy on the tummy.

Do a temporary hem. If your teen-ager buys a new pair of jeans that he or she just has to wear to a dance that night, but there's no time to get them hemmed in time, use duct tape on the inside to create a temporary hem. Then hem the pants for real after the dance is over (but before you launder them).

Label stored clothes. If you fold jeans and store them on a shelf, you can label each shelf with "good," "fair," and "poor." You won't have to go through all of the jeans to find the ones that you want to wear.

You can also label sheets and blankets with their size on a piece of masking tape so you don't have to unfold and check each item.

I.D. your jeans. If, like many women, your weight yo-yos, to avoid trying on jeans from your closet that might be too small or too large, mark in the waistband (with a laundry marker) the weight range for those pants. It saves time, since not all jeans of the same size fit the same way.

Color-code hangers to sort slacks. Black and navy blue slacks are hard to tell apart in a dim closet. Here's a timesaver for folks with failing eyesight, or those in a hurry. In your clothes closet, use one color hanger for navy slacks and another color for black slacks. The same can be done for different shades of red, green, and brown.

SHIRTS, BLOUSES, SWEATERS, AND DRESSES

Sort T-shirts with clever folding. Folks in Florida and other warm climates can wear both long- and short-sleeved T-shirts year-round. If you're tired of refolding long-sleeved tees, here's a way to tell the length of sleeve without unfolding the shirt. When you take the shirts out of the dryer, fold short-sleeved shirts in half lengthwise with the sleeves together and only half of the neck opening showing when the shirt is on the shelf. For long-sleeved tees, fold the tee at the shoulders, with both sleeves at the back of the shirt and the full neck opening showing.

Then let the family know that half the neck means half the sleeve!

Make a fake button. If you lose a large, white, plastic button from a blouse, you might be able to replace it by cutting out the bottom of a white medicine bottle.

Catch the light at night. If you are

going to a dressy evening event wearing a black outfit, make sure you are visible to cars in the parking garage or on the walk to the event location. Pin a crystal brooch to the lower back hip area of your jacket. It will pick up lights.

Color-code drawers. As you replace winter tops with ones for warmer weather, sort your shirts by color when you put them in the drawers. Put the black and warm-colored (pink, orange, and gold) shirts in the top drawer, for example, and white and cool-colored (blue, green, and purple) tops in the bottom drawer. Pretty soon, you'll get in the swing because you'll know what shade you're looking for and will have to open only one drawer to get it.

Keep threaded needles handy. Keep a pin cushion in your closet with a few needles threaded with various colors of thread. When a button comes off your slacks or blouse, it only takes 5 minutes to sew it back on. Doing it right away means you won't end up with a pile of repairs to do.

Get rid of annoying tags. If tags in the necks of your clothes drive you nuts, cut them off when you buy clothes. Then take a black permanent marker and make a dot where the tag was so you know which is the back of the garment.

Fix a troublesome tag. Have an annoying shirt tag that won't stay in place? Just use some iron-on hemming tape to keep it from flapping up, instead of cutting off the tag.

Pre-button a shirt. If your spouse or a relative has difficulty buttoning shirts because of an illness or injury, you can help when you do the laundry. When you take the shirts from the dryer, put them on a hanger and button all but the top two buttons. This allows your loved one to slip into the shirts, leaving only those two top buttons to fasten.

Alter clothes for elders. If your mother or another female relative is in a nursing home and confined to bed or a wheelchair, the aides may put her dresses on backward because it is easier for them to put the dresses on and take them off. A thoughtful gesture would be to rework the dresses so they open in the back. Each time you take some clothes home to launder, sew the front of each dress closed and cut the back open. Then sew the raw edges where you cut in the back, and put a snap at the top of the dress.

Stabilize sweaters. Sweaters that have dropped shoulders tend to fall off hangers. Sweaters with shoulder seams lines leave a "hang mark" on them. To alleviate both problems, slide a rubber band on both ends of the hanger to stabilize the sweaters and keep the clothing in place.

Recycle turtlenecks. When knit turtleneck shirts wear out, turn them into dickies. Cut off the sleeves and shorten the bottom of the top to end just under the bust line. When you wear them, the dickies stay in place better than the ones you purchase.

Preserve T-shirt designs. To preserve the design on the front of a T-shirt, turn it inside-out before laundering. Turn all dark shirts inside-out also, to prevent them from picking up lint from a previous load of whites.

Recycle your wedding gown. Many women save their wedding gown in a cedar chest for years, to perhaps hand down to a daughter to wear. Here is another way to give a wedding gown a new life.

Someone who can make clothes for dolls can make duplicates of the gown out of the material, using your wedding photos as a guide. The gowns can even be complete with veils. When your daughters get married, or daughters-in-law join the family, purchase for each of them a doll with the appropriate hair color and dress it in a gown made from your wedding gown.

One of my faithful newspaper column readers presented these dolls at wedding showers, along with photos and this poem: "This doll is a special doll/dressed up for your day./You see the gown that she has on/was made a different way./The material was not "borrowed"/and you can see that it's not "blue."/It's cut from something very old/and made especially for you!/ It once was part of another gown/worn on another day./And now this part is yours to keep./What more can I say?/I hope that you will treasure it/Tho' we are far apart./I hope you know that I will love you/forever, with all my heart." Add their names and wedding dates at the end of the poem.

Try on before removing any tags. When you order clothes by mail, always try them on before removing any tags or labels. If the garment does not fit when you try it on, many companies will not allow you to return it if tags have been removed.

If this happens to you and the company refuses to allow you to return the item, ask to speak to a supervisor. Give it another try and be firm. Tell them you only tried the garment on and that's it. It's worth another try.

SHOES AND SOCKS

 Save on shoeboxes. Instead of spending a lot of money on clear-plastic shoeboxes, a cheaper way to keep boxed shoes straight is to take a digital photo of them. Paste a copy of the printed picture on the end of the shoe box, and you'll always know which pair of shoes is inside.

Make shoes roomier. To stretch leather shoes, use a shoe stretcher in the desired shoe size, along with stretching spray formulated for leather. Or take them to a shoe-repair shop that has a stretching machine. It's not always possible to stretch leather shoes, so avoid buying pairs that aren't comfortable when you try them on.

Take scuff marks off shoes. Remove scuff marks from white leather shoes with the disposable erasing pads found in the cleaning aisle of most grocery stores.

Keep shoelaces out of bicycle spokes. To keep your shoelaces from getting tangled or untied when you're riding your bike, tuck the excess laces into your shoe.

Make heavy-duty shoelaces. If you seem to go through shoelaces fast because of those metal eyelets in hiking or industrial boots, make your own extra-tough laces. Purchase some parachute cord from a local military surplus store. Cut it to length and burn the ends (smelly but worth it). These homemade shoelaces are tough and long-lasting. The only downside is that they can come untied easily if not tied tight enough.

THE INSIDE STORY ON NEW SHOES

Have you bought shoes early in the day that felt tight when you put them on later that day? There's a reason! Experts say it's better to shop for shoes late in the afternoon because your feet are usually larger from water retention at that time. Here are some other hints about shoes:

- If your leather shoes or boots get wet, don't place them near heat or in direct sunlight to dry. Fill shoes or boots with newspapers or crumpled paper bags to help absorb moisture and to keep the shape.
- For smooth leather (not suede), you can do a quick polish by applying a light coat of petroleum jelly, mineral oil, or sweet oil and then wiping with a soft, clean cloth.

Another way to make your shoe-strings is to buy 100 percent nylon braided twine at a hardware or fishing supply store. (No. 24 is one usable size.) Cut off whatever length you need and seal the ends with fingernail polish, or use a match to melt the ends and seal them.

Lace a shoe. If a shoelace comes out of the loop and the lace is missing the aglet (tip), simply insert needle-nose pliers or tweezers through the eyelet and fish the lace through the loop. This saves a lot of aggravation.

Fix a shoelace with a candle. Here's another way to repair a shoelace that's lost its tip. If you have a candle that has been burning long enough to have a pool of liquid wax in the holder, just smooth out the end of the shoelace—or cut it evenly—and dip it in the wax. This might take several dips.

You might have to redo this repair several times over the remaining life of the shoelaces with the problem, but it works.

Fix a frayed shoelace. To thread a frayed shoelace, try using a match to melt the end. If the lace is nylon, it will melt very easily and can be reshaped as it cools. The shoelace will be very hot, so use caution.

Or try this: When the shoelace tips start to fray, twist them and carefully dip them in some clear fingernail polish. Lay the shoelaces on newspaper until they're dry, and they look great again! They also last a long time. The next time they fray, replace them with new ones.

Make your own shoe insoles. If you forget to put padded insoles into the shoes you wear to work, here's a substitute. Cut an old, clean, extra computer mouse pad that you have in your desk into the shape of insoles, and put them in your shoes. They are rubber on the bottom, so they don't slip, and just thick enough that they will give you instant comfort.

Make shoe treads. Leather-soled shoes can be slippery when you walk. Putting treads on the bottoms of your shoes is a big help, but they are expensive. Instead, buy tread for bathtub floors and cut it to fit the bottoms of your shoes. Most discount stores sell these for a couple of dollars, and one package has enough in it for several pairs of shoes.

No shoehorn, no problem. If you find yourself wanting to try on a new pair of shoes in a store, but there isn't a shoehorn in sight, make one from a pocket handkerchief. Just take the folded handkerchief, lay it in the back of the shoe, and the food slides in, maybe even more easily than with the conventional device.

If no hankie is handy, a dollar bill or a picture postcard will work also.

Make a shoe deodorizer. Here are the directions for a homemade shoe deodorizer using an empty film canister, a piece of pantyhose, and activated charcoal. These are easy to make and are reusable—just add more activated charcoal when necessary. You can find activated charcoal at pet stores that handle aquarium supplies. It's inexpensive and goes a long way.

Take an empty film canister and punch a couple of holes in the lid. Next, put a tablespoon of the activated charcoal into the film canister, stretch a small piece of pantyhose over the top, and snap on the lid (the pantyhose keep the smaller pieces of charcoal from coming out of the holes).

Put leftover activated charcoal in an airtight, self-sealing bag to keep it fresh until you need it again. As these "mini" deodorizers start to lose their effectiveness, replace the activated charcoal—it's that easy!

Make a shoe deodorizer, take 2. Here's another way to make your own odor eliminators for shoes, with just a few items. You'll need some scrap fabric, a sewing machine, and some cat litter.

Start by cutting several 6-by-8-inch or larger rectangles out of scrap fabric to make these odor absorbers. Fold each rectangle in half and stitch up the sides to form a pocket that's open at the top.

Be sure to use a tight stitch because your next step is to turn the pocket right-side out . . . and fill it about three-quarters with clay cat litter. Then stitch the top closed.

You can slide these little odor sachets into your shoes when you store them. The litter will absorb both odors and moisture. Just remember to keep your litter-filled shoes out of a cat's reach . . . or you'll have a whole new problem to deal with!

Deodorize shoes, take 3. Simply sprinkle a little baking soda in the shoes and then store. When the shoes are ready to wear, shake them out, and they should be odor-free. This is especially handy in the winter, when shoes are closed up in the closet.

Spray-on odor eliminators work. Just spray inside and let the shoes dry before you wear them.

You can also invert cone-shaped room deodorants in shoes and heavy slippers to eliminate odor issues.

Buy an extra pair of boots. If someone in your family wears work boots every day, you know that they can become smelly over time. Deodorizing them is a good idea, but here's another strategy. Having two pairs of work boots and wearing them on alternate days gives the boots time to really dry out between wearings. Work boots can be expensive, but you get better than twice the wear this way.

Repair slippers. When your cloth-soled bedroom slippers get holes in the heels, cut pieces of iron-on patch material to fit and iron them on.

Separate socks outdoors. Black and dark blue socks are maddening to separate under artificial room light, even if the light is bright. Instead, take them outside in daylight. In natural light they are easy to separate, and it doesn't even have to be sunny.

Use tall socks for first aid. If you have a football or baseball player in the family, hold onto long uniform socks that have lost their mates. You can use them to cover a wrist or an ankle, an arm or a leg, when you need to put an ice pack on an injury. Ice packs can really get too cold to be directly on the skin, so slip on the "odd tall sock" for a more comfortable way to apply ice to an injury.

Keep socks from slipping. If you have trouble keeping your socks from sliding down into your shoes, sew buttons on the back, and they will stay put.

HATS, SCARVES, AND OTHER ACCESSORIES

Store ball caps. To keep the bill of a ball cap shaped the right way, take the bill, curve it in your hand like a "C," and tuck it under and into the adjustable opening in the back of the cap. This also makes it easier to read the logo on the cap.

Store the folded caps in a clear, plastic shoe holder that you can hang on a door. Each cap fits into a compartment, keeping the dust off and allowing you to easily identify each one.

Unlimited hat bands. For collectors of Western hats, here's an inexpensive way to change hat bands on your hats to suit your outfits. Local thrift stores and garage sales always have belts of various colors and sizes. Just cut them to the crown size and presto! A new look!

Store scarves without wrinkles. If you have lots of scarves, storing them can be a problem because they get wrinkled in drawers. Try this:

Take a clothes hanger and hot-glue several clothespins to each side. Then hang your scarves neatly in your closet. They won't wrinkle, and when you're deciding what to wear, you can see them all at once.

Another good way to store scarves is to purchase a special hanger with holes for 24 scarves. Then buy a cheap, clear clothes-storage bag, put it on the hanger and over the scarves, then zip it closed. You will be able to see at a glance the scarf you need, and the bag will keep them clean while they are stored.

Keep gloves together. An easy way to find both your gloves is by pinning the pair together when putting them away. You then will have no difficulty finding them when you need them.

Give an old belt a new use. Instead of throwing away a belt you don't need any longer, hang it vertically inside your closet door and clip all of your hair barrettes onto it. Your barrettes will be organized and easy to see, access, and put away at the end of the day.

Different-size belts could be used for different-size barrettes.

Make a matching Western tie. Here's a tip for rodeo lovers. If you buy a Western suit for the rodeo and need to hem the pants, you can use the leftover fabric to make a matching tie. Sew the pieces together and you'll have a tie that perfectly matches the suit.

LINGERIE AND UNDIES

Stay warm. The prospect of walking the dog on a blustery winter day is chilling indeed. If you don't have any long underwear, find an old, worn-out pair of tights, cut off the toes, and wear them under your pants. They provide a great layer of insulation.

Secure bra straps. To keep the straps of a front-closing bra from slipping off your shoulders, sew a strip of elastic with one end halfway down one strap (around the shoulder-blade area when you're wearing the bra) and the other end directly across the back to the other strap.

The length of elastic and the position on the straps will have to be adjusted with each person, but it should prevent bra straps from falling.

Another tip is to try attaching rubber mesh. Cut a piece of rubber mesh into strips, double over a piece of mesh, and sew it onto the underside of each strap. The rubber mesh launders nicely until the bra is ready to be replaced.

However, if the bra fits correctly,

the straps should *not* slip. If you're having problems, it's probably time to get measured by a professional fitter.

Keep straps in place. Some knit tops tend to slide off your shoulders, exposing your bra straps. Solve the problem by sewing a 2-inch piece of self-gripping fabric tape on the outer side of the strap, facing the inner side of the top, to hold it in place.

Use tiny hangers. When you buy new bras, keep the tiny hangers and use them for hanging your bras to dry after you wash them. The hangers are so small and lightweight that you can even take them along on vacation. Wash the bras, hang them up on the shower rod, and they are ready to go in no time.

To get bras to dry faster, wash them and wrap them in a heavy bath towel before hanging them on the little hangers.

JEWELRY

Make your own jewelry cleaner. There is an easy way to clean gold and diamond jewelry right at home. Just mix equal parts of water and sudsy ammonia in a small container, such as a glass jar with a lid.

Warning: This cleaning solution cannot be used on turquoise, amber, pearls, coral, malachite, jade, lapis lazuli, opals, or any "soft" stones.

Drop in your jewelry and let it soak for a few minutes, then use a soft-bristled brush to gently brush away stubborn dirt. Rinse well and dry with a soft cloth, or drop into some rubbing alcohol, then buff to a shine.

Be sure to label the mixture, and when it gets cloudy or dirty, use it to clean the sink.

Hang earrings for easy access. You might like to keep a small rattan basket in your bathroom to store everyday jewelry. To avoid fumbling through it to find a pair of earrings, hang pairs of earrings on the side of the basket. It's decorative and makes it much easier to just grab a pair in the morning.

Transform an earring. If you lose one of a pair of dangly earrings with sentimental value, try turning the remaining one into a necklace. Go to a crafts store and buy a few beads and cords. Make a pendant out of the earring, adding beads and other embellishments.

Unknot your jewelry. When your favorite silver or gold chain becomes knotted, before you take it to a jeweler try this: Place the chain on a piece of waxed paper and drop a little baby or sweet oil on the knot. Use two straight pins to work the knot loose by gently prying the tangle apart.

You can remove the oil by rinsing the chain in a little warm water and mild detergent, then rinse in water and dry thoroughly.

Shorten a long chain. If the chain to your necklace is too long, just slide the chain through the label of your blouse or dress. If the label is not doubled, pin it with a safety pin to shorten the chain a little bit.

Store stretchy bracelets. If you have stretchy beaded bracelets and you need a place to store them, put them on a new, fluffy paint roller. It keeps them in one place and protects them as well. Just make sure that the paint roller isn't too much larger than the bracelets because over time it can stretch them out.

Hook on a bracelet. Here's how to fasten your bracelet or watch with one hand. Break off a small piece of tape and place it on your thumb joint to hold one end of the bracelet, then wrap the bracelet around your wrist to lock it into the tape-held end.

JEWELRY SHOPPING 101

If you're getting ready to shop for fine jewelry, make sure you know what to look for. Buying real jewelry can be a little intimidating, so here are some hints to help you find that perfect item:

• Start by dealing with a trained gemologist. Ask your jeweler if he/she is certified and has gemological training.

• Buy the best quality you can afford. Many times, a smaller stone of higher quality is a better value.

• Compare similar items when comparison shopping. Not all diamonds and other gemstones are created equal, thanks to Mother Nature.

• Make sure your precious metals really are precious. Remember, there are differences between electroplated, 18-karat, and 14-karat gold. If you don't know the difference, ASK!

• Be leery of big discounts. An item on sale could have been marked up many times its regular price before being marked down to a "sale price."

• Use caution when buying through the mail, online, or by phone. What you see might not be what you get!

If you don't have tape readily available, a rubber band (especially an elastic hair band) can also do the trick. Place the band around your wrist and over the bracelet to hold the end in place while you hook it.

Make a pin into a pendant. If you have a necklace that needs a pendant, use a nice dress pin. It really works and looks nice.

Display your brooches. If you have a nice collection of brooches, go into your old jewelry box and rediscover all the wonderful ones. If you don't dress up a great deal, you can display your brooches instead of wearing them. Get two very long red velvet ribbons (the kind with the wire down the sides to give it stability) and pin all those wonderful memories on the ribbons. Then hang them on your dressing-room wall with thumbtacks.

You can enjoy looking at them, and when you decide to wear one, just take it off the ribbon and replace it later.

My assistant, Kelly, says she likes to collect these types of pins, too, and puts them on a frilly pillow so that when she wants one, she can easily find it.

Keep track of rings. Rings look better longer if you take them off when you are working in the kitchen or outdoors in the dirt. Be careful taking them off when out in public, though,

---

How to Keep Tack Pins in Place

Here are a variety of ways to keep tack pins in place:

- Try using duct or adhesive tape—strength can vary depending on the type of fabric or thickness of the coat. Put tape on the underside of the material, push the pin through the material and tape, then place the back on the pin and cover with tape over all this.

- For a more permanent solution, take pliers and bend the stem of the pin slightly. Bending will keep the back on. If you do decide you want to move the pin, you can use the pliers to bend the stem back up again.

- Use the rubber mini-tubes you put on the backs of pierced earrings so they don't get lost.

- Use a pencil eraser. It will hold a tack pin tightly, but you can still remove it and use it on another outfit.

- Put a small drop of clear nail polish on the pin clasp to help keep it in place. If you don't intend to move a pin, you can try a bit of permanent glue to attach the back, but if you like changing the pins, this might not work.

as you might forget and leave them. At home, always put them in the same place so you know where to find them.

While washing your hands, put rings between your lips or put them in your pocket. Just be sure to put them back on your fingers!

STORING AND ORGANIZING CLOTHES

Scent clothing drawers. Open up perfumed inserts from magazines and place them in your clothes drawers. Men's cologne inserts can go into a man's shirt drawer.

Freshen a closet. A small walk-in closet can become stuffy. To freshen the air, leave a couple of bars of soap in the closet, and keep the door to the closet open as much as possible for air circulation.

A hint of perfume. If you find perfume too strong when you apply it, try this: Spray a little perfume in your closet and then close the door. The next morning your clothes will lightly smell of your favorite perfume. Just make sure you don't spray perfume

TIME TO BUY A WATCH

Here are some helpful hints about buying a watch. When you purchase one, there are several important things to consider. The price is a factor, but also think about the guarantee of accuracy and the cost of upkeep. Here's a checklist to help you make a "timely" choice:

- "Water-resistant" indicates that the watch can be submerged in fresh water up to 80 feet and in salt water to 75 feet without loss of accuracy or leakage. However, some watches aren't water-resistant after the cases are opened for battery replacement.
- "Shock-resistant" guarantees that a watch can be dropped from 3 feet onto a hardwood surface without damage.
- "Jewels" actually refers to the normally synthetic gemstones that operate the bearings inside a mechanical watch.
- "Anti-magnetic" indicates that the inside working parts are made of metal that won't magnetically attract each other, but rather operate independently.
- Check the cost of batteries, cleaning, new or replacement parts, and repairs. If you buy an expensive watch, read the guarantee carefully.
- If you buy an expensive watch that you wear daily, it's a good idea to find a trusted watch-repair person to take care of your watch.

directly on the clothes. The perfume can stain and eat the material.

Store seasonal clothes. Here's a great way to store off-season clothes. Suitcases are usually empty, so store your clothes in them. If you buy new suitcases, you can keep your seasonal clothes in the old cases without dumping out the clothes when you take a trip.

Use shoulder pads. Use shoulder pads you remove from clothing to pad plastic or wire hangers and prevent hanger bumps in your clothes.

Take a roll of double-stick adhesive tape and wrap the end of the hanger. Fold the shoulder pads over that and finish fastening the pads with self-gripping fabric tape, or sew them in place.

Make a padded hanger. Wrap the bottom of a plastic hanger with a piece of terrycloth and tape it in place to create a soft, round place to hang slacks so they don't wrinkle.

Find empty hangers. Tired of going through your closet looking for an empty hanger? Every time you remove clothing from a hanger, place the hanger on the rod at the front. When you need one, it is right there!

Hook it. An over-the-door hook is a handy place to hang an extra shirt. For a child's room, use a wreath hanger

KEEP MOTHS AT BAY

Did you know that moths can still damage clothing when it is stored? Our friends at the International Fabricare Institute suggest the following to keep moths from damaging your clothing:

- Have garments professionally cleaned and treated with moth-proofing solutions before storage.
- If home-washing, tumble dry at temperatures above 120 degrees F (if okay for the fabric) to kill larvae.
- Freeze garments in individual self-sealing storage bags at 0 degrees F for 48 to 72 hours before storing to kill larvae.
- Use cedar, eucalyptus, or lavender products to keep moths away. If using a natural repellent like lavender, cedar, or eucalyptus, remember to be careful that the garments don't touch the sachet. Also, note that these are repellents—they do not *kill* moths.
- Periodically vacuum floors and clean baseboards and walls in storage closets.

from a crafts store instead. It hangs down farther on the door, and kids are better able to reach it.

Get rid of old clothes. When you are cleaning out your closets, keep items that can be worn "one more time" and store them in your suitcase. Next time you travel, wear and toss.

Edit your wardrobe. Use key labels to decide how long it has been since you have worn something. Tag every single item after you have washed it and hung it up. Twice a year, go through your closets, and if something has not been worn for a full year, out it goes.

Weed out a closet. Is weeding out your closet a monumental task that you dread? Make it easier like this: Just choose what you are going to wear from the right side of the closet. When you try it on, either wear it or discard it. If you choose to wear it, it goes back on the left side of the closet. Keep something hanging in the center of the closet to separate the two sections. Eventually, empty the right side of your closet and get rid of the clothes you don't wear.

Have a clothing swap. Get rid of your unwanted clothes and never even leave your home! Call your friends and host a clothing-swap party.

Clean out clothing. Here is a fun way to weed out clothing from your closet. Invite a couple of trusted friends or family members over and do a "fashion review." Show them one piece at a time, and if your guests give it the thumbs down, get rid of it. If you are embarrassed to even show it to them, that's a sign to get rid of it!

Getting feedback from others eliminates the anguishing guesswork and "maybe I'll wear it someday" excuses. And this can be a fun process, with a lot of laughs and honest opinions.

Recycle clothes you don't wear. After you clean out your closet, remember to pass unwanted items to your church, synagogue, the Salvation Army, Goodwill, or one of the independent charity groups that help so many. School drama/theatrical departments also might want some clothes.

Edit your wardrobe, take 256! Nothing is more aggravating than to finish folding laundry and then be unable to fit it back into the drawer. When you find a drawer like this, turn aggravation into opportunity. Pull out the drawer and remove any clothes that you haven't worn in a while and place them in your "give away" box.

See how you look. Did you ever look at a picture of yourself and say, "What was I thinking when I wore that?"

When you are wearing an outfit and aren't too sure how it looks, take a picture with your digital camera using the self-timer. You can see how you look and can save or delete the picture. It will give you an accurate look at yourself.

I.D. clothes for patients. Here is a hint when you have a friend or loved one in a nursing home or other type of care facility. When you take clothing and other personal items, be sure to mark them clearly with the resident's name. This way, if things are lost or misplaced, they can be returned to their owners. This hint is especially helpful if the nursing facility does the laundry in-house. It's amazing how things tend to "go missing."

Label kids' clothes for camp. If you need to label your child's clothing for school or camp, write only the last name on the label (for common last names, also use the first initial). This way, it can be handed down to sibling after sibling without having to re-mark the entire label.

Treat stains right away. Always have a bottle of stain remover in your closet so you can treat stained clothing immediately after wearing.

Pre-thread some needles. Take the old saying "a stitch in time saves nine" an extra step: Keep three or four needles threaded in black, blue, and white and keep them stuck in the edging of your kitchen curtains. When a problem comes up, you're ready to sew.

Keep an extra button on your clothes. Many pieces of clothing now come with the extra buttons sewn on them. When an extra button comes in a little plastic bag, sew it on the clothes yourself instead of adding it to your tin of spare buttons that never seems to have the one you need.

Organize extra buttons. After you buy a new pair of pants or a top, remove the envelope with the extra buttons and staple it to the merchandise tag that it came with. When you need to replace a missing button, you can go to your sewing basket and readily find it from the description on the tag.

File clothing info. When you purchase new clothes, cut off the price tag, care-instruction tags, and extra buttons and place them in an envelope. On the front, jot a description and the color of the item and where it was purchased, along with a date. The sales receipt could be placed inside, too. File all the filled envelopes in a shoe box for easy retrieval when you need the extra button or a reminder of the washing instructions. The envelope can then be pinned to the item when it is given away years later.

DE-LINT, DE-STATIC, REPAIR

Use a sponge for lint. A damp sponge is just as effective as a lint roller, if not more so, for removing lint from clothing. Rather than buying the brushes or rollers, just keep rinsing the sponge and brush away.

And a way to remember that a sponge isn't for washing dishes is to clip off a corner, or just keep the "lint" sponge out of the kitchen.

De-lint and de-static. If you travel for business and rely on dark-colored coordinates for your work wardrobe, a lint roller is a must in your suitcase. The roller doesn't take up much room, and it has a bonus: You can take a clean dryer sheet and attach it to your roller with a couple of rubber bands. Rub over your pantyhose or whatever is clingy, and it will keep down the static from your skirts or pants. Also, you can roll it over the arms of your sweaters or blouses before you put on your jacket and get similar results.

Fix flyaway hair. Here's a quick fix for the static that electrifies your hair in winter when you remove your hat. Simply place a dryer sheet inside the top of the hat. It sticks to the hat when you take it off and leaves your hair static-free.

For heavy-duty de-linting. Use duct tape to get the lint off of a favorite fleece jacket or other fuzzy garment. Using a lint roller might barely put a dent in getting all the lint off, but duct tape can do the job.

Use a black washcloth. Keep a dry, black washcloth in both your kitchen

 Get Rid of Static Cling

To prevent a nylon slip from clinging to your body, use dusting powder (bath powder) inside your slip. Powder will also stop jersey dresses or men's trousers from clinging.

and your bathroom. Use them to remove spots and stains that mysteriously appear on your dark clothes just as you're ready to leave for a party or an outing. The cloths are also good for rubbing out "stuff" from any dark clothing—much better than leaving white lint from a white cloth.

Quick fix for eyeglasses. When the tiny screw falls out of the hinge on your eyeglasses, it'll probably bounce out of sight immediately. For a quick, temporary fix, take an earring post and pop it into the hinge to secure it until you can get to your optometrist.

Fix snags in clothes. Use a wire needle threader to get rid of unsightly snags on double knits. Poke the wire threader through the fabric on the inside of the garment, at the base of the snag.

Thread the snag back through the loop and pull the snag through to the back side of the fabric. Never cut the snag off; just leave it, now out of sight.

Quick fixes for garment mishaps. When you are traveling or on the go, sometimes things happen to the clothes you are wearing. Here are some quick-fix hints for handling emergency garment problems:

- If you spill coffee or water on washable clothing, blot the fresh spill with a cloth soaked with warm tap water.

- If you notice a spot on a garment while you are in a restaurant or hotel, rub the stain with white bar soap. Then wash and rinse. Some liquid hand soaps in restaurants

EMERGENCY CLOTHING REPAIR

Here are some quick fixes to repair clothing in an emergency situation:

- Buttons can be pinned back on temporarily with a safety pin.
- A waistband can be extended by looping two rubber bands through the buttonhole and then looping the bands over the button.
- If you can get to an iron, fusible tape can hold some fabrics, and fabric glue will do the job on others—test first on a seam.
- Safety pins or a stapler can restore a sagging hem—staple from the inside out to avoid snagging hosiery.
- Duct tape will fix most clothing mishaps!

can be used to quick-clean a spill. Hotel shampoo can be a good stain remover, too.

- If the garment you want to wear is wrinkled, hang it in the bathroom while you shower. The steam should take out most wrinkles.

Fix loose buttons. To keep buttons from falling off your clothes and getting lost, before you wear something sew the buttons on again with dental floss. The floss is really strong, and the buttons won't fall off. Also try putting a dab of colorless nail polish on the thread on top of the button. Do the same with any button you are replacing.

Replace a zipper pull. If the pull on your zipper breaks off, as frequently happens with children's coats, you can replace it with a promotional key ring with a decorative tag so you can keep on zipping.

LINENS AND BEDDING

Freshen the linen closet. Put an open box of baking soda in a seldom-used, musty linen closet to freshen the air.

Scent linens with soap. Buy your favorite bar soap in large quantities. Remove them from their wrappings and place them in your linen closet to give a pleasant scent to your linens.

Keep pillowcases fresh. When taking your bedsheets out of the dryer, don't discard the dryer sheet. Instead, place it between the folded pillowcases. The next time you use those sheets, they will have a fresh, clean smell.

Label linen sizes. If you have different-size beds in your home, it's not easy to remember which blankets, sheets, and bed pads go to which bed. Many may be the same color or style, and the attached label often does not note the size. As soon as you open a new package of bedding, use a permanent marking pen to write a large "K," "Q," "F," or "T" on the bedding tag.

When the bedding items are folded, put them on a shelf with the same marking. If they get missed on the shelf, it is easy to find the tag without having to unfold the entire item to determine the size. It's also easy to pick them out of the clean laundry basket and presort when folding.

I.D. sheets and blankets. To make it easier to find the top and bottom of a sheet, take a laundry market and write "LL" in the lower left corner. Next time you wash it you will know just how it goes on the bed.

Or, mark new fitted bottom sheets, top and bottom, with a black marking pen. Mark generously with about a 2-inch line on the elastic, top and bottom. You won't have to turn the sheet several times to find the right position.

Another way to I.D. sheets. To differentiate between the sizes of sheets for different beds, buy a different color for each size bed. Also, buy a striped pattern that runs from headboard to foot so you won't waste time when you make the bed trying to figure out which way the sheets run.

Organize sheets. To keep bedsheet sets together and neat, try this: When changing beds, put the dirty sheets back in the pillowcase to bring down to wash. When putting them away, do the same thing. Just fold the sheets nicely and put the whole set in the pillowcase. This trick keeps the sets completely together and easier to keep in the linen closet.

Keep sheets sorted. To keep sets of similar sheets and pillowcases from getting mixed up (because some are close but not all are the exact same style), fold everything small except for the fitted sheets. Then put the top sheet and pillowcases in the fitted sheet and fold it around them. This keeps them all together for storage.

Quit folding sheets. Wash and dry your sheets and put them right back on the bed. Eventually they will wear out, so toss them out and grab a fresh pair from the linen closet.

Roll up fitted sheets. Fold fitted sheets into fourths lengthwise and then roll. Easy to do and also easier to distinguish the fitted and flat sheets in the linen closet.

Save money on sheets. To save money on sheets, instead of purchasing a queen- or king-size sheet, buy two single sheets, and sew them together in a flat seam. Needless to say, two single sheets often cost much less than a queen or king.

Refresh your pillows. To refresh pillows, place them in the dryer on permanent press or low heat for 20 minutes, and check them often. They fluff up beautifully.

Reuse an old pillowcase. When a pillowcase is no longer "pretty as new" and you are ready to throw it away, you can use it as an extra protective case on a pillow and whipstitch the end. Put the regular case over it as usual, and it prolongs the life of the pillow.

We use a mattress cover to protect the mattress—why not pillow protectors?

Make special pillows. Turn favorite clothes you can no longer wear (especially cute, frilly little baby dresses and handmade items with sentimental attachments) into special pillows. After the garment has been washed, carefully stitch shut all the openings except one. Stuff the clothing item with polyester fiberfill or finely chopped old nylons, then sew the opening shut. Use baby clothes to make throw pillows and adult clothes for bigger pillows.

Make a pillowcase from a T-shirt. An old adult T-shirt with sentimental attachments can make a great pillowcase (for a regular bed pillow) once the sleeves and neck are sewn shut. If you want it to still look like a T-shirt, you can add a little stuffing in the sleeves. If you want it to look more like a pillowcase, tuck the sleeves into the body of the T-shirt, then stitch them into place (so they won't bunch up when you put the pillow in). Sew up the outside seam to make a square corner on your pillowcase.

LAUNDRY

Read clothing labels. Clothing has care labels, and they're attached for a good reason—to help you take the best care of garments so they will last as long as possible. What the labels *don't* say can be as important as what they do say. Here are some hints to help and guidelines to follow:

- By law, care labels are required to offer at least one acceptable method of care, even if others are safe. They must warn if there is no method of cleaning a garment without damaging it. Labels also must include warnings about methods of care that might harm the garment or other garments being laundered, cleaned, or dried at the same time.

- If the care label says "washable," it may or may not be safe to dry-clean.

- If the label does not mention a specific washing temperature, it is safe to use hot, warm, or cold water.

- If the garment calls for bleach, follow all bleaching instructions exactly, because there's a major difference between chlorine and non-chlorine bleach. If bleach is not mentioned, use any type of bleach that's needed.

Taking the Blue Out of Mondays

The column below was originally printed September 25, 1961, the second week of the first year that my mother, the original Heloise, was syndicated by King Features Syndicate. The advice is still good. Some research shows that many of us still do laundry on Monday or another specific day. Heloise Central started thinking: Where does the term "Blue Monday" come from? It seems it's because Monday was the dreaded all-day-long laundry-chore day back 100-plus years ago.

Read on:

"Dear Readers: Blue Monday? Do you know why Monday is a bad day for you? Because you always make it so. Monday need never be blue if you don't put everything off until that day.

"Laundry is what most of us do on Monday. We all dislike this chore but . . . why do it ALL on Monday?

"Did you know that Saturday is a good day to do your laundry? The children are home then and can help with it. Teach (notice I did not use the word "make") your children to help you hang up the clothes. Soon they will learn to separate them, too.

"As they go along the clothesline either holding the clothes or pinning them up (with your directions), you will find companionship with your children that you never had before.

"The children will actually enjoy helping. You will find that your laundry will not be burdensome but enjoyable because it will be shared. After the clothes dry, ask the children or Daddy (this works too, because I tried it) to help you remove the clothes from the line.

"You unpin them and let the family hold them as you load the clothes into their arms. You will find that you can take the clothes down three times as fast. Never let them put the clothes in your ironing basket. Put a sheet on the floor in front of the TV! This is Saturday night, and the entire family will be there. Leave the clothes there. I have a point here and will try to explain it.

"Psychologically, all the clothes that they have used during the week will be in front of their noses. Whether they are aware of it or not . . . they will absorb it. They are proud of the stack of clean clothes.

"Now, at intermission each person folds his own clothes and stacks them in piles. This can be done while the program is going on, too!

"When the program is over, each person can take his clothes to his own room and place them in the proper drawers. This saves Mother hours of work on Mondays."

I (Heloise the daughter) do remember folding laundry on the floor while watching TV! Maybe that's why I vacuum and dust during commercials today!

- If ironing instructions aren't given, the garment may not need to be ironed.

Make laundry easier. Don't let the laundry blues get you down! Here are some helpful Heloise hints to make your laundry day easier.

- Get everyone involved in the laundry process. Make sure that stains are marked (a clothespin works well for this).

- Make sure you check the garment pockets before adding the clothing to the washer. Nothing is worse than having shredded tissues or

LAUNDRY 101

Are your clothes getting as clean as possible? There are some things you can do to make sure that you and your washing machine are doing the best job possible! Read on for some Laundry 101 hints:

A lot depends on water temperature—did you know that . . .

- HOT WATER—removes dirt from heavily soiled clothes and kills more germs than cold water, but it can fade the dyes in some colored clothes and may cause wrinkling.
- WARM WATER—usually gets lightly soiled clothes clean and is safe for most colored clothes, but it doesn't kill germs unless a disinfectant is added.
- COLD WATER—requires cold-water detergent to get clothes really clean. You also can dissolve detergent powder in hot water before adding it to the wash water in a pinch.
- Whatever water temperature you choose, remember to use the right water-level setting for the clothes to move around freely, the detergent to work, and the clothes to be rinsed completely. Stuffing the washing machine full and cramming clothes in defeats the purpose!
- Set the water level of the washing machine to the load size. If you're washing only a few items, use the low setting.
- Separate the items into groups. Delicates, such as silky blouses, nylon slips, and some undergarments, should be washed on the delicate cycle. Make sure that all hooks are fastened and zippers are zipped.
- When loading the machine, place each piece of clothing in one at a time, laying them in a circle around the agitator in an even layer. Overloading can lead to dingy clothes. Start the water, then add the detergent when the washer is full.
- Add the right amount of laundry detergent. Too much is not always better! Read the detergent label to see what is suggested for the type of washer, temperature of water, and condition of the clothes.
- To prevent pilling on sweaters and printed T-shirts, wash them inside-out. Also, dark items will stay dark if they are turned inside-out and washed in cool or cold water.

other items end up all over clean clothes.

- Treat stains before washing. It might be a good idea to treat both sides of the stain.

- To prevent fading or bleeding of colors, wash only similar colors and fabrics together and turn dark garments inside-out.

- Always use the water temperature recommended by the manufacturer. Hotter is not always better! Trust me.

- Don't overload the washing machine or the dryer.

- Don't add wet clothing to a dryer full of partially dried garments. This makes the dryer work harder, and it takes longer for all of the clothes to dry.

- Don't put an item into the dryer until stains have been removed, because the heat from the dryer could set the stain and make it impossible to remove.

Use cold water when you can. Use the water temperature that is best for the load. Heavily stained clothing often needs hot, while you might be able to use cold or warm for items that are lightly soiled. Did you know that almost all the energy used by washers goes for heating the water? If you can use cold water, you can save quite a bit on your energy bill.

ORGANIZING AND SORTING THE LAUNDRY

Make laundry a family affair. In a busy family of four, everyone should help out with the laundry. Here are some procedures that make it easier for everyone, especially teenagers.

First, try to have loads separated by color into individual baskets. Designate one basket as "on deck," so everyone knows that it's the next to be washed.

If anyone puts an item in the washing machine that shouldn't be dried in the clothes dryer, the person is to stick a special magnet on top of the washing machine at the start of the cycle, so whoever puts that load into the dryer knows to look for an item that shouldn't be put in the dryer.

On the folding counter, everyone has a spot just for his or her clothes that is labeled with a sticker with his or her name. That way, everyone knows where to put the clothes as they are folded. And the family members are responsible for taking their own pile to their room.

Laundry at your house can become smooth sailing!

Use multiple laundry baskets. With a large family, laundry is a never-ending chore. To make laundry a little easier, buy three large, plastic clothes baskets, and have everyone put their dark, light-colored, and white clothes in the appropriate basket. When a basket is full, throw the clothing in the washer.

Or, give kids their own baskets. Put two clothes baskets in each closet for the kids to sort their own laundry, with darks and lights separated. When one basket gets full, the child brings it to the laundry room, you wash the load, fold it, and return it to the child to put away. This eliminates sorting, and the kids become more responsible.

Use dots to sort laundry. If sorting laundry is a challenge in your house, try this ingenious way to keep track of which items are whose.

Simply assign a number of dots to each child according to his or her birth order. The first child born gets one dot, the second born gets two dots, and so on. Then, using a laundry marker, mark each child's clothing with his or her assigned number of dots on a label or inside seam. This way, you let the dots be your guide when sorting and folding the laundry.

When you hand a piece of clothing down, you just add a dot, and you know that it now belongs to the next child in line.

Sort laundry more easily. To sort laundry into piles for washing with warm or cold water, you have to locate the care tag on the clothing. It may be on the side of the shirt, or the arm, or the lower hem. When the tag is on the collar line, sometimes the information is on the front, and other times on the back of the tag.

Use a fabric marker to write "warm" or "cold" on all your laundry in exactly the same spot to make sorting faster.

Don't tote the hamper. When the washer's far away, place a zippered bag (the kind blankets come in) inside your hamper. Empty the hamper into the bag and carry it to the washer.

Freshen with filters. Fill a clean coffee filter with baking soda, fold it in half, and staple it shut. Place this "sachet" in the bottom of the hamper.

Have a place for empty hangers. When it's laundry time, do you spend more time sorting clothes on the racks and looking for hangers than it takes to do the laundry?

Put all your empty hangers in one spot so you can find them easily. It'll save you loads of time.

Hook bras before laundering. When putting bras in the washer, always hook them first to keep them from snagging other garments.

Sort children's socks. If you've got several children, you may find it very difficult to keep track of their many sizes of socks. One solution is to put a small shoe box for each child on top of the dryer. As you fold a load of laundry, just toss the socks into the right box.

Keep socks together. Buy one or two mesh lingerie bags. Match socks, then put them into the mesh bag. Wash and dry the bags of socks, and you won't have any missing socks. It's a must for infant and toddler socks.

Match socks. If most of your socks are dark blue or black, it is probably tough to match them after washing. To keep them sorted, safety-pin the toes of each pair together when you take them off, before placing them in the hamper. You'll solve your matching problem.

Sort socks by using color-coded rubberbands. Use a rubberband or hair elastic to fasten each pair of socks together when they are taken off. Position the rubberband or elastic in the calf section of the sock pair so the foot section gets the full cleaning treatment. You can color code for each family member.

Sort hosiery in separate bags. To save time when you do laundry, sort your hosiery into plastic zipper-top bags that can be written on. Blacks and blues are hard to tell apart, so put them in separate labeled bags for storage when they're clean and dry.

You can have separate bags for sandal-toe hose of both colors, reinforced-toe hose, and knee-highs. Also keep a labeled bag for hose with runs that you can wear under pants.

Separate clothes that don't go in the dryer. When laundering garments that are machine washable but should not be put in the dryer, put them in a laundry bag (the kind used for delicates or hosiery) before putting them in the washer. Make sure the bag you use is large enough to allow the clothes to be washed and rinsed well.

When the wash is complete, it is very easy to identify the items that do not go in the dryer. This saves time and prevents you from accidentally putting the wrong item in the dryer.

LAUNDRY HOW-TO

What kind of detergent to use? Is there a difference between powdered and liquid detergent? According to the Soap and Detergent Association, the only difference is the texture. An added bonus with liquid is that it can be used to pretreat stains, too. But whichever type of detergent you use, always follow the dispensing directions on the product container to achieve the best results.

Don't overload your washer. Most washing-machine manufacturers have load information in their owner's manuals. Depending on variables, the consensus seems to be that a normal load is around 6 to 20 pounds of dry clothing, sheets, or other washables.

However, to tell how much will fit in one load, a better "measurement" is space, not just weight. Sheets (especially large ones) need more room in the washer than a piece of clothing to be able to move around and get clean and rinsed. So, if your machine states 6 pounds a load, it might mean that a large flat and fitted sheet, pillowcases,

and a few other items will make up a full load.

It's better to wash items of different sizes than all sheets or all towels.

Also, when you put linens or clothes in the washer, they should not be stuffed in! Pile them in loosely, so things can move around freely. To get the best results from your washer, loads should include items of different sizes and weights.

Learn laundry symbols. Universal laundering symbols that indicate how clothes should be cared for can be confusing. But knowing what those clothing-care symbols mean might be worth thousands of dollars in savings, too. For easy reference, go online to the Federal Trade Commission Web site at www.ftc.gov, where you'll find a printable version of Caring for Your Clothes in the Consumer Information area, under Shopping for Products & Services, Clothing and Textiles. Print out a copy and hang it next to your washing machine.

Extend your reach. If you have difficulty reaching into the bottom of the washer and the back of the dryer, use a pair of kitchen tongs to extend your reach.

Reuse hand-soap bottles. Recycle hand-soap dispenser bottles by filling them with laundry detergent and using them to spot-treat laundry. Use one filled with dishwashing soap on the kitchen counter—it is much neater than the usual dishwasher soap bottles.

Test for colorfastness. Before placing clothes that are new, dark, or bright-colored in the washer, test to see that they will not bleed on the rest of the laundry. This can be done by rinsing the garment in a pan of cold water. If it does fade, launder it with darker or similar colors the first time or two.

Don't set colors with salt. Years ago, salt or vinegar (my beloved vinegar that can do so many other great things) was used to set colors. Now, because

HOW TO LAUNDER HOME FURNISHINGS

Here are some hints on washing curtains and other furnishings:

1. **Clean dingy curtains.** When the weather permits, take down drapes, curtains, or sheers and shake them outdoors to remove surface dust. Then machine-wash at the highest water level, adding window coverings after the tub fills so they can move about freely. Remove from the washer. After washing curtains, dip them in a solution of 1 cup Epsom salts and 1 gallon hot water, and hang them over a shower rod or towel bar to dry. You won't have to iron them.

2. **Wash slipcovers.** Presoak washable fabrics in cool water with regular detergent for 5 to 10 minutes. Wash on the delicate cycle, then dry on the lowest heat setting. For a smooth fit, put slipcovers back on furniture while just slightly damp. Hint: Use a wooden spoon to tuck fabric into crevices.

3. **Perk up pillows.** Check care labels, but in general it's safe to wash polyester- or down-filled pillows two at a time in the machine on the gentle cycle for 2 minutes. (Be sure to check seams on feather pillows for any gaps and mend openings, or they may burst when immersed or during the spin-dry cycle.) Toss a couple of clean tennis balls into the dryer with pillows to plump them up. Hand-wash foam cushions in the tub or sink with a mild detergent and warm water. Air-dry.

4. **Launder comforters and blankets.** For cotton, rayon, or synthetics: Presoak or use a prewash spray on badly stained items. Then wash on the delicate cycle (check the label for water temperature; if not specified, choose the cold-water setting) for about 5 minutes with regular detergent and oxygen bleach, if safe for the fabric. Put in the dryer on the gentle cycle, or line-dry. For down-filled: Wash separately using a mild detergent and the delicate setting. Thick comforters may need an extra rinse cycle to remove all the soap. Add a clean sneaker to the dryer load to help fluff up the down.

of differences in fabrics and dyes, there isn't a "homemade" solution to set colors. However, there are specialized laundry products that help retain color. Check the laundry aisle in the grocery store for a product that works best for you.

More washing instructions. If you are bothered by the washing instructions on the label in the back of the neck of a new garment, remove the label from the back and sew it in the bottom of the side seam. You will still have the instructions and the label will no longer bother you.

Don't let denim roll up. The hems of denim clothes can curl up during washing. One solution is to put clothespins on the hems. Or, turn all denim clothing inside-out to wash it, and there won't be a problem with curling hems.

Don't fade your jeans. To help your jeans stay dark longer instead of fading, turn them inside-out before washing them, and use cold water. Air-drying or drying them on low heat (still turned inside-out) for a longer time will help some, too.

Be sure to wash all dark clothes

CARE FOR DOWN COMFORTERS

Have you ever wondered how to care for down comforters? What's the safest way to clean them?

- A down-filled comforter will stay fresher longer if it's protected from dirt and excess wear.
- Down comforters can be machine-washed, but only in a front-loading washing machine, meaning one in which there is no agitator. Otherwise, it should be professionally dry-cleaned.
- If you do the washing at home, dry the comforter on gentle heat. Make sure it's completely dry by removing, fluffing, and adjusting it several times during the drying cycle.
- Once the comforter feels dry, run it through another gentle heat cycle to make sure there's no trapped moisture.
- Then, if possible, allow the comforter to air-dry on a shower rod or clothesline for a day before putting it back on the bed.
- If you plan to store the comforter, avoid plastic storage boxes and bags that can trap moisture and cause mildew. Instead, keep down comforters in breathable cotton bags.

together, don't use too much detergent, and rinse twice to get all of the detergent out.

Get towels that match jeans. If you send your kids off to college, they might not take the time to separate their laundry. Shop for some good navy blue towels to match their jeans so they can wash them all together.

Unshrink a sweater. To try and restore a wool sweater that has shrunk in the wash, try the following method. It may help if the sweater hasn't shrunk several sizes, and it *only* works on natural fibers.

Pour 2 tablespoons of regular hair shampoo into a sinkful of cool water. Let the sweater soak for about 30 minutes, then, using gentle pressure, squeeze out the excess water. Do *not* rinse the sweater—just lay it flat on a towel and roll it up to absorb any remaining moisture. Now, place a fresh, dry towel down and lay the sweater out

again, then gently try to block and stretch it back to its original shape.

One way to wash a baseball cap. If you don't want to throw a baseball cap in the washer for fear of bending the brim, try shampooing it instead. Next time you take a shower, wear the cap; after it's wet, use a nailbrush with your favorite shampoo to clean the cap. Then you can let it drip-dry. After only a few minutes, the hat will be clean and will smell just like your shampoo. Just make sure the cap is washable and not an older or a collectible one.

Machine-wash delicates. Wash delicate undies in a mesh laundry bag on the delicate cycle, sending them through an extra spin cycle for quicker drying. Hang them to dry on multiple-bar pants hangers, one over the other. They can then be taken off and folded for putting in drawers, or just hung in the closet.

Give Jeans a Spray Treatment

Before laundering stained and muddy blue jeans, lay them out on the grass and use a garden hose to spray them for a few minutes, with the nozzle turned to "strong." This leaves the dirt on the ground instead of in the washing machine!

Are Laundry Detergents Safe with Ammonia?

You know that when cleaning the bathroom you must never mix cleaners containing chlorine bleach with ammonia-based products. Does this caution apply to laundry detergents, too?

The International Fabricare Institute knows of no laundry detergents that contain sodium hypochlorite (chlorine bleach). Laundry detergents may contain sodium percarbonate or sodium perborate, as these non-chlorine "bleaches" are safe for all fibers, but not necessarily all colors, even though they are advertised as color-safe. So laundry detergents would not be likely to react with ammonia.

But you should always read the con-

On the Light Side ～～～

Test Your Laundry I.Q.

Let's test your laundry I.Q. How many pounds of laundry does the average household do in 1 week?

　a) 25 pounds
　b) 50 pounds
　c) 75 pounds

Hmmm? If you guessed 50 pounds (according to our friends at the Soap and Detergent Association), then you must "b" the one who does laundry in your home.

tainer for any cautions, or call the toll-free phone number that is listed when in doubt!

Deodorize stinky towels. Sour-smelling towels and washcloths can be caused by many things. One is overloading the washing machine—a common mistake. Hint: Wash fewer towels at a time, and use a high water-level setting and even a second rinse.

To try to remove the sour smell, wash in hot water with the normal amount of laundry detergent. Add ½ cup of baking soda *or* washing soda (it's different from baking soda and is found in the laundry aisle) to the washer at the beginning, or you can wait and add it to the rinse cycle. If you live in an area with hard water, increase the amount of soda to ¾ cup.

After washing, put the towels in the dryer ASAP—don't let them sit. Do a sniff test and see if they smell fresh again. If not, repeat the above steps.

This should do the trick.

Freshen your towels. Here's how to give stored towels and comforters that fresh-out-of-the-dryer scent: Add a little fabric softener to an empty bottle, then add water and shake well. Spray this lightly on your linens.

Pretreat before washing. Stained

items should be pretreated before washing, and remember: Don't put items in the dryer until the stain is completely gone! The high heat from the dryer might set a stain, making it impossible to remove.

Find the spots. To help you know which shirts, pants, and other clothes have spots on them that need pretreatment before going into the washer, have your family tie that particular item of clothing into a loose knot before they put it into the laundry. When you are loading the washer and come to an item with a knot, untie it, find the spot, and treat it with prewash.

Use a salad spinner a new way. If you have a salad spinner that you never use, try putting it to work in the laundry room. When you hand-wash a delicate blouse, instead of wringing or trying to squeeze out the water, put it in the salad spinner.

WASHING MACHINES AND THEIR USE

Clean the machine. If your washing machine looks a bit yucky inside, you're probably seeing a buildup of laundry detergent, liquid fabric soft-

Towel Tutorial

Towels that smell bad may have a number of causes. If the towels do not absorb water properly, water cannot thoroughly penetrate and clean the towels when they are laundered, therefore causing a malodor. Towels can lose their absorbency for many different reasons. Older towels, through numerous baths and launderings, become thinner and less fluffy and can no longer do the job. Towels can also have problems absorbing water from oversoftening or undercleaning. Sometimes the cause is fabric softener (liquid or sheets). These softeners can cause a buildup, and the towels will not absorb water as well. Check the manufacturer's label on your towels—some even state not to use fabric softener.

However, fabric manufacturers state that at the recommended dosage levels, fabric softeners do not cause a buildup on towels or other fabrics.

The way that fabric softeners work is by providing a lubricating effect on fabrics, giving them similar surface characteristics and preventing a buildup of electrons, which cause static electricity.

If your towels are still in good shape, make sure you use softeners and detergents in the amounts as directed on the label. You can also help restore your towels' absorbency by washing them twice with double the recommended amount of a good detergent.

ener, and just plain dirt that accumulates inside the washing machine, especially on the top inner rim of the tub. A good cleaning is usually all it takes to get rid of that "yuck," but first check the owner's manual or go to the manufacturer's Web site for the recommended cleaning instructions.

Or, give this hint a whirl:

- Set the machine on the highest water level, put the water temperature on hot, and set on a "normal" wash cycle.

- Fill a gallon jug with hot tap water.

- When a cycle begins, stop it and add the gallon of water. Be careful not to overfill—you just want to get the water level up high enough to reach that yucky upper rim.

- Next, add 2 to 4 cups of household chlorine bleach. Close the lid and restart the wash cycle.

- After a few minutes, stop the cycle, but don't open the lid.

- Let the washer sit for 30-plus minutes to give the bleach and hot water time to work at removing all the "yuck" you did see, and also that you didn't see. Let the machine finish the wash cycle, and then open the lid to air out the inside.

Your washing machine should be squeaky-clean and ready to handle laundry.

Homemade Prewash Spray

This is an old hint from 30-plus years ago that is still good today! It's easy and cheap to make, and it'll save you lots of money!

You will need to combine equal amounts (meaning ⅓, ⅓, and ⅓) of:

*Non-sudsy household ammonia
*Dishwashing liquid (that you use to hand-wash dishes), not dishwasher detergent, liquid, or gel
*Water

Put these ingredients into a clean spray bottle and shake to mix. Be sure to clearly label the bottle with its contents and put in large letters "DO NOT USE WITH HOUSEHOLD BLEACH" or any other product containing chlorine bleach. *Caution:* Remember, ammonia and chlorine bleach SHOULD NEVER be combined; they will cause a toxic and harmful gas if they are.

To use this prewash, just spray on the stained area of clothing and wash *immediately*—do not let set for more than 5 minutes.

After this, to stay on top of build-ups that can cause odors, before doing a load of towels, take one and use it to wipe the inside rim of the washer tub, the fabric softener dispenser, and other areas where "yuck" seems to accumulate.

Another way to clean a washer. After years of washing dirty, grimy clothes, has your washing machine developed a bad odor?

To get rid of it, first try running a full-level hot wash with ½ gallon of vinegar and no detergent. If that doesn't do the trick, pull out the bleach and use the method described in the previous hint.

Always leave the lid of the washing machine open to air out in between uses!

Clean out the fabric softener dispenser. One possible cause of an odor in the washing machine is the automatic fabric-softener dispenser. Even if you don't use it, a buildup forms from spray from the machine filling and agitating. Periodically, you have to remove it and clean it out.

Reset reminder. Keep a small piece of colored electrical tape stuck near your washer. Whenever you change the load size or temperature setting, stick the tape on the control to remind yourself to reset it after the load is done.

Clean with a bottle brush. Keep a baby-bottle brush near the washing machine. It is very handy for cleaning, especially the fabric-softener and bleach dispensers. The type with a sponge on

---

BLEACH 101

When you walk down the laundry aisle of the grocery store, are you confused about which type of bleach to buy? Here is what the Soap and Detergent Association has to say:

- Chlorine bleach aids in soil removal, acts as a disinfectant, removes color, and generally whitens fabrics.
- Oxygen bleach is safe for most fabrics. It maintains color and whiteness.
- Don't pour bleach directly onto the clothing in the washer. Either put it in the bleach dispenser or dilute with water and then add to the washer after the clothes are wet and the washer has finished filling.
- Before using any laundry product, be sure to read the care label on the garment as well as the label on the product.

the end is useful for getting excess liquid out of hard-to-reach places.

Ventilate a front-loading washer. It is difficult to leave the door of a front-loading washing machine ajar when not in use because it tends to open wider than is safe. To keep the door open a bit to allow for air circulation, hot-glue two 1-inch tabs of hook-and-loop tape to the front—one on the door and one on the body of the washing machine—lining them up. Then cut a strip of tape to the desired length to keep the door open just a few inches. Hook the loops, and the door will stay just where you want it, and you will avoid the safety hazard of a fully open door.

Save steps to the laundry room. If your washer and dryer are downstairs, save yourself extra trips to check if laundry is finished. Use the timer on your microwave or oven and set it for the time of the washer's cycle, then go load the clothes in the dryer and use the timer again.

Have picture-perfect laundry. If you're out of commission after

WHY DO WHITE CLOTHES YELLOW?

Have you ever bought a piece of bright-white clothing and after a while it's no longer bright white, or you wash it and it comes out yellow?

Well, here's what the International Fabricare Institute says about this aggravating problem in an issue of *Clothes Care Gazette:*

"The most likely cause of the yellowing is a breakdown of the fabric finish used to make the garment appear brighter and whiter.

"Bright white is not really a natural shade of fibers, yarns, and fabrics. Many times, manufacturers brighten and whiten fabrics by using special fluorescent whitening agents or optical brighteners. Some of these brightening finishes have a somewhat limited durability to use and storage conditions. These finishes can yellow when exposed to light and atmospheric gases for long periods of time.

"The areas of a garment which receive more light exposure may show a more pronounced discoloration. In some cases, an entire garment may turn yellow or off-white.

"Dry cleaning can sometimes accelerate this process, though the change is not due to any improper action taken by a dry cleaner. Almost all white fabrics will eventually yellow to some degree from oxidation of the original finish, storage and care."

Read care labels carefully when buying clothes, and *don't* assume that all whites can be kept white by using chlorine bleach.

surgery and need family members to take over laundry chores for a while, here's how to help them get it right.

To make sure the washer and dryer are set on the appropriate settings for each load, have your laundry helpers set the controls and then take a picture of the washer with a digital camera. Have them bring the camera to you to check out the settings, and then delete the picture. It's an easy way for you to check that each load has the right settings.

Keep a magnifier near the washer. If you wear reading glasses, you probably never have them with you when sorting laundry. Buy a small, inexpensive magnifier at a bookstore or drugstore and clip it to a cord hanging from the rod above your washer/dryer, where it is always handy.

Use magnets. To keep track of how many "line-dry" items are in a load of laundry, keep a row of magnets on your washer. For every line-dry item that goes into the washer, move one magnet over to the dryer. Then, when placing that load into the dryer, you will know exactly how many garments should be hung up to dry.

Use all the detergent. Do you feel that you waste liquid laundry detergent because the measuring cup always has some left in the bottom? Put a washcloth on a small, plastic plate, and when you put the detergent in the washing machine, invert the cup onto the washcloth and let the remainder drain out onto the cloth. When the washcloth has enough detergent in it, place it in a load of clothes and use that detergent instead of adding any more to the wash load.

Use all the detergent, take 2. Another method is to just empty the cup into the washing machine and then throw it in with the wash. When you take the wash out, also remove the detergent cup—clean as a whistle and looking new.

Cue your washer cycles. When you buy a new washer and dryer, you have to figure out which cycles to use for which things. When you do, write items to use for each cycle on yellow sticky notes and tape them next to each cycle on both machines, for quick reference. Cover the note with clear plastic tape so it stays in place.

This will make doing laundry for everyone in the household easier, and who couldn't use the help?

STAIN REMOVAL

Clean up clothing stains. What's worse than discovering you've stained your favorite outfit? Maybe it's thinking about taking it to the dry-cleaner or maybe it's just getting the stain out yourself. Don't panic. You might have the perfect cleaning solution sitting in your cabinet right now.

First, read the care label. As long as it doesn't say "dry-clean only," there's hope. Next, figure out what the stain is—grease (butter, candle wax, chocolate), protein (baby formula, blood, cheese, grass), or sugar (fruit, juice, candy). The right formula or cleaning product just might make that darn stain disappear.

It's best to start with safe and environmentally friendly products before moving on to stronger commercial products. Many of these are common household items, such as ammonia, vinegar, lemon, and salt, which are usually on hand. Commercial prewash products are the next step.

Remember, for grease and oil stains, treat them with warm or hot water, if safe for the fabric. For protein stains, use cold water, and always try to get to the stain as soon as possible!

Keep clothespins handy. Keep a bag of clothespins in your closet, as well as next to the washing machine. Whenever something has a stain on it that will require special attention at wash time, mark the stain with a clothespin. That way, when loading the washer, you can quickly identify the things that require spot treatment.

Mark tablecloth stains. Before pretreating and washing a tablecloth, mark stain spots with a washable marker. This makes it a lot easier to find the stain if further treatment is needed.

Get rid of chewing gum. Next time your child gets chewing gum stuck to his clothes, don't worry—help is as close as your freezer. Freeze the garment to harden the gum (it usually takes about an hour or so). Then carefully remove the gum using a dull butter knife (don't use a sharp knife because you may damage the fabric). If any gum residue remains, treat it with prewash spray or sponge cleaning fluid on the back side of the fabric and launder as usual. Don't put the clothing in the dryer until the gum's all gone.

Banish formula stains. Formula stains are among the most difficult stains to remove. Always try to rinse the stained item in cold water immediately after the stain appears. Also, let the garment dry before putting it into a hamper or you will have a mildew stain to worry about, too.

One way to remove this stain from white washable clothing that can be bleached is to mix ¼ cup household chlorine bleach and 1 cup automatic dishwasher detergent in 1 gallon hot water and soak the garment.

When mixing this solution, use the sink or a plastic container. Do not use aluminum pans. Soak the clothing for approximately 5 minutes, then put it into the washer and wash as usual.

You may have to try this treatment more than once if the stains are persistent.

Remove lotion stains. Lotion spilled on an article of clothing can often be removed by scooping off the excess, then rubbing gently with a moistened towelette. Alcohol-based wipes will work

HOW TO GET RID OF MUD STAINS

Heloise Central gets a lot of questions about stains! One that comes in every summer is how to remove mud stains. They can be quite stubborn and are common with children's sporting events.

Our friends at the International Fabricare Institute have published the removal method in the *Clothes Care Gazette*, and I want to share it with you:

"Most mud stains can be removed by washing the item according to the care instructions. Let the mud dry, then brush off as much as possible using a soft-bristled brush, such as an old toothbrush. Wash as usual using regular laundry detergent.

"For those more difficult mud stains, try treating the stain using one of the many pretreatment products on the market.

"You can also use the following mixture of powdered detergent and ammonia as a pretreatment. *Important note:* This recipe works best if you are using a powdered detergent that does *not* contain a bleaching agent like sodium percarbonate or sodium perborate. Both of these bleaches release hydrogen peroxide, which is accelerated by ammonia and could cause color loss on some fabrics. Measure the amount of detergent needed for the load. Take a small amount of the detergent and mix with regular household ammonia (the non-sudsing type) to form a paste, and apply to the stained area. Let stand for five to 10 minutes, then launder as usual using the hottest water allowable for the garment.

"Remember to test for colorfastness before using any stain-removal agent. To test for colorfastness, apply a small amount of the product to an unexposed area of the garment. Let stand for about five minutes, then rinse. If the color is affected, don't use the product. Also check the label on your laundry detergent, as many give step-by-step pretreatment instructions."

on many stains and materials. However, use caution on silk, rayon, wool, and most "dry-clean-only" clothes.

Salad dressing SOS. Dribble a little salad dressing on your shirt while eating out? Scrape or pat off the "glop," then pat on some artificial sweetener and allow it to set and absorb the oil. Brush off, then launder when you get home.

Get sunscreen blotches off bathing suits. The oils in some sunscreens can leave dark marks on spandex and other stretchy fabrics. To get rid of the blotches, try this: Pour liquid laundry detergent onto the stain and work it into the fabric with your fingers so it penetrates. Wait 30 minutes before hand-washing in cool water. Let the suit air-dry. Repeat if needed. To avoid the problem, let your skin absorb the sunscreen (so it's not tacky to the touch) before suiting up.

Get marshmallow out of clothes. When marshmallow gets on clothes, you're dealing with a lot of sugar. To get it out, presoak the garment in the hottest water that's safe for the fabric, then wash as usual. Or try this: Stretch the shirt over a bowl in the sink. Heat water in a teakettle, and pour it from 6 to 8 inches above the shirt and directly onto the stain. The force of the hot water will remove the sugar.

Remove a colored stain. Confused about how to get a colored stain out of a white shirt? Here's a little Laundry 101. First, read the care label on the white shirt. Some of the newer white fabrics tell you *not* to use chlorine bleach. If the label does not say "no chlorine bleach," you can try some. If the shirt is made of a fabric that cannot be bleached, get a cotton swab and dab it in 3 percent hydrogen peroxide, then treat just the stains. Peroxide works slowly, so wait at least an hour, retreat the stains, and then wash in cold water and hang to dry. If this doesn't work and you're determined, try the recipe for Heloise's Last-Resort Stain Remover (page 152). It can be used for white and bleachable clothes, but not for silk or rayon.

Remove ink from clothes. If you need to get ballpoint ink out of a favorite washable blouse or shirt, here is a hint to try: Place white paper towels under the ink spot, and dab the stain with a clean cloth dampened with cleaning fluid, rubbing alcohol, or a petroleum-based prewash spray. Always start from the outside of the stain and dab in a circle toward the center. It might take a few attempts, but keep trying until all the ink is removed.

Before washing according to the care label, apply some prewash spray to the area.

Don't use hairspray on ink to remove it. This used to be recommended, but it won't work as well today with all the different types of hairspray and ink. It might even make the stain worse!

Remove mystery stains. Stains that you find on stored linens are called "mystery stains" because they seem to just appear out of nowhere. Usually the material looks clean when it is stored, but the problem is that it might not be completely clean. A clear spill that contains sugar is probably the culprit. As time passes, these spots start turning yellow and even brown, and become difficult to remove. Also, if you have laundered the item and put it in the dryer, the heat may have set the stain, making it more difficult to remove.

Stains on white linens can usually be removed by using 3 percent hydrogen peroxide. Simply dab a little on the stain using a cotton swab and let stand (it might take up to an hour or longer to work). Then launder using a product that is designed to "whiten and brighten," following the package directions. You can find the product near the laundry supplies where they sell dyes.

Remove bleach spots. If you try to remove stains from a white shirt by dabbing bleach on them, you may remove the stains but end up with yellow spots in their place. The white color in many fabrics is actually a fluorescent dye that can be damaged by chlorine bleach, just as bleach damages other colors.

HELOISE'S LAST-RESORT STAIN REMOVER

If all else fails to get rid of a stubborn clothing stain, try this recipe:

* 1 gallon hot water
* 1 cup powdered dishwasher detergent
* $\frac{1}{4}$ cup household liquid chlorine bleach

Mix completely in a plastic, enamel, or stainless-steel container. Let the garment soak in the mixture for 5 to 10 minutes. If there is still a stain, soak it a little longer and then wash.

The biggest hint of all is to treat the stain as quickly as possible.

The International Fabricare Institute offers this advice:

First, it is important to be sure that all of the bleach has been thoroughly rinsed from the fabric. Apply a few drops of white vinegar to the yellow spots, and allow it to remain on the fabric for a few minutes, then rinse thoroughly.

You also could try bringing the shirt to your dry-cleaner, who might have a professional product that could be more effective in removing the yellow spots. Be sure to point out all the spots so the dry-cleaner staff can mark them and deal with them appropriately.

Neither of the above methods might work, but it's certainly worth a try.

Remove gas fumes. To remove the odor of gasoline spilled on clothes, spread the clothes outside in the shade for a few hours to let the petroleum fumes dissipate. Then wash in the machine at the highest water level using regular detergent and ½ cup of washing soda. Air-dry only, and repeat the cycle until the clothes no longer smell.

Fine-tune stain removal. A great help in removing tiny stains is to keep a medicine dropper handy in the laundry room or in the kitchen. To use just one or two drops of a particular stain remover on a drop of blood or something similar is a real help.

Why use stain remover on a whole garment when a small amount will work?

Emergency stain control. If you spill food when you go out to lunch, here's how to attack the stain:

Blot up as much of the liquid as possible with a white absorbent cloth or paper towel. Make sure that you blot, and don't rub. Rubbing can cause the stain to spread and also could damage fabric fibers. Gently dab at the spot with some water on a cloth. If the stain is oil-based, open a package of sugar substitute and sprinkle over the stain; let it sit for several minutes to absorb the grease. Brush off the sugar, then treat the stain and wash the garment as soon as possible.

If the garment is dry-clean only, take it ASAP to the cleaner. For items that can be washed, treat the stain when you get home with a good stain remover. The longer a stain is allowed to set, the harder it may be to remove.

DRYING AND DRYERS

How to hang up sheets. If you use a clothesline, here's a good way to hang sheets: Before going outdoors, match up the top and bottom of the sheets and put the clothespins on in about four places so that the linens don't drag on the ground when you stand at the clothesline.

Create a handy clothespin caddy. Buy a small plastic bucket at a discount store and attach a shower curtain ring to it. Hang this on your clothesline and use it to hold clothespins. It slides up and down the line beautifully.

Dry a sweater. To dry a sweater, wash and rinse a window screen, cover with a large, thin towel, and place it across the backs of two chairs. Block (shape) the sweater on the screen and let dry. There's little drying time, and no need to turn the sweater as when drying on a flat table.

Line-dry pantyhose. When pantyhose are hung on a clothesline, they're apt to snag on the clothespins. Cut 2-inch squares from a used dryer sheet and put one between the clothespin and the pantyhose you're hanging to prevent snags.

Dry clothes in the shower. Add an extra shower-curtain rod at your bathtub to hang clothing you want to drip-dry. Make sure this rod is placed to the inside of the rod holding your shower curtain and liner.

Dry clothes on hangers. When hanging shirts or pants out on a clothesline to dry, put them on thick plastic hangers. They dry already on their hangers and in the shape they'll be worn. For the shirts, button the collar, the top button, and one of the lower ones. This way, they won't blow off the hanger. For thicker jeans-type pants, flip them over halfway through the drying to ensure even dryness. Once they are dry, it is easy to grab the hangers and go straight to the closet.

On the Light Side
Clothesline Controversy

Do dark-colored towels fade if they are hung out on the clothesline to dry? According to some major towel manufacturers, prolonged exposure to sunlight will cause most colors to fade over time—especially dark or bright colors. So, it might be a good idea to hang towels in an area where the sun doesn't shine directly on them, or only hang them outside every so often.

Hang knit tops to dry. Knit tops can shrink in the dryer. To prevent shrinkage (and save energy), let them dry on a clothesline in your laundry room. Don't use wire hangers because they leave marks in the shoulders of the tops. Instead, punch a small hole in the middle of the bottom of a small plastic bag (use the sealed side of the bag, and use a bag without writing on it). Put a padded hanger inside the bag and pull the handle through the small hole. Hang your knit tops on these padded hangers.

Block a baseball cap. After washing a baseball cap, place it over a large coffee can, and it will come out perfectly blocked.

Fluff pillows, but with caution. To fluff pillows, toss them in the dryer, along with a couple of tennis shoes, on the air-dry or no-heat setting. Just do not use tennis shoes with black soles, because they can stain the dryer drum.

Have fresh dryer sheets ready. To keep your dryer sheets fresh and easy to access, put them in a plastic con-

CLOTHES DRYERS 101

Aren't clothes dryers wonderful? They make laundry day a lot easier, so here are some helpful hints to get the best use from your dryer and save on your energy bill, too.

- Clean the dryer's lint screen after or before each load. This keeps the air flowing through the dryer. Also, a buildup of lint can cause a fire hazard.

- Dry full loads. Drying only a couple of things wastes money. But don't overload or stuff the dryer, either, because then it will take longer for your clothes to dry, and they will be terribly wrinkled.

- If you are doing several loads of laundry, empty the dryer and add the next load right away so that the heated dryer is put to optimal use. Dry heavy items first, lighter ones last.

- Don't put wet clothes in with partially dried items. And remove items as soon as they're dried to prevent wrinkling.

- Don't run your dryer when you're not home. Thousands of home fires every year are caused by dryers, many when someone left for "just a minute"! You don't want to take a chance.

tainer from disposable diaper wipes. Make sure the container is dry inside before adding your dryer sheets.

Reuse a fabric softener sheet. Put a used fabric-softener sheet to work again to clean the lint trap of the dryer. Just put the trap over your trash bin and wipe the lint right off with the sheet—no muss, no fuss.

Clean out all the dryer lint. Folks, how long has it been since your dryer vent has been checked? More than 15,000 household fires are caused by dryers yearly in the United States. Don't you become an awful statistic.

In addition to emptying the lint trap whenever you dry a load of clothes, check these other places periodically and remove any built-up lint:

- Disconnect the dryer hose from the dryer, and reach in and pull out as much lint as you can.

- Blow out the hose with a leaf blower, or use your vacuum cleaner or shop vacuum with the airflow reversed to blow outward. Put the hose end in the lint-trap opening, stuff a cleaning towel around the opening to avoid blow-back, and blow out the dryer-vent hose. Gather up the lint outside the outdoor dryer vent.

- Reach into the outside vent and pull out any lint you can find there.

- Have a repairer remove the dryer drum and clean out any lint lurking underneath and around it.

- Don't forget to check *under* the lint trap, too.

Keeping the dryer free of lint buildup can prevent a fire.

Brush away lint. Use an old toothbrush (first cleaned with soap and water) to help remove the lint from the dryer's lint screen. With the toothbrush you can "brush" the small crevices that are hard to get to, and this way the screen is really clean and ready for another cycle.

A lint-cleaning caution. If you clean your dryer lint trap with a used dryer sheet, also check the lint trap on a regular basis to make sure that the chemicals from the dryer sheet have not clogged the mesh on the lint trap.

All you have to do is take the lint trap over to your sink and run water over it. If the water drains through the trap easily, then all is well. If the water does not flow freely, you need to take a light brush, soap, and hot water and clean it to remove any buildup that might remain on the lint trap.

Prevent a dryer fire. Don't go to bed with the dryer running. And don't pile things on top of the dryer—one of them could lodge under the timer, jamming it and keeping it from advancing. The dryer will keep on running and could overheat, perhaps even causing a fire.

Another place to check for dryer lint. What appears to be the most common cause of fires in gas-powered dryers is lint in the burner-assembly compartment. Every gas dryer has a small door or a removable panel giving access to this area. At least once every year or two, this area should be checked, and any lint within should be removed. Otherwise, the lint accumulates and can be ignited when the burner lights.

De-lint a toploader. A top-loading dryer filter may allow lint to spread. Clean the lint filter by wiping it with a used dryer sheet, then wipe the top of the dryer, too. You might even make it a habit to leave a dryer sheet in the drum so you always have one handy and to remind you to clean the filter each time.

Dry wrinkles away. Here's an easy way to smooth out wrinkles in clothes after they've been hanging in the closet. Take your hair dryer and run it over the wrinkle for a couple of seconds. It's quicker than setting up the ironing board.

PREVENT DRYER FIRE

Did you know that dryer lint is a leading cause of home fires? Drying clothes in the clothes dryer is something almost everyone does without giving it a thought. You just drop the clothes in, turn the dryer on, and off you go to do something else. And how many of us even leave home while the dryer is on? This can be a very dangerous practice.

Here are some safety hints that will not only help prevent a home fire but also will extend the life of your dryer.

- Make sure the clothes dryer's vent hose is not restricted or crimped and that airflow easily passes through.
- Remove lint after each drying cycle, and remove it from around the drum—a buildup of lint can cause a fire.
- Have the dryer lint trap in place—never operate the clothes dryer without it.
- Don't connect a clothes-dryer power cord to an outlet that is not suitable for the dryer. Overloading electrical outlets can trip circuit breakers and blow fuses.

IRONING

Make ironing easy. After doing a load of wash that needs to be ironed, put the clothes in the dryer for 5 to 10 minutes and set the timer so you can't forget them. When the timer goes off, hang the clothes up, iron them one at a time while still damp, then hang to finish drying.

Set the iron on a grate. When you are ironing, put the grate from your gas stove or a metal trivet on the ironing board so you can lay the iron down flat. That way, the iron won't fall over and won't burn anything, either.

Clip threads as you iron. Keep a

On the Light Side

The Iron Age

We held a contest to find out which readers have the oldest iron, and here are the winners. So, if nothing is too "pressing," don't get "steamed," just "glide" through the list.

1. Avalon of Grapeland, Texas, said: "I have two smoothing irons that are 100 years old. Sometimes I'll heat an old iron to iron a ribbon or a quilt scrap."

2. Edna of Livingston, Montana, said, "This iron is over 100 years old and will work forever."

3. Helen of Bloomfield, New Jersey, said, "My irons date back to the early 1900s."

4. Linn of Meadowview, Virginia, said: "My old iron still works—no steam, of course! It was patented in 1908, 1914, and 1916."

5. Imogene of Bangs, Texas, said: "This electric iron with the trivet belonged to my mother-in-law. It was made in the 1920s. It still heats well."

6. Jerry of Anaheim, California, said: "My mother used this for as long as I can remember. This still works today, and it was bought in 1923!"

7. Wilma of Tyler, Texas, said: "This iron belonged to my granny. She bought it in the late 1920s, and it still works."

8. Bill and Shelby of Rochester, Illinois, said: "This is an old electric iron and is from the late 1930s. The iron still works and heats up very well."

9. Donna of Eden Prairie, Minnesota, said: "Here are two irons that I use. I am a quilter and need irons without steam holes in the plate. They are also very heavy and give a good, hard press. I never use them for everyday ironing because they are too heavy. They are both from the 1930s."

10. Gwendene of Bakersfield, California, said: "This was my mother's iron, used in the very early 1930s. It is a joy now to be able to use a lighter iron."

I have an iron from the late 1940s that was my maternal grandmother's, Amelia of Fort Worth, Texas. It's lightweight and easy to use. However, if I were going to use it more, I would have the cord checked or replaced.

pair of scissors on your ironing board while you iron so you can clip off any "extra" strings on the clothes as you're ironing.

Have accessories on the ironing board. When you iron, keep a spray bottle of water, a lint roller, and a pair of scissors on the ironing board. Use the scissors to snip stray threads from items you are ironing and "store" those loose threads on the lint roller.

Make your iron glide. Run your clothes iron over a sheet of waxed paper to make it glide easily.

Starch with ease. If you use spray starch when ironing, do it in a way that saves strain on your hands. Before laying down the garment to be starched, spray the entire top of the ironing board with starch, then lay down the garment and iron it. Or, spray the entire garment, then iron quickly. If the item is not large, this works well. The result will be a smooth, evenly starched garment with no blotchy spots from the spray starch.

Chapter 4

◼————————◼

Furniture and Furnishings

In this chapter you'll find hints on using and taking care of furniture, window treatments, bedding and linens, art and antiques, and candles.

Care for a leather sofa. When you get a new leather couch, the most important thing is to read all cleaning and care instructions in the manual that should have come with your sofa. Certain leathers might require different care, so it is always best to follow the cleaning guidelines suggested by the manufacturer.

Generally, you should clean up spills immediately. Dust and vacuum using the upholstery attachment. Don't use alcohol-based, abrasive cleansers or furniture polish, as they can contain solvents that might damage the leather.

Remove ink stains from leather furniture. According to the International Fabricare Institute, removing ink from a leather chair or couch is not easy. Stain removers containing dry-cleaning solvent or alcohol might work, but could leave rings or discolor the leather. If that happens, only a leather-care professional might be able to restore the color once the dye or pigment has been lost during stain removal. So, it's probably better to call a leather-cleaning specialist if you have ink stains on leather furniture.

Keep couch cushions in place. Do you have trouble with sofa cushions that will not stay in place? One solution is to place some rubberized mesh (the kind that is used as liner for cabinet shelves) under the cushions.

Another is to use very heavy self-sticking fabric tape that is sticky on both sides. Put three strips on each cushion and three on the couch or recliner to correspond.

Get rid of pet hair. The best way to

remove pet hair from furniture is to use a latex glove (normally for medical use). You can get a box of 100 latex gloves from a discount store, and they can usually be found in the pharmacy section near the bandages.

Make a decorator table. Instead of those small, unstable three-legged decorator tables, make your own from a new galvanized trash can and a round, wooden top. You can find precut rounds at home improvement stores, or if you're handy you can cut your own. Cover the wood top with a beautiful tablecloth or topper, and use the can for storage. No one will ever guess what's holding up the tabletop. Use the can to store holiday decorations or out-of-season clothes.

Figure out furniture placement.
Here's an easy way to find out if your furniture will fit in the rooms of your new home when you move. This trick is also a great way to try out different placements for furniture pieces without having to push heavy chairs and sofas around.

Measure each item and make an exact cutout—even of the bed—from newspaper (or use a roll of craft paper to make your cutout so you don't have to worry that the newspaper will leave traces of newsprint on your carpet or floor). You can then lay out the paper patterns, or "footprints" of your furniture on the floor. In this way, "furniture" can be moved easily to determine what will fit.

WICKER CARE 101

Wicker furniture is a lovely addition to any deck, patio or lanai, and cleaning is usually a fairly easy job. Here's some information to get wicker looking its best in no time:

- Keeping wicker furniture well dusted will keep the dirt from accumulating. You can use your vacuum and the upholstery attachment to get this job done quickly. Nooks and crannies can be dusted with a small, soft-bristled, clean paintbrush.
- To keep unpainted wicker from drying out, occasionally give it a mist of plain ol' water using a spray bottle. Since you want it lightly misted, stand a few feet away.
- Deep cleaning is required a couple of times a year, or more if needed. Mix together 2 pints of cool water and 1 tablespoon of salt. Apply to the wicker and let sit until dry, and then gently scrub the wicker with a soft-bristled brush. Rinse well and allow to dry.
- When wicker is not in use, it is a good idea to keep it covered. The elements are harsh, and wicker can fade, get out of shape, and break if not properly cared for.

The paper patterns are especially helpful when you are downsizing to a condo or an apartment. So many times, it's hard to pare things down, and this hint will surely help.

 **Take cell-phone photos of furniture.** Use your cell-phone camera to take pictures of some different styles of chairs for a homebound relative to see before buying. The buyer will be able to see the style and color without the hassle of going to the furniture store.

Make a chair stay put. To keep a recliner from sliding on the floor or carpet (and possibly blocking a walkway), cut strips from mesh place mats or shelf liner and tack them to the bottom of the chair.

Organize pieces before assembling furniture. Furniture often has to be assembled at home. Numerous items, screws, dowels, and other parts of various sizes are included in the kit.

Use a cupcake pan or an ice-cube tray from the kitchen to separate all of the different-size fasteners and small pieces, making them easy to count, keep track of, and use during the assembly process. Use a rectangular cake pan for the bigger items and the tools you are using. If you are pulled away from the job during the process, no bother—all the parts and tools will be just where you left them in the cupcake tray and cake pan when you get back.

Prevent houseplant overflow. To save your furniture from water stains and avoid messy cleanup when water-

FURNITURE ASSEMBLY 101

When you buy furniture that you need to put together, it can seem daunting to assemble all the parts. Following the instructions can sometimes be a real challenge. Here are some hints to make the task a little easier:

- Use a long screwdriver to give you more power or a short one to give you more control.
- Make a "starter hole" for a screw by using a small nail. To make a screw go in easier, lubricate the screw threads with a little wax or bar soap.
- To get a screw into a hard-to-reach place, put it through a slit in a piece of masking tape. Put the screwdriver tip into the screw slot and fold up the tape ends to make sure the screw stays with the screwdriver. Once the screw is in, the tape can be pulled off.
- To tighten a loose screw hole, insert matches or wooden toothpicks into the hole and squeeze wood filler into the hole. Drive the screw in before the filler dries.

ing houseplants, keep an old turkey baster handy. If the water threatens to overflow from the saucer, use the baster to draw it out and squirt it into a different plant. After the watering is done, store the baster in the watering can so it'll be there for the next time.

Find a new lid for a plastic cup. To replace a broken or lost lid from the type of plastic cups that come with lids, try using a new plastic lid meant for cat-food cans. They fit perfectly.

Locate china pieces. If you need to replace a piece of china or silverware from a discontinued pattern, you can

On the Light Side ~~~~~~~~~
Who Says Women Can't Put Furniture Together?

One reader wrote me to say that she had bought a large L-shaped computer desk, and the store put it in her car for her. She couldn't get the box out of the car when she got home because it was so heavy and awkward, so she cut the end of the box and removed each piece to assemble. It was a little difficult and a very slow process. But she scanned the directions and went to work. Several hours later, it was finished, and she was happily sitting on the floor looking at her handiwork. She reread the directions to be sure she hadn't missed anything. There was one statement she had missed: "Assembly work requires two men." She had a big laugh! That assembly requires two men *or* one very determined woman!

find advertisements for replacement services in the back of many women's magazines. Most companies have a toll-free number or Web site to use. You also can use your computer to check by going to a search engine and typing in "china dishes" or the specific name of the pattern you are looking for. Before calling, have handy as much information as possible on the china or silverware you are trying to match.

Keep sterling sterling. To keep sterling-silver jewelry looking beautiful, store it with your sterling flatware in a tarnish-proof chest.

Use a grapefruit spoon another way. A serrated grapefruit spoon works incredibly well for scooping a ripe avocado out of its peel.

Test new appliances. Make sure you test out every feature on a new appliance before the warranty expires. Many manufacturers will refuse to fix defective parts when the warranty expires. For instance, if you don't try to clean a self-cleaning oven for more than a year after you buy the stove, and discover that the door gets white streaks between the glass panes because it was not sealed properly, the company won't want to honor a 1-year warranty on it.

But if this does happen to you, you

can still call the manufacturer and stand your ground. If the oven door is defective, the manufacturer should solve the problem—it's not your fault.

Be careful disposing of appliance boxes. When you purchase new appliances, a computer, or other expensive items for your home, avoid placing the empty boxes out for trash pickup. This is not a good idea because it tells everyone what new items you have in your home, and can make your home a target for break-ins. Many times would-be burglars cruise through neighborhoods looking for targets. If boxes from electronics or appliances are sitting by the curb, you might as well put up a sign that says, "Come break in here."

Please take a few moments to cut up these boxes and give yourself peace of mind (plus, you'll make it easier for the trash collection if they're cut up and bundled together). Many localities accept cardboard boxes for recycling, but they must be broken down flat.

FLOORS AND WINDOWS

Keep throw rugs from sliding. Use leftover rubberized shelf liner on the bottoms of throw rugs in the bathroom and elsewhere to keep them in place. Cut the shelf liner to the shape you need for each rug, and the rugs will stay put.

Substitute drapery weights. If you buy new draperies that do not hang straight, putting some drapery weights in the bottom will solve the problem. If you cannot find drapery weights, try using instead the lead sinkers fishermen use to weight fishing lines.

Hang curtains more easily. Here are some tricks for sliding lace curtains onto a metal curtain rod smoothly, without snagging the lace:

- Put a table knife in the end of the rod and slip the curtain on.

- Wrap a small piece of plastic wrap around the end of the rod and hold it in place with a small elastic or rubber band. Now slip your curtain panels easily over the rod without catching.

- Put an adhesive bandage over the end of the rod.

- Cut fingers off a latex glove and slip them onto the ends of the rod.

Repair a screen with nail polish. Mend a small tear or hole in a window or door screen by applying several layers of clear nail polish.

Match fabrics. If you occasionally search stores for a certain item, like drapes or a comforter, to coordinate with another fabric or carpet in your home, carry along a small swatch of fabric from the items you are trying to match. Place the swatches in a small sandwich bag and just drop it in your purse. When you see something you think is in the right color or price range, you can quickly compare it with the swatch.

Replace folding doors with pleated shades. Install custom-pleated shades to replace cumbersome bifold doors and standard closet doors that block too much wall space when open. Choose a decorator color that coordinates with the room to assure a classy look. The shades will save space, and best of all, they never need refinishing.

I.D. ceiling fan controls. Here's a simple way to tell the fan switch from the light switch on your ceiling fan:

Fan-chain bobs come in a large variety of colors and styles. Use a white bob for lights and a dark bob for the fan—quick and easy to see, and they snap right onto your chains. There are no letters to try to read, and you can purchase any style to match your décor.

BEDS AND LINENS

Take care of your mattress. Ever wonder about the life span of an average mattress? Three years? Seven? Ten?

Buying a good mattress is well worth the investment, and, with proper care, it will hold up for about 10 years. Here are four things you can do to keep your mattress in good shape:

1. Make sure you have a good-quality bed frame. Keep in mind, though, that larger mattresses need extra center support to keep them from sagging.

2. Always turn a new mattress at least once a month to balance wear. You want to turn it from head to toe one month, and the next time, flip it from side to side. Some types of mattresses don't need to be rotated like this, so be sure to check whether yours does or not.

3. Use a washable mattress pad to keep the mattress clean and protect it from stains.

4. Keep the mattress tag attached or stored where you can find it—this tag has important warranty information that you'll need if there's a problem with the mattress.

Consider a low-profile mattress. When you shop for a new bed, be sure to inquire about the height of the mattress and box spring you choose. At the store, if you have a hard time getting up onto the display models to try them out, do not assume that the bed height is just for display in the store. If the bed seems too high for you, ask if a lower frame is available. You might be able to special-order a "low-profile" frame and box spring for an added cost.

Lengthen a blanket. When you purchase a new, taller mattress set, your old blanket will probably be too short. Here's how to make it fit the new mattress: After you purchase new sheets in the larger size, use the top sheet from your old set to lengthen the blanket by cutting off a large section of the sheet and sewing it to the end of the blanket.

It also will be easier to make the bed because the blanket will always be tucked in at the bottom.

Adjust sheets to fit. When you purchase a thicker mattress and the bottom sheet doesn't fit, purchase new bottom sheets in the same color. Then cut the old bottom sheets and sew a piece onto the top sheet to make it longer. From the leftovers of the bottom sheet you can make pillowcases and shoe bags for travel.

Cover king-size pillows. King-size pillows can be a tight fit in pillow covers.

PILLOW TALK

If you keep waking up with an aching neck or back, don't be quick to blame your mattress. Something else could be to blame—there's a good chance your *pillow* might be causing the problem!

If the pillow is not giving your neck and spine good support, you may feel it in the morning. Here's how to tell if your pillow is up to par:

Fold it in the middle and press down for a moment. If it springs back into shape, it's okay. If it doesn't, you probably need a new one for your head.

If you sleep on your stomach, a soft pillow would be a good choice so that your neck isn't hyperextended. For back sleepers, medium support usually works best. Side sleepers seem to get the best night's sleep from a firm pillow, which keeps your head lifted up off the mattress and aligned with your spine.

Do you sleep in more than one position during the night? Select a down or downlike synthetic pillow. The fill will automatically make adjustments as you do.

Try this when you buy new pillows. Put the pillows back onto the plastic packaging they came in (any plastic bag will work). Then start putting the covers on *over* the plastic bag (with the closed side of the bag at the end of the pillow that will be exposed). Slide it all the way on, then pull the plastic bag off.

Don't toss old pillows. Keep old pillows you no longer sleep on and use them for propping up a book or magazine, or to add as extra support while watching television. And your dog might appreciate an extra pillow in her dog bed, too.

Make the dust ruffle permanent.

Here's an idea for using a dust ruffle with a bedspread. Cut the dust-ruffle portion off of the center (liner) material, leaving just enough to make the ruffle hang to the length you need. Then tack the dust ruffle to the bedspread. You won't have to rearrange the dust ruffle when you change the sheets or turn the mattress.

Make bed making easier. Comforters and bedskirts are beautiful, but making the bed can be a dreaded chore for old, arthritic hands. Trying to stuff the top sheet and blanket under the mattress so that it doesn't show can hurt like the dickens!

CHECK THAT ELECTRIC BLANKET

If you own an electric blanket, be sure to inspect it when you pull it out of storage. Make sure there are no signs of wear or damage to the electric wiring or the power cord. If there are, throw it out or remove the wiring and control, and use as a lightweight blanket. Here are some other important things to remember when using an electric blanket.

- Always consider the health condition of anyone using an electric blanket. Avoid using one with infants and people who are bedridden, are sensitive to heat, or have poor circulation, especially people with diabetes who have lower-leg numbness.
- Never use pins of ANY KIND with an electric blanket. You could get shocked or even start a fire.
- Always place electric blankets on the bed completely unfolded. And don't tuck in the wired part of the blanket—you and the blanket could get overheated.
- Also, please note that electric "throw" blankets are intended for use on sofas and chairs. They should never be used on rocking chairs, recliners, or furniture with casters. Possible pinching or crushing could damage the wiring and create a hazard.

To ease the pain, pull up the ends of the top sheet and blanket and lay them on top of the mattress, making a flat fold on each side and the bottom. The folds don't show under the comforter; they just make it look plusher.

You won't have to jerk on the blanket to turn the bedding down at night. Just turn the folds down again.

Jazz up the couch. To add bright color accents to a couch, try recovering the old pillows. An easy way to do it is to shop for pillowcases on sale. Look for pillowcases with bold patterns and vivid and beautiful—even wild—colors. Purchase a few and slip them on your old sofa pillows. They'll slip off just as easily for laundering.

Dress up a doily. White plastic doilies placed under a table lamp can look a little plain. To make them look more decorative, take some ribbon and thread it around each doily. This technique works best with ruffled doilies.

Make special towels for children. When young grandchildren come to visit and stay over, it can be fun to provide them with a choice of solid-colored bath towels that you have trimmed with narrow decorative tape purchased at a fabric store. They will enjoy selecting their favorites, such as little bunnies or ducks, and other designs for different seasons.

Find fancy dish towels. If you like to use terrycloth dish towels but can't find them in the colors, textures, or patterns you like, try looking in the bath linen department (especially in the large discount stores) for hand towels. You will find more choices, and you may find better values, too. Lightweight, thinner hand towels are absorbent and wear well.

Unlimited Uses for . . . Plastic Tablecloths

Here are some hints for reusing old plastic tablecloths with flannel backing:

- Line the inside floor of pet houses, flannel side up.
- Use them to make dropcloths to protect surfaces used for children's art projects.
- Use them as covers for outside mowers, riding toys, or barbecue grills.
- Lie on one when working under a car—keep one in the trunk for emergencies.
- Line the bottom of a tent—flannel side up—to keep moisture from the ground away from bedding.

ART, ANTIQUES, AND COLLECTIBLES

Store art correctly. Here are some hints from an art conservator on storing framed and matted works of art. Long-term storage is entirely different from just putting something away for a while.

For long-term storage, it is not recommended to keep works in bubble plastic (the plastic is not chemically stable over time). Bubble plastic is safe to use for shipping, but never for long-term storage.

Pieces should *not* be tightly wrapped. Pictures and the material that is used to mat the artwork need to be able to breathe over time. But do not leave a piece uncovered or exposed to excessive air—storing in archival boxes in a vertical position is best for most pieces.

If you have a specific question about the care of a treasured keepsake, a museum conservator would most likely be happy to help. Check your telephone book for museum listings, call the local chamber of commerce, or use a search engine on your computer to find one.

CARE FOR ANTIQUE COLLECTIBLES

Caring for antique collectibles can be tricky, so I'd like to share some important do's and don'ts. When it comes to antique collectibles, making them look shiny and new is usually a big no-no!

- DO leave coins in "as is" condition. An old patina adds to their value.
- DO clean mildew on antique wooden furniture using a cloth dipped in a mixture of ½ cup white vinegar and ½ cup water. Then dry with a clean cloth.
- DO wash "hearty" ceramics with soap and water, but more delicate, painted, or damaged pieces should simply be wiped with a damp cloth.
- DO clean and lubricate antique clocks every 5 years.
- DON'T place grandfather clocks near a heat source—it will damage the wood.
- DON'T use bubble plastic to store silver or ceramics—heat and humidity can permanently discolor them.
- DON'T polish dark antique bronze. Just as with coins, destroying the old patina will lower the value.

Foil Kitty with Foil

If you do battle with pets that won't stay off forbidden sofas or chairs, place sheets of aluminum foil on the furniture. When your pet jumps up, the feel and crunch of the foil will spoil plans for nap time. Straighten the foil and reuse it over and over.

Use an antique iron. If you have an antique iron but do not use it for heating and ironing, try this: Stack some of your favorite books at the end of a shelf and prop your iron up on the other end. You now have a unique and functional bookend! The iron is heavy enough to hold just about as many books as you want and is a great conversation piece. Antique irons also make great doorstops.

CANDLES

Clean candleholders. Candles are delightful, but once the candle burns close to the bottom it can be a pain to get the wax out of the holder. Place a small amount of water in the bottom of the candleholder to loosen the candle. Or place the candleholder in the freezer to help remove wax. Remove them after a couple of hours; then turn them upside down, tap the bottom, and the remains of the candle will fall right out. If there is only a little bit of wax in the bottom you will be able to very easily pry the remaining wax from the holders when the wax is frozen.

Recycle candle pieces. Here's a way to reuse the leftover bits and ends of scented candles to perfume a closet. Cut off some old pantyhose about 6 to 8 inches above the ankle and put some candle pieces in the toes. Then tie a knot in the hose, leaving space to attach it to the closet rod and being careful not to place it near clothing.

When the closet door opens, you will be greeted by a soft, pleasing aroma. Upkeep is easy; occasionally shake or jiggle the bag to release the scent. Best of all, you will be recycling two things at once!

Remove candle wax from furnishings. Candles add a lovely light to a table, holiday centerpiece, or mantel. However, candles can leave an ugly mess if candle wax drips onto a tablecloth or even the carpet.

First, try to keep candles in holders with bobeches to contain that melting wax. But if wax lands where it shouldn't, try the following hints:

- To remove from a tablecloth, put the cloth into the freezer for several days until the wax hardens and dries out, then carefully scrape off the wax with a dull knife. Place paper towels on both sides of the stain and turn on your iron to a warm setting. Press over the stain to absorb all of the wax. Keep moving the paper towels to absorb the stain onto a clean area. Launder the tablecloth as usual.

- On carpeting, freeze the wax by putting a metal pan filled with ice cubes over the wax spill. When the wax has hardened, take a small hammer and hit to break up the frozen wax, then vacuum up the pieces. If there's a little left, cover it with paper towels and press with an iron set on a warm setting. Still a stain? Apply a bit of dry-cleaning solvent to a clean white cloth and blot the stain until it is gone.

Be careful with candles. Here's a candle caution—don't burn candles in unoccupied rooms. Too many devastating home fires have been started by a simple candle.

Clip a wick. Trim the wick with a nail clipper instead of scissors.

Practice healthy candle burning. The disclaimers on the bottom of candles recommend keeping the wick trimmed to ¼ inch and out of a draft so it will burn evenly. Pillar candles, when burned properly, will not drip wax on surfaces, but will burn straight down.

When burning pillars for long periods of time, never leave them alone, and when the flame becomes very long and nervous, trim the wick.

Put out a candle the best way. This is the best candle hint: Ask people how they turn their candles off, and the most common reply is "blow them out." Some stammer and suggest that the best would be a snuffer. Here is the best way to put out a candle.

Take a case knife, table knife, or any metal blade and push the burning wick into the pooled wax. The flame is immediately extinguished, with no smoke, and no smell of blown-out candles, and the rims of your candles will never be black from the soot. If you are using a hurricane-type glass chimney, you will not have your chimneys getting sooty, either. After extinguishing the flame, make sure your wick is standing straight and ready for the next lighting.

■————————————■

Chapter 5

Home Maintenance

Homes need regular mainte-nance—walls need to be painted (and repainted), chimneys need cleaning, light bulbs have to be replaced. Here are some tips on keeping your home in tiptop condi-tion, indoors and out.

Running the home front. Ladies should be fully involved with family finances and know how to run all sys-tems in the home. You need to know such things as how to turn off the water and electricity in case of emergency, and how to handle the water well, the septic system, the sprinkler system, and swimming-pool maintenance. You should also learn how to use the inside electronics (including that new televi-sion, with all its bells and whistles), what it takes to maintain the car, such as oil changes and air in the tires, and lots more.

In the business world, this is called "cross-training," and it's worth learn-ing how to do what appears to be a routine job or one you aren't always responsible for.

Devote a notebook to each topic, with directions on how to do these things. As you find out more, or when you buy new things, also add them to the notebook.

Organize a remodeling project. Use your computer to organize a remodeling or home improvement project. Get a three-ring binder, lined

On the Light Side ~~~~~
Home Maintenance Quiz
Okay, folks, here's a little test of your "what to do" IQ:

a) The toilet starts to overflow. How do you shut off the water?

b) A breaker "pops." What do you do?

c) The disposal gets stuck. What do you do?

If you know the answers, good for you. If not, maybe it's time to learn.

paper, and dividers with pockets, and use the binder to track all of the work going on at your home. Put every single thing that has to do with the remodeling in that notebook.

On your computer, create lists: of boxes of items you have to store while the work is going on, and the contents of each box, a list of any furniture you will sell, a list of things you will need to buy for the new space, and things you'd like to buy. Create a flow chart to show which contractors and workers will be on the job and when.

Keeping this kind of detailed notebook is also a good hint for anyone planning home repairs or organizing a move to a new home. The notebook will be valuable in years to come.

Touch-up trick. Keep a 96-count box of crayons just for hiding dings in furniture, countertops, and picture frames; bleach blotches; and other minor bumps and scratches.

Care for laminate floors. Laminate floors are very durable and, with the proper care, can look great for years to come. Here are some maintenance hints:

CONTACTING CONTRACTORS

If you're planning to build or remodel, make sure you hire the best contractor for the job. Here are some important questions to ask contractors:

- Are they licensed in your state?
- How long have they been in business?
- Have they done projects similar to yours?
- Will they be using subcontractors?
- Will your project require a permit?
- Are they insured and bonded?

Also ask them for a list of references—and check them! Ask former customers:

- Were they happy with the job?
- Was the work finished on time?
- Would they use the same contractor again?

Their answers should give you a good sense of whether the contractor is someone you should consider.

- Dirt is the number one enemy. If loose dirt, dust, or grit isn't removed regularly, the floor surface can become dull, and grit can leave tiny scratches when people walk over it. An electric sweeper or a padded floor duster works great, but if you use a vacuum cleaner, don't use one with a beater bar.

- Damp mopping every so often is suggested, but too much water can cause the floor to expand, so you want slightly damp, not wet. Go over the floor with a clean, dry cloth as soon as possible to make sure no water or water spots remain.

- Never use anything that will scratch the floor, like steel wool or scouring powder. Don't use wax, polish, or soapy detergent unless the manufacturer states it's okay to do so.

- Your best preventive strategy? Place doormats at every entryway to keep out as much dirt, grit, and grime as possible. And attach floor glides or protectors to the legs of furniture.

- To be on the safe side, check the instructions from the manufacturer, call the company's toll-free number, or visit its Web site. You'll find which commercial products are specifically recommended for you particular floor brand.

Maintain hardwood floors. To keep your hardwood floors looking beautiful for years to come, here are basic care hints to follow:

- Use throw rugs inside and outside of doors that enter onto the wood floor.

- Use floor protectors under the legs of furniture to prevent scratching the floor.

- Never slide furniture. Always pick it up to move it.

- Be careful of wearing high heels or sport shoes with cleats. You won't like the dents they leave behind!

- During the winter months, use a humidifier in your home to help minimize wood shrinkage and movement.

Lubricate sliding doors. Sliding exterior doors stick badly if not lubricated, so check them regularly. If you can't find the lubricating oil, you can use nonstick vegetable spray as a one-time fix. But over time the vegetable spray will attract dirt and gunk and will gum up, so don't use it on a regular basis.

Keep a door open. When a door keeps closing on its own and you don't want it to, here's a way to keep it open: Bend the hinge pin by crossing it over a screwdriver, holding the pin with your foot and giving it a few slams with a hammer. When you first see the huge pin, you may think "no way," but it should have just enough bend to work.

Refinish doorknobs. If your brass doorknobs are looking a little lackluster, don't replace them—refinish them. Over time, their protective coatings start to peel, and the brass underneath quickly tarnishes. But in many cases, you can restore a doorknob with a simple three-step process.

Before you begin, take off the doorknob, don some rubber gloves, and stage a cleanup area outside.

Then, remove the doorknob's old finish with lacquer thinner. Just wipe it on with a clean rag, and the finish should come off.

Next, polish what's underneath with a mildly abrasive polishing cream specifically made for brass and other fine metals.

Finally, spray on a high-gloss lacquer—you want two or three even coats. Let it dry, and you'll be in business. You'll probably have to repeat the process in a few years, but the shiny outcome will be worth the work.

Give Dad an IOU. Instead of older children giving their dads ties for Father's Day, have them write IOUs to wash the truck and do other maintenance chores. It's a good way for them to learn, and Dad will appreciate the gift.

Make roof repairs less troublesome.

PROTECT CULTURED MARBLE

It's a pretty good substitute for real marble, but, like the real thing, cultured marble is not damage-proof. Here are some hints on how to protect it:

- Avoid abrasive scouring powders, which will scratch the finish. Instead, use a nonabrasive spray or foam cleaner, or baking soda and water.
- Avoid setting hot items such as curling or flat irons and plates directly on cultured marble. They can scar and even melt the glossy finish.
- Nail-polish remover can also cause severe damage.
- Usually, scratches, chips, and minor blemishes can be fixed. A certified repair person can rebuff the surface with a special mixed gel-coat compound.

Having your roof repaired is a major project. Here are two hints to keep in mind:

- If you have a basketball hoop on your garage, let the roofer know whether you want to keep it for future use. Your roofer may otherwise haul it away with the trash.

- Protect items stored in your attic, such as Christmas decorations or seasonal clothes, and save yourself a lot of cleaning time by covering them with a tarp or sheet of plastic—a lot of dust and debris come into the attic as the roofers pound away on your roof.

PAINTING AND WALLPAPER

Take photos before painting. Before having your house painted by a professional, take pictures of trim, baseboards, and other areas to be painted, in case there is a disagreement about what was there before. If you use a digital camera, you can delete the pictures once the painting is done to your satisfaction.

Protect the phone from dirty hands. When you are painting or doing work that gets your hands messy, keep your phone clean by placing it in a clear plastic bag. If the phone rings, go ahead and answer it with your dirty hands—only the bag will get dirty. At the end of the day, take the nice, clean phone out of the bag.

Wear a painting shirt. When you paint, even if you are wearing your regular painting clothes, turn the shirt inside out. That way, only the inside of the shirt will be ruined, and you still might be able to use it again.

Apply light coats of paint, more often. A professional house painter in New Jersey says that it is far better to paint the outside trim or walls of a house once every 2 years with one coat of paint than to use two coats of paint at any one time. This gives the paint a chance to "season."

Many people think that the heavier the paint, the better. Not so. Thin the paint slightly until the brush does not "pull" and leave streaks.

Save time on painting. Here are two ways to save time when repainting: First, if you are installing new floorboard/trim, paint all of it at once, then cut it to size and touch up. Second, paint all doors at the same time (assuming they are the same color as the trim). Separately lean them to dry (leave some space for airflow). You will be able to get all of the trim and doors painted a lot faster, and the "touch-up" will also be quick.

Keep a paintbrush soft. If you have a small project that requires several coats of paint, instead of cleaning the paintbrush after every coat, put it in the middle of a sheet of stick-to-itself plastic wrap and seal it in. The wrap is better than putting the brush in a plastic bag because you can seal right around the bristles and press the wrap onto the handle of the brush itself so no air gets in.

Even after a day or two, the paint on the brush will be wet and fresh upon being unwrapped. You can use the same sheet of plastic over and over until the project is finished.

Get paintbrushes cleaner. Dried paint near the ferrule (metal band) on a paintbrush can be very difficult to get out. Adding a generous amount of

PAINTING POINTERS

Painting a room seems to be the number one do-it-yourself project in America! A simple can of paint can magically transform a so-so room into something wonderful. But good painters will tell you that it's usually more about the preparation work than the painting. Here are some general hints to make your next paint job go smoothly.

Before you begin painting, first:

- Empty the room. Remove everything you can, then cover everything else with dropcloths.
- Clean the walls with a mild cleaner to help the paint go on more smoothly.
- Cover stains with a good primer so they don't show through the new coats of paint.
- Clean off or cover mildew with a commercial product found at home-improvement and paint stores.
- Repair nail holes in the drywall. Sand and respackle areas that need it.
- Vacuum the room first to get rid of as much dust as possible—don't forget windowsills and baseboards.
- Mask off trim or other areas you need to paint around.

Preparation work takes time, but the result will be a paint job you'll be proud of!

liquid soap and combing the bristles vigorously with a dog's metal grooming comb will clean the brush nicely, and clean the dog's comb too!

Paint touch-ups. When touching up paint in small areas, use the small, plastic containers from takeout restaurants for the paint. They are wide enough for a small paint roller and can be tossed when the job is finished.

Make a paint notebook. It's a good idea to keep a small loose-leaf notebook that has a page for each room in the house. As you know, when you buy a can of paint nowadays, the salesperson sticks a label on the top of the can along with a dab of the paint.

When you buy paint, ask the salesperson to print an extra label for you. Stick this extra label on the appropriate page in your home management notebook along with another dab of paint. When you need more paint, you can take your notebook with you to the paint store. The salesperson will have all the information needed to duplicate the paint.

Get paint off your skin. An old way to remove paint from your hands and face: After you have finished painting, take a small piece of butter or a cloth dipped in baby oil and rub it on your skin wherever the paint has splattered.

Rub it in well and wipe it off. Then wash with soap and water. It is so much better for your skin than turpentine or other harsh paint remover.

Keep paint off the toilet. If you need to repaint the tight space behind the toilet, try placing an old T-shirt over the tank (neck up). Then use a sponge brush to paint those hard-to-reach spaces. The T-shirt will save you from getting paint on the toilet tank.

Keep outlets unstuck. When you paint a room, remove the electrical-outlet covers and place them on a sheet of waxed paper to paint. They won't

Prevent Paint Drips

When you are painting, always stretch a heavy rubber band or cord across the open top of your paint can. This allows for a place to wipe the brush gently each tine you dip for paint, and so it keeps the paint from dripping down the side of a small paint can.

stick to the waxed paper like they stick to newspaper after being painted.

Reuse window shades. Don't toss old roll-up window shades. They are perfect to use as a dropcloth when painting.

Store touchup-paint. Here's a handy use for empty prescription bottles: After you paint a room, fill one up with extra paint used in the room, dab some on the outside of the bottle or lid (so you know which color and room it's from) and keep it in the closet of that room. This way, you don't have to get out the paint can when touch-ups are needed, and you always know the extra paint is close at hand.

 How to pour and store leftover paint. Here's a hint that makes pouring and storing latex paint a breeze: Save all your liquid laundry-detergent jugs. Wash them out, and you won't find a better way to store paint. No more rusty, nonoperable lids, paint splatters from tapping the lids closed, dried-out paint, or runs down the side of the can when filling paint trays. The spout works great for dispensing paint. Use a funnel to fill the jugs, and you're good to go. You can use the cap as a paint cup when only small portions of paint are required. The handle is great to hang onto when it's time to shake up the next color.

This storage method is great for community theaters and other groups that need to store lots of colors. If you keep a lot of colors in inventory, set up a paint-chip catalog of all your colors. Give each chip a designated number that corresponds with the number on the container.

Make big paint chips. When reno-

Vintage Heloise: Keep Paint Out of Your Sleeve

If you put on a rubber glove when you paint ceilings and turn the cuff of the glove back an inch or so, the cuff will catch all the drippings!

The cuff trick is good for washing ceilings, too. The water just seems to drip, drip, and the cuff catches all the water that usually runs down your arm.

When the cuff is full of water, turn your hand down over the bucket and all the water will flow back into the bucket.

vating your home, you want to be sure to use just the right color paint. Small paint chips can be deceiving, so you might want to make yourself some bigger samples. Purchase a few quarts of paint and use just a bit of each to paint half a piece of poster board. Label each with the name, manufacturer, and paint color and then hold it up to the walls—at night and in the sunlight—to see which paint works best.

Keep paint off shrubs. When painting the outside of the house, throw an old tarpaulin with a rope tied to each end over nearby shrubs and stake the ends of the rope to the ground. The tarp holds the shrubs away from the sides of the house but does not damage them. If you don't have a tarp, substitute an old sheet or shower curtain.

Try an alternative tarp. When repainting the wood in a screened-in carport or other outdoor area, try turning over an old piece of indoor/outdoor carpet, if you have one handy, and using it as a dropcloth. Because it is heavy, it won't move around, and you won't have to spend time or pay for masking tape to tape newspaper to the floor.

Don't paint the pane. When you are painting windows, try this plan to keep paint off the glass: Take newspapers or any paper with a straight edge, dampen well with warm water and spread all over the windowpanes. They will cling there until you are finished with your job. When the papers are dry they are easily removed.

Or, instead of using newspapers or masking tape when painting windows, you can use a bar of softened soap. Paint will not stick to the glass, and the soap is easy to remove from the window. When the paint dries, just wash the window with a sponge. If it's an outside job, you can wash the panes with a garden hose.

Paint splatters on windows can be removed easily with nail-polish remover.

Remove a wallpaper border easily. A wallpaper border can be harder to

 Avoid Cleaning the Roller Pan

When you paint with a roller, put a large plastic bag over your roller pan before putting the paint in the pan. When you are through painting, just pull the bag off and the pan will be as clean as when you started.

remove than wallpaper on the rest of the wall because the water does not soak through as readily on the thicker border. Thumbtack wet washcloths along the border and let them sit overnight. When you get up the next morning, the border should come off more easily.

How to patch wallpaper. Here's an old trick for patching wallpaper: When you're tearing your paper to patch, always tear toward the wrong side of the paper. It makes the patch almost invisible.

PLUMBING, HEATING, AND AIR CONDITIONING

Check washing machine hoses. Check the hoses on your washer and dishwasher yearly. To be safe, these rubber hoses should be replaced anywhere from every 2 years to every 5 or 6 years. If a hose ruptures suddenly, your home can suffer serious water damage. Why take a chance?

Also, there are metal hoses that last longer, and you can consider replacing rubber hoses with metal ones.

Don't flush tissues. Only flush toilet paper down the toilet. Never dispose of facial tissues, paper towels, paper napkins, tampon holders, rags, cellophane, or plastic in the toilet because any of the above can cause the toilet to clog.

Clean drains with a "cocktail." Use my all-natural mixture of vinegar and baking soda to clear clogged drains. Pour ½ cup of baking soda down the drain and follow it with 1 to 2 cups of household vinegar. Put the stopper in the sink, fill the sink with water, and wait a few minutes. Pull the plug and let the "whoosh" push clogs through the pipes. Prevent these hair clogs by placing a used fabric softener sheet over the drain when shaving; just toss away the sheet when you're done.

Inspect the chimney, even if you don't burn wood. Hopefully, you have had your wood-burning chimney inspected every year, and cleaned if needed. But it is also important to have a gas log system inspected.

If the logs were installed in a fireplace that once used wood but was not cleaned before the installation, the creosote is still in the chimney, and the potential for a chimney fire still exists.

Another thing to remember is that birds will still build nests in a chimney—they care not what you burn. With a bird's nest possibly blocking the proper venting of the chimney, carbon monoxide (which is odorless but deadly) could be entering the living area. So have a professional chimney sweep check to see if you might have a potentially life-threatening problem.

De-bug fireplace logs. If you have a wood-burning fireplace, there's a good chance you have some logs stacked outside, and there's also a very good chance that there are bugs among them! To make sure you keep the bugs out when the logs come in, here are some simple hints to use:

1. Keep the wood outside in the cold until you're ready to burn it. Many insects that lay dormant in the cold suddenly spring to life when they enter your nice, warm home. So it's best to toss the logs right on the fire when you bring them in the house.

2. Also, store cut wood in loose stacks away from the house, off the ground, and under cover to keep it dry. If you use a tarp, make sure there's space between the tarp and the wood for air circulation.

PURGE INDOOR AIR POLLUTION

The air in your home can be polluted even more than outdoors, due to animal dander, house dust, dust mites, molds, mildew, pollen, bacteria, insects, and other nasties. Yuck and double yuck! Here are some hints to help you reduce and eliminate many indoor pollutants:

- Maintain the air-conditioning and heating systems. Have them professionally checked at least once a year, and clean or change filters monthly or as often as recommended.

- Control the humidity level by trying to keep it between 30 percent and 50 percent. Dampness serves as a breeding ground for mold, mildew, insects, and bacteria. Also, don't forget to ventilate the attic and crawl space!

- Dust and clean your home often to cut down on dust, animal dander, and pollen. Pay close attention to carpets, draperies, and bedding, and don't forget to vacuum your floors frequently.

- Use the exhaust fans in kitchens and bathrooms that vent to the outside. These can remove possible contaminants and moisture.

- Clean evaporation trays in dehumidifiers, in air conditioners, and under refrigerators frequently. The drip pan can harbor some really yucky-looking stuff.

3. Firewood can also be stored in a sealed box or container, as long as you spray the container with insecticide and let it dry thoroughly before putting the wood inside.

4. Never spray the wood itself! When burned, pesticides can release poisonous gases.

LIGHTING AND ELECTRICITY

Find the right circuit breaker. Suppose you want to install a ceiling-light fixture on the second floor of your home, but the circuit-breaker box is located outside on the ground floor. How can you tell when you've found the right circuit breaker to shut off the current? Instead of having to go upstairs to see if you have pulled the correct circuit breaker, open the window and plug your vacuum cleaner into the outlet in the room and turn it on. You will know you have the right breaker when the sound of the vacuum stops.

Handle hot bulbs with care. To change a light bulb that is hot, take the cardboard sleeve from the new bulb, slip it over the hot one, and unscrew. Set the hot bulb on a pot holder or other heatproof surface until cool and then dispose of it properly.

Prepare for power outages. Keep a flashlight and fresh batteries in every

INSULATING HINTS

Weatherizing and insulating can save up to 35 percent on your utility bill. Besides saving money (which we all want to do!), you might also get more years out of your heating system. Here are a few hints to get you started:

- Insulated window treatments can really make a difference in keeping cold temperatures out and warm heat in.
- Check for drafts, and weatherstrip any doors or windows that might be letting cold air in. Don't forget about fireplaces, electrical outlets, cabinets, and other places where pipes or wires enter your home that might also need to be sealed—you can pack these areas with insulation or caulking.
- Insulate hot-water pipes wherever they are exposed in unheated areas—check the garage or attic. And, while you're at it, wrap insulation around your hot-water heater.
- Every year, do an energy check to make sure your home's heating system is in good and safe working order.

room (or at least know where they are) so you will be prepared whenever the power goes out in a storm.

MAINTAINING APPLIANCES

Keep manuals with appliances. Take a gallon-size, self-sealing plastic bag and use duct tape to fasten one side of the top opening to the unit, then put the owner's manual and all service records and bills in the bag. This way, whenever the unit is serviced, all the paper-

work and past records are right there. Do the same with large electronics.

"Correct" a chip. Use white typewriter correction fluid (yes, it's still made) to paint over chips on a white enamel stove. This fluid is also handy for covering a mark on woodwork.

Check your freezer. A freezer that you use for food storage should be checked regularly. If the freezer develops a problem, you might not discover it for days, or weeks, until maybe one day you find a chicken or roast thawed in the working freezer.

If the thermostat has a default that

SAVE ELECTRICITY IN SUMMER

Here are some simple ways to save big bucks on your electric bill in summer. If you're looking for ways to keep cool during hot weather without running your air conditioner nonstop, consider some of these helpful hints:

- Drink a lot of water. It will keep you cool and hydrated. Keep in mind that caffeine and alcohol have the opposite effect.
- Dress for the heat, both indoors and out. That means loose-fitting clothing made of cotton and other breathable fabrics. At night, use lightweight cotton sheets.
- Create more indoor shade with curtains, window blinds, and solar window screens.
- Keep the air moving when you're home. You can create nice cross breezes with ceiling fans and rotating fans. It can make the house feel almost 10 degrees cooler.
- Use a toaster oven rather than the oven, and you'll save money and keep the kitchen cooler.
- Minimize heat buildup from appliances by limiting use of the clothes dryer, dishwasher, and oven. Instead, air-dry dishes, drip-dry clothes, and consider cooking food outside on the barbecue.

is causing it to turn on and off randomly even though the unit is still on, food can freeze and thaw randomly.

If this happens you will need to have the unit replaced. But here is a way to monitor your freezer to make sure it's working properly. Pour ¼ inch of water in one compartment of an ice-cube tray, cover the surface with aluminum foil, and stick a toothpick in the center. Once frozen, pop out the cube and place it in the freezer.

Check this cube every time you take food out of the freezer. If it's still frozen, all is well.

Test an old microwave. The best way to check if an older microwave works is to simply plug it in, set the clock, and then put 1 cup of water in a 4-cup or larger microwave-safe bowl and microwave for 3 minutes on high power. Three minutes should be enough time for the water to boil. Check to see if it is. Remember, the water will be *very hot*. Don't remove the container or break the surface of the water by putting a spoon or anything into it, because it could boil up and burn you.

If the water boils, then the microwave should be okay and you can cook with it. Most microwaves have a safety switch that should automatically turn off the oven if it isn't working properly.

If you're still unsure, you can contact a repair shop in your area to send

MAINTAIN YOUR FREEZER

It's easy to forget that your freezer needs regular maintenance and cleaning, but a few minutes of effort can save you money in the long run.

Freezers have to work harder when dust and grime cling to the condenser coil or when a thick frost builds up. So, every few months, scrub the floor underneath and then vacuum the coil at the back or bottom of the freezer, and defrost when you see that the frost buildup is ¼ inch thick.

While you're at it, clean and deodorize the inside with a solution of 4 tablespoons baking soda and 1 quart warm water. Wash well, rinse, and wipe dry. Stubborn stains can usually be removed by scrubbing with a little baking soda on a damp sponge.

Before you put everything back in the freezer, now would be a good time to think about organizing the different types of food in clear, plastic storage boxes, which you can find at discount stores. Meats in one, desserts in another, and so on. Labeling each will make it easy to keep track of items that might otherwise get lost in the back of the freezer.

someone out to take a look at it, or if it's a portable model, take the microwave to the shop.

TOOLS AND EQUIPMENT

Clean up small screws quickly. To pick up small screws, nails, and tacks while working, try this. Invert (inside out) a zippered sandwich bag and place a magnet inside the inverted bag. Draw the bag with the magnet over those tedious, countless, metallic bits. After they are gathered, simply invert the bag right side out. Zip the bag shut, and you can store it for later use.

Carry a little duct tape. You usually don't need much duct tape for an emergency repair, so instead of carrying an entire roll of it, cut up an old broom handle into 3-inch lengths and wrap about 2 feet of duct tape around each piece. How handy to just toss one in

the glove compartment, purse, or tackle box and always have a little bit there when you need it.

Retrieve broken glass. To remove pieces of broken glass from the bottom of a deep, narrow stone vase, try this: Get a wooden dowel and securely attach a piece of duct tape, sticky side out, to it. Place the dowel down into the vase, push against the glass and lift it out. Or, use ice-cube tongs to pull out the glass. Try to grab the edge of the glass and carefully remove it.

Use a dolly for lots of things. Furniture dollies aren't just for moving furniture. You can use a dolly to:

- Haul a heavy briefcase around.
- Carry shopping bags.
- Move a plant.
- Carry a heavy box home or into the office.

Reuse an old luggage cart. Before wheeled luggage was invented, we had carts to carry our bags. If you have

Unlimited Uses for . . . Duct Tape

Duct-tape the handles of your brooms, mops, garbage can, or even the children's baseball bats when they start to wear out, to extend their life.

Temporarily reattach a broken mailbox door with vertically placed strips of duct tape on both sides of the door bottom and the mailbox.

one sitting in the closet, it can come in handy to transport your garbage to the trash bin. It can hold quite a bit of weight and is probably very sturdy.

HOME SAFETY

Paint a stairway. Having a basement stairway well lit is helpful for elderly people whose eyesight is dimming. Here's another way to make the stairs easier to see: Paint every other step on the basement stairway a bright color.

Keep smoke detectors current. If the smoke alarms in your home begin to have false alarms, even after you replace the batteries, check their expiration dates. According to the U.S. Fire Administration, a smoke alarms life span is 8 to 10 years, after which time it should be replaced. To keep track, write the purchase date on the inside of the smoke alarm.

Folks, a smoke alarm is of no use if the batteries are dead, so take a minute now to test your smoke alarms, and replace the batteries in all your smoke detectors once a year.

Note when to change batteries. When you change the battery in each of your battery-powered smoke

LADDER SAFETY

It's one of the most dangerous tools around the home, even though it uses no electricity or moving parts. What is it? Whether you're painting, hanging, or reorganizing around the house, chances are you'll be using a ladder this summer. But be careful—more than a quarter of a million people are hurt on ladders every year! Here are some important hints to follow:

- Always read the warning label attached to your ladder for weight and height limits. This seems obvious, but there are many different types of ladders.
- When working near electricity, use a fiberglass ladder, *not* a metal one.
- Always inspect the ladder rungs before climbing to make sure they're sturdy, clean, and dry.
- Keep the ladder on a firm, level surface—no loose or wet dirt or gravel.
- Never overextend your reach. It's safer to just move the ladder!
- Use both hands to climb. Carry your tools or supplies on a tool belt, or have someone else hand things to you as you need them.
- Paint every other rung with bright paint as a visual clue!

alarms and carbon-dioxide detectors, write the date you changed it on the outside of the unit with pencil. Mark the date so you can easily see it from below without needing to stand on a ladder. Use pencil so you can erase the old date and enter the new one.

Use the garage door safely. Electric garage doors are a wonderful convenience, but they can also be a danger. Taking the time to test the door every few months can be a true lifesaver. Here are some important safety hints if you have an electric garage door:

- Make sure the door will reverse within 2 seconds after coming in contact with someone or something. To test this, lay a 2×4 flat on the floor directly under the door so that the ends are pointing straight in and out of the garage. Then activate the door opener. The garage door should reverse as soon as it hits the objects—if it doesn't, disconnect it until it can be adjusted by a professional and then test it again.

- Have the door inspected by a professional every so often to check for wear and tear that could affect the door's speed and sensitivity.

- Keep remote controls away from children.

- Teach children by example by not attempting to run out of the garage as the door is on the way down.

- And for heaven's sake, *don't* let your children play with an automatic garage door!

Check window locks. Always check to make sure your windows are locked after even the most reputable companies leave, including carpet cleaners and all repair people.

OUTDOOR MAINTENANCE

Clean patio pieces. White resin (plastic) patio furniture may get black stains on it—they look like mildew. Cleaners made with bleach may make the furniture "chalky." The soap-and-water method doesn't do the trick.

Usually, the furniture looks dirty because dust, dirt, and grime settle into surface grooves or scratches and won't just rinse off. It could also be mildew.

You can make a solution of:

- ¾ cup regular household bleach
- 1 tablespoon powder or liquid laundry detergent
- 1 gallon water

Wear rubber gloves to protect your hands, and test the solution on a small spot to make sure it doesn't harm the surface. Next, apply the mixture to the furniture with a sponge or soft brush and let sit for a few minutes, then rinse away.

You might also have good luck cleaning the furniture with foam bathroom cleaner and a battery-operated scrubber. After scrubbing, simply rinse the tables off with the hose.

Touch up outdoor furniture. Use appliance touch-up paint to cover marks and scratches on metal-framed outdoor furniture.

Clean the spa. Use a sponge mop to first clean most of the dirt from your spa's vinyl cover, then spray cleaner on it and rinse. It's much easier on your back than continually reaching over with a sponge or towel.

Swab the deck with detergent. Here's an easy cleaning formula to use on an outdoor deck. All you need to do is mix detergent with 1 gallon hot water, then apply with a soft-bristled brush or a push broom. Allow the solution "work" time, about 10 to 15 minutes, then rinse well. Stubborn stains might need to be scrubbed a little to completely remove them. For really stubborn grime, you might need to repeat.

If mild mildew is a problem, you can add 1 cup household chlorine bleach to the above mixture, or use a detergent that "whitens and brightens." Just use caution with your clothing, and wear gloves to protect your hands, as well as eye protection.

Make sliding glass doors visible. Children can walk into sliding glass doors and injure themselves (birds can fly into them, too). To make the doors visible, put a couple of bathtub appliqués right at eye level.

Help a tablecloth stay put. To keep a tablecloth on an outdoor table on a windy day, weight it down like this: Sew a "sleeve" on the underside of the tablecloth on all four sides. Then cut a 1¼-inch round wooden rod (any size rod can be used) to insert into each of the sleeves to put equal weight on all four sides. Make the sleeves approximately 2 inches shorter than each measured side so the rods don't show, and position each sleeve so that when the rod is inserted, it hangs just past the bottom of the tabletop and well above the knees of anyone sitting at the table. Place the sleeves where there is enough of the tablecloth to drape over them and hide them completely.

Cover a small pool. An inexpensive plastic tablecloth makes a great cover for a small children's pool. To secure it to the ground, cut two metal clothes hangers into four Vs and reinforce the corners of the tablecloth with duct tape. Then secure the tablecloth to the ground using the hangers. The tablecloth also makes an effective solar water heater for the pool.

Keep a flag flying. Outdoor flags may get wound around the pole because of the wind, but here's a way to keep them flying. Cut some advertising refrigerator magnets into strips and glue them inside the seams.

Melt snow, save your back. Save your back after snow is cleared from your driveway or sidewalk. Put a large container of an ice-melting agent in a two-wheeled shopping cart. Walk up and down the driveway, spreading the ice melter on the ice with little effort.

Ward off burglars with smart gardening. When working on your landscape, think about crime prevention.

Plants and shrubs may not seem like crime deterrents, but where you plant them can make a big difference in protecting your home by giving—or not giving—a burglar a place to hide.

- Don't plant large shrubs against the house foundation—especially near windows and doors. These large shrubs may give someone a hiding spot.

- Do plant thorny shrubs under windows. Getting stuck or scraped by a bush or cactus isn't in the game plan for most thieves.

- Light up the yard. Install motion-sensor lights and spotlights in dark areas.

- Keep shrubs and trees trimmed so there is an open, no-hiding-places feel for the bad guys.

Get rid of weeds. To kill unwanted weeds and grass between patio stones and pavers, pour on a little vinegar.

Water plants the smart way. To water small planters and pots that dry out quickly, layer the surface with ice cubes each day. The water will melt slowly and won't just drain through the soil and run out the bottom of the planter.

Chapter 6

⎯⎯⎯■⎯⎯⎯

Home Office Matters

Welcome to the world of the home office. Whether you have your office in a separate room or a corner of the kitchen, here is where you run the business of your life—paying bills, filing receipts and papers, and keeping in touch with friends and family. This is also where you use and maintain an ever-expanding assortment of machines—computers, cell phones, fax machines, and all the other gadgets of modern life. The

SET UP A HOME OFFICE

More and more people are working from home these days. If a home office is in your future, will you have the space? It might be easier than you think to get set up. Here are some hints to help you set up a home office space:

- Look around for nooks and crannies that could serve as an office area if you don't have a separate room to use, and make sure the space is away from distractions.
- All you would need is a space for a fold-up, built-in desk so that you can confine work and cover it when you want to protect it from curious children or pets. A closet can be ideal, either walk-in or standard size—both can be transformed into a work space by adding a custom-sized desktop, shelves to fit, and electrical outlets. Two filing cabinets and a smooth piece of wood can quickly become a desk. When you are ready to work, just open the door(s) and pull up a chair.
- Or, you can easily hide an office area in the corner of a room with a three-panel screen.
- If your dining room isn't in the mainstream of traffic and you seldom use it, then the dining-room table can be a great work space.

Wherever you find the space, make sure it is bright, cheery, and organized!

hints in this chapter will help you manage it all.

Hear the buzz. If your home office is upstairs but your laundry room is downstairs, you might not be able to hear your dryer's buzzer going off when you are working in your office. To get to the dryer quickly so your clothes don't wrinkle, purchase an inexpensive baby monitor. Place the child unit in the utility room and the parent unit in your office.

Turn these units on when you're doing work on your computer at the same time you are doing laundry and you won't miss hearing the dryer buzzer.

Measure with a bill. When you need an approximate measurement but haven't got a ruler handy, use a dollar bill. U.S. paper currency is a tad more than 6 inches long and just a bit more than 2½ inches wide.

Prop up a binder. If you have to read many pages in a large, three-ring binder, put a length of nonabrasive rubber shelf liner on the table and stack up a couple of large books to prop the binder on. When you open the binder, it will not slide on the table. It will make the reading easier.

Write clearly. University administrators are expressing amazement at the illegible handwriting they see from their students, both young and older adults. Very pertinent information, such as their name, Social Security number, and phone number, is often illegible. This leaves the school unable to contact the students.

If you are filling out a form, it behooves you to write clearly or print important contact information.

OFFICE MACHINES AND EQUIPMENT

Label cords for tech gear. With all the new technology, you probably seem to have a computer cable, power cord, or recharge cord for every small appliance, cell phone, digital camera, MP3 player, and toy. To avoid confusion, whenever you get a new electronic device, label the accessories right away so you'll be sure to use the correct ones. Using the wrong wiring can cause a fire or burn up the device.

A good way to label these "wall warts" is to keep a silver permanent marker available, and every time you get a wall wart, label it with the electronic device it belongs to and the date you bought it.

This I.D. is also useful when several

wall warts are plugged into a surge protector.

Another way to I.D. chargers. Write on a small slip of paper which device the charger or plug-in belongs to and tape it to the power supply. Or, label the cord of each new electronic device with a piece of tape and a permanent marker. Attach the tape like a flag and write on the flag what the cord is for.

Color-code chargers. Use a color-dot system to identify chargers and plugs for cell phones and other devices. Place a dot of the same color on the power supply, the item, and the plug. If there is a "top" to the plug, always put the dot on the top side so you know which way to install the plug into the device. You can use just about any color/dot combination. Use different colored dots for each item you have.

Mark the charger. Use a glob of white typewriter correction fluid on the top side of your cell-phone charger plugs. You won't have to look at the little connectors to see which way the plug fits into the phone; just look for the white dot and plug it in.

Organize your tech gear. Electronic devices come with a wide collection of accessories: cables, earphones, carrying cases, straps, software, manuals, and more. Keeping track of all the pieces can be frustrating, but you can store them together in a clear, self-closing plastic bag. The contents are readily visible, making identification easy. The bag stands up on the bookshelf, especially if you use heavier freezer quart-size bags.

Quart-size bags are good for all sorts of accessories, such as small electronic devices like cameras or music players, while gallon-size bags hold larger items, such as computer equipment.

This is a wonderful and cheap way to organize all of those accessories that come with today's new gizmos!

Unplug, plug, and play. Many times, if an appliance or gadget won't work all of a sudden, unplugging it and counting to 10 just might do the trick. It's worth a try before calling a repair person or taking it to a repair shop.

Stabilize your keyboard. The slide-out keyboard trays on many computer desks have a tendency to slide in while you are working. You will be typing away and find yourself trying to get your fingers under the desk where your keyboard has gone. Here's a cheap and quick way to keep the tray in place without buying a new desk. Clamp a large binder clip onto the track right next to where the tray slides in.

Clean the keyboard. If your

keyboard is sticking, try cleaning it before you go and buy a new keyboard. You can, if you are careful, remove the space bar. Carefully remove the dirt, lint, and other gunk you find.

Just be careful when you start popping off the keys because some, such as the space bar, might have small springs and other parts that could easily be lost. An old makeup brush is great to use to dust off the keyboard. You can use canned air, too. Also, turn the keyboard upside down once in a while and watch all the junk come tumbling out.

Reduce work stress. Feeling stressed after sitting at your work computer all day? Job experts say to get up, stretch, and move around every hour or so. Make certain you are sitting properly in your chair (and not hunching over), and that your keyboard is at the right level.

Solve computer problems. If your computer, printer, or other digital device stops working properly, before you call a repair person, try shutting it down completely for a couple of minutes, then restart it to reboot the system. While the device is off, check all the connections to make sure plugs are secure in their outlets and wires are

not loose. Try this first—you might just be able to save a service call.

Buy the right ink cartridge. When your ink cartridge runs out, take a cell-phone photo of it, take the empty cartridge with you to the store, or write down the number.

If you do get to the store unprepared, try to find a machine like yours in the store, and then you will be able to find the correct cartridge.

Make a printer cheat sheet. Next time you go to print labels or pictures from your computer and find yourself wondering which direction to load the paper so that it prints correctly, take notes. Then, tape a small piece of paper stating the instructions to your paper tray, such as "load label paper face down in paper tray." We all think we will remember till next time, but seldom do. It also can help others who use that printer.

Change font size. To enlarge or reduce the size of type shown on your computer screen, hold down the control key while turning your mouse wheel. It works on nearly all computer programs and Web pages.

Be thrifty with scratch paper. When you print out an e-mail or a recipe from the computer, there is usually some plain white space left on the paper. Cut the paper off and cut it into strips to use for a grocery list or other notes.

Forward calls when online. Here's a hint for dialup Internet users who also have mobile phones. It is a way to have uninterrupted online connections without the expense of a second phone line.

Some phone companies have a feature that automatically forwards incoming calls to a second number when your phone is busy. You can use your cell phone as the forwarding number, and use your cell phone's voice mail feature to take messages when you are busy online. Just be sure to remember to "un-forward" calls when you're offline.

It is also possible to have a second phone line just for the computer, as long as you have regular phone service; the cost can vary.

Protect your privacy online. If you post messages on public message boards related to a hobby or subject of interest to you, such as arts and crafts, fishing, or genealogy, and you include your name and phone number, there's a possibility that your contact information can be snagged by a search engine and made available on the Internet.

Use larger font. When composing written information on a computer to be sent to someone who might need reading glasses, it's thoughtful to increase the size of the font. That way, the person can read it more easily without hunting for those glasses.

Encrypt stored passwords. Many online Web sites require you to have a password in order to use the site. If you know how to use encryption software, you can start a file in your word-processing program listing all your passwords, sign-on IDs, and account numbers, then save it by encrypting the file.

To check a password, you will only have to remember the one to access the file. Just be sure to choose a password that you can remember. And don't create this kind of file unless you can encrypt it to keep it secure.

Test your e-mail server. If you aren't sure how quickly businesses or acquaintances receive e-mail when you send it, try this: Test the server to see how fast it works by sending the same e-mail to yourself. You can check to see if you received it and know that it should arrive shortly at its destination.

Make up a password. For a password, first select a couple of numbers or letters you'll never forget, like favorite numbers or your dog's birthday (it's not a good idea to use your own birthday). Then use the name of the company you need a password for. Your password would be something like 06Heloise14. The 06 would be June, Heloise would be the company, and 14 is the day of the month. You would always use 06 and 14, but the name of the company would change.

Keep passwords on paper. Make a list of all accounts, I.D.s, and passwords on a piece of paper (*not* in your computer) and store it in a safe place away from the computer. In case your computer crashes (or you upgrade software), it will help you recover.

I.D. e-mail attachments. If your friends and relatives are reluctant to open your e-mail attachments because viruses and worms are often sent that way, you could put a small personal thumbnail photo of your family below your signature. When your recipients see that photo, they will know that you are indeed the one who sent it and that it is safe.

Find a message easily. When you get a forwarded e-mail or a reply to an e-mail, the note written by the sender can get lost on the page because it is

STOP SPAM

When you go to retrieve your e-mail, is the box filled with spam, those unwanted commercial e-mail messages? Because we use e-mail so much these days, marketers are also using e-mail to pitch their products. You can reduce spam, and here are some steps to get you pointed in the right direction:

- E-mail spammers buy lists of e-mail addresses from list brokers, who harvest addresses from the Internet. The marketers have special software that sends out thousands or millions of e-mails at one time. So, don't post your e-mail address in chat rooms, Web sites, or newsgroup postings.

- Read the privacy policy before you give your e-mail address to a Web site. Does it let the company sell your address?

- Consider setting up two e-mail addresses—a personal one and another for chat rooms.

- Get an e-mail filter that weeds out spam. Some Internet providers have a "report spam" program in place, so be sure to use it.

- When you do get spam, hit the delete button.

the same size, color, and type as the original message. Solve this problem by making the size of the reply larger and changing it to a different color.

Clean up e-mails when forwarding. When you forward an e-mail message, try the following to get a really clean message. First, set it up for forwarding. Delete all those long lists of names that are on the e-mail. If you look at the attachments and there are several, all the same, delete all but one, because they are the same attachment. This not only cleans up your e-mail, but it also makes it quicker to send and receive, especially for those friends who have dialup—not high-speed—Internet connections.

These little hints take only a moment, but they sure can make a big difference in the appearance and reception of your e-mails.

Remove the hard drive before you donate or dispose. Before an old computer is disposed of, the hard drive should be removed and destroyed or retained by the owner. Even if the hard drive is erased or reformatted, files and data stored on the hard drive can be retrieved.

Before you donate your old computer to a local organization, have someone remove the hard drive from it and either destroy it or install it in a spare port in your new computer. Putting it into the new computer will give you additional storage space and allow you to keep old files you may need.

Dispose of computers safely. Computers and electronic equipment contain all sorts of hazardous materials, including lead, cadmium, and mercury. That's why it's important that you dispose of old or broken electronic items safely. We don't want that stuff in our landfills and polluting our drinking water.

Try to find someone who can either refurbish and reuse the item or dispose of it properly. A good start is your city's recycling center or department of household hazardous waste; if it won't take your items, someone there should be able to tell you who will.

The Environmental Protection Agency has information about programs around the country. You can learn more about its "Plug-In to eCycling" at the EPA Web site, epa.gov. Look for eCycling in the A to Z directory of topics on the site.

Be prepared to pay recyclers and refurbishers a fee for their services. It's a small price to pay to protect our environment, don't you think?

Save on fax cover sheets. When you work at home, office expenses add up fast. Here's a way to use fewer cover sheets with your fax machine. If you make a fax sheet and place it in a plastic sleeve, you can write with a dry-erase marker the date, the recipient, and other information. After you have sent the fax, simply erase the sleeve and reuse it.

Remind yourself when you need paper. To remind yourself when your printer or fax machine needs more paper, place several sheets of colored paper in the bottom of the tray, with a lot of white paper on top. When a document prints on colored paper, you know it's time to add more paper.

Make a phone button easy to see. Say you are on the phone and another caller beeps in; if you don't have your glasses on, by the time you find "flash" to take the call, the caller may have hung up. Solve that problem by dabbing a dot of bright-red nail polish on the "flash" button on your phone.

Reset a telephone. If you are trying to reset a phone that isn't working properly and the telephone is plugged

STOP THE CALLS

If you don't like getting those annoying telemarketing calls that usually seem to disturb you when you are eating dinner, you can do something to stop them from coming into your home. Here are steps you can take:

- Add your phone number to the National Do Not Call Registry by going online to: donotcall.gov, or call (888) 382-1222. If you register online, you will get an e-mail confirmation. You must click on the link to assure that your number is added to the registry.

- When your number has been in the registry for 3 months, most telemarketing calls should stop.

- But be aware that not all of the calls will stop, since not all are included. You can still receive calls from charities, telephone surveyors, or political organizations. Calls also might come from companies that you do business with or from companies that you have given permission to.

- If you are still getting calls and feel that they may be fraudulent, file a complaint with the Federal Trade Commission at (877) 382-4357.

- Remember, it's okay to hang up on an unwanted telemarketing call. The telemarketer called you, not the other way around!

into electric power as well as the phone line, unplug both cords. The phone line is also a power source and might keep some circuits from resetting. Leave the appliance unplugged for at least 10 minutes. This gives some components time to fully drain their charges and allows the appliance to start up as though brand new, provided further damage hasn't been done.

If the phone rings, don't get hurt. Say you are standing on a ladder when your phone rings. If you are smart, you will take your time to get down before heading to answer the phone. Courteous callers will let it ring 10 times before hanging up, giving you a reasonable amount of time to reach your phone. Or say that your hands were messy and you had to clean them off before heading for the phone.

No one should ever risk his or her safety by hurrying to answer the phone. Too many injuries have happened that way.

Include cell phone area codes. When you are putting cell phone numbers into your phone, include the area code. If you're out of your area, the number will still work.

Calculate with a cell phone. When you go out to dinner, use the tip calculator in your cell phone to figure out how much to leave the server. Many cell phones come with this feature.

Use your cell phone as a ruler. To use your cell phone as a ruler, measure your phone, memorize the measurements, and if you need to measure something small, just pull out your phone instead of trying to locate a ruler.

Donate an old cell phone. Some volunteer groups collect old cell phones and donate them to women's shelters for survivors of domestic violence. The phones can call 911 in an emergency but cannot otherwise make calls.

If you want to donate your phone, contact "Call to Protect," a program run by The Wireless Foundation at www.wirelessfoundation.org/CallTo-Protect. Or you can call (202) 785-0081 to find out more about donating used cell phones. Also, call the closest fire station to see if it collects cell phones.

Other uses for old cell phones. Keep an old cell phone by your bedside—if the weather is bad and there's a possibility of power failure, you can set the alarm on the cell phone as a backup, just in case.

Take along the old phone while on vacation to use as an alarm clock.

Keep an old cell phone for backup. If you lose or misplace your cell phone, your provider might be able to reactivate your old phone; if your new phone miraculously reappears, the provider can reverse the process. Check first with your provider to make sure this will work for you.

Save the cell phone. If your cell phone has capabilities that you do not use, such as Internet, pictures, and text messaging, call your service department and have these items blocked. Should your phone be lost or stolen, a large bill can be run up in a hurry if these services are used.

Find a lost cell phone. When you get

Unlimited Uses for . . . Cell Phones

Cell phones are not just phones anymore! They have morphed into cool tools for many uses. Here are some hints on using cell phones:

- Whenever you meet someone and you want to exchange phone numbers, put the new number in your cell phone, along with the new acquaintance's name.

- When you can't explain style, color, shape, size, or specific brand or pattern to someone who is going shopping for you, take a picture using your cell phone to show exactly the piece of furniture or item you're requesting. This will help the person buying get the correct item, and it could also help with comparison shopping.

- If you have an allergy to metal and are not able to wear a watch, let your cell phone be your watch.

- When you're at home, use cell phones to talk back and forth when one person is outside working.

- Use your cell phone to store your car and truck license-plate numbers in case the plates are stolen or you need the numbers when filling out forms.

- Use the calculator on your cell phone when you do all your running-around errands each week. Not only will it help you keep track of what you're spending, but it also will help you determine which size product is the best deal.

- When you need to give someone an address over the cell phone and the other person has no pen and paper, do this: Agree that you will hang up; then, when you redial the person, he or she will not answer. Leave the address as a message on the other person's cell phone to be retrieved when needed.

- Use a cell phone to entertain a fussy baby in the car. Show her the lights and go through the ring tones, and she may seem to be amazed at all the lights and sounds.

- Use the bright screen as a flashlight to help you see when moving around the room while your spouse is sleeping and to look for things when you drop them in dark places like a movie theater.

a new cell phone, you can program a greeting. Put in a lost-and-found message, such as "If found, call Libby at (your home or work phone)." You may never need this, but if you do lose your phone, a Good Samaritan who finds it may call you, and you will get the phone back.

Keep the phone in your pocket. If you carry a cell phone in the front pocket of your pants, rather than on a belt clip, the phone can fall sideways in your pocket.

To keep it upright, sew a 2-inch strip straight up and down through the bottom of the pocket. This divides the bottom of your pocket into two compartments, and the cell phone can slide into one area and stand straight up. It will be easier to reach for.

Make your cell phone easy to find. Quit digging in your tote bag or purse for your cell phone when it rings— here's an easy way to find it. Use a bright-colored child's slipper sock as a carrier for the phone. It provides a soft sleeve for the phone, and it's instantly visible in your purse.

Remember your cell phone. To make sure you remember your cell phone when you leave the house, put your car keys on top of the cell phone. You won't leave home without it.

Take a message. Are you always searching for paper and a pen when you need to take a phone message? Try this: Put a pad with a sticky back on the wall right next to the phone. Then get a pen and tie it onto a ribbon, and attach it to the pad.

When someone calls, you'll have everything ready to take a message.

Leave your number first. When leaving a message on an answering machine, say not only your name but also your phone number at the very beginning of the message. Then the person getting the message doesn't have to listen to the entire message over again to get your number.

Leave a clear message. When leaving a message on someone's answering machine, always speak slowly and clearly. It takes a lot of time to replay a message over and over again just to try to understand the name or the phone number of the caller.

Make the outgoing message helpful. It is frustrating when you call a number and aren't sure whom you've reached. On your answering machine's outgoing message, if you don't want to give your name, at least state your number so callers will know they have reached the right number. Leave this message on the machine: "You have reached XXX-555-1212, please leave a message."

Leave yourself a message. Here's another use for a cell phone. When you're away from home and remember that you need to water the plants, make an important phone call, or put out the trash, call home on your cell phone and leave a message on your home phone. When you retrieve your messages you'll get your reminder.

When you're home and need to remember to do something at work, call your work number and leave a message on your voice mail.

You also can leave yourself a message on your cell phone.

Text yourself. When you remember something you need to do, but don't have a pen and paper handy to make a note, send a text message to your home e-mail account from your cell phone. When you get home or to a computer, everything you need to remember will be in your mailbox.

Make a camera case. Compact digital cameras are usually sold alone, without protective carrying cases. Instead of purchasing the manufacturer's protective case, slip a clean tennis wristband or a child's athletic sock over your camera. This protects the camera and screen from scratches, is inexpensive, fits in your pocket, and is easily replaceable.

I.D. your camera. Here's a clever way to put identification *into* your digital camera in case you lose it. Take the first picture of your business card, with your name and

---

SUMMERTIME CAMERA CONCERNS

Here are some important summertime care hints for digital cameras. You can fight off sand, heat, humidity, and water with the following ideas:

• Keep your camera out of the heat. Indoors is best, but when outdoors, avoid leaving cameras in a hot car or in direct sunlight. When there's no shady place, make your own with a T-shirt or towel.

• Moisture can also make digital cameras malfunction. When swimming or boating, keep your camera in a zipper-top plastic bag until you're ready to snap a picture.

• If moisture does get into the camera, turn it off and take out the batteries and memory card. You'll want to air-dry them for about 24 hours.

• And be careful when you have sunscreen on your hands. Getting it on the lens can damage it. To be safe, use a clean, soft cloth—not your fingers—to wipe off the lens.

phone number showing. Someone who finds your camera would be able to return it to you.

Repurpose an eyeglass case. Do you have an extra soft eyeglass case with nothing to put in it? Don't fret—try using it to hold a cell phone, MP3 player, or small personal data organizer.

Print a sample picture. Digital cameras allow you to print your own photos on your computer's printer. If you are going to print several copies of the same photo, run it on plain paper first to make sure it looks exactly like you want it to. That way you won't waste the expensive photo paper.

STORING AND EXCHANGING INFORMATION

Computerize your address book. Entering your address book in a word-processing table or spreadsheet on your computer can make your life easier. This is definitely a timesaving hint when you have lots of envelopes to address.

Use the "Help" section in your word-processing software and type in "labels." Stack envelopes with new addresses after the holidays and update the list all at once. You will be more likely to keep addresses up-to-date as the year progresses and people move, too.

If you don't know how to do this on your computer, ask a friend or family member to show you how easily it can be done.

More things to do with your address list. You'll find many uses for your computerized address list. Here are just a few:

- Keep a copy at work, another at home, and one with a trusted friend in case your address book is lost.

- When traveling, take a copy with you to send postcards or to contact someone who lives where you are visiting.

- Use it to create mailing labels for holiday cards or party invitations.

- Make a set of labels for thank-you notes, for the kids' birthdays.

- E-mail or send the documents to family members and friends to update contact information for one another.

Label phone numbers. When a family member dies, the family may have a hard time trying to figure out who some of the people in their address listings are. When you set up a new address book, put a category after each name (such as coworker, friend, or church member).

If anything ever happens to you in the future, your family will find the notes helpful.

Update your address file. An easy way to update your address file (if you keep it in a book or card file instead of on the computer) is to clip the return addresses from incoming mail. Tape them over the old addresses in your address file.

Organize e-mail addresses. Here is a handy way to organize the e-mail addresses of people you frequently contact, such as relatives and close friends.

When you write a new e-mail or forward one, your list of contacts probably appears somewhere on the screen. If you put an "a" or an "aa" before those names you contact most often, they will appear at the top of the list, and you will save time by not having to scroll down and hunt for the address of the person you wish to contact.

Find a small address book. If you have a small address book that constantly gets lost under piles of papers on your desk or phone table, take a large silk flower and stick the stem down the spine of the book. It'll be easy to find.

Jot quick cues on business cards. Do you attend events for a company and get lots of business cards from people you meet there? After a week or so, it's impossible to remember who the people were or, sometimes, where you met them. As a memory booster, after arriving home or at your hotel room, take a couple of minutes to write some information on the back of the card. You could write the date, event, what you and the person discussed, or a descriptive fact, such as "sales" or "has three dogs." The info will come in handy when you need to call that person.

Store passwords and photos. Keep all your passwords and other information filed with "invisible ink" on your PC. Simply change the font color to white, and the page looks blank. Just highlight and change the font color to black to see the information. While this might not fool hackers, it might keep your passwords safe from others who share your computer.

Remember your passwords. If you have a home computer and have many passwords and online names to remember, keep an address book in the drawer of your desk especially for computer use.

Address books are inexpensive and make for quick alphabetical access, and they take up less space than sticky notes all over your desk. However, it might not be a safe idea to keep one at the office or anyplace someone you don't know could get hold of your passwords.

Make a portable password file. If you teach or work in different locations, you can make a small, portable file of the various passwords and user names for the computers you use. Just write the Web site or account number name and then the password. File them alphabetically, and they're much easier

On the Light Side
The Lighter Side of Passwords

Here's a humorous computer story. A reader reported to me that during the initial training for the newsroom on the computer system at *The Houston Post* starting back in 1975, the trainer always emphasized that it was important for passwords to be secret, although usernames were public. When the *Post* closed in 1995 and the trainer had to clear everything before shipping the system (when it was sold to another paper), it was discovered that more than half of the newsroom's staff were using the word *secret* as their password.

to find than all those scraps of paper you probably used before. It can also be tucked safely away out of sight or even locked in a drawer of a filing cabinet if necessary.

Dispose of paper. To reduce your chances of falling victim to identity theft, shred credit card applications, bank statements, and other documents containing sensitive information. Mix the shreds in with the litter from your cat's box. Or, divide the shreds between two or three plastic grocery bags and add some water to them before tossing into the garbage can.

Another approach is to take a permanent black marker and mark out all sensitive information. On credit card applications, for instance, black out your name and address, and scribble all over the application blank. Then tear it into small pieces if you don't have a shredder.

Really get rid of paper. To destroy documents without a shredder, tear them up, then put them in a dishpan and run hot water on them. Let soak for a couple of hours, then wad them into a ball of mush and put them in the trash.

Destroy that label. To further protect your privacy, when discarding prescription medication bottles, make sure you remove the label and destroy it first. A dishonest person could use much of the information on the label to get a start on stealing someone's identity!

There is a lot of personal information on a prescription label—your name, address, doctor's name, and maybe your insurance number. To be on the safe side, it sure can't hurt to destroy the label. Some pharmacies have started to put easy-to-remove labels on the bottles, and I want to thank them, since this now makes removing a label a snap.

Guard credit card numbers. Here is a caution about copying the backs of credit cards in addition to the fronts.

In an effort to control fraudulent use, merchants have been asking for a control code number on the back of the card when you order by phone. Any copy with this number makes it easy to use the card if it falls into the wrong hands. Complete copies of credit cards should be guarded like a real credit card.

Collect shredded paper fast. If your paper shredder has a wastebasket for the catch bin, place a paper bag inside the basket. When the bag is full, just pull it out, fold over, and toss in the recycling bin.

"Bury" the numbers. Shred your old documents that are no longer needed and that have credit card num-

---

PROTECT THAT PURSE!

What would happen if your purse, wallet, or briefcase were stolen?

When you leave home, do you carry your whole history with you? You don't need to. To protect yourself, take the following steps:

- Monitor the contents of what you carry with you. Experts say to take only what you need each day, if possible. Make copies of all your credit cards (front and back), and update these when a new card is received or a card is canceled.

- Do carry your bank card, driver's license, a multipurpose credit card, and affinity cards, such as frequent-flier cards.

- Do *not* carry your passport, Social Security card (you very rarely need this), or credit cards from stores you visit infrequently.

- Never write your PINs on a piece of paper and carry it with your credit cards.

- Do *not* carry original family photos that cannot be replaced.

- If your purse, wallet, or briefcase is stolen, call credit card companies and banks ASAP.

bers, Social Security numbers, and bank account numbers on them. If you want extra protection, put the shreds in a brown paper grocery bag, half full. Then scoop cat waste from the litter box on top of the shreds. Roll up the bag and put it in the trash.

Use shredded papers for mulch. Here's another way to keep your shredded secrets out of the hands of others: Save the shreds in a large bag, and, when it's full, sprinkle them in a thin layer under and around fruit trees and vegetable plants as mulch. A great way to hold moisture, and it is biodegradable.

Be careful with restaurant receipts. If you pay by credit card in a restaurant, don't sign the receipt and leave it on the table when you depart. How easy it would be for anyone to just grab the receipt. If you do leave a receipt behind, make it a habit to cross off your account number. Take a close look—most receipts should have only the last four numbers printed. If the entire number appears, scratch it out. Or avoid the entire problem by handing the receipt directly back to the waitstaff.

Tear bar codes from recyclables. As you go through your mail, magazines, and especially catalogs, cut out or tear off not only your name and address but also the bar codes—and not only on the back, but in the middle and the front. Some catalogs provide your name, account number, and amount they allow you to charge on the front. Shred everything that has your name or information on it to help prevent identity theft.

Beware of phony calls. Telephone con artists often make urgent calls and leave messages on people's phones or cell phones claiming they are from your service provider, and are calling regarding your bill. When you call back to straighten out the misunderstanding, the person on the other end uses high-pressure tactics and asks—rapid-fire—for personal information. They can hit you so fast that you may be on the verge of giving them your Social Security number. Don't fall for this! If a call seems strange to you, hang up immediately. Phone companies do not solicit your personal information over the phone—they already have what they need.

Don't get taken! Protect your personal information, and don't give your Social Security number to anyone who calls you!

Vacuum-seal documents. Use your food vacuum sealer not only for food storage but also for important documents. Here's how:

- After completing your IRS return, seal all forms with supporting records in the required length of the 11-inch roll of plastic. This ensures a complete file in the event of an audit and greatly reduces the space required for the information in the file cabinet drawer.

- After sorting the papers for your safety-deposit box into legal envelopes by categories, list the contents on the front of the envelope, then seal and trim away the excess. This space-saving technique will enable you to maintain everything in the smallest (and cheapest) bank box, expedites record retrieval, and prevents damage to your records in the remote event of a flood at the bank.

- As part of your hurricane evacuation preparedness plan, seal updated insurance policies, your will, and other important papers before filing them. If evacuation becomes necessary, quickly remove from the file cabinet only papers you have previously sealed. This process will take only seconds, and you will have peace of mind knowing that these important decisions have been made without the stress inherent when a storm is threatening.

File online shopping receipts. If you do a lot of shopping online, create files for the receipts. When you receive confirmation of an order from a company that you haven't previously done business with, create a new folder in your inbox and put this information in the folder. All correspondence regarding it is then placed in this folder. If you later buy more merchandise from this company, add the new information as well. It is easy to look up something if you need to because each company you buy from has its own folder.

I.D. phone books at a glance. If you have a shelf full of thick phone books, make it easy to select the one you need. Use a felt-tip marker to write the date and area covered on the bottom edge so the identity is visible when the book is lying flat on the shelf.

MAILING AND SHIPPING

Check *all* your mail. Make sure that you always check all your mail before you discard it. Occasionally checks or other important mail can become stuck between the pages of catalogs or magazines as the mail carrier sorts the mail and places it in your box. To make sure you don't miss any mail, thumb through those magazines before setting them aside.

Write mail dates on your calendar. It's handy to highlight occasions and appointments in your calendar, but you can also pencil in a mail-by date. This will remind you when something has to be mailed.

Put junk mail to use. If the paper received in junk mail is not printed on both sides, you can cut it into four pieces, attach it together with a large paper clip, and use it for scratch paper.

Pre-address a postcard. When you receive a letter from a good friend and you do not want to search all over for the address, tape the return address to a blank postcard. The address will be there when you need to write back.

Stamp out a mystery. If you have old, nondenominated stamps that you bought when the postage rates changed (and they are not the "Forever" stamps the postal service has sold in recent years), it's easy to lose track of their face value. You can call the post office or go online to find out the value of those stamps.

The U.S. Postal Service Web site—www.usps.com—can help. Just go to the site and select "Buy Stamps & Shop." Type "nondenominated stamps" into the search window.

From now on, when you purchase a book of stamps, write on the cover what the stamps are worth.

Dispense stamps. If you keep a 100-stamp roll in a small dispenser, when you put a new roll in, remove the 10th stamp from the tail end to let you know when it is time to reorder.

If you don't use a dispenser, open the roll from the inside instead of the outside. The stamps will stay in a neat roll, and they can be pulled out as needed, right side up for "righties" or from the bottom for "lefties."

Helpful holiday card hint. When addressing envelopes for Christmas cards, sometimes we make mistakes and end up with more cards than envelopes. To solve this problem, you can use colored dot stickers from the stationery store to "seal" the cards. Then address the backs of the cards and add a stamp to mail them. Just make sure the cards are addressed properly and sealed well.

Return to recipient. When you send a get-well card to someone in the hospital, the intended recipient may be sent home before a card reaches him or her. When addressing a card, put the recipient's home address in the return address area instead of your own. If the person already has been discharged, the card will be returned to him or her. This way, you can be assured that your card gets delivered.

Seal an envelope. To reseal an envelope, if you can't find any glue, try using clear fingernail polish instead.

Reuse envelopes. Here's a good use for the backs of envelopes from bills and junk mail. When you are paying bills, working in your checkbook, unscrambling words for a puzzle, or writing a quick note, you look around for scratch paper. These envelopes are the perfect answer. Rather than throwing them away, save them and use them for this purpose. Look at it as recycling.

Keep in touch. Many of us still like to keep in contact by writing letters, especially to loved ones who are very far away. Time just slips by, and the longer you don't write, the more there is to write, and the more difficult it becomes to even get started. To solve the problem, keep a pad and pencil handy. The first day, do nothing but address the envelope and stuff the letter to be answered in it. Then every

day, write down a sentence or a thought. In 2 weeks, this amounts to a one- or two-page letter.

The moment you seal the envelope, start a new letter. On the place where the stamp goes, write the date on which the previous letter was finished and mailed. That way you can easily keep track of the time that elapses between letters.

To save time rereading letters you've received, read each letter with a red pen in your hand. As you read it, underline every point you want to answer.

Fix an envelope error. Have you ever made a mistake while addressing the envelope of a greeting card before sealing it—with no replacement envelope? It is possible to carefully open the glued parts and turn the envelope inside out and glue it again with a glue stick. The original glue on the flap—now on the outside—can be wiped off with a slightly damp cloth.

Reuse plastic shipping envelopes. Save plastic shipping envelopes that you receive. To return items, turn the plastic envelopes inside out and attach the return label. This way, you won't have to worry about the post office getting confused by too many shipping labels on the package.

Recycle shipping boxes. To remove

a shipping label so you can reuse the box, use a hair dryer to warm the shipping label, and it will easily peel off. The hair-dryer method works for taking labels off of anything.

 Pack with popcorn. When mailing a package, instead of using plastic foam peanuts, use popped and butter-free popcorn as packing material. The popcorn then can be fed to birds, squirrels, and other wildlife.

Make space-efficient packages. When mailing packages to out-of-town relatives for birthdays and holidays, you can get more articles into a box if you soft-wrap the gifts when possible. Do not use individual gift boxes, if you can avoid it, and instead use tissue paper and then wrapping paper. You will make better use of space and also cut down on the final cost of the shipment.

Use plastic bags for shipping. Here's another way to recycle plastic bags: Take the plastic bag from your Sunday paper and stuff it full of other plastic bags. When it's full, clothespin the bag to a clothesline in your garage. When shipping packages, instead of using foam peanuts or buying packaging with air bubbles, grab one or more of your tubes of plastic bags, tie a knot at

FIND USES FOR ADDRESS LABELS

Many of us receive unsolicited address labels from charities seeking donations. In addition to using them on envelopes, there are many other things you can do with them. Just be cautious—you would not want to put your name and address in a public place where strangers could use them to gain access to your personal information. Here are some possible ways to use address labels:

- If office coworkers share a refrigerator, use the labels to identify beverages that you bring from home as well as your brown-bag lunch.
- If you live in an area subject to tornadoes, use the labels to identify personal belongings in your home that could not be easily replace in the event of a storm. Paste one on the inside of each photo album you have, and also on the back of framed photos you display in your home. If the photos ever are lost people will know to whom they belong.
- Use them on all of your small electronics (laptop, camera, music player).
- You can also use them to place on return envelopes and postcards, and in place of business cards. When traveling and meeting new people, if you don't happen to have a business card you can place one of the labels on a blank piece of paper.

the open end and stuff it (or them) into the box.

When the recipient gets the package, he or she can take the bags to the nearest recycling center.

Check address labels before using. Before using any of those address labels, double-check the spelling of your name and address to make sure they are correct.

Send address labels to camp. When your child goes to camp, print some address labels to give to each new friend your child wants to keep in touch with. Also send some blank note cards for the child to use to get addresses from his or her new friends.

Walk with I.D. If you walk or exercise regularly and don't like to carry your driver's license with you, use an address label. Peel one off and stick it to your T-shirt or sweatshirt.

Provide an emergency address. If you use babysitters or have in-home care providers for children or elderly family members, it can be a good idea to put an address label on your phone in case of emergency.

Use address labels for merchandise returns. Use labels when returning

---

Unlimited Uses for . . . Address Labels

Carry some address labels in your purse and you're bound to find new uses for them. Here are a whole bunch of places to put your labels:

- At the top of the shafts on golf clubs
- Inside the covers of books you lend out
- On the backs of photos
- On the backs of greeting cards for quick identification
- On bags of homemade goodies
- On items taken to gatherings (such as chairs, tables, or coolers)
- On plastic containers for taking to family, church, or work-related events. Place a sticker on both the lid and the container, and also on spoons and ladles.
- On CDs and DVDs, when you lend them out to family and friends
- On canes, walkers, and scooters
- On suitcases
- On each piece of data needed for rebates
- On your cell phone and charger
- On raffle tickets
- On film rolls to be developed
- On hand tools
- On a dog tag when your pet is away from home

items to department stores where you are asked to fill out a short return form with information that includes your name and address.

Instead of writing down all that information, which often takes a couple of minutes to complete, stick one of those labels on the form. It saves time for you, the salesperson, and the people waiting in line behind you.

ID your umbrella. Put your address label on your umbrella handle. Include all of your telephone numbers (home, work, cell) so that if the umbrella is lost, the finder can call you! Since we don't use our umbrella every day, we tend to forget it. (Write the phone numbers on the label first, then peel and attach!)

Donate labels to a daycare center. Cut off your name and address, and give what's left to the teachers. Kids love getting stickers and putting them on everything.

Use labels on Halloween treats. For Halloween, make up bags of treats with a small toy inside, seal each bag, and affix your address label so parents know its origin.

Hand out labels when you move. If you move after staying put for many years, carry some address labels with you so that when you run into old acquaintances who lost touch, you can stick a label with your new address in their address book, check register, or whatever they have handy—usually a shopping list.

Send labels to a correspondent. Exchange address labels with a relative or friend you correspond with often. It will save time for both of you.

Take address labels to a convention. Whenever you attend a convention where there are many booths and forms to fill out, stick an address label on each form.

Label wrapped coins. When wrapping pennies and coins (especially from garage sales and charity benefits), put an address label on the wrapper. It will help identify your money when taking it to the bank.

OFFICE SUPPLIES

Recycle envelopes for shopping. If you receive bills that include a window envelope for the return payment but you pay your bills with your own envelopes or online, don't waste those window envelopes. Instead, save them and use them for your grocery lists. Write your shopping list on the outside, and put your coupons inside.

Recycle your own paper. Recycle your used computer paper by cutting it in half and using it for scratch paper. You can also put a stack of used paper in your home fax machine if you get a lot of junk faxes.

At Heloise Central we recycle paper, too, and reuse the side without printing. We simply load the used paper back into the printer to print on the other side. But we have put a note on the printer about which way the paper should go to prevent printing something over the original item.

Store felt-tip pens. Felt-tip pens dry out quickly if their caps fall off. If you have felt-tip pens or markers whose caps fall off very easily, wrap an address label right where the cap sets on the pen. The caps stay secure, and you can store them point down in a container, which allows the liquid to drain to the point. This method is good for pens you don't use regularly, perhaps those for decorating holiday cards or making Halloween decorations.

Recycle junk faxes. If you receive many junk faxes and some pages with a heading or an ending on a single page, reuse them in your plain-paper fax machine. To conserve paper, turn these barely used pages around (or print side down) and feed them back into the fax machine.

Organize with a napkin holder. If you've got a napkin holder you never use, you can put it on your desk to hold bills and other mail or papers that need attention.

Attach a notepad. If you can never find a notepad when you want one, glue a magnetic strip on the back of the pad and stick it on a metal paper stand or filing cabinet on or near your desk. The pad will stay put.

Use correction fluid. Here's a hint for those of you who use correction fluid. The liquid takes a while to dry, and if you need to photocopy a document after applying the fluid, it may leave spots on your photocopier glass. If you are in a hurry, put a piece of transparent tape over the fluid, and it's good to go!

Or, use peel-off correction tape. The tape won't interfere with the scanner or fax machine and prevents white spots on the photocopier as well.

Make your own correction tape. Don't buy expensive correction fluid. When you are through with a sheet of labels from your computer, cut off the white edges that are left (which you would normally throw in the trash). Drop them in a folder, and then when you need to cover up a mistake, tear off what you need and stick it over your mistake.

Stash pens in a soup mug. If your hands will not handle a heavy, decorative soup mug full of soup, use it instead on your desk to hold pens and pencils. It won't tip over, and it looks nice.

CONSUMER CONCERNS

Don't use highlighter on receipts. If you need to save a receipt for a possible return or tax-deductible purposes, don't highlight the item or you might erase your proof of purchase. Instead, circle the item with a ballpoint pen.

File receipts on the computer. Don't print receipts for online orders—just highlight the information, copy, paste, and save to a computer file. Label the file by the vendor and date so you can find what you're looking for if necessary. You will save paper, printer ink, and clutter, and save yourself a lot of filing.

When the item is delivered, you can make a note in the file, along with any remarks about the item, such as quality and shipping comments, as well as pros and cons of ordering from the particular company, for future reference.

Organize catalog shopping. Here's a system for catalog shoppers that keeps all your information in order. When you place an order, write on the front of the catalog the order date, dollar amount spent, confirmation number, and any other relevant information. Then dog-ear the pages and put the catalog in a specific pile.

Every so often, sort through the pile and recycle the catalogs from which you have received your order. If the transaction is incomplete (for instance, if you had to return something), put the catalog back in the pile until it is done. You can see at a glance what you ordered and when, and whether an order is overdue. Having the info easy to find will save you a lot of trouble if there is a problem with an order.

Keep mail-order info together. When sending a mail order, write the complete address and phone number in your check registry. Often the only address given is on the part of the order form that you send back (then it's gone). This way, if you need to correspond with the company for any reason, you will have everything in one place—date, check number, address, phone number, and amount of purchase.

Keep the balance. It's hard to keep track of the balances on gift cards.

When you receive one, place a piece of masking tape on the front of the card, on the opposite end from the magnetic strip. As you use the card, write the remaining balance on the piece of tape. You will always know what your balance is, and you won't waste time trying to find out.

Be smart with gift cards. A gift card that becomes misplaced or forgotten often becomes subject to handling charges that vary from $2.50 after 6 months to a number of other combinations from the issuing company, allowing the company to whittle the card's value considerably.

When it comes to giving gift cards, beware! Since gift cards are the latest rage in gift-giving, there are a few things you ought to know. Some of these cards do come with catches, such as expiration dates, handling fees, monthly administrative fees for inactivity, lost or stolen replacement fees, and a charge for an expired card.

If you receive a gift card, take a look at the fine print to make sure you know the stipulations. Many cards state that you should register your card in case it's lost or stolen. Also, laws vary by state.

Put receipts in your checkbook. If

HOW TO COMPLAIN

If you bought something that does not work or you are dissatisfied with a service from a store or business, keep the receipts and the item purchased, and make a note of the service not performed. You should respond in a cool, businesslike way—don't be emotional in a written (or verbal) complaint. Here's a checklist for making an effective complaint that should get you a refund or the results you expect:

1. Give your name, address, and work and home telephone numbers.
2. Include the date and place of purchase.
3. Note the serial and model numbers of the merchandise.
4. Cite the name of the person(s) who did the work, if it's a service complaint.
5. Make several copies of your complaint letter, and allow a reasonable amount of time for a response.
6. Follow up until you get the satisfaction you want.
7. If you do not get results, you can contact the Better Business Bureau or state agencies that handle consumer complaints. Most newspapers and TV stations have consumer reporters who might be able to help as well.

On the other hand, if a business or employee does a good job, hey, give a compliment!

you use a debit card for many purchases, entering each receipt in the checkbook at the time of purchase is not always convenient. Instead, put that receipt in your checkbook. When you enter that purchase in your checkbook, put a check mark on the receipt, fold it, and put it in the back of your checkbook until "cleaning day." Then check each receipt for the check mark and put it in a storage box in case you need it later. If there is no check mark, check the register to see if it has been entered; if not, do so, and your records will be straight.

Make a backup gas receipt. Sometimes when you fill up at a gas station, the pump does not provide a paper receipt. Rather than go inside and wait in line, take a snapshot with your cell phone or digital camera of the readout on the pump. Within seconds, you're on your way. Later, copy this amount into your checkbook register.

Keep tabs on gas purchases. Never can find those flimsy little receipts from gasoline stations for a double-check? Fold them so that only brand, date, and amounts show, and tape them to the correct date on your calendar. When bills arrive, just compare and pluck the receipts off. You'll know what's still outstanding at one glance.

Also, total all purchases monthly and write the sum in the right corner of your calendar. Maybe those figures will inspire you to plan your trips to the supermarkets more economically.

With the price of gasoline these days, it is very important to check your billing, and this is a good record of gallons used and how much you paid per gallon.

Monitor gas purchases. Here's a simple way to do a quick check on your credit card statement for your gasoline purchases. Whenever you fill up, always end the amount of the purchase with the number 7. The pump stops when the tank is full, and you can carefully press the trigger to move the last cent to 7 (such as $15.67).

When your credit card statement arrives, check the gasoline purchases, and all the amounts should end in 7s. If you find any that do not, you know that you need to call and check on them.

Preview the returns policy. Our job as consumers is to ask a company about its return/exchange policy *before* we make a purchase. It doesn't matter how many receipts you have—if the company has an exchange-only policy, you won't get your money back. So ask before you buy.

File receipts by month. At the beginning of each month, take an envelope and write the month and year on it. Put all receipts in that envelope for that month, and do the same for each month in the year. Whenever you need a receipt for a return or a reference, it's right there at your fingertips.

Pay as you go with credit cards. Each time you make a purchase with a credit card, enter the purchase amount into your checkbook (just as if you had written a check). At the end of the month, when the bill comes, there are no surprises as to how much you owe, and you will know there's enough in your checking account to cover the bill.

Find government information online. Here's a very helpful Web site to know about: www.usa.gov—the U.S. government's official Web portal from the U.S. General Services Administration.

At this site you'll find all sorts of information. You can apply for college loans, purchase savings bonds, contact elected officials, and much more.

This trustworthy site brings together a gold mine of resources from federal, state, local, tribal, and territorial government Web pages. The site has a fast search engine that gives timely and relevant information, news, and pictures, such as the local forecast or photographs taken on Mars.

With www.usa.gov, you can find local farmers' markets, get lottery results, and learn how to adopt a lighthouse. You can even find recipes there (just type "recipes" into the search box).

HELP FOR CONSUMERS

Scams and frauds plague all of us—whether we're shopping at the mall, the grocery store, or online. And even without worrying about shady offers, it's complicated getting the best deals and making smart choices. The Federal Citizen Information Center in Pueblo, Colorado, has lots of helpful information available free for consumers.

Go online to www.pueblo.gsa.gov and click, or call (888) 878-3256 to see what's available. You can order a copy of the 2009 *Consumer Action Handbook* and search for information on topics such as preparing for retirement, and saving and investing.

These terrific publications from our friends in Pueblo are loaded with hints that will help you protect your family, save time, save your hard-earned dollars, and learn about cell phones, indoor air hazards, and much, much more.

BANKING AND FINANCES

Monitor bills and bank accounts. Identity theft can occur in a number of ways. One scheme involves people using some software to come up with names and numbers. When a name and number match your name and credit card number, the transaction can go through. This type of identity theft is much different from finding something in someone's trash or not shredding statements. To decrease the chance it will happen to you, monitor or close out bank and credit card accounts you don't use often or at all.

 The benefits of direct deposit. Here is a timesaving hint from a former U.S. Department of the Treasury official for people who get Social Security and other federal benefit checks: Switch to direct deposit. Using direct deposit means one less thing to worry about. It also safeguards against identity theft, which can be traumatic, costly, and time-consuming to resolve.

Plus, direct deposit eliminates the risk of stolen checks and forgeries. With direct deposit, you also will have more control over your money and immediate access to funds from almost anywhere.

For all these reasons, the U.S. Department of the Treasury and the Federal Reserve Banks are sponsoring the "Go Direct" campaign to encourage all people who receive federal benefits to use direct deposit.

ORGANIZE THE CHECKBOOK

If your monthly checking-account statement doesn't quite add up to your calculations, then maybe a little checkbook organization is in order. Here are several hints for eliminating those bank-statement surprises:

1. Your check register is a good record of deposits and spending—if you record *all* transactions. Include the date, check number, name, and, if applicable, an invoice number.
2. Include payment information on the line at the bottom left corner of your check.
3. Save time by paper-clipping the check register on the page where you are working.
4. Make sure your math is correct! It is helpful to keep a small, thin calculator with your register if you aren't good at adding and subtracting.
5. You can also round up check amounts to the nearest dollar to make the math easier and have a little extra in the account.

It's easy to sign up for direct deposit of your Social Security or Supplemental Security Income payments—simply call the Go Direct toll-free helpline at (800) 333-1795, or sign up online at www.GoDirect.org. You also may visit your local bank, credit union, or Social Security Administration office.

Track transactions with ease. Bank deposit envelopes are handy for recording credit card and debit card transactions, and for saving the corresponding receipts. When you travel for business or are on vacation, you will be able to keep personal and business transactions easily separated—with a separate envelope for each check card. It's a handy option in lieu of carrying a checkbook or stuffing receipts in pockets.

Sign in blue. When signing legal and financial documents, use a pen with

CREDIT COUNSELING 101

Here are two things to be aware of pertaining to your credit report. It is always a good idea to close unused accounts, but if you close all those accounts, you actually could damage your credit rating (score) by lowering it. Almost any action you take in regard to your credit will have an impact on it. For instance, if you are shopping for a car or other product and go to different dealers to shop for the best deal, each time a dealer makes a credit inquiry, it could drop your credit score a few points. If you go to a lot of places, it could dramatically impact your credit score. Then, a couple of weeks later, if you make an application for a large purchase, such as a new home, you could have a lower credit score, which could affect your interest rate.

Multiple inquiries from certain sources, especially in a short time period, might negatively impact your credit score—even if it's to buy a car or television, or shop for credit cards. There are ways of shopping around without letting anybody make an inquiry about your credit. For instance, when you check your credit report (which should be done once a year) to make sure everything is current and correct, make a copy of it and carry it with you when planning to make any major purchase involving credit within the next year! This should suffice until you make your final decision, and then the company you choose would probably need to verify the credit information you had on hand.

There are so many variables in the calculation of a credit score that it is always a good idea to contact a credit consultant (someone who reviews credit daily, or a lender or banking institution) with any questions.

Your credit history and score really are your lifelong "permanent" record, so take care when using credit cards.

blue ink to distinguish that original signature from the black photocopies. I also try to mark the copy with a "C" in the upper right corner to make it easy for me to identify which is the original and which is the copy.

Make a creditor report. To handle the finances in the family, create a record (on paper or on a computer worksheet) of your creditors—name, address, account number, when started, and when paid off. Keep up this record through the years, highlighting each account as it is successfully paid off. This record makes for easy reference, and may prove to be beneficial if you are ever a victim of identity theft and need to review your history with the three major credit bureaus.

Store credit cards. To keep track of your credit cards and other cards of similar size, purchase a 4-by-9-inch business-card-holder notebook. In addition to filing the card, also file a slip of paper identifying the item (Visa, Social Security, insurance, debit card). Each card goes back to its proper spot after use. Keep a typed list of everything in the box in a separate location.

Color-code transactions. Color-coding is one way to help keep transactions straight. Use a different color

of highlighting pen each month when you reconcile your bank statement. Highlight the transaction on the bank statement and in your register with the same color each month. This method makes it easier to see which transactions had not gone through at the time of the statement.

It also makes it easier to find a bank statement. First, find the transaction in your register to see which color highlighter was used, then look in your statements for that color. This will also work for tax deductions—use one color the whole year just for deductions, and other colors for your regular transactions.

If you use duplicate checks, you can sit down at one time and make all the entries at your desk where you have the various colored pens. Enter the balance after each subtraction or addition in pencil so it can be changed easily if there is a mistake.

Organize your checking account. Each month, use a different-colored pen to write checks, letters, and lists. It will help keep things organized.

Donate online. Online banking is a godsend for many people, who like the convenience when paying bills.

You can add your favorite charities

to your list of online-banking payees. That way, whenever you have extra money, you can send a donation their way, too. It saves time over the regular check writing and mailing process.

Use labels on checks. If after moving you have checks preprinted with your former address on them and your account will still be with the same bank, put address labels with your new address over the address printed on your checks instead of scratching it out and writing in the new address.

Get ATM deposits ready. To save time at the ATM (for yourself and the people behind you in line) take a few deposit envelopes and put them in your glove compartment or desk drawer. The next time you go to make a deposit, you can do all the preparation at home, at work, or in your car. It will speed up the line at the ATM and reduce the frustration of others.

Make sure you have checks. Ever been in the grocery store and started to write a check only to see you were out of checks?

When you put a new book of checks in your checkbook, list all the check numbers in the check register. As you write checks, you can tell when you are getting to the end. When you get

down to two checks, get out another book and do the same on the check register.

This system also helps you remember to post a written check.

Checkbook reminder. In your checkbook, put a little sticky note about the third check from the end to remind you to get more checks. When you get a new book of checks, transfer that same note to the new group of checks.

Register the year. As you use your checkbook, write the year as well as the date of your checks. At least indicate in the register where the year begins and ends.

If you become disabled and need someone to manage your finances, he or she will need to know which year expenditures have occurred. When someone passes away, the executor of the estate will need this information.

Start a new record book. To keep track of checks for each year, at the beginning of each year, begin a new checkbook register. On the front, write the year and the beginning check number. At the end of December, write the last check number and place the book with the year's tax papers. Then you are ready to begin a new year and a new record book.

Pay bills on time. As bills arrive, open them; on the response envelope (in the corner where the stamp will go), write a date 5 to 7 days earlier than the due date; write the check; put the check and payment stub in the envelope and seal it up, ready to go. Place the envelope in a binder clip in "mail date" order with other outgoing mail. Then, as the mail date rolls around, add a stamp and return-address label and mail the payment. Never a big chore at once, bills are always ready to go, and you won't have late payments.

It's prudent to mail payments earlier rather than later, so take note of weekends and holidays. A credit card payment that is just 1 day late (and in some cases an hour!) can cause a late-payment fee and even a jump in your interest rate. Check the fine print on your bill—you might be shocked. At Heloise Central we looked at three issuers, and the cutoff times for payment due were all different—noon, 2 p.m., and 3 p.m. Also, one stated that if the payment is stapled, folded, paper-clipped, or not in the provided envelope, the payment might not be credited for 5 days.

Don't miss hidden treasure. If an elderly relative passes away and you need to clean out the house, search

FINANCIAL PLANNING

If you think you need help with planning investment decisions, you might want to find a financial planner to help you and your family. Here are some steps you can take to find good financial planning services:

- Get recommendations from relatives, friends, and business associates.
- Examine the licensing and education credentials of the person, along with his or her professional experience and track record.
- Make sure the financial planner will consider your opinions and needs.
- Ask for a written analysis of your financial situation, and get a written summary of fees and service. Don't sign anything until you understand everything clearly.
- Request that the planner document the reasons for decisions.
- Think about your goals and priorities—how much, how long, and why you are investing. Think about how much risk you want to take, and let the planner know your "comfort level." It's your money!

carefully for any hidden cash he or she may have left behind. Some of the older generations didn't trust banks and hid money at their home, as my mother did also.

Some places to check: flip through old books and magazines; the little drawer found under many old dining-room tables; under the paper lining and underside of drawers; in old, unpaid bills; and pockets in clothing. One elderly couple had money taped to roll-up window shades. Some folks even put money with food in the freezer.

The search is a time-consuming job, but leave no stone unturned before you sell the house or any of the furnishings.

Chapter 7

Moving, Buying, or Selling a Home

Whether you are selling a house, buying a house, or renting a house or an apartment, moving is stressful. Here are some hints to help you reduce aggravation and make the process go more smoothly.

Make a change of address easier. If you will be moving, plan ahead for the address changes you will need to make. Several months before the move, take a large, bright-colored envelope and label it "Moving." Collect return addresses from current subscriptions, bills, and memberships. This will make it easier to announce your new address (either online or via snail mail) when the time comes.

You can also collect clippings and hints regarding making moving easier, including your own "to do" list as the ideas pop up.

The material inside the envelope helps keep all the loose ends in one place!

How to change your address. It seems like such a simple thing to change one's address, but really it is quite a chore remembering all the companies and places that will need your new address.

Start a list in advance—about 2 months before moving—and keep it on a notepad near the phone. Every time you think of a new one, jot it down—credit cards, doctors, retirement accounts, alumni groups, employers. Four weeks before moving, start to contact them. Some will be easy, and you can make the change via e-mail.

MOVING 101

Here are a few hints that just might make moving day less stressful:

- Start early to eliminate unneeded items. Take 10 minutes a day and clean out a drawer or cupboard. Toss what you don't need and pack what you will take with you. Label each box with the contents.

- Keep a folder with address changes you might easily forget to make. Use the U.S. Postal Service's address-change packets and moving coupons.

- Arrange for transfer of your medical records.

- Get referrals by asking around town about good movers—and check out your choices with your local Better Business Bureau.

- Never book a move over the Internet.

- Start collecting boxes now—you will be shocked at how many you'll need. If you have to buy boxes, they can be expensive!

- Get several estimates from movers who will come out and physically take a look at everything you plan to put on the truck.

- If one bid is way below the others, be very careful unless you know whom you're dealing with.

- Months before your move, start to use up cleaning products and chemicals.

- Make sure all items you will be taking yourself are out of the way before the movers arrive.

- When packing, color-code boxes so you can tell at a glance which room they go in. Colored stickers serve this purpose well. This will make unpacking easier, as you won't have to carry items from room to room to place them where they belong.

- If you don't use color coding, at least identify the room to which the box should be delivered.

- Place address labels on the inside and outside of each box.

- Keep an inventory list of boxed items—number each box and identify contents on the inventory list.

- Don't overpack each box. Keep the weight to 50 pounds or less. Reinforce the bottoms of boxes with super-strong tape.

- Put items for donation in one bag and keep a list for tax-deduction purposes.

- Keep valued items and medicines with you, and your moving papers, too.

- Before moving into your new residence, perform any painting and carpet cleaning to avoid having to move furniture later.

Others will have specific forms that need to be filled out, some will want letters, and others let you change the address with a simple phone call.

You'll be glad you started well in advance.

Get a mover's guide. If you are getting ready for a move, go by a post office for a Mover's Guide packet found in the lobby, or visit www.usps. gov for the Mover's Guide online to file a change of address. You can also call (800) ASK-USPS.

Get moving boxes for free. The best place to get free cardboard boxes is the local liquor store. The boxes are stronger than commercial boxes, resist modest amounts of moisture, and have dividers to hold small, delicate items.

Organize what's in moving boxes. To keep track of boxes and their contents when you are moving or putting boxes in storage, number the boxes with a felt-tip marker and list the contents of each numbered box in a notebook. It takes only an extra minute, but it saves time if you need to retrieve something.

Make photographic labels. When packing for a move, use a digital camera to photograph the items that you packed. Then print the photos on labels using your computer and put them on the boxes. You know what they say—a picture is worth a thousand words.

How to pack china. If you need to pack china dishes for a move, try using plastic foam plates to separate the china plates. You won't get ink on the plates, as you could if you packed with newsprint, and the foam plates will cushion the china and protect it from chipping.

Prearrange furniture. To make moving day easier (for you and the moving company) make copies of the floor-plan layout of your new home, if you have one. Then pencil in where you want to place the furniture in each room.

Moving clothes. When moving, lay a bathrobe on the bed, place up to 20 shirts (or blouses) on hangers, hooks at the top, on top of it, then close the robe, fold up the bottom, cross the arms, then tie the belt. This will allow you to carry the shirts without wrinkles, sore fingers, or entangled hangers.

Get ready for bed in the new home. Put a set of bed linens in a clean trash bag and then place that in a dresser drawer for each bedroom you will be using after the move. That way, you won't have to dig through boxes to find sheets to make the beds after you've had a very long day.

Buy three batteries. When you move, purchase three 9-volt batteries for the smoke detectors—one for immediate replacement in the smoke detector in your new home, one for backup, and one to leave behind in your old home or apartment for the new owners or tenants.

Stash stuff in wheeled cans. If you buy new trash cans when moving to a new house or apartment, get big ones with wheels. Since they're new, put them to work and move unbreakable items (like books or holiday decorations) in them. You can just wheel your belongings into the new place rather than carrying heavy boxes.

Sequester valuables when you move. Make a list of your valuables and where you plan to leave them during the move. Use a cabinet, closet, or room that can be locked, and limit access to that area.

Make an easier transition to school. Moving day can also be a school day. Getting everyone "up and going" is bad enough on a normal day, but on the first day in a new house, it can be even worse. To make it easier, pack school clothes in a suitcase just as you would for a vacation, so that everyone will have everything together for school.

SELLING A HOME

Create sales appeal. Are you thinking about selling your home? Here's a checklist that will make it more appealing to buyers:

- First, get rid of any clutter inside and out! An uncluttered area appears larger and less busy.

- Add flowers to your garden, or hang flower baskets near the front entrance.

- A fresh coat of paint inside and outside, if necessary, is always a plus.

- Clean doors and windows, and sweep sidewalks, driveways, and patios. Power washing will remove most stains.

- Clean the entire inside of the house, paying special attention to the kitchen, bathrooms, and master bedroom.

- Remember that clean, orderly closets and cabinets make the whole house appear less cluttered.

- The day of a showing, make sure all beds are made, clothes and shoes are put in their places, and curtains are opened to let the sunshine in. Take a quick walk-through to ensure that your home is presentable to the potential buyer.

Entice a buyer. When prospective buyers are coming to see your house, real estate agents suggest sprinkling some cinnamon in a disposable pie pan and putting it in the oven at a very low temperature. You'll get the appealing scent of baking without the cleanup. Also, spray a bit of your best cologne or perfume in the bathroom.

Be a kind home seller. Here are some hints to help make move-in day a little easier for new homeowners. One of the nicest things you can do as a seller is to make sure the house is spick-and-span for the new owners. Here are some other kind gestures:

- Leave a roll of toilet paper in the bathrooms and a roll of paper towels in the kitchen.

- Place all extra keys, appliance warranties, codes, and other information that go with the house together on the kitchen counter.

- Consider leaving a list of names and numbers of trusted repairmen, landscapers, veterinarians, and other professionals in the area.

- If the new owners have children, consider including the names of doctors, schools, and babysitters you recommend.

- You could also leave details about the days and times of garbage and recycling pickups, neighborhood amenities, and any other information you think would be helpful.

- And it's a good idea to leave your name, phone number, and forwarding address as well, in case the new owners come across items or mail that belongs to you.

What *not* to do when selling your home. Some folks disagree with the advice to leave your phone number and address for the buyers of your home. Some new owners will call you every time something goes wrong in the house or they have a problem with a neighbor.

To prevent being pestered, you might tell your buyers that if they need to get in touch with you, they can do so through your real estate agent instead of giving them the information directly.

BUYING AND RENTING

Be a considerate home buyer. When you are shopping for a home, it's basic good manners as a prospective buyer to show up—on time—when you schedule a showing. If you do buy a house, wait until after the closing to try moving in your things or showing the house to friends. Until closing, the house is the property of the sellers, who are probably very busy getting ready to move!

 Be a savvy tenant. When going through a new rental property, take a notepad and pencil along to note things that need to be repaired or replaced by whoever is renting the property to you. It's a good idea to do this when walking through with the agent, and do the walk-through in daylight. Many problems are not as noticeable at night. In addition, take along a digital camera and photograph any potential problems to document that they were there when you moved in.

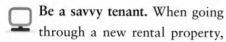

BUYING A HOME

I would like to share some sound advice about probably one of the most important purchases of your life: buying a home. This can be a scary proposition, but it doesn't have to be if you do your homework in advance and have a checklist, which could help eliminate some of the worry.

Here are some hints that I think you'll find helpful:

- In general, the proposed monthly mortgage payment, electric, water, and maintenance bills should not be more than one-third of your total income.
- It is always a good idea to get prequalified by a local lender so you have an idea of the price range in which you will be eligible to purchase.
- Hire a licensed home inspector to look for flaws, damage, and possible future repair problems . . . unless the price is such a bargain that repair costs would not be a factor.
- Consider the distance to schools, availability of bus service or other public transportation, and how long it will take you to get to work. Also, are shopping malls, grocery stores, a post office, or hospitals nearby?
- Figure out how high your taxes will be. Most counties have a Web site where you can find the amount of property taxes that were paid for the previous year.
- Talk to neighbors—they can fill you in on any unique neighborhood problems or perks. Go to the city's Web site to find out (usually by ZIP code) about any crimes or registered offenders in the area you are considering.

Happy house-hunting!

Don't be shy about checking to see if large appliances work, doors latch, and toilets flush. Is there cable for the TV? Where are the meters? After all, a year's lease is a large investment, and you might not have time to find everything that needs attention within a few weeks after moving in.

Don't go overboard with rental complaints. It is wise to make sure a house is in good repair before you rent it, and to take note of any existing damage or appliances that don't work. But don't go too far. If you look at a house and later return with three typed pages of things you find wrong with the house, the owners may not want to rent to you.

If you have a lot of problems with the house, just don't pursue the rental further. Look for something else.

PART 2
Life, Simplified

In part 1 of this book you found loads of tips on taking care of your stuff—your home and your belongings. This section is all about you. There are hints on cooking and storing food, entertaining friends and family, crafts, holidays, taking care of your health and appearance, family activities, caring for pets, and a chapter on coping with storms, emergencies, and other difficulties. These hints will let you have a richer, more satisfying home life. Enjoy!

Chapter 8

―――――――――

Cooking Hints

This chapter is all about cooking. You'll find hints and recipes for different food groups, including snacks, sweets, and leftovers, plus shortcuts and substitutes for when you run out of time or ingredients. There are also ideas for using kitchen tools and appliances in new ways, and for how to keep and organize recipes and cookbooks. Happy cooking!

SUCCESSFUL COOKING 101

The recipe for a successful dish starts before the cooking even begins. If you are a beginner or are making something for the first time, you don't want to miss these helpful hints:

- With most dishes, the recipe holds the key to your success. So, don't skim through it. Take the time to get it right.

- Read the recipe all the way through at least twice before you start, to make sure you understand the instructions. You don't want any surprises up ahead.

- Make sure you have all the ingredients. Sounds obvious, but many a good cook has discovered he's out of a key ingredient halfway through the process.

- Have all your ingredients accurately measured. Too much or too little of some things— like baking powder—can ruin a dish.

- Make sure you understand the measuring instructions. Half a cup of nuts, chopped, is not the same as half a cup of chopped nuts. Make sure you know whether to chop and then measure or the other way around.

- "Beat two eggs separately" means to separate the whites from the yolks and beat—*not* put an egg in each of two different bowls.

Plan meals. When you have a very busy household, it helps to take turns with meal preparation, say, making breakfast and dinner one day a week. The family can work together once a month to come up with a menu, and adults can help children choose meals appropriate to their skill level. Give each person one "free pass" to eat out. This way, only one person has to get up extra early one day a week.

An added benefit is a new understanding and appreciation for all the effort that goes into a home-cooked meal.

Make meals for one. It's hard to cook for one person, but if you're cooking for one, you can still enjoy great home-cooked meals. Prepare food as usual, and after you finish your meal, divide the remainder into individual TV dinners to store in the freezer. You'll have a variety to choose from whenever you want (label each meal so you will know what you have). And best of all, you can always invite someone over on your big-meal day.

Conquer cooking odors. When you're cooking strong-smelling foods like cabbage, onions, or fish, your kitchen and home can fill with those unpleasant odors. Here are some easy and cheap odor-eliminating hints to

help you freshen the air in your kitchen:

- When frying food, put a small bowl of white or apple cider vinegar next to the stove to help prevent that nasty "fat is cooking" smell.

- If you have burned food, place several lemon, orange, or grapefruit slices in a pan filled with water and bring to a boil.

- If your home smells like smoke, dip a towel in vinegar and wring until lightly damp. Wave it through the air to help eliminate the smell. My mother, the original Heloise, used this hint in the sixties when more people smoked indoors.

- If something has dripped onto the bottom of the oven during baking, cover the burned gunk with table salt and clean up when the oven is cool.

- If the garbage disposal smells rotten, grind a bunch of citrus peels (lemon, lime, grapefruit, or orange) inside. Then flush with lots of cold water. Several drops of peppermint or other extracts added with water will also help deodorize the disposal.

Ask about food allergies. When you invite non–family members over for a meal, ask if they have any food allergies. That way, you'll never serve anything that would be a problem for an invited quest.

Label food allergens. When baking for your community, church, or friends and using nuts as an ingredient in the goods, also sprinkle the nuts on top of the brownies, cookies, or cakes so that those with an allergy to nuts will see them immediately. If the nuts are inside the food and not visible, make a small sign (using a square, white card and a toothpick) stating "contains nuts." This ensures that those with allergies to nuts will not accidentally ingest these foods and become ill or worse.

Be mindful of leftover jars. If you reuse peanut butter jars for leftovers, be aware that even after thorough washing, traces of peanut proteins could remain in the jars, resulting in cross-contamination of food that could be lethal for allergy sufferers.

Douse a small kitchen fire. Baking soda makes a good fire extinguisher, especially for small oil or grease fires

FOOD SAFETY 101

Food safety is very important because perishable food can cause food poisoning. But there are ways to prevent foodborne illness. Here are some important hints to keep your kitchen safe:

- Place meat and poultry in the refrigerator or freezer as soon as possible. After grocery shopping, put perishables away first.
- Don't thaw food on the counter or in the sink for more than 2 hours. When the temperature is high (85 degrees F or above), don't leave food out for more than 1 hour.
- Cook meat and poultry thoroughly to kill bacteria. Meat should be cooked to 160 degrees F, poultry to 170 to 180 degrees, and fish to 145 degrees. Although meat might look "done," it should always be checked with a meat thermometer.
- Store leftovers in small, shallow containers and place in the refrigerator immediately so they cool quickly.
- Wash cooking utensils that come in contact with raw meat, poultry, and fish. Cross-contamination is always a concern, so don't use the same utensils or platters for raw and cooked meat.

These hints will help keep your food safe.

in the kitchen. It's a good idea to keep a box of baking soda in a cabinet near the stove and oven just in case there's a flare-up.

But be sure to *turn off the heat*, stand away, and gently toss a handful or two at the *base* of the flames, not over the top. If it's a deep-fat fryer, don't try this because the fire could spread. Turn off the heat and cover the fryer with a large metal lid. If it gets out of hand, don't wait—call 911 ASAP!

Call to complain. The solution to a complaint about any product is to call the toll-free number on the label. The companies are grateful for our com-

ments and most of the time will send a replacement coupon. They pass the information on to their consumer quality-control department.

SHORTCUTS AND SUBSTITUTES

Easy doughnuts. Here's a shortcut way to make doughnuts. Get generic dinner rolls. Pop a vanilla chip in the middle of each one, gently drop them in hot grease for about 45 seconds, and turn when golden. Take a brown lunch bag and fill with sugar, cinna-

COOKING OUT OF THE BOX

Here are some ideas for when you're making a "budget" meal, to make a packaged entrée taste more like homemade:

• Add onions and other veggies to boxed pasta mixes that are added to hamburger or tuna. Add the onions while browning the meat. Add some spices, too, to give it more of a homemade taste.

• Have a box of instant mashed potatoes and a jar of ready-made brown gravy? In a baking dish, put a layer of browned ground beef seasoned with your favorite spices, then top with the gravy, a can of corn, and a can of peas, add the prepared mashed potatoes, and sprinkle shredded cheese on top. Bake in a 350-degree oven until the cheese melts and the dish is heated through.

• The new packaged rice dishes that take only 90 seconds to make in the microwave are great. Add some browned ground beef or strips of grilled chicken breast with some favorite spices, and voilà—dinner in a snap!

• Chop up leftover steak or similar meat and heat. Also prepare a box of beef-seasoned boxed rice mix. Combine the two in a skillet and stir in a bag of mixed veggies. Heat and enjoy. Three food groups in one!

mon, or powdered sugar, and put the "doughnuts" in and give them a shake. Delicious!

Make burgers fast. When you're in a hurry to make hamburgers with ground beef, just add a little mild, chunky salsa. Salsa has everything you need: tomatoes, onions, and peppers.

Have fun with oatmeal and yogurt. Here are some delicious yogurt and oatmeal variations:

- Add bite-size pieces of fresh fruit.

- Put yogurt in ice-pop containers and freeze.

- Quick cobbler—add one package of instant cinnamon oatmeal to 3 to 4 ounces of applesauce in a casserole dish and bake in a 350-degree oven for about 25 to 30 minutes, or until slightly brown.

- Sprinkle yogurt with granola cereal.

Jazz up instant rice. When preparing instant rice, use Bloody Mary mix as the liquid ingredient. It makes a very tasty and easy-to-prepare dish. Another option is to use a can of vegetable juice as the liquid.

Make quick garlic toast. To make garlic toast for dinner in a hurry, put bread in the toaster. When it's done,

take it out, brush with melted butter, and sprinkle on some garlic powder.

Freeze flavoring and save time. To save time when cooking, do the following:

- Reconstitute about 2 cups of your favorite dried mushrooms. Put them in a blender and then pour the mixture into ice-cube trays and store the mushroom cubes in a plastic bag in the freezer. You will always have a quick flavor addition to any dish.

- This method works for tomato paste, too. Freeze tablespoons of tomato paste on a tray and store them in a plastic bag in the freezer. When a recipe calls for a tablespoon of paste, there is no need to open a whole can.

Enhance potpies. Cheap potpies don't contain a lot of chicken or veggies. To make them better, prepare small packets of bite-size cooked chicken and frozen peas and carrots (in sandwich bags) and freeze them. When baking potpies, microwave the packets and add to the potpies. It costs very little and makes the pie more of a meal without adding too many more calories or much more fat.

TASTY TIDBIT

Do you love pancakes? Well, here's a pancake pop quiz to see how much you really know about those golden, fluffy "cakes" most of us have come to love.

Question: Ready-made, self-rising pancake flour (a.k.a. pancake mix) was first introduced in what year?

a) 1889

b) 1900

c) 1923

d) 1951

The answer is "a." Pancake mix was developed way back in 1889 and has been a staple on pantry shelves ever since!

Substitute for maple syrup. For folks who do not care for maple flavoring in anything, or who are diabetic, here's an alternative to maple syrup. Melt butter to pour over your waffles or pancakes and then sprinkle with a mixture of cinnamon and sugar substitute.

Make yummy pancakes. When you get really hungry for pancakes but find that you're almost out of pancake mix, you can add white cake mix to the pancake flour for the recipe.

The pancakes will be very sweet, so skip the syrup and just put a bit of butter on them.

Pinch-hit for flour. In a pinch, you can substitute some pancake mix for flour in a recipe. Just keep in mind that the mix already has baking powder or soda, so don't add any.

Baking powder substitute. If your baking powder is bad (see the Baking and Bread section in this chapter for a way to test your baking powder), you can make some up in an emergency by mixing ¼ teaspoon baking soda and ½ teaspoon cream of tartar for each teaspoon of powder needed. Make up only as much as you need—it doesn't store well.

It's really not a good idea to refrigerate baking powder or baking soda that is used for baking. The moisture from the fridge can cause the products to react in the can or box, thus making them unusable.

Substitute for self-rising flour. If a recipe calls for 1 cup self-rising flour and you don't have any at home, you don't need to run out to buy some. You can use 1 cup all-purpose flour and add 1½ teaspoons baking powder and ½ teaspoon table salt.

Turn bread heels into buns. Bread heels make great hamburger buns. They do not get all soggy and squashed flat like store-bought buns. Brown the cut side a little in the oven broiler. Keep them in the freezer until you're having hamburger for dinner.

Substitute lemon juice. If you have no fresh lemon juice for a pie or other dessert recipe, substitute a little bit of powdered lemonade mix.

Disclose secret ingredients. If you are making an unusual substitution in a recipe that is going to be eaten by people other than your family, please, please don't keep it a secret!

There are a lot of people with fairly serious food allergies and sensitivities, and not knowing that you've substituted A for B in a dish could be fatal. At least, please let the host(ess) know what you put in the food; the host(ess) can then let anyone who is not supposed to eat a particular food know to avoid your dish, or, if someone inquires, you can answer the question.

BREAKFAST

Make instant oatmeal better. To cut the sugar in flavored instant oatmeal packets, add an equal amount of unflavored instant oats to the flavored oats. For the liquid, use all milk. It's still plenty sweet, and more economical as well.

HELPFUL SUBSTITUTES

Who hasn't been in the middle of making a recipe only to find that you are out of an ingredient? So, you are either forced to rush out to the store or attempt to find something that you can substitute.

Here are some substitutions that you might find helpful. But keep in mind that sometimes when you substitute, the flavor and texture of a recipe might not be the same:

- Apple-pie spice—For each teaspoon of seasoning, mix 1 teaspoon ground cinnamon and ⅛ teaspoon nutmeg.
- Baking powder—For each teaspoon needed, mix ¼ teaspoon baking soda and ½ teaspoon cream of tartar.
- Bread crumbs—Crush crackers, cereal, or chips to use in place of them.
- Buttermilk—For 1 cup, mix 1 tablespoon vinegar and 1 cup regular milk.
- Chocolate—Don't have a square of unsweetened chocolate for baking? Substitute 3 tablespoons unsweetened cocoa powder and 1 tablespoon cooking oil (or shortening) for one square.
- Cornstarch—For each tablespoon of cornstarch, use 2 tablespoons all-purpose flour.
- Tomato sauce—For 1 cup, mix ½ cup tomato paste and ½ cup water.

Make oatmeal in bulk. You can find numerous recipes online for making oatmeal in a slow cooker. You cook the oats overnight with water (with a variety of nutritious add-ins like dried cranberries), then add the milk in the morning—and eat all week!

Pre-prep oatmeal. To save time in the morning, make a batch of whole-grain cooked cereal for the week on Sunday. Prepare each bowl by portioning the cereal for one day at a time into microwaveable bowls, adding raisins, nuts, or sugar as desired. Then cover the bowls with plastic, refrigerate, and heat as needed in the morning before adding milk.

Give pancakes some zing. Add a teaspoon of vanilla to pancake batter to bring a zing to breakfast.

Try Oval Hot Cakes

Here's one of my mother's first syndicated columns, from September 1961, and it's perfect for today:

"Did you know, have you ever thought of, or have you ever tried . . . oval-shaped HOT CAKES?

"When you cook them in a round skillet or round grill, an oval shape will fit better and you can get more in! And besides . . . who ever said that pancakes had to be round? Grandmother? Oblong hot cakes also fit better on the plate. This leaves space for the bacon without all the syrup spreading into it.

"Another hint: If hot cakes stick to the grill . . . try adding more shortening to the batter.

"And did you know that any recipe that says 'and add one egg' could be made better by separating the white and the yolk? This includes cakes, waffles, hot cakes, etc.

"This white, when beaten separately, adds bubbles, tenderness and makes the finished product lighter. This is true for nearly all boxed items.

"The next time you have hot cakes, try adding two eggs with the whites and yolks separated. Beat yolks into batter as usual and then whip whites until stiff. Fold these egg whites into the batter just before cooking; even though the recipe calls for one egg . . . try using two."

Doesn't an oval- or even crescent-shaped pancake make sense, especially if you are serving other food on the plate? Give this a try, and I bet you and your family will love it.

TASTY TIDBIT

Here is a trivia question to add to your food knowledge: In the late 1800s, while trying to make cheese with cream and whole milk, a dairy man came up with what popular, multipurpose dairy product we use today?

Well, what do you think? The answer is cream cheese! And aren't we all glad this happened? Cream cheese makes a tasty, quick spread covered with salsa or chutney (I like to use a fork and make grooves in it first) and gives many desserts that extra-delicious taste.

Make shaped pancakes. Who said that pancakes had to be round or oval? When your kids are little, make them in animal shapes. It just takes a little imagination, and the kids love them!

Repackage pancake mix. Big boxes of pancake mix with the plastic bags inside always seem to make a mess when you try to fill measuring cups.

So, buy a large, inexpensive plastic container and fill it with the pancake mix. Then cut the original label off the pancake box and tape it onto the new plastic container. Everyone in the family will know what type of mix it holds.

Mold pancakes with cookie cutters. To make special pancakes for a special child when you don't have a shaped pancake mold, here's an idea. Spray the inside of a metal cookie cutter of the desired shape with cooking spray. When the skillet is hot enough, fill the cookie cutter with the batter. Just be sure to be careful if your cutter doesn't have a handle on it. When the pancake is cooked on one side, lift the cookie cutter (take care, it's hot!) and let the pancake drop out. Flip the pancake over to cook the other side.

Flavor cream cheese. Here's a way to make a breakfast English muffin a little more flavorful. After toasting the muffin, add some cream cheese and then sprinkle some berry-flavored gelatin powder over that.

Get the toast out. Here's how to get smaller-than-usual toast out of the toaster. Have you tried unplugging the toaster, turning it upside down or trying to flip the toast out? Use a wooden clothespin to grab it instead. You probably already have some in the kitchen to fasten opened chips and other foods.

Scrape the toast. When toast gets scorched or burnt, scrape the burnt part off while holding the bread upside down. It keeps the burnt crumbs from falling into the holes in the bread, leaving no burnt taste on the toast.

HELOÏSE WAFFLES

This waffle (or pancake) mix is a longtime favorite with my readers. To make waffles, you will need:

- 2 cups good biscuit mix
- 1 egg
- ½ cup oil
- 1⅓ cups club soda

Combine the above ingredients and use a large spoon to blend—don't overmix! Then simply add to a hot waffle iron, and when done you will have delicious waffles; or make as pancakes.

Keep in mind that this mix doesn't keep, so only make as much as you are going to use at one time. Remember, cook them ASAP so they will be fluffy! Don't let the batter set and go flat.

To make the waffles a little more healthful, add ½ cup each of wheat germ and flaxseed (it will make the waffles a little crunchy).

Save the sausage. If you like to have a sausage biscuit for breakfast once in a while, what can you do with the rest of the sausage roll after you cut a slice or two? Slice the rest into serving pieces, cover them with waxed paper, and put them in the freezer. After they are frozen, put them in a plastic freezer bag. When you want sausage, just remove what you need from the bag.

Mix up the cereal. If your kids love to eat cereal for breakfast, when you have several nearly empty boxes, let them mix up the cereals in their bowls to make something new.

They might even get excited about coming up with new names for their concoctions.

EGGS, MILK, AND CHEESE

Mark the oldest eggs. When you have several eggs in your refrigerator, put an "X" on the ones to use first. Or go one step further, and write on the shells in pencil the carton expiration date. The pencil marks do not penetrate the shell or rub off, even when you soft- or hard-boil the eggs.

I.D. hard-cooked eggs. Keep a couple of hard-cooked eggs on hand to

---

EGG-PEELING SECRETS

What's the secret to peeling hard-cooked eggs? Peel an egg by cracking the shell all over and rolling it between your hands to help loosen it. Hold the egg under water and start at the large end to begin peeling.

Source: The American Egg Board

TASTY TIDBIT

Did you know that certain hens can lay colored eggs? The eggs of different breeds of chickens can be blue, green, yellow, and even red. While you might be able to find only brown and white at the grocery store, the colored eggs are interesting.

make a quick lunch. So as not to confuse them with fresh eggs in the refrigerator, add some dry onion skins to the water when cooking the eggs. This colors the eggshells. It's a natural dye and makes it easy to tell which ones are the hard-cooked eggs.

I.D. hard-cooked eggs another way. When boiling eggs, put a few drops of food coloring and a splash of vinegar in the water. Let the eggs stay a bit longer in the water until you can see the color on them. It makes them easily identifiable as hard-cooked eggs, and it takes only a few seconds.

Heat up the sauce. If you love picante sauce on your scrambled eggs but don't like to put cold sauce on hot eggs, here's a solution. You can try putting the sauce in the eggs while cooking, but you might not care for the texture or color of the eggs. So, after the eggs are out of the pan, pour some of the sauce in the skillet for a few seconds and stir—hot sauce! Your eggs will stay hot longer.

Keep egg yolks intact. To prevent broken yolks when frying eggs, when it's time to flip the egg, pour a little water into the bottom of the pan and cover it. The top of the egg will cook a bit from the steam, making it stronger, and then it's safe to flip the egg.

Peel hard-boiled eggs with ease. Hard-boiled (technically called hard-cooked) eggs are usually hard to peel if the eggs are fresh. So, when you plan on hard-cooking some, buy them about a week ahead of time if you can. The American Egg Board suggests the following method to get perfect eggs:

Put the eggs in a pan in a single

TASTY TIDBIT

Here's some "egg-stra" information about eggs and their grading. According to the American Egg Board, there is no nutritional difference between grade AA, A, and B eggs, and no difference between brown- and white-shelled eggs. The breed of hen determines the color of the eggshell. For instance, brown eggs are produced by hens with red feathers and earlobes, while white eggs are from hens with white feathers and earlobes.

When most recipes for baked goods (such as cakes, casseroles, and custards) call for an egg, they mean a large egg.

layer, add enough cold water to cover by about 1 inch, then bring them to a boil. Cover, remove from the heat, and let stand 15 to 17 minutes. Pour off the hot water and cover with cold water.

I've been experimenting, and here is what I now do: I cook the eggs as described, pour off the hot water, shake the pan to crack the shells, then add ice cubes and water, replacing them when the ice melts. Let the eggs sit about 30 to 45 minutes, then peel. You just might be surprised at how easily they peel. Many times the eggshells just float off.

A secret ingredient for deviled eggs. To make egg salad "egg-stra" special,

On the Light Side ~~~~~~~~~~

Don't Call Them Deviled Eggs

A reader sent in this funny story: "My niece, Sara, and I made deviled eggs quite a bit because she loved them. One time I mentioned that they were just too delicious to be called 'deviled.' I thought for a moment and then said, 'Let's call them angel-ed eggs!' We just loved that suggestion and have called them that ever since. I've told the story to friends across the country, and many now refer to them as 'angel-ed' eggs." Another reader's young daughter, Audrey, called them "doubled eggs" because they seemed to have double the yolk in them when they were prepared.

add a small can of deviled ham to the yolk mixture.

If you add a large can of the ham, you will have extra left over that you can put on crackers and eat as a snack.

Another filling for deviled eggs. Coleslaw dressing is thick and creamy, and makes a nice change from mayonnaise in deviled eggs. Another one of my faves is blue-cheese dressing.

Fill deviled eggs easily. When you make more than six deviled eggs, it's hard to keep them from sliding around when you fill them. Put them in minicupcake papers to makes the eggs stay in place.

To make the egg mixture, put cooked egg yolks in a zipper-top bag. Seal and mash until they are all broken up. Add the rest of the ingredients, reseal, and keep mixing thoroughly. Cut off a corner of the bag and squeeze the mixture into the hollowed-out eggs. Just throw the bag away when done for an easy cleanup.

Transport deviled eggs. When you need to transport deviled eggs to a gathering, spray a length of plastic wrap with cooking spray, to prevent the eggs from smearing in transit, and cover the eggs with the wrap. Or, lightly smear some solid shortening on the plastic wrap instead of the cooking spray.

Transport deviled eggs, take 2. If you are making a large amount of deviled eggs and you do not have a plate large enough to hold them all, use an 18-egg foam carton, place the eggs in the hollows, and close the cover. You can refrigerate and transport them that way.

Just be sure either to wash the carton well with soap and water and then dry it or to line it with plastic wrap before putting the eggs into it.

Make lots of egg salad fast. Here's a hint for preparing large amounts of eggs. After boiling, cut the eggs in half

TASTY TIDBIT

Does the shell of an egg protect it from bacteria? We went to the experts at the American Egg Board. What did they have to say? Well, they say yes and no! "The egg has many natural, built-in barriers to help prevent bacteria from entering and growing. These protect the egg on its way from the hen to your home. But, although it does help, the porous shell itself is not a foolproof bacterial barrier." For further safety, government regulations require that eggs be carefully washed with special detergent and sanitized. Then, the hen's original protective shell coating is generally replaced by a thin spray coating of a tasteless, odorless, harmless, natural mineral oil. A shiny shell indicates oiling, rather than an unsafe or old egg.

TASTY TIDBIT

Let's test your Heloise Hint egg IQ. Is the following statement true or false? You might crack a raw egg and find no yolk or two yolks.

This is "no yolk"! If you chose "true," then you are one smart egg! Double yolks are common in young or old hens. And although rare, a young hen might lay an egg with no yolk at all!

with a sharp knife and scoop from the shell with a spoon (yellows and whites can be separated). To chop, use a potato masher to make the job go a lot faster.

Mix up eggs. Use an electric mixer to mash peeled, hard-cooked eggs for egg salad. Add a little mayo or salad dressing before beating. This also works for mashing the yolks to make deviled eggs.

Make fast egg salad for one. Yet another, very simple suggestion for chopping an egg for egg salad: Place a peeled, hard-cooked egg in a coffee mug. Take a sharp steak knife and chop away! No mess, and in moments, you can add mayo and mix.

Here's another quick way to make egg salad for one: Scramble an egg or two, cool, then mix with mayo, seasonings, onion, and celery.

Soften butter. When butter is too cold to spread, turn a hot bowl over it and it will barely soften, but not melt. Your bowl can be made warm by filling it with hot water from your tap for a few minutes.

Shave butter better. If a recipe calls for finely shaved butter, use your cheese slicer—the result is nice, even slices to cover the mix you are making.

Tame hot peppers with milk. Did you know that milk is the best thing to drink when you've taken a bite of food that is too spicy hot? The casein in the milk helps quickly cool down your mouth. So, give it a try the next time those jalapeños are too hot!

SALADS

MY MOTHER'S COLESLAW

This slaw is better if made a bit ahead of time so that all the flavors have time to blend together. It's a tasty side dish.
You will need:
  1 head cabbage (about 2 pounds)
  Ice water to cover
  2 ounces vegetable oil
  1 ounce vinegar, lime juice, or lemon juice
  (not all three)

½ teaspoon prepared mustard
½ teaspoon celery salt
1 ounce mayonnaise
Salt and pepper to taste
Dash of paprika

Shred the cabbage and soak in the water for 30 minutes. Meanwhile, mix together the remaining ingredients. Drain the cabbage and mix in the dressing. Refrigerate until ready to use.

Put the potatoes in last. When making potato salad, put all the ingredients for the potato salad except the potatoes in a bowl and mix thoroughly. Then put the potatoes into the bowl and stir into the ingredients. This method ensures that all the potatoes are coated with the salad dressing. If you put the potatoes in the bowl first and then add the dressing, the potatoes may break up from all the stirring.

TASTY TIDBIT

Did you know that cabbage is part of the Brassica family? What other veggies share the same family?

a) cauliflower

b) broccoli

c) Brussels sprouts

d) all of the above

  If you guessed "d," all of the above, you are right!

Simplify potato salad. When you're in a hurry to produce a large amount of potato salad, here's a timesaver. Instead of boiling the spuds in the jackets, cooling, then cutting them into pieces, peel and chop them, then steam the pieces in a steamer basket for about 20 minutes. No burned fingers, no mess, and no mushy, water-logged potatoes.

RED, WHITE, AND BLUE POTATO SALAD

This recipe came from a reader in Hawaii who sent in a recipe for the Great Heloise Potato Salad Challenge. It is delicious! You will need:

2 pounds small red-skin potatoes (unpeeled), washed and boiled
1 bunch green onions, sliced, saving the tops for garnishing
1 can water chestnuts (drained), diced
8 ounces blue cheese, crumbled
10 ounces sour cream
½ cup white-wine vinegar
1 tablespoon celery seed
1 tablespoon dillweed
Salt and pepper to taste
Paprika (optional)

Slice just-cooled (but not cold) potatoes and put into a large bowl. Add green onions and water chestnuts to potatoes. Mix blue cheese, sour cream, vinegar, celery seed, and dillweed together and pour over potato mix. Stir gently. (Warm potatoes absorb the flavors better.) Add salt and pepper to taste. Sprinkle paprika and remaining green-onion tops over potato mix. Chill for 2 hours or overnight, which is best for flavors to blend.

Use chilled tuna for salad. If you love tuna salad, keep a couple of cans of tuna in the refrigerator so that when you make the salad, it's already cool.

And keep a can of peas in the fridge standing at the ready for a quick chilled pea salad.

Use a fork for tuna salad. When preparing tuna salad, it's easy to get the proper amount of mayo out of the jar with a fork. Tap the fork against the top of the jar, and most of the mayo is released. Tap the base of the fork prongs to release the rest of the mayo from the fork. Use two forks to really "toss" tuna salad—they work much

TASTY TIDBIT

Test your milk IQ: How many pounds of milk does it take to make 1 pound of cheese?

a) 1

b) 5

c) 10

d) 20

The answer is "c." It takes 10 pounds of milk!

better than a spoon. Not only is it more economical to use a fork, but you will no longer have a yucky spoon in the sink or dishwasher.

SOUPS

Make soup from leftovers. Have you ever come home from work and realized that you have nothing planned for dinner yet, and everyone is asking, "When are we going to eat?" Sound familiar?

Instead of ordering fast food, you can whip up a healthy and hearty soup with all those leftovers in the refrigerator. Just grab a big pot or saucepan and add a few cups of water and some beef, chicken, or vegetable bouillon. Look in the fridge for any leftover chicken, and cut into bite-size pieces. Season with your favorite spices and simmer for a few minutes. Hopefully, your family won't recognize the leftovers, and you will have saved time and money.

You can also make this "refrigerator soup" by starting with a few cans of chopped tomatoes, water, and bouillon, then adding fresh, frozen, or canned vegetables. Sprinkle each bowl

SOUP'S ON

When cooler days are upon us, doesn't a nice, warm bowl of soup sound perfect? Soup can be a light snack or a main meal when combined with a sandwich and salad. Here are some quick soup ideas from Heloise Central:

- Here's a quick soup from the pantry: Use tomato or vegetable juice as the base, add a cube or two of beef bouillon, and then toss in whatever fresh veggies you have on hand. Let simmer and enjoy!

- To make a quick egg-drop soup, use chicken bouillon for the base and add seasonings (my favorite is Italian seasoning, which has a blend of about five spices), then swirl in a beaten egg or two and cook.

- A great soup meal is to use a bean mix package and pop it into a slow cooker with water according to package directions. You can add cooked hamburger meat or even some sausage, and it is delicious. This will need to cook all day—but it is worth the wait! And it can be cooking while you are working.

- To stretch soup or make it into more of a meal, add rice, noodles, macaroni, or barley. Always keep your pantry stocked with some of these staples, and you can whip up "almost from scratch" soup.

with some Parmesan cheese or croutons. Add a salad and rolls or crackers, and you're all set.

Make a quick soup. When you are in a great hurry, make a quick version of egg-drop soup. Take one can of green peas, rinse them off (to lower the salt content), and place in a pot. Add water or chicken broth, and after it comes to a boil, turn it off and add two soft-scrambled eggs to make a quick soup. With a slice of crusty bread, it will satisfy you until you can cook a full meal.

Two variations: Beat two raw eggs together, then swirl them in the liquid a few times and cover to finish cooking, instead of adding cooked scrambled eggs. Or, mash the peas before you put them in the pot.

Strain your broth. If you should happen to run out of cheesecloth to filter the broth for your homemade soups, you can use a coffee filter.

Use vegetables trimmings to make compost. If you like to cook soups, try making several kinds on Sunday and having them on hand for the rest of the week. If you end up with a lot of vegetable trimmings, don't put them in the garbage.

To make cleanup quick and easy, take a plastic grocery bag and line a

TASTY TIDBITS

Did you know that cheddar cheese is the most popular cheese in the world? Cheddar is a hard, natural cheese that can range in color from white to yellow. The strong yellowish orange color is usually produced by a color additive. Cheddar has a slightly crumbly texture and is delicious added to just about anything—salads and scrambled eggs, for instance—and is part of one of my favorites, a grilled cheese sandwich with tomatoes and jalapeños!

large bowl to put your peels and trimmings in. When you are finished, take the organic waste from the vegetables and use the bag to carry it to your compost pile. Then properly recycle the plastic bag. The bowl that you used only needs a wipe and it's clean.

GARDEN CHEDDAR SOUP

There's no better way to warm up a chilly day than to make a delicious pot of soup. And so I have a recipe for you that's a little bit different. It's Garden Cheddar Soup, and to make it, you'll need:

2 carrots, peeled and sliced
2 small zucchini, halved and sliced
2 tomatoes, peeled and cut into wedges
1 celery stalk, sliced
1 cup portobello mushrooms, sliced
1 onion, halved and sliced

2 cloves garlic, minced
4½ cups beef broth
1½ cups tomato juice
1 tablespoon fresh basil, minced
½ cup dry red wine
½ teaspoon salt
½ teaspoon ground pepper
2 tablespoons fresh parsley, minced
1 cup shredded cheddar cheese

In a stockpot, add the first nine ingredients and heat to boiling. Reduce heat and simmer, covered, for 30 minutes or until vegetables are tender.

Stir in basil, wine, salt, pepper, and parsley just before serving. Sprinkle the top of each serving with a little cheddar cheese.

Cool soup quickly. Is your soup too hot to eat? Simply toss in some frozen veggies, an ice cube or two, or even a dash of tomato juice, milk, or cold bouillon, depending on the soup base.

FAT-FREE CREAM SOUP BASE

To try this recipe, you'll need:
1 cup nonfat dried milk powder
1 tablespoon dried onion flakes
2 tablespoons cornstarch
2 tablespoons chicken bouillon powder
½ teaspoon dried basil
½ teaspoon dried thyme
¼ teaspoon black pepper

Put all of the above ingredients in a large saucepan with 2 cups cold water. Cook on medium, stirring *continuously*. Once it becomes thick, add your main ingredient—

2 cans of artichoke hearts (pureed in the blender or food processor), broccoli, leftover shredded chicken, chopped celery, sliced mushrooms, or whatever you like.

Thicken a soup. If you need to thicken a soup, just add some instant mashed potatoes, a little at a time (you can use them to thicken stews and gravies, too). Or puree some vegetables, like broccoli, with some bouillon and add that.

PASTA, PIZZA, AND RICE

Give someone a home-cooked meal. Double your sauce recipe the next time you make spaghetti and make a batch

TASTY TIDBIT

Here is a question Heloise Central received: Can you eat canned soup right out of the can, cold? A major soup manufacturer we contacted said yes! Soup can be eaten from the can because it already has been cooked and then packed into cans. The manufacturer did admit that it is usually better when warmed up.

It is always best to check what the manufacturer of the brand of soup has to say. The soup usually has contact information on the product label. Give the manufacturer a call, or check the Web site. And enjoy the soup!

of lasagna to take to a son or daughter in a nearby college, a homebound relative, or an elderly neighbor. Just add a loaf of fresh garlic bread.

Quit twirling spaghetti. If you like to cut up spaghetti to eat it, cutting it up with a knife and fork can be time-consuming. To save time, grab the pizza cutter, and, after a few quick "run-throughs," your spaghetti will be in small, manageable bites. The pizza cutter works great for slicing garlic bread as well.

Shorten spaghetti all at once. When you break long spaghetti over the pot of boiling water, it can go every which way. Instead, bend the cardboard box before you get to the pot, then just pour in the spaghetti.

Signal if you've salted the water. As busy cooks put water on to boil for pasta, there always seems to be some kind of interruption. When you return to the pot, the question is, "Did I salt this or not?" To eliminate this problem, when you add salt, throw in a few grains of black pepper. This is not enough to alter the taste, but it is visible when you're ready to add the pasta.

Prevent boil-overs. To keep pasta from boiling over, give the inside rim of the pot a good coating of nonstick vegetable spray. Also, if you give the colander a light spray, none of the pasta will stick to it, either. You can also add a tablespoon of cooking oil.

Keep lasagna from tearing. Here are some ways to keep cooked lasagna noodles from tearing:

- You can boil them in a 13-by-9-inch oblong pan that is safe to put on the stove. Make sure the pan is safe for the stove top or the heat will crack it.

- Or, add oil to the water to keep the noodles separated. The real trick is to slowly pour them out into a colander and pour cold water on them. I used to take them out one by one, and they always ripped.

Cover with a cookie sheet. Use a cookie sheet to cover lasagna (or any

TASTY TIDBIT

Did you know that there are more than 300 types of pasta? Cooked pasta without sauce or filling is relatively low in fat and calories, and has very small amounts, if any, of sodium and cholesterol. It is what you put on or in the pasta that affects the final calorie and fat counts. Pasta is available dried or fresh. Fresh pasta should be refrigerated (up to 4 days), and it can even be frozen for up to 2 months.

So, use your noodle and get creative the next time you have a penchant for pasta!

TASTY TIDBIT

Let's test your pasta IQ. How many different pasta shapes are available around the world?

a) 200

b) 400

c) 600

The answer is "c," according to the National Pasta Association.

other casserole) to be baked in the oven. It's better than fooling with aluminum foil.

Get the last drop. Get the most from a bottled pasta sauce. Put some of the cooked noodles in the jar to "rinse" the bottle out. It is better than using water because you get more of the sauce without watering it down.

If the bottle needs further rinsing for recycling, then use water.

Doctor jar sauce. Pasta sauce in a jar is convenient, but it can be watery. Adding a 6-ounce can of seasoned tomato paste to a 26-ounce jar of pasta sauce is an easy way to make a much thicker and richer sauce.

Reheat pizza. Here's a great way to reheat a slice of pizza. Heat a small amount of olive oil in a heavy or nonstick pan. Set the heat to medium-low and heat until warm. Place the pizza slice in the pan, taking care not to burn the bottom of the pizza as you reheat it. You can even use this method on pizza that is a few days old. This method keeps the crust crispy, and the pizza tastes like it just came fresh out of the pizza oven.

Reheat pizza in a microwave and pan. For pizza with a crispy crust, microwave one or two slices at a time for 15 to 20 seconds, to heat the toppings. Then place the slices in a nonstick frying pan to get the crust crispy. No more soggy crust, and you don't have to heat your entire oven. Cleanup is easy, too.

Keep rice from sticking. When cooking rice in a rice cooker, spray the bottom with a nonstick spray so that the rice does not stick to the bottom.

Make an extra portion. When you cook rice, make more than needed for one meal. Put the remainder in a gallon-size freezer bag, flatten, and freeze it. When a recipe calls for rice, simply break off what you need.

TASTY TIDBIT

Did you know that more than 2.5 billion pizzas are sold yearly in our 50 states? That's a lot of pie! What do you think the favorite topping is? The answer is pepperoni.

Make easy Spanish-style rice. Use a can of diced regular tomatoes and green chiles to make a simple Spanish-type rice. If you use a rice cooker, the liquid part of the tomatoes can be used as part of the measured water that is

Italian Spaghetti Sauce

My mother, the original Heloise, printed her Italian Spaghetti Sauce recipe in the early sixties, and it has been a favorite of readers for many years.

You'll need:

¼ cup olive oil
½ cup butter
1 cup finely chopped onions
1 pound ground beef
4 strips finely chopped bacon
4 cloves garlic, finely chopped
3 tablespoons finely chopped fresh parsley
1 bay leaf, finely chopped
1 tablespoon salt
Freshly ground pepper to taste
1 teaspoon crushed dry red pepper
2 ounces red wine
2 15-ounce cans whole tomatoes or tomato sauce
1 small can tomato paste
1 cup water
1 carrot, finely chopped

Heat olive oil over low heat in a pot large enough to hold all the ingredients. Add butter and simmer until melted. Add onions and sauté until lightly browned. Add ground beef and bacon; sauté until browned, stirring occasionally.

Add garlic, parsley, bay leaf, salt, pepper, and red pepper. Cook over low heat for 10 minutes. Add wine, cover, and "steam" for a few more minutes.

Add tomatoes, tomato paste, and water. Bring to a boil and add the chopped carrot. Cover and cook over low heat, stirring occasionally. Remove the bay leaf and discard. Get ready to enjoy this tasty sauce! It seems to get better the next day.

A nice gift for a new mom would be to fill a large jar with this sauce, write out the recipe, add a box of pasta and a loaf of Italian or French bread, and put it all in a pretty basket.

TASTY TIDBIT

Are you ready to test your Heloise Hint IQ? Here's your question: What is wild rice—just another variety of rice? Well, what do you think? If you determined that they are not the same, then you are right on the money. Wild rice is not even related to rice. It is the seed of an aquatic grass that grows in swampy areas. The good news is that you can add it to plain rice to liven it up a little by giving it a crunchy texture.

added to the rice. Lightly sautéed onion (and, if desired, bell pepper) may be added to the uncooked tomatoes.

Spanish-style rice, take 2. There are many variations of Spanish rice. You can make instant "Spanish" rice with Bloody Mary mix or vegetable juice.

Here's another variation: Use the desired amount of dry rice (either quick-cooking or converted), and use a mixture of half water and half salsa for the liquid. Add a tablespoon of margarine per cup of rice and have a perfect accompaniment to any meal. If you use a "chunky," thick salsa, you may find that the dish needs more water or broth. So, folks, you need to test this yourself and undercook it a little so you can add more water if needed.

MEATS

Another way to cook bacon. Take a piece of bacon (not frozen) and dip it in nothing but flour and then fry as usual. Flour gives it more body and makes a beautiful crust!

Freeze bacon. Whenever bacon goes on sale, buy several pounds. Then take the bacon and roll it in waxed paper one slice at a time until you have a large roll. When you want a slice or two, just take it from the freezer and unroll.

Freeze bacon strips, take 2. Always have some bacon in the freezer. When you buy a package of bacon, tear off several pieces of waxed paper and lay about five strips across one of the pieces of waxed paper, then top it with another piece of waxed paper and repeat, until all the bacon has been separated. Then slide the stack into a large plastic bag and place it in the freezer. When you need a few pieces of bacon for a special recipe, simply grab what you need out of the freezer, without having to defrost an entire package of bacon.

Freeze a taste of summer. When cooler weather arrives in fall, many people get ready to put their grills away for the winter. Before you do, buy a couple packages of hamburger, make into patties, and fire up the grill one last time. After cooking and cooling, put the patties in sandwich bags, then into a large freezer bag and freeze.

After the holidays, when the winter blahs set in, 2 minutes or less in the microwave will give you a juicy, just-off-the-grill-flavored hamburger for an indoor picnic to remind you that spring is just around the corner

Drain fat easily. To drain the fat from ground beef, put a spaghetti drainer (colander) inside a bowl and dump the meat into the drainer. Put the meat into whatever you are cooking. Let the fat cool and put it in an empty butter or cottage cheese carton for disposal—don't let any of the fat go down the drain.

Make no-stick meatballs. To keep hamburger meat from sticking to your hands when you are forming meatballs, simply run your hands under water. The meat will not stick to your hands.

Mix meatballs in a bag. Use a plastic bag to mix meatballs. Then cut off the corner of the bag and "pipe" the meatballs onto the baking pan. Throw the bag away when you are finished. It's neat and easy.

Stretch meatloaf. Here are some fillers to add to meatloaf to help stretch it and give it a special flavor and texture. Give one or more a try:

- Crushed cornflakes

- Oatmeal

- Bread crumbs

- Grated carrots

- Dried bread cubes

- Crushed potato chips or corn chips

- Crushed crackers

- Cornmeal

- Croutons

- Pretzels

 Curl-Free Bacon

When you fry bacon, keep it from curling. Fry it in your regular frying pan and place the bottom of another pan directly over the bacon itself, then put it over very low heat. Result? Nice, flat pieces of bacon that have not shrunk.

An unusual meatloaf additive. One more add-in for meatloaf is sugar-coated flakes of breakfast cereal. It might sound strange, but the sugar takes the edge off the ketchup if you also use that.

More meatloaf additions. When you make meatloaf, you can use instant potatoes and vegetable juice.

Try a different meatloaf sauce. When making meatloaf, try using your favorite barbecue sauce or salsa instead of tomato sauce.

Spice up meatloaf. Add finely chopped jalapeños to your meatloaf mix and to your taco meat when you're cooking it.

A secret meatloaf ingredient. Here's a novel twist on meatloaf. To make it, prepare your usual mixture, but spread it thin on a sheet of waxed paper, then spread a thin layer of drained sauerkraut over all of it. From one edge, roll up (it helps if you chill it a little) like a tube. Bake as usual. Even folks who don't like sauerkraut love this meatloaf. You can also use this trick with grilled burgers—mix up some sauerkraut in your ground-beef patties.

Make a better meatloaf. Beans make a better meatloaf filler and are much healthier and tastier than bread, cereals, or oatmeal. Add a cup of canned

TASTY TIDBIT

Let's test your ground-beef (hamburger) knowledge. In 1888, an English doctor prescribed three hamburger meals a day as a cure for various ailments. His name is remembered today as the name of a seasoned ground-beef patty served with gravy. What's the doctor's name? Salisbury!

Thanks to the Iowa Beef Industry Council for this piece of trivia.

black or pinto beans (or replace half a cup or so of the hamburger if you don't need a large meatloaf) to your regular meatloaf. Beans add vitamins, fiber, and protein, and are tasty, too.

Mix meatloaf. Try using regular household rubber gloves when mixing up meatloaf. Your hands will stay clean, and, if you have mild arthritis, they might not hurt as much while you mix the meatloaf.

Make unsoggy meatloaf. When you cook a meatloaf, put two slices of bread on the bottom of the pan first. The meatloaf won't cook in the drippings and get soggy. It makes for a faster cleanup, too.

Make small loaves. If you love meatloaf but don't want to make a large loaf, make up your favorite recipe and form the meat into patties a little thicker than ordinary ground-beef patties. Separate them into small plastic bags, or use plastic wrap, and freeze. Then, you can take out and thaw only as many as you need for your meal. They cook a lot faster than a big meatloaf.

Make meatloaf more appealing. To make meatloaf more appealing to non–meatloaf lovers, try this twist. Make the meat mixture and put half of it in the loaf pan, then sprinkle a generous amount of cheese on top of the mixture. Put the rest of the meat on top of that.

Make a meatloaf sandwich. Cut meatloaf into slices and make a grilled cheese and meatloaf sandwich. Put a slice of cheese on each slice of bread and top with a slice of meatloaf. Spray each side of the bread with butter spray. Grill as you would any grilled cheese sandwich.

Vintage Heloise

Meatloaf Mania

My mother, the original Heloise (1919–1977), started this column in 1959. In her book *Hints for Working Women* (1970), she had a lot to say about meatloaf—who knew? Here's the short version:

"Dear Readers: When all else fails (including your brain and budget!) and the prices of other meats are the cost of gold inlays . . . remember hamburger, and let's make meatloaf.

"Speaking as a working woman, let me say that one should never make one loaf at a time. Always make at least two. You can freeze one of them uncooked, cooked completely, or partially cook it and then freeze. I like the last way best because on our 'tired days' it takes less time to cook if we are in a hurry. And just who isn't nowadays?

"Meatloaf is great when served hot the first night with baked potatoes (and always throw in a few extras because they can be pan-fried or used for making potato salad the next day). As long as that oven is going, utilize that heat at the same time. Saves more money.

"The next night you can slice your loaf in thick pieces and broil under your broiler. Delicious when spread with oleo [oleo margarine, meaning margarine], barbecue sauce, or chili sauce. And what a change it makes for your taste buds, as it disguises the hamburger in a big way.

"It can always be pan-fried quickly for either open- or closed-faced sandwiches; diced and when slightly browned, scrambled with eggs for a quick hot meal."

Can't you just hear her chatty voice and smell the meatloaf? Good advice then, and good today!

TASTY TIDBIT

Let's check your Heloise Hint IQ for black beans. What else are they sometimes called?

a) bird beans

b) dog beans

c) turtle beans

If you picked "c," turtle beans, then you are right on target. They are sometimes called this because they are dark black, shiny, and look kind of like a turtle shell.

When using leftover meatloaf that has been refrigerated or frozen, warm the slices for a few seconds in the microwave to make sure the meat is warmed through. You can make a meatloaf for just this purpose to experiment with using different seasonings.

Frost a meatloaf. Here is a way to serve meatloaf and potatoes all in one. Make the meatloaf and let it cook through. Then make mashed potatoes and "frost" the meatloaf's top and sides, just like a cake, and then put it under the broiler to brown the top just a little. After it's sliced, you have the meat and potatoes.

Defining the fajita. Fajita literally means "little belt" or "little strips," and therefore any meat that can be cut into little strips can be called fajitas. The classic cut of beef for fajitas is skirt steak.

Make tacos healthier. When making tacos at home using a seasoning packet, replace half of the ground beef with the same amount of black beans. It is delicious and more nutritious, and kids love it. It is cost-saving, too.

Use cereal bags to pound meat. Instead of using plastic wrap for pounding meat, use the waxed bags from cereal boxes. They are much stronger and do not tear when you flatten meats or poultry.

Contain meat juices. When you carve meat, first place a cookie sheet under the cutting board. The juices will go on the cookie sheet instead of all over the counter.

Save meat juices. Use tongs rather than a fork when turning meat to save the juices.

Wrap individual dogs. When you buy a package of hot dogs, the first thing to do is get the hot dogs ready for the freezer. Lay out a piece of plastic wrap, place a hot dog on the end and roll it over, then place another hot dog and roll it, and repeat using as many pieces as you need. Then place the wrapped hot dogs in a self-sealing, plastic freezer bag. Then you can remove one or two as needed, and they won't stick together.

Seal your own meals. When you're a retired empty-nester or single, you don't have to give up buying the economical family-sized bargain packages of meats. Divide them into meal-size portions and use a vacuum food sealer. If you like, you can season the meat before sealing it. Buy several pounds of salmon when it goes on sale, sprinkle it liberally with lemon pepper and dill, seal it in meal-sized portions, freeze, and it's ready to bake when thawed.

Buy hamburger on sale. Buy hamburger when it is on sale to save money. Brown most of it in a pan and package it for the freezer.

Another strategy is to buy 10-pound hamburger packages and cut through the plastic packaging into convenient sizes for different dishes. Put the smaller portions in freezer bags for meals later. It's easy to package that way.

TALKING TURKEY 101

Heloise Central has helpful hints to help you prepare the perfect turkey.

- Don't know how big a turkey to buy? You will need about 1 to 1½ pounds of uncooked turkey per person if you want leftovers. Don't want leftovers? Then buy only 1 pound per person.
- If you buy a frozen turkey, be sure it's frozen solid and the wrapping isn't torn.
- If you buy a fresh turkey, don't buy or pick it up until a day or two before you plan on cooking it.
- When turkey shopping, take the bird home right away and keep it in the refrigerator.

How to defrost the bird? For defrosting in the refrigerator, you need to allow about 24 hours' thawing time for every 5 pounds. Be sure to place the turkey on a platter or on a baking sheet with sides to contain raw juices. *Never* thaw a turkey at room temperature! You can also thaw a turkey in a sink full of cold water, but you must change the water every 30 minutes or so when it warms up. The turkey will take about 60 minutes per 2 pounds to thaw in the sink. For example, a 20-pound turkey would take 10 hours.

And lastly, how do you know when the turkey is done? The turkey should be cooked until a meat thermometer reads 180 to 185 degrees F and the juices run clear. Place the thermometer deep in the thigh of the turkey without touching bone. Allow the turkey to rest for 15 to 20 minutes before carving so the juices will settle and carving will be easier.

POULTRY

Cook and freeze chicken. There are so many great recipes that call for cooked chicken, like chicken and noodles, chicken salad, and many, many casseroles and dips. To save money and time, buy chicken on sale and cook it in a slow cooker with onion, celery, and carrots. When cooked and cooled, shred the meat and put it in sandwich bags, 1 cup in each bag. Freeze the small bags in a large freezer bag.

On days that you are busy, work late, or just don't want to fuss with cooking, the bags take only a few minutes to thaw in a microwave.

Freeze meat in portions. Wrap chicken parts, steaks, pork chops, and other meats individually with plastic wrap, then put in a freezer bag. Not only can you remove just the number of pieces you need, but they thaw quicker, too.

Roast half a turkey. When you purchase a Thanksgiving turkey, ask if the turkey has a leg clamp, and if it does, have the butcher cut the turkey in half. This can be done to fresh or frozen turkeys. Also ask the butcher to put some plastic between the halves, and when you get home, separate them. Freeze the second half to enjoy later. When you roast the turkey, place it on foil, cut side down. You get to enjoy fresh-roasted turkey twice for the same price and half the roasting time. This way, you can purchase a larger turkey that gives a better yield of meat per pound.

SEAFOOD

Seafood should be separate. Did you know that you should never buy cooked seafood if it is displayed in the same case as raw fish? The reason is that the raw fish can contaminate the cooked.

Keep the instructions. After you remove some frozen fish sticks from their original box to cook for your kids, put the remaining fish sticks in a plastic freezer bag for future lunches.

Before throwing away the empty box, cut out the cooking preparation panel from the box so that you can reference the cooking instructions when you cook more fish sticks.

Fry fish the old-fashioned way. For an old-fashioned fish fry, instead of dredging in flour or bread crumbs, use crushed potato chips. The flavor is

Ageless Chicken

Here's a blast-from-the-past column that my mother, the original Heloise, wrote more than 30 years ago. I had to edit it down because of limited space in today's newspapers, but her voice and the "meat" of her hint are as valuable and enjoyable to read today as they were then.

"Dear Chicken Lovers:

"I have been test-cooking 2- and 2½-pound broilers (split in half) for four days now, trying to find a way that was fail-proof for tender chicken . . . chicken that could also be barbecued without using a barbecue grill.

"And, so help me, I have tested so many chickens that I'm beginning to cackle!

"But since chicken is just about one of the most inexpensive meats on the market, I think this is a fantabulous recipe for you folks, so here goes . . .

"First, remove your broiler pan and set it aside.

"Second, turn your oven to 325 degrees. (Set the shelf in the center of your oven.)

"Rub the inside AND outside of the chicken halves with softened oleo [margarine]. Then salt and pepper well.

"Lay chicken skin-side DOWN in a shallow pan with sides.

"Then completely cover the pan of chicken with foil, making sure that all the edges are tucked under thoroughly.

"Now you are ready to put the chicken in the oven. The important step is [that] your oven is preheated to 325 degrees. Put the pan on the center shelf, set a timer for 50 minutes and don't peek.

"When the timer rings, remove the pan and take off the foil. If you want to use barbecue sauce, this is the time to spoon some in the cavity of each half. Place the chicken back into the oven until the chicken is slightly brown. Then pull out the pan and, using your tongs, turn the lovely things over so the breast sides will be UP. If you are using barbecue sauce, spoon more on the breasts and add a dash of paprika. Then return the chicken to the oven until slightly brown. (This takes from 5 to 10 minutes, so keep both eyes open, because thermostats do differ.) Then use your spatula to remove the beautiful bird and put it on your plate (or platter if you are having company).

"Add some water to the good, gooey, sticky sauce that will be left in your pan (now on top of your stove), and let it boil down until slightly thick, then pour over each half of the lush thing. If you are using barbecue sauce, add some of that to the gravy. This gravy goop can also be served on the side instead of poured over the chicken.

"If you are not using barbecue sauce, still use the dash of paprika on the bird to give it that reddish tint and professional look.

"Folks, keep in mind that I was using 2- and 2½-pound broilers. If your bird doesn't weigh that much, it will take less cooking time to keep it from literally falling off the bone."

really great, and it is a terrific way to use the broken chips in the bottom of the bag. Also, try frying fish on the side burner of your patio barbecue to keep the fried-fish smell out of the kitchen.

Make a quick dinner for one. Single professionals on the go find it difficult to make a quick dinner for one without a lot of leftovers. So, purchase a value pack of salmon, wrap each individual cut in foil and place in the freezer. When it is time for dinner, you can simply grab one of them and place it on your indoor grill.

Eliminate shrimp odor. When you peel raw shrimp, nothing is worse than the smell when you put the shells in the trash! If you put the shells in a plastic bag with a little vinegar, they won't smell as much.

Also, double bag if you can.

SHRIMP DIJON

For a change from your usual dishes, why not "stir" things up a bit and serve something a little different, such as Shrimp Dijon? It can be an appetizer or a main dish when served over rice or noodles. To make this scrumptious shrimp recipe, you'll need:

½ cup butter or margarine
1½ pounds shrimp, peeled and deveined
1 onion, thinly sliced
½ cup flour
1½ cups milk
2 tablespoons Dijon mustard
½ teaspoon nutmeg
½ teaspoon salt
⅛ teaspoon pepper
1 6-ounce package cream cheese, softened

Melt butter in a frying pan; add shrimp and onion, and sauté for about 3 minutes. Do not brown. Sprinkle a little flour at a time into the mixture. Add a little milk slowly, continuously stirring to avoid lumps. Add mustard, nutmeg, salt, and pepper, and cook for 3 to 5 minutes. Stir in cream cheese (cut into thin slices) until completely blended, then warm through, but *do not boil*.

If you like, add a few drops of yellow food coloring to the water for the rice or noodles to make the dish eye-appealing.

Since shrimp can be a little pricey, buy an extra pound and freeze it. Shrimp Dijon may become a family and friend favorite.

HELOISE SALMONETTES

This recipe was a favorite of my mother's and her readers, as well as of my readers today. It's pretty easy to make and is quite yummy, too.

You will need:
vegetable oil
1 14-ounce can salmon or tuna
1 egg, lightly beaten
½ cup flour
1 heaping teaspoon baking powder
¼ cup liquid from the salmon or tuna
Fill a deep fryer or skillet half-full of oil.

Preheat this while you are mixing the salmonettes.

Drain all but ¼ cup liquid off of the canned fish and set it aside. Put the salmon in a mixing bowl and break it apart with a fork until you have no big flakes. Add the egg and flour. You can add a dash of pepper if you like, but no extra salt is needed. Blend with a spoon until all of the flour is mixed in, but don't overmix.

Add the baking powder to the liquid that was set aside and beat with a fork or whisk until frothy. Immediately pour this into the fish mixture and stir until well blended. It is important not to let the baking powder and liquid mixture sit after mixing. Pour it into the fish immediately.

Carefully drop the mixture by spoonfuls into the hot oil. They will brown very quickly, so watch them closely. Lift them out with a slotted spoon and drain on a paper towel.

You must cook this right away—it cannot sit. Serve and enjoy these tasty treats.

VEGETABLES AND FRUITS

Hide the veggies. If your family just won't eat their veggies, try "hiding" them. Puree vegetables like peas, carrots, and broccoli with mashed potatoes and some sour cream. The potatoes will look a little green, or orange, but they still taste good. Green mashed potatoes would be just right for St. Patrick's Day!

Another tactic is to add vegetable puree to meatloaves, including salmon and turkey loaf as well as the conventional hamburger meatloaf.

Shop the salad bar for soup. When you want to buy only enough of a

A SHOPPER'S GUIDE TO PRODUCE

Here are a few hint to help you get your money's worth when buying fresh produce:

- Broccoli with little yellow flowers trying to poke through the green head is older than broccoli that has no flowers. The same goes for asparagus, so skip these.

- You can usually guess how long vegetables with cut ends have been in the store by looking at the cut end. Is it a fresh cut, or is it brown and dry?

- When you see delicate leaves on the ends of carrots or radishes, you know they didn't just fall off the vegetable truck yesterday . . . they are sprouting and, therefore, older.

- Pick the best quality that you can afford, but avoid overpriced, out-of-season produce most of the time.

- As a courtesy, don't press your thumb into produce! Bruising causes a lot of waste and spoilage that the consumer ends up paying for.

TASTY TIDBIT

Soup is delicious as a snack or a meal. Let's test your Heloise soup IQ: What percentage of U.S. homes serve a minimum of one bowl of soup every 2 weeks?

a) 45 percent

b) 55 percent

c) 65 percent

If your choice was "c," 65 percent, then you are "soup-er" smart. Puts you in the soup mood, doesn't it? Soup can be a starter, a light meal, or a thick-and-chunky main meal! Add a small green salad and some delicious bread (I love warm corn bread), and it's that easy to serve a nutritious meal.

variety of vegetables to make soup and you don't care for the prepackaged selections, go to the salad bar. You can get what you're looking for, and they are already chopped up.

Scrub veggies. Washing vegetables and fruits is a favorite use for baking soda. Always scrub potatoes before baking so the skin can be eaten. Scrubbing with baking soda and a brush is the perfect nontoxic method

Roast asparagus. A delicious way to prepare asparagus is to roast it. After the asparagus is prepped, place it on a cookie sheet, spread just a little olive

DEMYSTIFY ASPARAGUS

Many people consider asparagus a "luxury" vegetable, but it's such a delicious addition to most any meal . . . treat yourself often!

Don't let the mystery surrounding asparagus intimidate you. It's easy to cook and is good for you. Here are some hints to get you started:

- First, buy the thinnest asparagus you can find; it's most tender when cooked. Look for straight, firm spears with closed tips.
- Keep asparagus refrigerated upright, preferably in a tall container with about an inch of water.
- You should plan to cook it within a couple of days.
- When you're ready to cook it, rinse the asparagus well and then snap off the woody bottoms.
- To steam, tie together with string and place in a pot with a couple of inches of boiling water. Cover and steam for 5 to 8 minutes, or until tender.
- You can also boil asparagus in a large frying pan filled with about an inch of water. Bring the water to a boil first, then add fresh asparagus and return to a boil. Next, reduce heat to medium and cook about 5 to 10 minutes, depending on the stalks' thickness. The asparagus should be tender but not mushy.

BOOTLEGGER BEANS

TASTY TIDBIT

Did you know that it takes three growing seasons before asparagus can be harvested? It actually looks like a filmy fern during its second year, but by the third year it has the stalks that are ready to eat (after washing, of course).

This is a favorite reader recipe and an old one to boot! It's easy to make, and you can expand the dish by adding more beans, some chopped green pepper, or other ingredients. You'll need:

3 strips bacon
Chopped onion (any kind, small to
   medium)
1 can pork and beans in tomato sauce
1 tablespoon brown sugar
2–3 tablespoons ketchup

Fry the bacon in a medium saucepan over medium-high heat until almost crisp. Add the onion and continue frying until the onion starts to brown. Pour off almost all of the grease. Dice the bacon, then add the remaining ingredients and stir.

oil over it, and place it under the broiler until it is cooked (with a little crispness left). Another option is to either add a little salt and pepper or sprinkle on a little Parmesan cheese before broiling—delicious!

Don't cook asparagus at all. Just wash tender asparagus in cold water, snap off the ends, and then eat it raw. It is crispy and full of flavor, not mushy. Sometimes it's a little stringy, so you might want to use a potato peeler to peel off the outer skin. You get all the vitamins and minerals, as they are not left in the cooking water.

Try tofu. Is tofu good for you? It is made from soybeans, is very versatile for cooking, and comes in various forms of texture, such as extra firm, firm, soft, and silken. It can be used in anything from soups to desserts.

It also comes in a "light" version,

BEAN TIPS

Beans are nutritious and can add great flavor to any meal. Here are a couple of suggestions from Heloise Central:

• When making vegetable soup, add a can or two of different types of beans for a delicious taste and added nutrition.

• Add cold kidney or garbanzo beans to a salad.

• Make "no-fat refried" beans from a store-bought can of pinto beans. Use your potato masher to mash to the desired consistency.

TASTY TIDBIT

Let's test your celery IQ. What is a celery heart? A celery heart is the inner ribs of celery that are usually tender and not bitter tasting. You can buy just celery hearts, but they are pricey. Celery is available year-round and is economical, so when it's a bargain, buy several stalks and treat yourself to a heart-of-celery appetizer plate.

which is lower in calories and fat. You can marinate, stir-fry, grill, or broil it, depending on what you are making. The silken tofu is creamier and is best for dips, puddings, and sauces. It can be substituted for yogurt, salad dressing, mayonnaise, or sour cream. So, try it—you might like it.

Get rid of vegetable odor. Brussels sprouts, cauliflower, and broccoli steam beautifully in the microwave, but they can really stink up the house. To eliminate much of the odor, light a match near the microwave oven as soon as you open the door. Or, light the match and then blow it out.

Keep celery fresh. Celery is one of my favorites, and a good snack all by itself or with a little cream cheese, peanut butter, or pimento cheese. To keep it at its best, store unwashed celery in a plastic bag in the refrigerator.

Or, stand stalks upright in about 2 to 3 inches of water in the refrigerator.

If celery is left uncovered, it loses moisture and wilts. All you need to do is place it in a little water to revive it.

When buying celery, look for a bunch that doesn't have yellow or brown spots on it. It should be compact, crisp, and bright green.

If you need only a couple of stalks, check your produce department—many times it has celery sticks available in small or large quantities.

Keep celery handy. The best container for cleaned celery just might be a glass loaf pan. It's deep enough to hold the celery and doesn't transfer any taste. Just fill it with cold water, and the celery is up for grabs.

Take corn off the cob with no mess. When removing cooked corn from the cob, hold the cob on the inner ring of a

TASTY TIDBITS

Which bean is red and named for its shape? It is a favorite in salads, soups, and chili. What is your guess? The answer—and I'm not "kidneying"—is the kidney bean.

Also, did you know that there is a white kidney bean that is sometimes referred to as a cannellini bean and is often used in minestrone soup?

sponge-cake pan. You can easily cut the kernels off, and they fall into the pan, making no mess at all.

Get rid of corn silk in a flash. If you get tired of trying to pick off the corn silk before making corn on the cob, try this. Grab a dampened paper towel and brush downward on the ear of corn with it until every strand comes off.

Core lettuce fast. Here's the secret to coring a head of lettuce. You don't have to search for a nonmetal knife or corer. Hold the lettuce in both hands, core side down. Give it one or two quick raps on a solid surface, such as a countertop. Turn the lettuce over and pull out the core with your hand. Wash well and then drain.

Handle an onion. Leave the "head" on one end of an onion when you grate it and use this as a handle. That way you will save your fingernails.

When the onion is grated down near to the end, just discard the rest. No waste really, because this part is usually cut off and thrown away.

Store onions in pantyhose. To store onions, put them in the legs of old pantyhose, then put a knot in the hose after each one. As the onions hang, when you want one, just cut one off—the rest stay knotted in the pantyhose!

Don't cry over onions. This makes a lot of sense if you think about it: People wear goggles at the beach to keep saltwater out of their eyes. So wear goggles while slicing, dicing, or cutting onions to keep the fumes out of your eyes and to stop the crying. It might look funny for a few minutes, but it saves a lot of crying and suffering. You could also try wearing safety goggles—the plastic type that fit completely around the eye area and have a strap to tighten them. You can keep your own pair hanging in the pantry. When you grab an onion to cut up, grab the safety glasses as well.

TASTY TIDBITS

Let's test your onion IQ. What are the three colors of onions available?

a) red, white, and yellow

b) red, white, and blue

c) red, white, and green

What color choice did you pick? You are "a" winner if you picked red, white, and yellow. Did you know that Americans typically eat more than 18 pounds of onions every year?

But don't let your dogs eat any onions, as onions can make them sick.

Don't cry over onions, take 2. When you peel and chop onions, turn on the vent fan over your stove. The vent takes up the fumes and prevents tears.

You could also take the onions outside. Take your cutting board, knife, and onions to a table out on your porch and chop away without a tear in sight. Added bonus—no strong onion odor in the house.

Chop onions less often. Do you hate to chop onions? To lessen the frequency of the task, use your food processor to chop five or six cooking onions in one session. Place the pieces in ½-cup portions in plastic sandwich bags, then place the bags in a heavy plastic freezer bag and freeze. The onions are thus measured and ready to pull out as needed for casseroles, meatloaves, and other dishes. In the same freezer bag, you could also keep a sandwich bag of chives that you've washed, dried with paper towels, and chopped to be available as needed.

Freeze an onion. If you use little fresh raw onion, slice or chop the whole onion, and put what is left into a freezer bag and put it in the freezer. This saves the onion and also makes it easy when you need a small amount to cook with.

Freeze onions and celery. When you have celery or onions you need to use

MUSHROOM MANIA

Do you love mushrooms, whether white button, portobello, or shiitake, but find yourself in the dark when it comes to keeping them fresh? If so, here are a few basic dos and don'ts for cleaning and storing mushrooms:

- Do refrigerate them as soon as you get them home.
- Do store them in a paper bag or spread them out on a cookie sheet lined with a paper towel in the refrigerator. If you keep fresh mushrooms dry, they should last 5 days or longer.
- Don't store mushrooms in an airtight plastic bag. They will spoil more quickly if condensation is allowed to build up.
- Don't clean them until you're ready to use them. And, when you do clean them, use a damp cloth, paper towel, or soft brush, then rinse quickly with cold water and dry with paper towels.
- Don't soak fresh mushrooms. They are porous and will absorb water, which will affect their flavor and texture.

up, cut them into pieces for stuffing or stir-fry and freeze the pieces in freezer bags. Bell pepper can be cut into strips and frozen also. When needed, a gentle tap of the bag on the counter breaks the clump of frozen vegetables apart, and you can pour out what you need.

Store onions and peppers. Partially used onions and peppers keep better when first wrapped in paper towels and then in foil rather than in plastic wrap or bags.

Freeze hot peppers for cornbread. For a family that loves Mexican cornbread, here's a way to cut up hot peppers without worrying about getting the hot juice on your hands (which usually ends up on your face).

Pick the peppers and freeze them, but don't wash them before freezing. As you use them, wash them, peel and de-seed them, and cut them up frozen into the batter. They work just as well as fresh peppers, without the burn.

Remove pepper seeds. Here is a hint for removing seeds from peppers, especially the small ones, like serrano: Cut the top off with a sharp knife, then slice the pepper in half lengthwise. Use a grapefruit spoon with a serrated edge to scrape off the membranes inside the pepper. Also, you should probably wear gloves when handling hot pep-

TASTY TIDBIT

Did you know that the taste and texture of a properly grilled portobello mushroom have been compared to eating a steak? Next time you're at the grocery store, pick up a portobello and give it a try. If you are grilling, heat the grill and prepare the mushroom by washing, rinsing, and drying. Place the portobello, stem side down (stem is usually removed), on the grill and brush the top with olive oil, Italian dressing, or butter. Grill for about 4 minutes, then flip, brush the other side, and continue cooking for 4 to 5 minutes, or until tender.

pers. This will prevent hot hands or the transfer of hot stuff to other parts of your body.

Tame hot chile oil. The best way to remove the oil from a hot chile pepper from your hands is to soak your hands in some whole milk. The milk will help "tame" the burn. Milk is also the best beverage to quickly cool down your mouth after you have bitten off more than you can chew. Another effective and fast way to rid your hands of chile oil is to fill your palm with baking soda and add vinegar to moisten. As it bubbles, rub it all over your hands. Leave it on for 1 minute, then rinse.

There are numerous other folk remedies for taking away the pepper burn from your hands. Try lemon juice, tomato products, milk, used coffee grounds, rubbing alcohol, vegetable shortening, degreasing shampoo, or white vinegar.

Neutralize hot pepper juice. The solution to getting hot pepper juice off your hands is not to get the juice on your hands in the first place. Coat the fingers of the hand with which you hold the pepper with a small amount of cooking oil (coat the whole hand or both hands—depending on how involved you're going to get). Then chop away. Immediately afterward, put a dab of dish soap on the hand(s), rub it around, and rinse. No spreading! No sting! No nada.

Cut peppers in half for stuffing. When you prepare peppers to be stuffed, cut them in half lengthwise, then remove the seeds and membranes. Fill each half with the hamburger mixture and bake them as the recipe directs for time and temperature. Much easier to handle and serve.

Clean up peels fast. Lay a paper towel flat in the sink when you are peeling vegetables. The paper catches most of the peelings, making for quick cleanup.

Keep potato peels out of the disposal. When you're peeling lots of potatoes, don't run the peels through the garbage disposal unit. Instead, line the sink with plastic wrap, and when the peeling is done, put the pile of peels in the trash or on a compost pile if you have one.

Mashed potato tricks. When making mashed potatoes, drain the cooking water into a pan. Season potatoes with salt and butter, and sprinkle with powdered milk equivalent to the amount you would use if mixed. Add the hot liquid to moisten the mixture and continue to add liquid until the potatoes whip up light and fluffy. The powdered milk is cheaper, you can give your family extra calcium, the potatoes stay hot (instead of using fresh cold milk), and you've saved the nutrients cooked out of the potatoes.

Make potato pancakes with leftovers. For a tasty way of making potato pancakes, plan for leftover potatoes when you make scalloped potatoes and ham.

Make the scalloped potatoes as usual. Use three layers of thinly sliced potatoes sprinkled with pepper, dried onion, and flour. Sandwich some ham pieces between the two bottom layers and cover with the top layer, then pour milk over the potatoes and bake for an hour and a half (check and see—it

might need a few more minutes) at 350 degrees F.

Serve the top layers of potatoes along with all of the ham, and refrigerate the bottom-layer potatoes in the dish. To make the pancakes a day or so later, coarsely mash (lumps are good) the refrigerated layer and include any browned bits clinging to the sides of the dish. Mold the mixture into balls and flatten into pancakes, then dust each side with flour and fry in a little butter (or light margarine) for about 15 to 20 minutes, until nicely browned.

Discover picante sauce. When you are watching your calorie intake, instead of butter or sour cream on baked potatoes, use picante sauce. It is delicious and adds only a few calories.

On the Light Side ~~~~~~~
Prepping Baked Potatoes

A reader shared this story about asking her son to get some potatoes ready for baking.

"When my son was a teenager, I called from work one day to check on him after school. I asked him if he'd mind preparing the potatoes for dinner, and I would bake them when I got home from work. I told him to 'wash them, oil them, and poke each one with a fork.'

"When I got home, he'd done exactly that—four potatoes sat on the counter washed, oiled and with a dinner fork sticking out of each one."

TASTY TIDBIT

Okay, who would you guess gets the credit for being the first American to introduce french fries at a dinner party?

a) George Washington

b) Abraham Lincoln

c) Thomas Jefferson

Yes, it was one of these presidents. And the correct answer is "c," Thomas Jefferson, who served the fries at a White House dinner.

You can choose mild, medium, or hot, depending on your taste. Give it a try!

Make your hash browns golden. You know how delicious the golden hash browns always look in a restaurant? Well, it's simple and easy to do at home. While your hash browns are frying, just sprinkle them with a little paprika. It makes them brown as they fry. The results are the same as in a restaurant—delicious and golden brown. Paprika is the trick!

Get potatoes out of plastic bags. Potatoes stored in plastic bags often seem to quickly grow eyes, or just don't keep well.

Years ago, potatoes were sold in paper bags with a window, or in netting. The packaging allowed air to circulate. Empty your potatoes out of the plastic bag and they'll keep much better and longer in either a cupboard or a pantry.

Store potatoes. The United States Potato Board recommends that you store potatoes in a dark, well-ventilated area with a temperature between 45 and 50 degrees F to keep the potatoes from sprouting.

Don't store potatoes in the refrigerator. The potato starch converts to sugar, and when you cook the potatoes, that converted starch can have an effect on the flavor and color.

Want more great potato information? Visit the U.S. Potato Board's Web site: www.potatogoodness.com.

Grate butter on yams. While making candied yams, try grating cold butter onto the yams instead of using little cut-up chunks. Not only does it take half the time, but it looks great as well. The butter has to be right out of the fridge.

Cook pumpkin. Buy pumpkins after Halloween at reduced prices, cut them in half, and scoop out the insides. Place them in a roasting pan and bake in a slow oven until very done. Let them cool, then peel and put in a food processor in small amounts. Drain the puree for a couple of hours in a colander and place 2 cups in a freezer bag—

the amount called for in most recipes. This will keep well in the freezer. It's a bit of work, but well worth the time. Compared with canned pumpkin, the taste is wonderful.

Make a one-dish meal. Stuff a seeded acorn squash with your favorite meatloaf recipe, replace the top, and cook uncovered in a 350-degree oven for 2 hours. The squash can be cooked ahead, frozen, and microwaved for those with limited preparation time.

It's delicious served with a green salad.

Scoop seeds from squash in a flash. To scoop out the seeds and pulp from butternut squash, use a serrated grapefruit spoon (which you probably never use for grapefruit anyway). That pointy, serrated tip is sure to make the job quick and easy.

Ways to use tomatoes. Many gardeners are overrun with tomatoes in the summer. In addition to the obvious—using them in salads and on cold sandwiches, or eating them plain—here are more uses:

- Skip the bread and simply toast a slice of ham and/or cheese atop an extra-thick slice of firm tomato. The toaster oven works great for this (be sure to put the tomatoes on aluminum foil to catch drips). Cook at 350 degrees F until desired doneness.

- Add to grilled and ham and cheese or tuna sandwiches.

- Use in salsa.

Make tomato juice. Here are some variations on basic tomato juice:

- Mix up the juice in a salsa container. No need to add salt or seasonings. Salsa is the healthiest of condiments.

- Add other vegetables to your liking—makes a great generic vegetable juice.

- Tomato juice is also delicious mixed half and half with vegetable juice.

A way to avoid blanching. Our mothers always blanched peaches, tomatoes, and other soft fruits for easier peeling. If you just do not seem to have the time to boil water for the one tomato you need immediately, a quick run over a ripe tomato with the back of a paring knife will release the skin.

Put fruit stickers to work. Here's a way to use those pesky stickers on fruit—remove them when you wash the fruit. When the stickers are gone from the fruit in the refrigerator, it means the fruit is washed and ready to eat.

Keep apples bright. To prevent peeled apples from turning brown, use water containing some lemon, lime, or orange juice. Here are some other options:

- Cover the apples with apple cider, seal, and refrigerate.

- Use pineapple juice whenever you make a dish of cut fruit.

- Try a splash of white vinegar and a pinch of canning salt in the water.

- Use honey to keep apples and pears from browning.

Flavor applesauce. Add dry gelatin (any flavor) to a bowl of applesauce to give the applesauce a whole new flavor. It's amazing how different a recipe can

TASTY TIDBITS

Here's an interesting question about tomatoes: Is a tomato a fruit or a vegetable? Here's what the California Tomato Growers Association, Inc. has to say: "Technically a tomato is a fruit, since it is the ripened ovary of a plant. But in 1893 the Supreme Court ruled that tomatoes were to be considered vegetables." So, now you can have your fruit and veggies, too!

change in taste and texture by adding or substituting only one ingredient.

Avocado facts. Here are some interesting facts about avocados:

- Is an avocado a fruit or a vegetable? The answer: It is a fruit. Avocados are available year-round, and California is where the majority of them are grown in the United States.

- Do you know what else avocados are called? They are called alligator pears! I guess when you think about it, they do have a bumpy, rough skin, resembling an alligator's.

Pits don't prevent discoloration. The idea of putting an avocado pit into guacamole to keep it from turning brown has been around a long time. I hate to be a hint-buster, but it really doesn't work. Experts say putting the pit in guacamole does no good, and

---

TASTY TIDBIT

How many apple varieties are grown within the United States?

a) 25,000

b) 2,250

c) 2,000

If you picked "a," you get the apple for the day!

leaving the pit in half an avocado protects only the area the pit covers.

Once an avocado is cut, air becomes its enemy! The air is what causes the flesh to turn brown. To keep your avocado green, sprinkle lemon or lime juice or vinegar over an exposed avocado and store in an airtight container in the fridge. You also can use plastic wrap. Just press it tightly over the avocado or a bowl of guacamole and store in the refrigerator. If the guacamole turns brown, just scrape that layer off, and the guacamole is still yummy!

Keep avocados fresh. When you cut open an avocado, cut it all the way around, lengthwise, then "twist" it open. The pit usually remains in one half. Use the pitless half now and put the half still containing the pit in a resealable (vacuum pack) plastic bag and vacuum-seal it. The pit prevents the avocado from getting mushed, and the air-tightness of the package keeps the avocado fresh and green for more than a week.

For those who don't have a vacuum sealer, take the seed out, press plastic wrap tightly against the flesh, put the seed back in, put the half in a zipper-top bag, and then put it into the fridge. Air is the culprit in turning avocados brown.

PICK THE RIGHT AVOCADO

Choosing an avocado depends first of all on when you want to use the avocado. If you plan on using it right away, you will need one that yields to gentle pressure, but don't choose one that is too soft or has bruises or dark spots. If you are going to use it in a few days, you can select one that is somewhat firmer.

Uncut, fresh avocados can be stored in the refrigerator for up to 2 to 3 days. If you have some slices left over, sprinkle a little juice on them from a citrus such as lime or grapefruit, or use some vinegar. Wrap well in plastic wrap or put in a sealable plastic bag or storage container—these should be eaten within a day or two.

Do you need to ripen an avocado quickly? No problem. Place the avocado in a brown paper bag with an apple. The apple releases ethylene gas, a natural ripening agent.

Use ripe bananas. Lots of us use too-ripe bananas in muffins, but you can also mix an overly ripe banana into a cake recipe.

Keep gnats off bananas. When you buy bananas, hang them on a banana hanger and set them in the sink. Run water over the entire stock of bananas. Leave them there to dry and then put them on the counter. No more gnats flying around the kitchen.

Mash bananas. When mashing bananas, tear a piece of paper towel and place it under the finger holding the fork, and your finger won't slip.

Be ready to use overripe bananas. For those very ripe bananas that you always seem to have, keep several prepackaged zipper-top bags of the dry ingredients for banana bread in your cupboard (premeasured flour, baking soda and powder, sugar and salt). When you have the ripe bananas, add them, along with butter and eggs, to the bag. Knead them in the bag, cut a hole in the corner of the bag, and squeeze the mixture into a loaf pan, then bake. You won't have to measure ingredients or dirty a mixing bowl.

Save a banana. To save an uneaten half of a banana for another day, spraying the cut end with olive oil spray will keep the banana half from

TASTY TIDBIT

Do you know that avocados have consistently tested as having the lowest levels of pesticide residues than almost all other fruits?

TASTY TIDBIT

Let's see how much you know about bananas. What do they call a cluster of bananas? Let me give you a hand—that's right, they are called "hands"! And the individual bananas are called "fingers." So, grab a hand or a finger and enjoy this sweet treat with no fat!

discoloring or getting mushy for 24 hours.

Freeze bananas. When your bananas ripen too quickly, peel the overripe bananas and slice them into rounds. Put the pieces in a plastic container and then in the freezer. They make a nice, healthy treat.

Use lots of lemons. Here are some ways to use lemons:

- Lemon juice makes a delicious and healthy substitute for salt and salad dressings. Just squeeze it on steamed vegetables, seafood, and salads. Place a piece of nylon net over the cut end of a lemon and squeeze—the net keeps the seeds from falling into the salad as well.

- It's also yummy in tea. A favorite tea recipe is to combine 1 to 2 teaspoons finely chopped mint, 3

tablespoons lemon juice, and three to five tea bags. Just add hot water and steep for about 5 minutes, strain, then add lemon and sweetener if you like.

- Lemons also can be used to help keep potatoes and cauliflower white by adding one to the boiling water. Rubbing a little juice on your hands will remove odors from onions and fish.

- The zest of the lemon, which is just the outside colored part of the fruit, is used in many recipes. Use a grater to remove the zest, being careful not to include the white part underneath, which can be bitter. Store the zest in plastic sandwich bags and freeze.

- Lemon juice can be frozen in an ice-cube tray or in small amounts to use later. Removing the juice is easy if you use a nutcracker. Just cut the lemon in half and give it a squeeze.

Make lemon cubes. Here's a hint on keeping lemons. Squeeze and strain lemon juice, then freeze the juice in ice-cube trays. After the cubes are frozen, store them in freezer bags. They keep very well and are useful for tea, lemonade, water, and baking.

Discover a mangosteen. Have you ever tried a mangosteen, and do you even know what it is? This is a delicious tropical fruit that can be found in the produce section of your grocery store. To give one a try, cut off the red rind and enjoy the juicy segments inside. One note: The sap from the fruit might permanently stain clothing or anything it comes into contact with, so use care when peeling. It is called the "queen of fruits," so treat yourself like royalty.

Olive ABCs. What fruit can be used on everything from tossed salad to pizza? Want to add some pizzazz to that hors d'oeuvres tray or pasta sauce? Some would argue there's no better way than to bring on the olives. There are plenty of varieties, but the most popular in the United States are plain old black olives, which are the ripened siblings of green olives.

You can keep canned, unopened black olives on the shelf for 2 or 3 years. Once the can is open, refrigerate unused olives right in the can with the brine and lightly cover the can with plastic wrap. They'll be good for about a week and a half.

TASTY TIDBIT

Did you know that you can ripen a mango by placing it in a brown paper sack (at room temperature)? Keep an eye on it, because it can ripen quickly. Ripe mangoes can be kept in the refrigerator for about 5 days. You can tell when a mango is ripe by gently squeezing it to see if it gives just a little (similar to an avocado), and it should also smell delicious.

Avoid storing olives in an airtight container. If the original brine has been tossed out, store the olives in a solution of 1 cup water and ½ teaspoon salt. This will keep them moist and free from refrigerator odors.

I'm a real olive lover. Black, green— you name them, I'll eat them. My husband even thinks I'd put them on top of ice cream. Hmmm.

Save orange peel. Before you peel an orange, wash, rinse, and dry it thoroughly. Then remove the zest with a grater and store it in plastic bags in the freezer. You will always have fresh-tasting orange rind for flavoring in baking and marinades.

Peel peaches. To peel peaches without immersing them in hot water, try using your potato peeler. It really does a nice job.

Cook hard pears. Here's a very tasty way to prepare hard pears. Peel and cut the pears to bite size, and boil them in a little water. Add cinnamon candy and cook until they are tender. The cinnamon candy gives the pears a very good taste and turns them a pretty color. You don't need to add any sugar, as they are sweet enough. This is very good with chicken dishes.

Enjoy pomegranates. Here's an easy way to remove pomegranate seeds from the pulp. A grapefruit spoon with a serrated tip works perfectly for scooping out the juicy seeds.

Hull strawberries. An easy way to hull strawberries is to push a straw into the pointed end of the berry; the

On the Light Side ~~~~~~
Making Pear Sauce the Hard Way

In Texas we have hard Kieffer pears that are large, extra firm, and gritty. They are used mainly for canning and baking but are not very good to eat by themselves. One of my secretaries picked a bunch of pears and wanted to try a recipe for pear sauce, which is likened to applesauce.

So, she put the pears on to cook. Well, hard pears are *hard,* and it took hours and hours to cook them until they were soft enough to put through the food mill. She says she will never do that again!

TASTY TIDBIT

Here's a Heloise Hint IQ question for you: When a farmer crossed a blackberry, a red raspberry, and a loganberry, what did he end up with? The answer—a boysenberry! The berries are large and juicy, so watch your grocer's shelf for availability. Pick berries that are firm and dark-colored. These are a "berry" good choice.

leaves and the core will come out the other end. Or, use the end of a potato peeler.

Slice lots of strawberries. When you have too many strawberries to eat fresh, slice them for freezing in order to enjoy them on your cereal during the next few weeks.

After washing and hulling the berries, use an egg slicer to slice them. You'll have all the berries sliced and in the freezer in less than half the time it would take to wash, hull, and slice them by hand.

Use this method the next time you prepare berries and kiwis for a fruit pizza.

Store berries in balsamic. Strawberries, boysenberries, and blueberries are great fresh, but they get mushy and moldy too quickly. Here's how to extend their life: Slice the strawberries (leave the other berries whole), then mix a teaspoon of sugar per 8 ounces of berries into ½ to 1 teaspoon balsamic vinegar until the sugar is almost dissolved, and then mix it into the berries. You might want more vinegar—it's a matter of taste. This may sound odd, but the flavor is good, especially if you like balsamic vinegar.

The vinegar arrests mold growth before it starts and keeps the berries firm. Treated this way, the berries can last a week or more in the refrigerator.

How about mixing up a homemade vinaigrette with your choice of berry, balsamic vinegar, and a little sugar to taste blended in a blender for a minute or so?

TASTY TIDBIT

If you lined up all the strawberries grown in California in one straight line, they would wrap around the whole Earth 15 times, so says the California Strawberry Commission.

Now let's see if you are "berry" smart! How many seeds are there on the outside of a strawberry?

a) 100

b) 200

c) 300

Well, if you guessed "b," then you are the number one berry in my book!

Store strawberries longer. Fresh strawberries seem to deteriorate rather quickly when they are allowed to touch one another in the store packaging. Therefore, to extend their life and freshness, use a no-longer-needed egg carton. Place one strawberry per egg space in the carton and store in the fridge. Do not wash until ready to eat.

Prevent watermelon mess. Here are a couple of watermelon hints: When storing halved watermelons in the refrigerator, put them in a turkey-roasting bag. The bags are big enough, are easy to close with a twist tie, and can be washed out and reused.

When cutting a large watermelon, place it on a turkey platter. It saves cutting the countertop and helps keep the mess confined.

How to have watermelon anytime. Here's a tip to make eating watermelon convenient. When you buy a watermelon, cut it into bite-size pieces immediately, removing all the seeds. Drain in a colander, then put the pieces in a bowl, cover, and refrigerate. Now you can have watermelon anytime!

Cool a watermelon. Here's a way to cool a watermelon for a picnic when you're short of ice. Line a cooler with freezer packs. Cut the watermelon into

TASTY TIDBIT

Here's a tasty tidbits quiz: What berry has seeds on the outside? I'll give you a clue—it is the most popular berry around, and it's red in color and contains vitamin C. What's your guess? The answer: the strawberry!

serving slices, place them in plastic bags, and then lay them in the cooler. A couple of hours later, the watermelon will be ice cold and delicious.

SWEET STUFF

Save bread ends. Instead of slicing the crust off heels of bread, save all the heels in the refrigerator until you have enough to make bread pudding. It's delicious with warm maple syrup over it.

Save money on chocolate syrup. To beat the high cost of chocolate syrup, take 4 tablespoons cocoa, 1½ cups milk, and 1 cup sugar. Heat it and reduce by about half the amount, then pour it hot or cold on vanilla ice cream.

Make richer chocolate pudding. Make chocolate pudding (for pies) richer by adding a handful of chocolate chips when cooking.

Don't worry about chocolate bloom.

If you receive a beautiful box of chocolates as a gift but the chocolate looks gray or whitish, it doesn't mean the chocolate isn't good. The grayish tinge is called "bloom" and occurs when the cocoa butter in the chocolate rises to the top because the chocolate was stored in too warm or humid an area. The good news is that there is nothing wrong with the chocolate, so feel free to have a piece.

Keep candied fruit unstuck. When making a flourless, no-bake fruitcake, spray the blades of the food processor with nonstick cooking spray before chopping the candied fruit. The spray will keep the fruit from gumming up the food processor.

Making funnel cake. When you're making funnel cake, try using a kid's sipping cup (the ones with the little straw) instead of a funnel to drop the batter into the hot oil. It is easy to handle, and you'll have a place to keep any unused batter.

You could also use a funnel to fill an empty, plastic, squeeze syrup bottle. It leaves one hand free, makes the batter easier to control and ration, and keeps your "squeezing hand" at a safer distance from the oil, which might pop. And you can put the unused batter in the refrigerator for later use.

Make funnel-less cake. Want to make funnel cake but haven't got a funnel? Pour all the ingredients into a gallon-size freezer bag. Mix them all up by smooshing the bag around, then cut out a tiny corner of the bag to squeeze the batter into the oil. When finished, just throw away the bag. No mess to clean up.

Mold gelatin for the holidays. Buy candy molds for whichever holiday is coming up and use them to make gelatin molds. Just spray the mold with nonstick vegetable spray and then fill with your favorite flavor gelatin and chill.

Keep your hands warm. When you enjoy a cold bowl of ice cream while sitting on the couch watching a favorite TV show, instead of resting the cold bowl on your hand, rest it on a hot pad or an oven mitt.

When you slide your hand inside the hot pad, you can hold the bowl without your fingers becoming too chilly.

Keep ice cream in the cone. To keep ice cream from soaking through the bottom of an ice-cream cone, put a layer of miniature marshmallows in the bottom of the cone first. (Just one works great in a pointed-bottom cone.) The marshmallows soak up the melting ice cream before it drips through.

Save leftover ice cream cake. If you end up with more than half of a large ice-cream cake after a party, it won't easily fit in your freezer. So slice it and wrap the individual pieces in waxed paper and put them into quart-size zipper-top bags. It will give you great flexibility to find space in the freezer. When you want to serve the leftovers, the waxed paper comes off easily and makes serving the leftovers easy.

Make ice-cream servings a snap. Here's a way to easily serve ice cream. First, buy ice cream in a cylinder-shaped container. On the days you are going to serve the ice cream, remove it from the freezer and let it soften slightly. Then, with a sharp knife, cut the carton in half lengthwise. Cut the half "barrel" of ice cream into half-moon serving sizes. It's oh-so-easy.

Keep the cone upright. Have trouble scooping ice-cream cones? Put the cone into a baby bottle (without the top). It stays up easily, and you can make more than one cone at a time.

Make healthy ice pops. When making ice pops at home, use half cherry drink mix and half grape juice. It's a good way to sneak in a little nutrition.

Get marshmallows unstuck. It's

TASTY TIDBIT

Let's test your marshmallow knowledge. Here we go: How many small marshmallows equal one large one?

a) 5

b) 7

c) 10

Do you think "c" is the answer? That's right.

Okay, let's try one more time: How many large marshmallows equal a 10-ounce bag? Give up? About 38 to 40!

marshmallows are coated. Most of the marshmallows will fall apart, but there might be a few that remain stubborn, and you should be able to gently pull them apart.

To keep marshmallows fresh and unstuck, put them in a freezer-safe plastic bag or a container with a tight-fitting lid, and store them in the freezer. When needed, remove and thaw at room temperature, and they are as good as new.

Here's a hint if marshmallows are too dry: Make sure you have a sealable container or bag and add a piece of white bread. The moisture from the bread will help soften the marshmallows.

usually pretty easy to unstick marshmallows that are stuck together. Just pour a little confectioners' (powdered) sugar or cornstarch into the bag, close and shake, shake, shake until the

Vintage Heloise

Pistachio Ambrosia

Ambrosia has been a favorite Heloise recipe for a long, long time, and it's one that is easy to make and so delicious that it won't last long!

To make the pistachio ambrosia, you will need:

1 16-ounce can chunky pineapple

1 8-ounce can crushed pineapple

1 small package instant pistachio pudding

1 cup chopped walnuts or pecans

1 cup shredded coconut

12 to 16 ounces nondairy whipped topping, thawed

1 cup miniature marshmallows

In a large bowl, mix the contents of the pineapple cans. Next, sprinkle pudding on top, and don't stir or mix for 2 to 4 minutes. Combine nuts and coconut, and slowly fold into mixture. Last, carefully stir in whipped topping and marshmallows (don't overmix). Refrigerate for 2 hours or longer before it's ready to dive into!

PEANUT BRITTLE

What makes this delicious recipe quick and easy is that it's made in the microwave.

You'll need:

1 cup granulated sugar

½ cup light corn syrup

1½ cup raw (skin on) peanuts

½ teaspoon salt

1 teaspoon vanilla extract

1 teaspoon butter

1 teaspoon baking soda

Cover a cookie sheet with some aluminum foil and spray lightly with some nonstick cooking spray.

In a large, microwave-safe bowl (one with straight sides works best), combine sugar, light corn syrup, peanuts, and salt, and mix together. Place in the microwave and heat on high for 8 minutes, stirring well halfway through.

Stir in the vanilla and butter (leave the bowl in the microwave to do this) and microwave for another 2 minutes on high.

Carefully take the bowl out—it will be extremely hot!

Add the baking soda and immediately stir until you see the mixture is foamy and light, but don't overstir!

Quickly pour onto the baking sheet, using a *metal* knife. It's really hot and can be a little hard to handle.

Evenly spread to about ¼ inch thick. Let it cool, then break the peanut brittle into big pieces. Store in an airtight container or zipper-top bag. This recipe yields about a pound of peanut brittle.

Since microwave wattages vary, you might need to adjust the times a little. You must watch carefully or the peanuts will burn—trust me!

Make a dessert as easy as pie. Here's an easy "pie" dessert: Break two to four graham crackers into a bowl, add a tablespoon or two of pie filling, and then top with a tablespoon of whipped topping.

Clean up crispy treats. Before you make rice-cereal treats, spray the mixing pot with nonstick vegetable spray. The pot will be easy to clean, and you won't have such a sticky mess with the melted marshmallows and sticky rice cereal.

A variation on s'mores. For a fun twist on s'mores, substitute the cute yellow marshmallow chicks sold at Easter for the marshmallows in your treats made with chocolate bars, graham crackers, and marshmallows.

The family who invented these calls them "smeeps." You can purchase the marshmallow chicks after Easter at very economical prices and freeze them to enjoy year-round.

Make simple s'mores. To make s'mores while camping, instead of using graham crackers and chocolate bars, buy chocolate-coated pinstripe cookies, put a marshmallow between the two cookies, and enjoy. They are easier and cheaper.

A secret for strawberry shortcake. Here is a great hint for preparing strawberries for shortcake. Always buy a container of frozen, sliced berries with juice. Thaw this. Take a box of fresh strawberries, hull, wash, and slice. Add these to the thawed frozen strawberries. Voilà! Now you have plenty of berries and juice to put over your cake. No need to bother with additional sugar.

Fill a tart easily. To fill graham-cracker tarts with a favorite pudding quickly and easily, use a turkey baster. No mess to clean up on the counter or the outside of the bowl. Just be sure to clean out the baster right away. Remember, pudding soft-sets in 5 minutes, no matter what's in it. And for added appeal, if there's a tart shell left over, crush it up into fine pieces and sprinkle on top of the others. Add a dollop or two of whipped topping and you're all set.

BAKING AND BREAD

Test your baking powder. If your cookies, muffins, cakes, and biscuits do not rise enough, your baking powder may no longer be fresh. To test it, just add 1 teaspoon baking powder to ¼ cup hot tap water (the water must be hot, not warm). The more bubbles, the fresher the baking powder—it's that simple. No bubbles? Time for a visit to the grocery store. Not-so-fresh baking powder will produce not-so-good results in baking.

Keep baking soda fresh. Baking powder comes in an airtight can, while baking soda comes in a box. It is hard to measure from the box, and the box is not sealed tightly unless you over-wrap with a plastic bag. For a better alternative, store baking soda in a clean, dry, empty grated Parmesan cheese container. Or, take the label off an empty baking-powder can, fill the can with baking soda, make a label, and store it like that.

Understand cocoa. Is cocoa powder the same as cocoa? Here's what a major cocoa manufacturer had to say: Cocoa powder and cocoa are the same thing. Unsweetened cocoa powder is usually sold in a can and is found in the baking aisle of your grocery store.

Keep raisins from sinking. The way to keep raisins from sinking to the bottom of breads and cakes is to lightly dust the raisins with whatever flour is used in the bread or cake. The dusted raisins will stay suspended in the batter.

Write the oven temperature. Write

on the upper right-hand corner of recipes the temperature you need to set the oven to bake the recipe. That way, you won't have to hunt when you want to preheat the oven.

Don't scratch your nonstick pans. The instructions for heavy-duty, dark, nonstick baking pans direct you not to use anything metal or sharp on the inside to avoid scratching. When you make a batch of brownies in this kind of pan, after cooling completely, cut the brownies with a plastic (disposable) knife, and you won't scratch the pan.

Keep your hands clean. If you put a plastic sandwich bag over your hand when patting sticky cookie dough into a pan, the dough won't stick to your hand.

Pick up dough. Do you roll out your biscuit dough right on the counter? If you use your dishcloth to clean up the residue, you end up with gooey globs of dough on the cloth. Instead, take some flour, sprinkle it over the bits of dough, rub with your palm, and you'll be left with little bits that you can brush into your hand and dispose of.

Use spoons to drop cookie dough. Use two regular-size eating spoons to drop cookies onto a cookie sheet. Scoop the proper amount of batter in one,

and use the other to scrape it off onto the baking sheet. That way, you won't have sticky dough on your fingers afterward. It also works great for deviled eggs.

Slice with floss. Use dental floss for cutting unbaked dough for cinnamon rolls, biscuits, and everything else. Just slide a long string of unflavored, unwaxed dental floss under the roll of dough, cross the ends, and pull in opposite directions.

Fill the whole tin. If you don't have enough batter to fill all the cupcake tins in your pan, pour 1 tablespoon water into the unfilled spots. This helps preserve the life of your pans.

Use a baster for batter. When you are baking a lot of small items, like cupcakes or mini-cheesecakes, for a bake sale or an event, fill a turkey baster with the batter and squeeze it into the cupcake papers or miniature tins. It's quick and neat.

Customize bread dough. Most supermarkets sell white French bread dough that you pop open and bake for 30 minutes. To add some whole grains to the white bread dough, smother the dough with lots of rolled oats, flaxseed, and wheat germ and a bit of olive oil. Then bake as directed.

Stash hot bread. When your bread has just come out of the bread machine and it's too hot to put away, place it on a small cooking rack in the microwave (off). Then you can go to bed without worrying about the bread getting hard sitting out or getting soggy if enclosed. It's perfect in the morning.

ANGEL BISCUITS

These Heloise's Angel Biscuits are a favorite of my readers. They are easy to make, and the dough can be kept for up to 3 days in a covered bowl in the fridge.

You'll need:

1 package dry yeast
$\frac{1}{4}$ cup warm water
$2\frac{1}{2}$ cups flour
$\frac{1}{2}$ teaspoon baking soda
1 teaspoon baking powder
1 teaspoon salt
2 tablespoons sugar
$\frac{1}{2}$ cup shortening
1 cup buttermilk

Dissolve the yeast in the warm water; set aside. Mix the dry ingredients in the order given, cutting in the shortening as you normally do for biscuits or pie dough. Stir in the buttermilk and yeast mixture, and mix thoroughly. The dough is ready to refrigerate.

When it's time to make the biscuits, turn the dough out onto a floured board and knead lightly. Roll out and cut with a biscuit cutter, placing them in a greased pan.

Let the dough rise slightly before baking in a 400-degree oven for about 12 to 15 minutes. Enjoy!

HELOISE BISCUIT MIX

This old-time recipe is easy and makes delicious, light biscuits.

You will need:

8 cups all-purpose flour
$\frac{1}{2}$ cup baking powder
2 teaspoons salt
8 teaspoons sugar (optional)
1 cup solid shortening

Blend together flour, baking powder, salt, and sugar. Cut in shortening using a pastry blender. When the mixture looks like coarse meal, it's ready. Keep the mixture in a tight-sealing container and keep it in the refrigerator.

To make biscuits, preheat the oven to 450 degrees F. Mix 1 cup biscuit mix and $\frac{1}{3}$ cup milk. Drop biscuits by tablespoons onto a cookie sheet and cook for 12 to 15 minutes.

MONKEY BREAD

This is a great recipe and is really easy to make, too. It's a favorite around our office.

You will need:

$\frac{1}{2}$ cup margarine or butter (don't use diet)
$\frac{1}{3}$ cup granulated sugar
$\frac{1}{3}$ cup brown sugar
$\frac{1}{4}$ cup finely chopped nuts
1 tablespoon cinnamon
3 cans buttermilk biscuits

Preheat oven to 375 degrees F. Spray the inside of a Bundt pan with nonstick cooking spray.

Next, melt the margarine in a bowl. Mix sugar, brown sugar, nuts, and cinnamon in a separate bowl.

Open the biscuits, separate, and cut

each into 4 sections. Roll each section into a ball and put into the sugar mixture to coat. Place the balls into the pan and drizzle a little melted butter evenly over the top of this first layer, which is one can of biscuits. Repeat until all three cans of biscuits are used.

Sprinkle remaining sugar mixture over the top and bake for 30 to 35 minutes. Let cool for a minute or two before turning the bread onto a plate and carefully removing the pan. If you leave the monkey bread in the pan much longer, it will stick and be hard to remove.

Hint: Most canned biscuits have a "use by" date on the can. It's recommended that refrigerated products be baked by the "use by" dates. Products used after that date might not rise or might have poor texture.

Monkey bread shortcut #1. If you don't have the patience to roll each piece of biscuit into a ball and put it in the sugar mixture to coat it, here's a shortcut.

Put the brown sugar, nuts, and cinnamon into a plastic bag, and as you cut each tube of biscuits, just drop them into the bag and shake, making sure they are all coated with the sugar mixture. Then just pour the bag full of biscuit pieces and all remaining sugar into the pan, and pour the melted butter over the top and bake. Just slice it and eat.

Monkey bread shortcut #2. When you make monkey bread, don't bother to coat all the biscuits with the sugar-and-cinnamon mixture. Just put pecans on the bottom of a tube pan, layer some of the cut-up biscuits, sugar, cinnamon, and pecans, and then pour one-third of the melted butter over it. Then repeat the process, and bake as directed in the recipe. The butter and sugar will melt and spread over the biscuits.

Mash bananas for bread. When making banana bread, instead of mashing the bananas with a fork, use a pie-crust blender and a round-bottom bowl to mash them thoroughly and quickly.

Make crispy cornbread. Make cornbread batter by whatever recipe suits you, then bake it in a Belgian waffle maker. After it's baked, brush it with melted butter or olive oil. It turns out nice and crispy, as if it had just been taken out of a cast-iron skillet.

Line brownie pans for easy removal. Line the baking pan for brownies with parchment paper. When cool, lift out and cut with a pizza cutter. Very easy to cut, and the pan is spotless!

CAKE MIX BROWNIES

The recipe for brownies from a cake mix is a winner. You will need:

1 egg
¾ cup water plus more as needed
½ cup chopped pecans (optional)
1 18.25-ounce box devil's food cake mix
Nothing else!

Preheat the oven to 350 degrees F. Grease a 13-by-9-inch pan. Mix the egg, water, and nuts in a large bowl. Add the dry cake mix; stir well, but don't overbeat. If the batter needs a little more water, add a teaspoonful at a time. But don't add too much, because the batter should be thick. Don't overmix—just mix enough so that there is no "powder" showing.

Pour into the prepared pan, being sure to smooth the top evenly. Bake for 20 to 25 minutes for chewy brownies; if you like them a little drier, bake a few minutes longer.

A cold glass of milk is a perfect match. In fact, put the milk in the blender, add an ice cube or two, and whir—it's even better.

Make mini-brownies. Always keep lots of your favorite brownie mix on hand for when you need to send a treat to school or for a last-minute dessert or potluck. Make the brownies in mini-muffin tins. It makes it so easy to send in the brownies, teachers do not have the hassle of cutting them, and adults love "just a bite."

Flour a cake pan with cocoa. If you are preparing to make a chocolate cake, use some dry cocoa to "flour" the pan. There's no white residue, and the bottom looks as good as the top.

Flour cake pans a new way. When a cake recipe calls for flouring the baking pan, use a bit of the dry cake mix instead—there won't be any white flour on the outside of the cake when it's baked.

Line pans with cereal paper. Use waxed paper cereal box liners to line cake pans. Trace circles on the paper using 8- or 9-inch baking pans. Cut these out as needed to line the pans before baking cakes. You still need to grease and lightly dust each pan with flour first, but the added waxed paper liner guarantees easy cake removal every time.

Make an extra cupcake. Each time you bake a cake, remove enough batter to bake one cupcake.

TASTY TIDBIT

What is a brownie? Well, this became quite difficult to research, as the origin of brownies is not clear, but they have been popular in the United States since the 19th century. Some say it was the result of a chocolate cake recipe error, but they certainly are delicious, aren't they?

Put the unfrosted cupcake in the freezer, and before long you will have an extra batch of cupcakes. Frost them all at the same time, but you'll have a variety of cake flavors.

Keep cupcakes neat. Use a glass measuring cup or any container with a pour spout to fill cupcake liners with cake batter—it results in fewer drips.

Sometimes a ladle works well, too.

Fake a homemade cake. When you make a cake from a mix, add a teaspoon of vanilla extract or flavoring to the batter to give it a made-from-scratch flavor.

Sift cake mix. If you don't have a hand mixer, it can still be easy to make a cake from a mix. Use a mesh strainer and, with the back of a spoon, sift the cake mix into the bowl.

After adding the eggs, oil, and water, the mix will stir up beautifully in just seconds.

Test a cake. If you find that you have no toothpicks to test a cake you're baking, use a dry piece of spaghetti. When batter appears on the strand, simply break it off at the end, reset the timer, and try it again. When the spaghetti comes out clean, the cake is done.

You can also use a metal skewer to check for cake doneness.

CHOCOLATE CAKE 101

What is the difference between a plain chocolate cake mix and a devil's food cake mix? The ingredients on the boxes are the same. How is a German chocolate cake mix different?

According to a representative of a leading manufacturer of cake mixes:

- German chocolate is usually a milder chocolate flavor and a lighter color than other chocolate varieties.
- Devil's food cake mixes have a stronger, richer cocoa flavor and are darker.
- Plain chocolate mixes usually have a milk chocolate flavoring.

A lot of times, these varieties are different because of the frostings used. German chocolate cakes usually are served with a coconut-pecan frosting, while devil's food cake has a fudge or white frosting. Plain chocolate cakes can have a variety of different frostings.

So, bake a cake today and enjoy!

TASTY TIDBIT

Cakes with creamy frostings can be left out on a counter in a covered container, but cakes with cream cheese, whipped cream, or cream filling should be kept in the refrigerator.

BAKE A WARTIME CAKE

This recipe came about because of the food shortages during the World War II years. Items like eggs, milk, and butter were not easily available. So, the women of this era came up with the following recipe for cakes. Mix together:

2 cups brown sugar
2 cups hot water
2 teaspoons shortening
½ to ¾ cup raisins
1 teaspoon salt
1 teaspoon cinnamon
1 teaspoon cloves

Preheat the oven to 350 degrees F. Grease a tube pan. Mix the brown sugar, hot water, and shortening in a medium saucepan. Add the raisins, salt, cinnamon, and cloves. Mix and boil for 5 minutes after it first bubbles. Remove from the stove and let cool completely (very important).

After the mixture is cool, add 3 cups flour and 1 teaspoon baking soda that has been dissolved in a couple of teaspoons of hot water. Mix well. Pour into the prepared pan and bake for 1 hour.

Keep extra icing on hand. Lots of kids love canned cinnamon rolls for breakfast, but there never seems to be enough icing in the little container that is provided.

Solve that problem by supplementing the frosting with vanilla icing from a can that you always keep on hand. The rolls are delicious with extra icing. Keep the can in the fridge until needed again.

Make quick drizzle frosting. To drizzle frosting over cookies or cakes easily and mess-free:

Put three or four squares of almond bark in a glass bowl and microwave to melt the bark. Once the bark is melted, dip a spoon into the melted chocolate and drizzle the chocolate in a decorative pattern over the dessert.

Make colored frosting. You can easily make colored frosting for cakes or cookies by sprinkling a little bit of cherry, strawberry, or other powdered flavored drink mix into plain white or butter-cream frosting. It adds just a hint of tartness as well as coloring.

Stretch cake frosting. When you buy a container of cake frosting from the store, whip it in your mixer for a few minutes so it doubles in size. You get to frost more cake or cupcakes with the same amount of frosting, and you also will eat less sugar and fewer calories per serving.

TASTY TIDBIT

Did you know that you can quickly frost cupcakes by putting a few chocolate chips on the top of each one and heating for a few seconds? Delicious!

Use corn-on-the-cob holders a different way. To keep plastic wrap from sticking to a frosted cake, you can use corn-on-the-cob holders to keep the plastic from touching the frosting.

Or, you can use toothpicks or raw spaghetti, broken off at whatever length you need.

CANDY CANE COOKIES

These cookies are just perfect for the holiday season. You will need:

- 1 cup butter
- 1 cup confectioners' sugar
- 1 egg
- 1 teaspoon vanilla extract
- 2½ cups flour
- Red food coloring
- 1 cup candy canes, crushed into small pieces

Preheat the oven to 350 degrees F. In a large bowl, mix the butter, sugar, egg, and vanilla. Stir in the flour to make a dough. Divide the dough in half and add a few drops of red food coloring to one half of the mixture and mix well. Take 1 teaspoon of each dough and roll into strips about 4 inches long and ¼ inch thick. Twist the strips around each other and form into the shape of a candy cane on an ungreased cookie sheet.

Bake 15 to 20 minutes. Remove from the oven. While the cookies are still warm, sprinkle some crushed candy canes on each one.

Premeasure and freeze cookie dough. When school-age kids are selling cookie dough, buy several flavors. Use a cookie scoop and cover cookie sheets with balls of dough. Put them in the freezer and, after they are frozen, transfer them to freezer bags. That way, you can take out just two or three of several flavors to bake at a time instead of baking a whole batch of one kind of cookie before trying another.

Freeze cookie dough. When you overestimate how many cookies to bake and have a *lot* of dough left, freeze some to use later. Here's what to do: Roll the dough into a tube, wrap it in waxed paper and then in aluminum foil, and put it in the freezer. You'll be creating your own "slice and bake" homemade cookies. You can bake as many or as few as you want.

Make extra cookies. Nothing tastes quite as good as warm chocolate chip cookies (or any freshly baked cookies, for that matter). When making a batch of cookies, bake a few and drop the rest of the dough in balls onto the cookie sheet (you can place them close together). Put the cookie sheet into the freezer until frozen, then put the cookie dough balls into a zipper-top freezer bag and put them back in the freezer.

When you want just a few fresh cookies, take out as many dough balls as you need, and then bake as usual.

You can always have fresh-baked cookies in just a few minutes' notice without having to take time to mix up a new batch.

Frozen dough is especially handy for those times when you need cookies to take to someone or have unexpected guests and need a little sweet snack.

Bake cookies on foil. When making cookies, especially cutout cookies, bake them on foil (on your cookie

CAKE MIX COOKIES

I get so many requests for this recipe—it might be because you can use any flavor cake mix and add a multitude of goodies. The possibilities are endless. And it is easy:

- Start by preheating the oven to 350 degrees F. Then mix *only* ½ cup vegetable oil and two eggs with a box of regular cake mix. *Do not* add any water!
- Add ¼ to ½ cup "morsels"—chocolate or peanut-butter chips, chopped nuts, or raisins—and mix well.
- Place the dough by the teaspoonful on an ungreased cookie sheet, about 2 inches apart. Bake 8 to 10 minutes. Let cool.

When using powdered cake mix, put the liquid in the bowl first, then the dry mix. This will help prevent powder pockets.

Customize your cake mix cookies. Use different flavorings, along with nuts, raisins, and chocolate chips, to make cookies different for special occasions. Just to make the dough festive, divide it and add a few drops of food coloring for a fun look. You can also sprinkle the cookies with different-colored sugar to dress them up.

If your kids like cutout cookies, here's how to adapt the recipe so it can be used for that purpose as well. To the regular recipe, add 2 heaping tablespoons flour, which stiffens the batter so it can be rolled out on a cutting board. Flour the cutting board, cookie cutters, and rolling pin. Everything else in the recipe stays the same, and when the cookies have cooled, they can then be decorated according to the holiday you need them for.

sheets). When baked, you may slip the foil with the cookies off the cookie sheets onto the counter to cool.

When cooled, your cookies should be in perfect shape, since you aren't disturbing the cookies with a spatula.

Keep cookies soft. Have you ever made a batch of cookies that got too hard? Put them in a sealable tin as usual, but add a slice of bread. This will soften the cookies.

Package cookies better. To store or ship homemade cookies, try to make them a uniform size. After cooling, gently put them into a clean, empty potato-chip tube. To mail the cookies, tape the lid on securely and mail in a padded envelope. Or use extra bubble plastic and mail them in a box.

Roll bananas for muffins. To entertain children when you're baking, let them smash the bananas with a rolling pin. Pull out a gallon-size, reclosable plastic bag, peel the bananas, drop them into the bag, and roll the pin right over them. It's lots of fun, and the muffins are a treat.

ELEPHANT EARS

This is a favorite recipe in my office and it's oh-so-easy to make, too. All you need is:

½ cup cinnamon

1 cup sugar

1 can cinnamon buns (found in the dairy case)

Preheat the oven 375 degrees F. Mix the cinnamon and sugar together, then spread it evenly on a sheet of foil or waxed paper. Take one bun at a time and lay it on the sugar/cinnamon mixture. Now, use a rolling pin to roll each bun out, turning often so the dough absorbs as much sugar and cinnamon as possible. You want about a 6- to 8-inch circle. Place on foil-lined cookie sheets (only 3 "ears" might fit) and bake on the center rack or as close to the center as possible. Check often so they don't scorch or overbake—they are very thin.

When you shop, watch for specials and pick up a few extra cans of the cinnamon buns to keep on hand. You can always make a batch of elephant ears for breakfast or as a dessert.

TASTY TIDBIT

When was the original chocolate chip cookie invented?

a) 1920

b) 1930

c) 1940

If you want to "b" the smartest cookie of all, then your answer should be 1930!

Make a perfect pie. Here is a suggestion if you bake a pie that has a runny filling—examples are pecan or pumpkin—and you're using a disposable pie tin.

Those tins are very flimsy, and when they are filled with a runny filling before baking, they tend to bend, leak, and make a mess when you're trying to put them in the oven.

So, use two or three pie tins for filling and baking. When the pie is done, remove the extra pans.

MOCK APPLE PIE

This recipe has been a Heloise reader favorite since 1959. It is a hoot to serve—and don't tell until after your guests take a bite!
To make one pie, you will need:
pie pastry to make double-crust pie
2 cups water
1¼ cups sugar
2 teaspoons cream of tartar
20 whole soda crackers* (see note below)
Butter (for dotting)
Ground cinnamon (for sprinkling)
Preheat the oven to 375 degrees F. Line the bottom of a 9-inch pie pan with pastry. In a medium saucepan, boil the water, sugar, and cream of tartar. Add the soda crackers and boil only 1 minute (the mixture will be a little soupy, but it will thicken). Spoon gently into the pie shell. Dot the top with butter and sprinkle on the cinnamon to taste. Cover the pie with the top crust and cut vents in it.

Bake 35 minutes. Let the pie cool completely so it can firm up. Put the pie in the refrigerator for a "quick cool." You'll swear this delicious pie really had apples in it!

*The crackers are the small, square ones with four sections to a "sheet." Break each sheet into the four crackers and stack until you have 20 total.

Make a crumb crust. When making a crumb pie crust, spread the buttered crumbs evenly in a 9-inch pie shell with a fork. Then place an 8-inch pie pan in the center and press firmly to compact. No fuss or messy hands.

Dress up pumpkin pie. To dress up a store-bought pumpkin pie, just place pecans or walnuts around the edge and add a little cinnamon and whipped cream in the center of the pie.

Make easy caramel rolls. You can easily turn the ready-made cinnamon rolls found in the freezer case into caramel rolls. Melt a tablespoon or so of butter in the bottom of the pan, then sprinkle with brown sugar and—the big secret—drizzle with syrup! Any kind of syrup will do, but pancake syrup works especially well. Place the rolls on top and bake as directed. When done, turn the pan of rolls upside down onto foil to allow caramel to run down over the rolls.

Make tart shells faster. When you

need to make tart shells in a hurry, use the cap end of an unopened water bottle as an aid. Put the pastry dough into each of the tart cups, clean the bottle with hot water and soap, dip the dry bottle cap into a small bowl of flour, and then "stamp" out the tarts. It takes a fraction of the time that finger-pressing would take.

TASTY TIDBIT

Did you know that the first pies were usually made with meat instead of fruit? When fruit pies were first introduced, they were usually served with breakfast. Now that sounds good, doesn't it? Americans' favorite pie is apple pie, followed by pumpkin. So, why not have a nice, warm slice of apple or mock apple pie right now?

COOKIES 101

Here are some simply delicious hints to make baking cookies easy:

- Before baking the whole batch, test one or two cookies first to make sure you are using the correct baking time and temperature.
- Be careful when substituting ingredients, as it could change the taste or texture.
- Use powdered drink mix instead of colored sugar when topping sugar cookies.
- If cookies get burned on the bottom, gently grate off the burned portion to make them "great" once again.
- A cheese slicer is handy for cutting refrigerator cookies.
- To keep cookies soft, place a piece of bread in the container with them.
- To make sprinkles stick to cookies, slightly dampen the top and then sprinkle with decorations.
- To keep cookie cutters from sticking to dough, spray them with nonstick vegetable spray before use.
- When making cookie dough, make extra to freeze so that you can bake another batch quickly.
- A potato-chip can is an ideal container to mail cookies in.
- Use a melon-baller utensil to scoop out dough and put on a cookie sheet when making drop cookies.
- Use a potato masher to form the design on peanut butter cookies.

BEVERAGES

MOCHA COFFEE

Here's a Heloise mocha coffee blend that we have been printing for more than a decade, and it is perfect for chocolate lovers. Try this:

½ cup instant-coffee granules

½ cup sugar (or equivalent measure using sugar substitute)

1 cup powdered milk or powdered creamer (nonfat can be substituted)

2 tablespoons cocoa powder

Mix all of the ingredients together and put it in a coffee can (that you have labeled) or other container. This dry mixture can be stored and made up quickly when needed, and you'll avoid all the hassle of cleaning up a coffee machine. This mixture would also make a great gift in a pretty apothecary jar.

To add a special touch to your cup of mocha coffee, drop in a few mini-marshmallows or a dash of cinnamon or nutmeg. This mocha blend is delicious when made and then chilled by pouring over ice for a glass of iced coffee.

To make a cup of chocolate "Joe," start with 2 teaspoons to a cup (6 to 8 ounces) of hot water. You will need to adjust for your taste. If you have used sugar substitute, you will use less.

Mocha coffee, take 2. Pour a packet of dry hot chocolate mix into a cup, and instead of hot water, pour in coffee. Instant mocha coffee.

While you're at it, you can stir in ½ teaspoon cinnamon, and you'll have your own Viennese blend.

Mocha coffee, take 3. Add a teaspoon of cocoa to your coffee filter for each cup of coffee you make. Tastes great!

Make your own mint coffee. As the Christmas holidays draw near, coffee lovers may discover that they like peppermint-flavored coffee. If you want to make your own, put a couple of miniature candy canes in the coffee filter with the coffee and let the hot water melt and combine them with the coffee grounds. Voilà! Instant peppermint coffee at a fraction of the price of gourmet coffee from the grocery store. (After Christmas, stores have boxes of miniature candy canes on clearance, so buy then and save.)

Also, try adding them to a freshly brewed cup of coffee or hot tea—a kind of flavored stir stick!

Make crazy coffee. I buy several bags of gourmet coffee during my shopping. When I get down to the last little bit of a couple of bags, I mix the dibs and dabs together to make what I call "crazy coffee." It's never the same twice!

Make iced coffee. Here's an ultra-simple recipe for iced coffee that helps beat the heat. It is so good on a hot day, and so easy. It also "recycles" any coffee left in the pot after breakfast. You can save leftover coffee in the fridge and when you have a pitcher, just whip it up!

You will need 6 to 10 cups of coffee (depending on how strong or weak you like your coffee) and one 14-ounce can of sweetened condensed milk. Stir together in a pitcher until well blended, and refrigerate.

Make iced-coffee cubes to use instead of plain ice.

Iced coffee, take 2. Here's a great way to use leftover coffee. After you have your morning coffee, pour the leftover coffee into an ice-cube tray and freeze it. Whenever you want a nice, iced coffee, pop out the cubes and put them in a blender with some milk, sugar, and a little chocolate syrup. Mix it up and top with whipped cream.

Pre-measure coffee. To save time and aggravation in the morning, separate a month's worth of coffee filters, and pre-measure the coffee into each. Then nest them together and store them in a sealed plastic container.

Stash coffee pods in less space. Pod coffee machines are great, but those bags of pods take up too much room. One solution is to transfer the pods to an empty tall potato-chip can. Then, cut out the front of the bag and tape it to the can.

Remove a coffee filter. To get a new coffee filter, turn the stack of filters upside down. Slightly moisten your clean fingertips, and the filters easily slide off, just one at a time.

Warm your cup. If you like your coffee to stay hot, warm the cup up first in the microwave by putting some water in the cup and microwaving for 30 seconds (or longer, depending on your microwave). Pour out and add the coffee.

Warm your coffee cup another way. If you have a hot-water attachment on your sink, fill your empty coffee cup with hot water from this faucet and wait a few seconds. Dump the water and then pour your coffee as usual. This keeps the coffee warmer longer.

Cut caffeine but not flavor. Are you a coffee lover who's trying to cut down on your caffeine? When you make a pot of coffee, make it with half regular coffee and half decaffeinated coffee. You will still get the same flavor and enjoyment, but with half the caffeine. You can even mix flavored coffees.

Measure coffee an easier way. Do you get tired of measuring 12 scoops of coffee grounds each morning to brew your daily pot of coffee? Measure the 12 scoops into a 1-cup measure and find out how much those scoops add up to. Then measure with a bigger measuring cup. You may only have to measure one or twice to brew a perfect pot of coffee.

Separate filters with a fingertip cover. A rubber fingertip cover, like the ones secretaries use to flip through papers, is an efficient way to separate coffee filters. An added advantage is that the finger cover can be left nesting in the filters and is not so likely to be removed.

 Save time on morning coffee. Here's a time- and effort-saving hint for making morning coffee.

If you use a mixture of regular and decaf, instead of dragging both big cans of coffee out of the pantry each day, purchase seven ½-cup plastic containers with lids. Each cup holds enough coffee for brewing one pot.

Once a week, fill all seven containers (two scoops decaf, one scoop regular, or whatever you like). Put the lids on and stack the cups on the left side of the cupboard shelf.

When you empty a container, place it on the right side of the shelf. There is no need to wash the cups each time if you are going to refill them with coffee each week.

This system saves fumbling around with the big coffee cans and scoops when you are still half asleep.

Cool coffee or tea in the cup. Keep two stainless-steel teaspoons in your freezer for those occasions when you're in a hurry and don't have time to wait until a freshly poured cup of coffee or tea is cool enough to be drinkable.

After you fill your cup, submerge one icy-cold spoon into the beverage (or two, if you're in a BIG hurry), and in only a minute or so it will cool down to an acceptable temperature.

COFFEE 101

Wake up and smell the coffee! It can be even more enticing if you do something a little extra to that cup of java. Here's a little Coffee 101, so you can sound like an expert when you step up to the coffee bar to place your order.

Espresso is a popular coffee drink that is concentrated, strong, and rich-flavored and usually served in small demitasse cups. It is a basic ingredient for cappuccino, café latte, and café mocha. By adding spices, milks, and syrups, you can make your own specialty coffee.

Necessity and burned lips—the mothers of invention.

Use coffee grounds for fertilizer. Save up your used coffee grounds and sprinkle them in your flower beds—they're good for the soil. If you do want to dispose of them, try putting them in a plastic newspaper sleeve for less mess in your garbage can.

Give flowers some coffee. Instead of throwing coffee grinds or leftover coffee away, mix a little of the liquid coffee with water and feed your azaleas. They are acid-loving plants, and coffee will add a little acid to the soil—and also help nourish it. Spread the coffee grounds on the soil around the azaleas.

Make flavored hot chocolate. Buying flavored hot chocolate, such as raspberry or orange, can be quite costly. Here's a frugal way to make your own.

Scoop hot-cocoa powder into a cup per directions, then add 1 level teaspoon of raspberry, orange, or cherry gelatin powder. You can use any flavor you want—let your imagination go. It is delicious.

Make bigger ice cubes. Take empty plastic containers that you get with applesauce or puddings. Fill them with water and freeze. The cubes pop out easily when frozen and are a great size. Freeze as many as you need and store in the freezer.

Make fancy punch bowl ice. Here's how to make an attractive ice float for a punch bowl instead of using ice cubes. Take a flower-shaped gelatin mold, fill it with water, and freeze it. Then, dip it in hot water for a second or two and it will come right out—looks lovely in the punch bowl.

Forget punch rings. An alternative to using ice rings in punch bowls (because they dilute the punch and the punch ladle never fits the hole in the ice ring) is to use the little fluted cups from fast-food places that hold small sundaes. Freeze some of the juice you are using in the punch, and use several of these cups to freeze fancy ice cubes.

Make ice to match your drink. Avoid having melting ice cubes watering down a drink: Make ice from the drink mix you are consuming.

Make a lemonade ice cube. When you're serving a big bowl of punch at a party, use lemonade, frozen in a small tube pan and with cherries in the bottom, as an ice cube. The ice cube won't dilute the punch, and it will also look pretty.

Make juice cubes. Freeze different flavors of juice in several ice-cube trays, and then use the frozen juice cubes in your juice. It is also fun to try different combinations of juice and juice cubes. You can make "tomberry" juice (tomato and strawberry) or "grapple" juice (grape and apple). Get creative!

Make a healthier drink. As a healthier alternative to drinking soda, take your favorite juice and mix with half club soda.

Make your own tomato juice. Make your own tomato juice with tomato paste. Here's the formula:

Use 1 part tomato paste to 3 parts cold tap water (more or less—you can adjust to your taste); blend in blender (this makes it completely smooth and creamy), and add salt and pepper to taste.

Not only is it cheap, but it's also rich and delectable.

Mix lemonade. Instead of a large glass pitcher to make frozen lemonade, use an empty 96-ounce (3-quart) plastic juice container. It is easier to use because it has a closed cap and allows you to shake the ingredients.

All about milk. Milk is "udder"ly fascinating and is a good source of calcium and protein in the American diet. It comes in four basic varieties: whole, 2 percent, 1 percent, and nonfat (or skim) milk. They vary in calories and fat grams. Milk contains nine essential nutrients and is fortified with calcium. The milk must indicate on the label if it has been fortified with vitamins, calcium, protein, or minerals.

P.S. What goes best with a piece of chocolate cake? A cold glass of milk!

Make flavored milk. How about using common kitchen extracts to flavor milk? Flavor extracts are a real treat in cold milk. If you use instant powdered milk, mix a pitcher and let it sit until cold, or put some ice cubes in the drinking glass. You will have to find the quantity of flavoring you like. Determine the number of glasses your pitcher holds and take it from there. The flavorings could also be added to regular processed milk.

Also, for a refreshing hot drink during the day or night, put a cup of the flavored milk in the microwave and heat. Try whatever flavors you like—banana, vanilla, coconut, lemon, peppermint, peach, rum, walnut, butterscotch, or blueberry—use your imagination. You can mix flavors, too, such as blueberry and banana or coconut and pineapple, for a different taste. You can use cinnamon, nutmeg—anything you like!

Use the extracts or spices to flavor coffee, too.

Keep soda fizzy. Take a 2-liter bottle of soda and fill up several smaller bottles for ease of portability. If you fill up all your smaller bottles at the same time and replace the lids securely, the soda stays fizzy quite nicely. It's opening the big bottle repeatedly that makes it go flat.

Make a quick cup of hot tea. If you're a tea lover, keep a pitcher of iced tea in your fridge. When you feel like having a cup of hot tea, just pour a cup of iced tea and put it in the microwave. It's a timesaver.

FRIENDSHIP SPICED TEA

This favorite recipe is delicious, and it also makes a great hostess or housewarming gift when put in a pretty jar along with directions on how to make it. To prepare this friendship tea, you will need the following:

2½ cups powdered orange-flavored breakfast drink

1¾ cups powdered instant tea (not sweetened)

2 to 2½ cups sugar

1 small package unsweetened lemonade mix (small packet that makes 2 quarts when mixed with water)

1½ teaspoons ground cloves

1½ teaspoons ground cinnamon

Mix together all the ingredients and store in a container with an airtight lid. You can put the ingredients in a blender to make the tea smooth and creamy-looking. Or, make a sugar-free version by using sugar substitute, diet powdered orange drink, and sugar-free lemonade.

To make a glass, add 1 to 2 rounded teaspoons (the sugar-free is more concentrated, so you will probably need less) to 6 to 8 ounces of water. Stir well and add ice.

There are all kinds of things you can add to hot or cold tea to give it a little more flavor. How about trying a lemon-drop candy, chocolate morsel, or sprinkle of cinnamon?

SPICED TEA NO. 2. Here's another way to make spiced tea:

Wrap six (about 2-inch-long) cinnamon sticks, I teaspoon whole cloves, and a whole nutmeg in a double thickness of cheesecloth. Now, give it a good whack or two using a meat mallet or hammer to crush the contents.

Combine the crushed spices with 2 cups tea leaves, 2 tablespoons grated orange peel, and 2 tablespoons grated lemon peel. Mix well and keep in a jar with a tight lid.

When you're ready for a cup of this delicious tea, you'll need to "warm up" the teapot by rinsing it with boiling water, then pour out the water. Next, spoon in a teaspoon of the mixture for each cup you want to make, and also add the appropriate amount of boiling water. Let the tea stand for 2 to 5 minutes, then strain it into teacups. Yummy!

Tips for tea. Two hints for relaxing with a hot cup of tea: To avoid frustration while using a tea bag to make a cup of tea, clip a clothespin to the tag to keep it from falling into the hot water. Also, use a metal tea-bag squeezer to keep from burning your fingers.

Make sun tea. Sun tea is an energy-saving (and easy) way to make tea, and those of us who live in Southern climates can make it year-round.

Sweet treat tea. Fill a glass jar or glass pitcher with water and 3 or 4 regular tea bags. Set it in the sun until the tea is brewed, about 2–3 hours.

You can use frozen ice pops to keep your iced tea cold, and the added flavor from the flavored pops is delicious. And did you know that more than 80 percent of tea served in the United States is iced—so swizzling with an ice pop is a sweet idea!

Have milk and lemon. A cup of hot tea is so comforting on a cold winter day. If you like both milk and lemon in your tea, but the lemon curdles the milk, here's an alternative. If you put a scant teaspoon of lemon extract in the cup of hot tea, you can enjoy both flavors without the curdling.

Label iced teas. At a family gathering or party, it's nice to serve a few types of flavored iced teas in attractive glass pitchers. The problem is that the teas all look alike. Labels can fall off, and tags tied to the handles can be hard to read. Try washable paint to label the tea containers. Simply write directly on the pitcher and, when it is empty, wash the paint right off.

Use Christmas candy canes. A great way to use up candy canes hung on Christmas trees is to use about one-quarter of a candy cane to sweeten a cup of tea. The candy canes melt faster if you break them up and cover them with boiling water.

Make "drip" tea. When brewing iced tea, rather than having to keep an eye on a teapot or a pot of boiling water on the stove, use an automatic-drip coffee maker. Make sure the basket is clean of any coffee residue, put the tea bags in the carafe, and run water through as usual. The tea steeps really well because the water in the carafe is kept hot automatically for a couple of hours. Add extra water and sugar later, whenever it's convenient.

TASTY TIDBIT

Here's a bit of information for you tea lovers—did you know that tea bags were introduced more than 100 years ago?

Considering that Americans drink billions of cups of tea a year, that's a lot of tea bags!

Remove tea residue. When you decide to make sun tea in a gallon container, tea residue can build up on the inside of the wide-mouth jug. If you fill the container with hot water, add a denture tablet, and let it sit overnight, the residue can easily be wiped away.

Put a teakettle to work. Even if you're a coffee person, a teakettle can still come in handy. Keep a teakettle full of water on the range. After you pull a pan off of the stove, cover the hot burner with the teakettle to protect yourself (and others) from potentially nasty burns.

TASTY TIDBIT

Do you know which country consumes the most tea on a per-person basis? Look at the following countries and see if you know the right one:

a) Great Britain

b) Canada

c) Ireland

d) United States

Do you think it's Great Britain? Well, according to the Tea Association of the USA, the British consume 3.2 cups per day, per person, and people in the United States consume much less. But the answer is "c," Ireland, where nearly 4 cups per person are consumed each day.

Reuse wine bags. Wine bags can be reused several ways—just fill with air and . . .

- Use as a pillow while soaking in a hot bath.

- Use for lumbar support at your desk or in your vehicle.

- Pack in your suitcase (deflated) and use as a travel pillow.

- When summertime comes around, use in a friendly game of pool "catch."

SANDWICHES AND SNACKS

Get the sandwich in the bag. When you cut a kid's lunch sandwich in half or in quarters, getting it into the sandwich bag after it is cut can be quite messy. Use a wide spatula to pick up the sandwich and place it in the bag. The spatula slides right out with no mess and the sandwich stays intact.

Make a PB and J sandwich. When making a peanut butter and jelly sandwich, pull two pieces of bread out of the loaf. Spread the peanut butter on the downside of the top piece and the jelly on the upside of the bottom piece. This allows the pieces to fit together perfectly when pressed, and will save embarrassing jelly drops on your shirt.

Squeeze out the mayo. Here's a great way to pack condiments when you'll be making a sandwich away from home: Get a sealable plastic sandwich bag and squeeze the mayonnaise into the corner. When lunchtime comes, simply punch a hole in the corner of the bag and squeeze the mayo out with ease and without a mess.

Make a thick sandwich. Have you ever bought wafer-thin sliced, chopped, pressed, or cooked sandwich meats in a sealed envelope?

Don't try to separate the meat. Just cut it up in slices, the whole wad, and then separate and pile it on the bread. It makes a thick sandwich.

Make sandwiches fun. When you're serving children, cut grilled cheese sandwiches, pancakes, and waffles into three sticks. Also cut peanut butter and jelly sandwiches with cookie cutters that reflect the season, or into smaller squares or diagonally into four pieces. Kids love them.

Store snacks in the freezer. Keep your boxes of snacks in the freezer. You'll never need to worry about stale treats! Just take out what you want.

Great for cereal and for sale items you won't use soon.

Prepackage snack servings. Do big bags of snacks disappear like magic when you bring them home? When you buy a bag of chips or other snack food meant for school lunches, fill some small plastic bags with the chips according to the single-serving info on the bag. Then take all the little bags you've made and put them back into the original bag.

Your snacks will last a lot longer because your family will tend to stop eating them after one serving.

Make yummy healthy snacks. If you have to curb sugars, starches, and

---

TASTY TIDBIT

Let's test your snack food knowledge. Which snack food do Americans consume 17 billion quarts of annually? One more clue: Most of this snack is grown in the United States.

a) tortilla chips

b) pretzels

c) popcorn

Do you "c" the right answer? Has it "popped" into your head yet? Popcorn is the answer! Scientists have found popcorn ears or cobs while excavating in New Mexico sites that are nearly 5,600 years old. So, it's safe to say that popcorn has been around for a long time.

other refined products from you diet for health reasons, here's a great substitute for snack crackers.

Put anything you would have put on a cracker on a thick slice of cucumber instead. You'll have the crunch you liked from the cracker, and the toppings you normally enjoy, like tuna, shredded chicken, or cheese. Slice the cucumbers and put them into a plastic bag, then eat them at your desk for a snack.

Snack on garbanzo beans. For a very healthy snack, rinse and drain garbanzo beans (also called chickpeas) and spread on a cookie sheet. Spray with cooking spray and sprinkle on some grill seasoning. Cook at about 300 degrees F for 30 minutes or until crunchy, stirring occasionally.

You can also "roast" the beans at 350 degrees F for 30 minutes and use a Greek seasoning.

Make party mix. If you love to make big batches of party mix, finding a container big enough to mix all the ingredients in can be a challenge. You could mix it in a big, metal popcorn tin, and then store the mix in the tin until needed. Don't use a trash bag to make up your party mix—they aren't made of food-grade plastic, and may contain chemicals that you don't want food to come into contact with.

TASTY TIDBIT

Let's test your popcorn IQ. Which term is used for popcorn kernels that don't pop?

a) old maids or spinsters

b) toothbreakers

c) pop duds

If you picked "a," then you are right; however, they have been known to break a tooth or two.

Make a quickie pizza. To make a quick pizza, get an English muffin, split it in half, and top with pizza sauce, cheese, pepperoni, or anything you like best.

Put it in the oven for about 10 minutes at about 350 degrees F. It's great homemade pizza!

Make your own popcorn salt. An air popper is a great way to make popcorn because you can use less salt, oil, and butter than the microwave kind has.

Regular salt does not stick very well to the popcorn. Solution: your single-serving coffee grinder! It grinds approximately ¼ cup regular salt at a time. The finely ground salt sticks better to popcorn, and is great on french fries, too.

Dress up plain popcorn. If you love

chocolate-covered raisins, try adding some to popped corn. Kids love it.

Flavor your own popcorn. To make French toast popcorn, pop some popcorn in an air popper. Add five to 10 pumps of spray butter, then sprinkle with ground cinnamon and powdered sugar.

It's a nice change of pace when you are craving something a little bit sweet but are still trying to keep it healthy and low-cal.

Share movie popcorn. When you take kids to the movies, instead of buying each of them a "kid's popcorn combo," bring some cone-shaped coffee filters, and buy one medium popcorn for all of you to share. Each person can use a filter as a popcorn holder—it's less messy than trying to

POPCORN POINTS

Who doesn't love popcorn? It's delicious and high in fiber, and it can be a low-calorie snack. So, I thought I would share some hints and a recipe for a great snack—popcorn:

- Put popcorn into resealable plastic bags after it's cooled. Cut a small hole in the corner of the bag and give the whole thing a good shake so that unpopped kernels fall out of the hole.

- Popcorn should be cooked only in microwave-safe containers or prepackaged microwave bags. Kernels can scorch and catch fire if cooked in other containers, such as brown paper bags. And don't reheat popcorn in the microwave.

- Popcorn kernels should be stored in an airtight container on a pantry shelf, not in the refrigerator. Too much moisture could prevent the popcorn from popping.

- Try sprinkling with seasoned salts, salt-free herb blends, dry salad-dressing mixes, taco or chili seasoning mixes, grated hard cheeses like Parmesan or Romano, or the powdered cheese from macaroni-and-cheese dinners.

- Serve popcorn to guests with several bowls of different toppings so they can make their own special blend.

- When you make a batch at night, save some for workday or school lunches. Put the cooled popcorn in a large, resealable plastic bag.

- Don't salt popcorn before popping—it might actually toughen the kernels.

- To make edible holders for party munchies, shape popcorn-ball mix over the bottoms and sides of glasses that are well-greased with margarine. After the mixture hardens, remove the "cups" and fill with nuts or other treats.

balance popcorn on a flimsy napkin.

Unsalt your nuts. If you love mixed nuts but need to watch your salt intake, here's an idea. Fill a jar of salted mixed nuts with warm water and rinse all the salt off the nuts. Then place them in a shallow dish with a couple of paper towels and put them in the microwave for a minute.

Use chip bits. Don't throw away those last tiny chips in the nacho-chip bag because they are too small to dip into the salsa. Sprinkle them over chili or any kind of Southwestern stew or soup.

EXTRAS—SAUCES AND GRAVIES, CONDIMENTS, DIPS, AND SPREADS

Make a marinade. Don't let marinades intimidate you. Why buy expensive bottled marinades when it's so easy to make your own? Be creative—mix various flavors of mustards (dill, Dijon, or honey) and vinegars with your favorite fresh herbs, olive oil, Worcestershire sauce . . . even a splash of white wine. Experiment with a little before you make a lot. When it's to your liking, whisk it all together and

On the Light Side

What's the Most Popular Barbecue Sauce?

Did you ever wonder what the most popular flavor of barbecue sauce is? Well, according to the Hearth, Patio & Barbecue Association, hickory flavoring is the favorite, followed by tomato-based sauces. An empty, well-washed ketchup bottle is a great container to store your homemade barbecue sauce, and it's handy to use.

baste those kebabs, chickens, turkey breasts, pork chops, salmon steaks . . . the sky's the limit!

"SWEET" BEER MARINADE

Marinades can add great flavor to meat, pork, chicken, or just about anything! Here's a "sweet" beer marinade for pork or chicken that you can whip up in a few seconds. Combine:

¼ cup soy sauce
1 cup beer (or nonalcoholic beer), at room temperature
2 tablespoons brown sugar
2 teaspoons grated fresh or finely chopped candied ginger
1 or 2 drops hot sauce to add zip

Mix well. Put four chops or chicken breasts in a self-sealing plastic bag and pour in the marinade. Seal and put in the fridge for 4 to 24 hours—then they're ready to grill.

Remember that after using marinade with raw meat or chicken you must boil the used marinade for 2 minutes or longer if you are going to use it as a sauce for the meat. Toss it when done—it's not safe for a third use.

Freeze in a marinade. If you buy flank steaks or London broils at a warehouse club where they come in large packages, freeze some. When you get home, prepare your favorite marinade in gallon-size freezer bags. Put one steak in each bag and then place it in the freezer. When you are ready to use a steak, take it out of the freezer and thaw it overnight in the refrigerator. The steak will be full of flavor from the marinade and very, very ten-

Heloise's Jamaican Barbecue-Sauce Recipe

My mother, the original Heloise, printed this Jamaican recipe in her column in the sixties. The story goes that she sweet-talked a chef when she was visiting the islands.

Combine:

1½ cups apple-cider vinegar
3 tablespoons Worcestershire sauce
4 teaspoons lemon juice
2 teaspoons brown sugar
1 tablespoon prepared mustard (yellow)
1 tablespoon liquid smoke
1 teaspoon garlic powder
1 teaspoon cayenne pepper
¾ teaspoon salt
½ teaspoon flavor enhancer (this is monosodium glutamate flavoring, which was popular in the sixties; you might want to omit it from the recipe)
1 cup ketchup
½ cup tomato puree

Mix all of these ingredients together (sometimes I use a blender—just make sure the brown sugar is dissolved). Put in a clear container with a tight-fitting lid—a clear mayo or spaghetti-sauce jar is perfect. This sauce needs to be stored in the refrigerator or used immediately.

Once you have had a taste of this spicy concoction, you'll want to make a double or triple batch!

der. This works great for a quick dinner when you are in a hurry. Just throw the steak and some corn on the grill and open a bag of prepared salad.

Make gravy taste better. Any brown gravy tastes better when you add a little leftover coffee from breakfast. How much? When making brown gravy, start with a little and then adjust to taste.

Make gravy without all the fat. After a turkey or a roast is removed from a roasting pan, drop ice cubes into the drippings to quickly solidify and remove the fat. Use a fork to lift out solid grease, and as the ice cubes melt, add more. Use the de-fatted drippings to make gravy.

Store leftover gravy. When you have a lot of gravy left over after cooking a turkey or a roast, freeze it in a clean ice-cube tray. After it freezes, just pop the cubes out and store in a freezer bag. They will defrost in a microwave fast, whether you are using one cube or many.

Make easy gravy. The water in which you cook potatoes is great for making mashed potatoes. And it's great in gravy, too. When you make fried chicken, use browned pieces from the chicken and any reserved flour coating mixture. Brown this and then add the liquid from the potatoes, supplemented with enough milk to make your gravy bowl full.

Of course, you have to have hot biscuits and mashed potatoes to put the gravy on!

Spice up nonfat mayo. Since nonfat mayonnaise does not have much taste, add a dash of hot pepper sauce to give it some zip.

Freeze cranberry sauce. Fresh cranberries aren't available all year long, so do the following: When you are preparing cranberry sauce for Thanksgiving or Christmas, buy four or six bags of cranberries and cook them, two bags at a time, then freeze them in 8-ounce yogurt cups.

You can enjoy fresh cranberry sauce all year.

Use the last of the jelly. When you have used up all of the jelly or jam, put

---

TASTY TIDBIT

Let's test your apricot IQ. Which of the following words is the Latin meaning of the word *apricot*?

a) love

b) precious

c) tender

It's nice to "b" right! Fresh apricots are available from February through August, so why not buy some to enjoy?

a little bit of very hot water in the jar, place the lid back on, and shake it really well until all of the jam has loosened enough to pour out and use. You can add it to all kinds of things, like tea or flavored waters.

Re-liquefy crystallized honey. Here's some helpful information from the American Honey Producers Association about sweet honey. It is natural for honey to granulate over time. You can easily re-liquefy honey by placing the container in a bowl of warm water and letting it sit until the honey is clear. Once the water starts to cool, replace it with more hot water. Be careful not to overheat, as this can caramelize the honey, which can change its flavor and texture.

Did you know that storing honey in the refrigerator can actually speed the crystallization process? So, store honey at room temperature, out of direct sunlight.

Clean up condiments. Take a minute to remove the screw-on caps from ketchup, mustard, or similar items and give them a quick rinse under hot

Apricot Jam

Here is a flashback recipe from my mother, the original Heloise, that we think was printed in the mid-seventies or earlier. It is a delicious apricot jam made from dried fruit that is different, tastes good, and takes little effort. Here it is, in her voice:

"Buy some dried apricots. Put them in a big fruit jar. Pour boiling water over them and let sit overnight. Remember, they will swell. Fill the jar about half full of fruit.

"The next day put these apricots in the refrigerator. Let them sit one more day. By then, they will have become swollen and juicy. Pour the water off, put the apricots, as is, into your blender (or electric mixer) and give them a whirl. At this time one may add a few spoons of sugar or a sugar substitute. You will come out with the thickest, most exciting jam you have ever tasted.

"If you like a wee bit of a sour taste, slice four or five slivers of fresh lemon and put in the jar before pouring the boiling water over the fruit.

"I have also tried this with other dried fruits such as pears and peaches. This is wonderful when put on waffles or pancakes. –Heloise"

I remember my mother making this many times! It was kinda fun to do and yummy to eat.

water. Have you ever taken a look at one that hasn't been "treated" for a while? Unappetizing, to say the least!

Make martini olives. Many of us like the biting, briny taste of martini olives. When you get a new jar of olives, pour out about one-quarter of the jar juice and replace it with vinegar. Then put the jar in the refrigerator. The olives are ready in 2 to 3 hours.

TEXAS CAVIAR

This recipe can be made ahead of time and refrigerated for at least 24 hours before serving to allow the flavors to blend, or you can mix it up and serve it fresh as a side "salad."

You will need:
1 large jar medium or hot picante sauce
2 16-ounce cans black-eyed peas, drained
1 16-ounce can white hominy, drained
1 cup green bell pepper, diced
1 cup white onion, chopped
1 cup fresh tomato, chopped
½ cup fresh cilantro (Chinese parsley), finely chopped
¼ cup jalapeño pepper, seeded and chopped
1 cup scallions (include green tops), chopped
1 tablespoon sugar
1 tablespoon salt
2 tablespoons coarsely ground black pepper
2 tablespoons ground cumin (comino)

Combine all the ingredients in an extra-large bowl. Use as a dip with tortilla chips or crackers.

Olive Nut Spread

This original Heloise recipe was first printed more than 45 years ago, and it has been a longtime favorite of readers (and mine). To give it a try, you will need:
6 ounces cream cheese (regular or low-fat), softened
½ cup mayonnaise or light mayonnaise
1 cup chopped green salad olives (buy the least expensive kind, since you chop them up anyway; the jar will say "salad olives," and they are usually small pieces of olives and pimentos) and their juice
Dash of ground pepper (but no salt)
½ cup chopped pecans

Combine the softened cream cheese and the mayonnaise in a bowl. A fork works well to get it all mixed together. Add the juice from the olive jar and a dash or two of pepper, then mix. Now, fold in the pecans and olives.

This can be served as a thick dip, or used as a nice spread on toast or on bread with some tomatoes and lettuce for a tasty sandwich.

Peanut butter—should it be refrigerated or not? Well, here is what a leading manufacturer had to say: Unused or opened jars do best when stored at room temperature. Temperature fluctuation, hot or cold, can change the peanut butter, but it's still safe to eat. Now I'm hungry for a peanut butter and jelly sandwich, with a little shredded apple for crunch.

Reuse pudding cups for dips. When serving hors d'oeuvres, aside from the dip container in the middle of the chip tray, there never seems to be enough holders for other sauces, like mustard for cocktail franks or pasta sauce for mozzarella sticks. But little plastic pudding- and fruit-cup containers work great when they're washed out. They are small enough to fit on a serving tray and can just be tossed out after a couple of uses.

CINNAMON BUTTER

Cinnamon butter is delicious and easy to make. It can be spread on toast, bagels, waffles, pancakes, baked sweet potatoes, or any other food you'd use a sweet-flavored butter on.

All you need is:

½ pound butter or margarine (not diet)
3 tablespoons cinnamon
½ pound confectioners' sugar

Combine the ingredients, mix well using an electric mixer, and place in a labeled airtight container. Store in the refrigerator. This butter won't last long, so keep these three ingredients on hand.

Stretch pimento cheese spread. To help "stretch" your favorite commercial cheese spread, add some reduced-fat mayo and a few extra olives. It goes a little further, is creamier, and helps cut a few fat calories, too.

Soften natural peanut butter. When using natural peanut butter, if it gets a little hard at the bottom of the jar, just take out what you need and microwave it for a couple of seconds, and it'll be spreadable again.

Want to know the difference between green and black olives? Even though they differ in taste and color, they are from the same tree. The only difference is the ripeness—green olives are picked when they are immature, and black ones stay on the tree longer. Unopened cans of olives have a shelf life of 3 to 4 years if stored on your pantry shelf. Once a can has been opened, the olives will stay edible for approximately 10 days in the original brine, loosely covered with plastic wrap.

SPICES AND SEASONINGS

To make your own homemade seasoned salt, you will need:

½ teaspoon cayenne pepper (more if you like a little heat)
1 teaspoon dried parsley flakes (ground well)
1 teaspoon garlic powder
1 teaspoon chili powder
2 teaspoons paprika
1 tablespoon celery seed (ground well)
2 tablespoons onion powder
1 cup salt (or salt substitute for salt-restricted diets)

Mix the ingredients using a spoon or fork, or just put them in a clear jar with a lid and shake, shake, shake to mix. You can alter the recipe by adding or subtracting some of the spices to suit your taste.

Fix a saltshaker. Here is an idea for those stubborn tiny corks that are used to plug up saltshakers and pepper shakers. Often the corks dry up and shrink or get pushed into the container so far that it is impossible to get them out without damaging them. Buy soft foam-rubber earplugs to replace the corks. Squeeze the rounded end, push into the hole, and it will expand to fit the hole. To get the plug out, simply squeeze it together.

Refill shakers with no spills. When refilling salt and pepper shakers from the bottom, put a piece of plastic wrap on the top of the shakers, then turn them upside down and remove the stoppers. Fill the shakers, insert the stoppers, and turn them right side up again. Remove the plastic wrap, and none of the salt or pepper will have spilled.

Fill a saltshaker. Filling bottom-loaded saltshakers can be a trial. But if you cover the holes at the top of the shaker with a bit of tape, you can fill it from the bottom without any spills.

Make salt easy to see. For a family member who has difficulty seeing salt on his or her food, try coloring the salt. Fill the saltshaker, pour the salt into a mug, and add two drops of food coloring. Stir until it the color is even, let dry, then refill the shaker.

The salt will be easy to see, and guess what? Blue salt on green or yellow food (especially eggs) sure helps you cut back on using the saltshaker.

Make a saltless surprise seasoning. Mix up salt-free seasoning by combining 2 teaspoons garlic powder, 1 teaspoon basil, 1 teaspoon oregano, and 1 teaspoon powdered lemon rind (dehydrated lemon juice can be used instead). Mix ingredients in a blender, then transfer this wonderful salt-free seasoning to a glass container with a tight-sealing lid. Enjoy!

Make salt boxes easy to open. Here's a way to tame those nasty salt box tabs that break your nail when you open the box. When you get a new box of salt, use pliers to bend the rounded end of the tab to about a 45-degree angle. This allows it to still close, but it can be opened easily and quickly with your thumb and not your fingernail.

Get pepper for less. Grind (in an electric coffee grinder) whole black peppercorns that you can buy very inexpensively at discount stores. You will get two to three times the amount you'd get of fresh ground pepper for a very low cost.

ALL ABOUT SALT

Salt is an ingredient in most recipes, and it can also be used around the house as a cleaner.

Salt varies in color—it can go from colorless to brown. And did you know that salt is an essential element in most diets?

There are a few different types of salt. Here they are, along with their definitions:

- REGULAR SALT is granulated and has a free-flowing agent added. Keep in mind that this salt still might clump. Used for table seasoning, cooking, and baking.
- IODIZED TABLE SALT got its name because iodine was originally added to salt to reduce the incidence of simple goiter. All salts that contain iodine will be labeled "iodized."
- CANNING AND PICKLING SALT is granulated and doesn't have any preservatives or free-flowing agents added to it. You can use it in cooking, pickling, and canning.
- KOSHER SALT is a coarse flake with a free-flowing agent added. It can be used in cooking and when making kosher meals.
- POPCORN SALT is superfine and made specifically for popcorn and other snacks. It is also delicious on corn on the cob and french fries.
- SEA SALT is the natural salt left behind when seawater evaporates. It contains sodium chloride and trace elements, but no iodine, sugar, or anti-caking ingredients.

Here are some other "salty" hints I'd like to share:

- Pour salt and other spices into your hand or a spoon first instead of sprinkling them directly onto steaming foods because they absorb the steam and deteriorate faster, not to mention get all clumped up.
- The classic way to keep salt from clumping is to put a few grains of uncooked rice in the shaker. Some people add crushed crackers.

Make cinnamon sugar. Make a cinnamon-sugar mixture by combining 3 cups sugar with ½ cup ground cinnamon. Mix well and store in an empty, clean spice container, preferably one with a shaker top.

Pack brown sugar. To really pack brown sugar in a measuring cup, spoon the sugar into a 1-cup measuring cup, place the next-smaller size cup on top, and press down. Continue adding sugar and pressing until the cup is filled to the brim and packed firmly.

Keep brown sugar soft. After you remove the amount of brown sugar you need, fold the inner plastic bag over the sugar and tape it closed, removing the air. Then use sealing plastic wrap and wrap the sugar bag. The sugar stays soft for a long time.

Or, for boxed sugar, put the box into a plastic freezer bag and keep on the pantry shelf. It will be easy to scoop every time.

Keep brown sugar soft, take 2. To keep brown sugar from getting hard, while the sugar is still fresh, transfer it to a glass jar (or jars) with a snug-fitting lid and store in your cupboard.

Soften hard brown sugar. If you find your brown sugar in rock form in your pantry and you need to use it right away, break off a few smaller "rocks" and grate them down quickly until you have the amount you need.

Here are some other ways to soften hard brown sugar:

- Put a piece of bread on each side of the sugar chunk. The sugar will suck the moisture out of the bread.

- Put some candy jelly orange slices into a zippered lunch bag or plastic container with a lid, along with the hard brown sugar. The sugar should soften up in a few days.

- Get a paper towel and fold it into quarters, then wet it. Put it in a small plastic bag and leave the bag slightly open, then put the bag in the brown-sugar container, sealing the top of the container. A few days later, when the brown sugar is soft again, remove the bag.

On the Light Side ~~~~~~

The First Spice from Columbus

Let's talk spices! What spice did Christopher Columbus discover on his first voyage? According to the American Spice Trade Association, allspice! ASTA said, "The Spaniards were so eager to bring back this spice from the New World, they labeled the dried berries 'pimiento,' which means 'pepper,' based on its similar appearance to black pepper."

Save on spices. Do you get sticker shock at the prices of spices? Keep the empty containers and refill them with spices sold in bulk (they are sold in the ethnic area of the supermarket and are more economical).

Help herbs and spices last longer. Spices and herbs will last a long time if they are stored in airtight containers away from heat, light, and moisture, so don't store spices above the stove, oven, sink, or dishwasher.

Keep 'em away from steam. Try not to sprinkle spices or herbs over a steaming pot, as the moisture will seep into the jar and cause the contents to spoil rather quickly.

HELOISE'S NO-SALT SUBSTITUTE

This is a favorite. You will need:
   5 teaspoons onion powder
   1 tablespoon garlic powder
   1 tablespoon paprika
   1 tablespoon dry mustard
   1 teaspoon thyme
   ½ teaspoon white pepper (can use black)
   ½ teaspoon celery seeds
Mix all of the listed ingredients and store in a tightly covered, labeled container in a cool, dry place. Put in a saltshaker for table use.

Freeze cilantro. If you buy a bunch of cilantro, chances are some of it will go bad before you can use it all. To avoid wasting it, freeze what you don't

THE AGE OF SPICES

How old are some of the spices in your kitchen? How do you know if the spice or herb is "past its prime"? It should have a good fragrance and fresh color, and taste flavorful. If you can't taste the spice, replace it! Here's a hint: Mark the date of purchase on the spice so you'll know how long you've had the product.

Storage is one of the most important factors in the life of a spice or an herb. So, keep the following in mind:

- Keep away from heat and strong, direct light.
- Replace the lid immediately after using.
- Don't sprinkle spices directly into steaming or boiling water (use a measuring spoon). Make sure the spoon used is completely dry before dipping it into the spice or herb jar; otherwise, the moisture will speed the "demise" of the spice or dry herb.

Spices can make a wonderful addition to many dishes. So, why not do a little research, buy a new spice, and give it a try? Buy the smallest bottle when trying a new spice, just in case it doesn't suit your taste.

use right away. When you need some, just pull it out. It is easier to chop, too.

PUMPKIN PIE SPICE

Here's a recipe for pumpkin pie spice, and you might already have the ingredients on hand. You will need:
 $\frac{1}{2}$ teaspoon ground cinnamon
 $\frac{1}{2}$ teaspoon ground ginger
 $\frac{1}{8}$ teaspoon allspice
 $\frac{1}{8}$ teaspoon nutmeg
This makes enough pumpkin-pie spice for one pumpkin pie. If you want to make more, just double or triple the amounts. Store in a clean, labeled spice container.

Find spices fast. To find a particular spice or seasoning bottle in a hurry, put a label on the top of the jar or can. You'll be able to easily find what you're looking for. Alphabetizing helps, too.

TASTY TIDBIT

Here's some helpful information on spices:

- Buy the smallest amount of spices so that you can use them quickly, and buy fresh ones often.
- To keep spices from clumping when adding them to a dish, pour them into your hand first and then add them.
- If spices smell "off" or the color has changed, you probably need to replace them.

CLEVER WAYS WITH LEFTOVERS

Keep track of leftovers. When you clean out your refrigerator, do you discover leftovers you could have eaten or frozen? Here's a solution: Label each container with the contents and the date of preparation, place a sheet of paper on the front of the fridge with the leftovers listed, and place all leftover food containers on the same shelf. Result: Less waste of food, time, and money, and better eating!

Store leftovers in an ice cream carton. When you empty any ice cream carton (the premium kind with lids), wash it instead of throwing it away. Then when you need to throw away old leftovers from the fridge, put them in the carton, put the lid on it, and then throw it away.

Freeze extra meal portions. When you make a large dinner, freeze a couple of portions before you eat for times when you need just one or two portions.

Freeze leftover dinners. When you cook big meals on holidays and special occasions, make the leftovers into TV dinners and freeze them.

Pack leftovers to go. Send leftovers

home with your dinner guests in the plastic containers that cottage cheese, margarine, and yogurt come in. The guests get a container they can keep that is filled with an edible snack.

I.D. leftovers. To identify leftovers stored in see-through containers, use painter's blue tape and write with a permanent marker what is inside (such as meatloaf). Also use a small piece of tape on the lid to mark the date the item was refrigerated or to identify "sugar-free" foods specially made for a diabetic family member. The labels are easy to read and the tape comes off easily.

Label all the leftovers. Cut 1-inch squares of masking tape and put them on a large sheet of waxed paper. When you have leftovers or anything else that needs a label, use a marking pen to write the items on one of the pieces of tape, date it, and stick it on the lid of the container before refrigerating—it sure beats wondering what's inside the container or how old it is.

How long to store canned foods. I'll bet on your pantry shelf right now there are cans of food that have been sitting there for quite a while, but how do you know if you've kept them a little too long? Here are some helpful guidelines:

- Canned goods should be kept in a dry, cool room with a temperature of about 70 degrees F. Never store

Make Your Own Croutons

Here's a simple way to make delicious homemade croutons anytime you want them. Croutons can make a so-so salad really wonderful. And they're quick and easy to make. By experimenting with different herbs and spices, the sky's the limit for possible flavors.

To get started:

- Cut day-old (or older) bread into small cubes.
- Mix your favorite herbs and spices with about ¼ cup olive oil, then lightly brush the oil on all sides of the bread cubes.

- To sauté them, put them in a pan over medium heat for about 5 minutes, tossing frequently. They're done when they look toasted and golden brown.
- To bake them, spread the coated bread cubes on a baking sheet and bake in a 300-degree-F oven until they're crisp and dry—about 45 minutes.
- Let the croutons cool completely. Then garnish your salad right away, or store the croutons in an airtight container. They'll keep for about a week on the shelf or up to 6 months in the freezer.

canned goods near steam pipes, furnaces, or kitchen ranges or in the garage because extreme temperatures—hot and cold—will have a negative effect on their quality.

- As for how long you can keep them, acidic foods, like canned tomatoes and fruits, are safe to store for 18 months.

- Nonacidic canned foods are safe for 2 to 3 years, with some vegetables—like potatoes—keeping as long as 5 years.

- If you see rust, discoloration, or bulges on a can, bacteria may have gotten inside. So throw it out! Better safe than sorry.

Reuse plastic bags. One of the handiest bits of kitchen equipment to come along in ages is the resealable plastic storage bag, which comes in all sizes and can be used in many ways.

If you want to reuse the bags, add a drop of dishwashing liquid to a used bag, seal it, and squish it around in a massaging motion until it's clean, then rinse and dry thoroughly with a paper towel.

However, if the bags have held raw meat, poultry, or fish, they should not be used again for any food item.

I.D. freezer food. To keep from having outdated food in your freezer, try this organization method. When wrapping new, leftover, or frozen packs, place a number on each pack on a strip of masking tape. In a 5-by-7-inch notebook, enter the number, date, and identification of the contents. It's easy, and prevents old, forgotten items. Cross out items as they are removed.

Use stale bread. Here are a few more uses for leftover bread crusts, bread ends, or stale hamburger or hot dog buns that are stored in the freezer. There's no reason to throw away perfectly good bread:

- To make breadsticks, cut bread into strips, brush with melted butter or olive oil, sprinkle on spices, and bake until crispy.

- To create inexpensive croutons, cut stale bread into cubes and add seasonings.

- To enhance brunch casseroles, layer bread with beaten eggs and browned sausage.

- To spice up meatloaf, cut into cubes and combine with prepackaged stuffing (you might need extra seasonings). Add chicken broth, browned sausage, and sautéed mushrooms, onions, and celery.

Save bread ends. Don't throw away those end pieces of bread just because your kids don't like them. Save them in a bread bag in the freezer. When you have collected enough, defrost and use to make stuffing or croutons.

Use leftover buns. Freeze leftover hamburger and hot dog buns to use later as garlic bread. Texans call them Texas breadsticks!

Use extra chips. When you go out to eat Mexican food and do not eat all the chips that come with the salsa, take home the extras, crush them, and freeze them. They make an excellent topping for casseroles, squash, taco bake, hash browns, or any of your favorite casseroles.

Another use for leftover meatloaf. Here's another way to use leftover meatloaf: Crumble or cut it into small pieces and pour a jar of spaghetti sauce over it. Cook some spaghetti and heat the meat sauce, add a salad and garlic bread, and you have a good dinner.

Transform leftover pizza. Heat leftover slices of pizza in the microwave, scrape off the toppings, and use them as omelet stuffing. Top with a little Parmesan cheese, and you have a quick and easy treat for breakfast. Way better than cold pizza.

Reheat leftover french fries. To reheat leftover french fries brought home from a restaurant, fry them in a little oil and drain between paper towels. They come out like fresh ones.

Use leftover veggies. When you have leftover salad vegetables, throw them into a blender for mixing (not too fine).

ANOTHER ROUND FOR FRENCH BREAD

Don't throw out that stale French bread. It is still good for eating. Most French bread, if not eaten the day it's baked, will be hard as a rock the next day. But you can turn it into something wonderfully edible. Here's how:

- Slice it, then bake it until it's brown and hard. Sprinkle the slices with some yummy grated cheese and let the cheese melt for a few minutes in the oven. I like to float the crispy, cheesy bread in a bowl of soup.

- You can make croutons for salad, soups, or snacks by baking French-bread cubes in a 275-degree-F oven for 30 to 45 minutes, or until golden brown and crunchy.

- For a quick breakfast or light supper, cut stale bread into cubes, mix with beaten eggs, and fry in a small amount of butter, margarine, or vegetable oil, as you would French toast. Serve with syrup. This is easy for little ones to eat—no cutting needed!

It's a wonderful mixture to add to salsa, gazpacho, or just about any non-creamy soup. It's also another way to get your family to eat more vegetables.

FOOD STORAGE

Stamp the date. If you have a date stamper you can stamp the date of purchase by the bar code on grocery items that you store in the refrigerator or freezer. This way, you know where to look to see when food expires.

Keep some spare caps. Keep a small box in a drawer to hold plastic tops for ketchup, mustard, milk, and other con-tainers. After you use a ketchup bottle and there is ketchup all over the top, just put the messy cap in the dish-washer and put a clean one back on.

Close plastic bags of food. When opening plastic bags of food that you know you won't be finishing right away, like frozen veggies, cut the top off and use that strip to tie the bag closed.

No searching for bread ties or chip clips. The ties stay secure and are easy to remove.

Fill storage bags easily. When you're filling gallon-size zipper-top freezer bags with liquids such as soup or chili, insert the bag inside a large coffee pot.

IDEAS FOR LEFTOVER VEGGIES

Do you wind up with leftover cooked vegetables at the end of the week? Here are some delicious ideas for leftover vegetables:

- Think of them as the original precooked convenience food—by adding some freshly browned onions or garlic, you'll have a new dish your family will love.
- Heat up a can of broth or make some beef, chicken, or vegetable bouillon; add spices and let all those veggies simmer until hot, and you'll have a fast and healthy vegetable soup.
- Mix leftover chilled, already-cooked veggies with salad dressings or sandwich spreads, or just arrange them on top of lettuce and add your favorite dressing.
- Cut or dice leftover potatoes, brown them with some onion, and add eggs or egg substi-tute for a hearty breakfast or light supper. You can add diced red or green pepper for color or top with salsa or picante sauce.
- Make a vegetable hash by frying leftover vegetables—such as corn, peppers, potatoes, peas, and beans—with some seasonings.

It holds the liquid steady and keeps the zipper clean.

When the bags are filled, place two of them flat on top of a cookie sheet and freeze. Once they are frozen, remove the cookie sheet, and the filled bags will lie flat inside the freezer.

Label freezer bags. When you purchase meat in bulk that has to be repacked for freezing, individually wrap each portion in plastic wrap and then pack them all in gallon-size zipper-top freezer bags.

Rather than write the type of meat

On the Light Side

Fossils in the Fridge

What is the oldest thing in your refrigerator? Here's what some readers have said:

- Dr. Charles of Minnesota says: "I think I take the cake with the oldest refrigerator item. I have a couple of bottles of 74-year-old dandelion wine! My mother and grandmother made it."

- Marion of Arizona says: "I have a 59-year-old jar of strawberry facial mask!"

- Dorothy, who reads the column in California, says: "I have a 56-year-old unopened bottle of beer. This bottle was the last one of a case that was sent to me from Munich, Germany, shortly before a friend whose enlistment was up was due to come home. When he got back, some friends and I had a welcome-home party, and all but this one bottle was consumed.

- Leno of California says: "The oldest thing is a piece of our wedding cake (from 1955!). It was an Italian rum cake, and I guess the rum really preserved it well."

- Carol of Texas says: "I have a sliver of cocoa butter given to me when I left a hospital in May of 1955!"

- Sandra of Arizona says: "Almost 50 years ago, my two sons had their tonsils removed. Their father gave each a chocolate character. Well, as soon as they saw their new candy, they wanted to eat it. I told them they had to wait until their throats healed. They are still waiting."

- Steve of Illinois says: "Stored safely in a remote corner of my refrigerator's freezer compartment is a half-eaten buffalo barbeque sandwich that will be 47 years old this coming September! I 'salvaged' it after then-Vice President Richard M. Nixon left it on his picnic table during a political stop in my hometown in 1960. I have no plans to discard this historical piece of memorabilia, so it will probably outlive me."

- Mary Ellen of Virginia says: "I have candy birds and dolls that were decorations on my baby-shower cake. They have been in my refrigerator for 44-plus years."

So, there are some old things in those refrigerators, aren't there?

and date on the bag, you can cut out the original label that is on top of the store package and insert it inside the bag. It shows the weight, date, and type of beef, chicken, or fish.

Cook for two. Cooking for two can get boring, so cook in bigger quantities and freeze enough leftovers to serve two people. You can have your choice of mashed, fried, boiled, or twice-baked potatoes, wild rice or rice pilaf, corn off the cob, crisp summer green beans, and more, to go with grilled chicken breasts, pork, beef, or lamb roasts, all from the freezer. Pasta doesn't freeze well, but lasagna and manicotti do. You'll save lots of time during the week.

Easy-open jar. Put a piece of plastic wrap on the jar top before replacing the lid, and you will be able to open the jar easily the next time.

Close with clothespins. Use wooden spring clothespins to close the waxed bags inside cereal, cracker, and cookie boxes, and to close bread wrappers (after removing those pesky twist ties).

If you have both sweet and hot onions that you cut and keep in plastic bags in the refrigerator, write "hot" or "sweet" on a clothespin and clip it to the top of the bag.

Give bowls a cap. When staying in motels, pick up the unused shower-curtain caps that are provided in the bathrooms. They work perfectly to cover the tops of bowls that are placed in the refrigerator.

Store leftovers in glass jars. You can use any jar to store food or leftovers in the fridge, and you can see what's inside the jar. Remember, though, that you should only use canning jars that are labeled specifically for canning or freezing to store food in the freezer. Other glass jars should not be used in the freezer, as they can break easily.

Use a lid. The plastic lids on top of large coffee cans may fit plastic soup bowls or other bowls so you can use them to store leftovers.

Avoid tomato stains. To keep your plastic food container stain-free from tomato-based sauce, mold a piece of

TASTY TIDBIT

Let's check your food IQ. When cleaning up after a meal, should you put the hot food into the refrigerator right away or let it sit out on the counter and cool first? The answer? Place in the refrigerator right away! The food should be divided into small portions if it's a large pot or pan (such as soup or lasagna). You want space around the containers for cold-air circulation to prevent the refrigerator's temperature from rising.

plastic wrap inside the container. Pour the cooled sauce in and freeze. When ready to use, remove from the freezer and pull off the plastic wrap before thawing.

Keep counters clean. Keep a few of the round plastic lids from empty containers of tea, coffee, or vegetable shortening. Place them upside down under your stored cooking oil bottles to catch drips and keep shelves and countertops clean.

Keep a freezer full. When kids go off to college it may be hard to keep your freezer full. Freezers work more efficiently when full, so you want to keep yours working well without filling it with unneeded food.

You can continue to make large meals that can be frozen, and freeze them in containers to use later. To take up the rest of the space, freeze containers of water, placing them directly underneath frozen foods, to help keep the freezer running efficiently. Other benefits include always having ice to put into coolers and clean drinking water should the need arise.

Bulk up. Many individuals have a small family but require bulk ingredients for large family gatherings. You can put flour, margarine, meal, sugared cereal, candy ingredients, sugar, and other bulk foods in the freezer to be sure of having ingredients on hand. After the holidays, when flour, nuts,

KEEP FOOD FROZEN

Dear Readers: When you bring frozen food home from the supermarket, it's important to make sure your freezer is working properly in order to keep frozen food frozen. Here are some things you should know, from the American Frozen Food Institute:

- Maintain your freezer at 0 degrees F. If the temperature fluctuates, it will cause frozen foods to lose moisture faster, and they will become dry and rough.
- Keep your freezer full to maintain the temperature.
- Don't add too many items to the freezer at one time because the heat given off by non-frozen food can increase the freezer temperature.
- Store food in moisture-proof containers with airtight seals so it will retain nutritional value and good taste.
- Place the items you use the most in the front or on the door so you don't have to dig around—which will cause the freezer temperature to increase.

and various items are cheaper, buy them and stock them in the freezer, out of sight and away from insects.

Keep baking powder out of the fridge. Don't store baking soda or powder that you're going to use for baking in the refrigerator—the moisture can make the products unusable—and always use a clean, dry spoon to measure.

Wrap bread without twist ties. If you've misplaced the twist tie from your bread wrapper, just tightly twist the empty end of the wrapper, turn the wrapper end inside out, and pull it back over the loaf.

Keep buttermilk on hand. If you use buttermilk for baking but no one in your family drinks it, buy some and freeze what you don't use in muffin tins. Each tin holds about ¼ cup. When the buttermilk chunks are frozen, remove them from the muffin tins and put them in a freezer bag for later use in a recipe. They are easily removed from the muffin tins. Just let them sit out for a few minutes, then run a knife around the edge of the frozen milk— they pop right out.

For others who seldom use buttermilk, there is also dehydrated or powdered buttermilk

Another way to freeze buttermilk. Freeze buttermilk in ice-cube trays, then transfer the frozen cubes into freezer bags. Use as many cubes as a recipe calls for. You will always have buttermilk!

Freeze a cake. If you are going to freeze a cake for later use, don't frost or fill it first. After thawing, it can then be frosted or filled.

Can in a hard-water bath. Here's a home-canning hint for folks in hard-water areas. When processing jars in a boiling-water bath, add a few tablespoons of vinegar to the water. Jars will come out sparkling clean, with no hard-water scum.

Store celery and lettuce. To keep celery and head lettuce fresh and crisp for a long time, trim the cut end (root end). Place a wet paper towel, folded into a square, over the cut end. Put into a plastic bag and place in the vegetable drawer of the refrigerator. If the

TASTY TIDBIT

Here's how to keep butter at its best: Butter should be stored in the original container or wrapping until needed. You can freeze butter—its freezer life is about 2 months or so. To make butter easier to spread, leave it on the counter for a few minutes. It can sit at room temperature in a covered dish for 3 to 5 days.

item, particularly lettuce, has a lot of moisture on the surface, wrap a dry paper towel around it.

Freeze cheddar cheese. Cheddar cheese, and other kinds, too, will dry out or become moldy if you try to store it for a long time. If you freeze it, the cheese won't slice as well when thawed out.

What you can do is cube most of the cheese as soon as you purchase it, keeping some in a bag in the fridge and freezing the rest in a plastic container. Layer it, using waxed paper in between each layer.

Store cheese. Unwrap cheese immediately when you bring it home. Take just enough paper towel to wrap the cheese. Soak the towel in vinegar and squeeze until almost dry, then wrap the cheese in it. Place in a plastic bag. It will last for weeks. It won't go moldy, and it won't taste of vinegar.

Double-wrap cheese. For most cheese—especially hard cheese—keeping the air out is the key to keeping them mold-free. To keep a block of cheese fresh in the refrigerator, take a square of foil and lay a square of plastic wrap on top of it. Wrap your cheese in this two-ply wrap. It will stay fresh and mold-free for weeks. The foil and plastic wrap together work better than either does alone.

Store shredded cheese. After shredding cheese, sprinkle with a little flour and toss. The shredded cheese will not stick and can be stored in a plastic bag in the refrigerator for later use.

Store condiments. Before returning condiment containers like ketchup, mayo, mustard, or barbecue sauce to the refrigerator, take a second and wipe off the bottom. This will keep those icky spills away, and cleanup is a snap.

Store condiments. To store ketchup, salad dressing, squeezable jelly, and other condiments upside down in the fridge door so they don't fall over, reuse the cardboard six- or four-pack bottle holders from beer or wine coolers.

Freeze fresh corn. Every time you serve corn on the cob during the summer corn season, cook an extra dozen ears. It takes very little time to prepare them and cut the kernels off the cob, and in the end, you'll have a few bags of corn in the freezer to enjoy later.

Store crackers as you do chips. To keep soda crackers from breaking, store a sleeve of crackers in a potato-chip tube. They remain fresh and are easily accessible.

I.D. your eggs. When you buy a dozen eggs and store them in the fridge, it's easy to tell them apart from the previous ones if you alternately buy white eggs one week and brown the next.

You can also mark the older ones with a pencil to identify them. When storing eggs, according to the American Egg Board, they should *not* be stored in the fridge door because of the constant exposure to temperature change and vibrations due to the door opening and closing. The best way to store these little morsels is in the original carton, on a middle shelf in the refrigerator. Storing them in the cartons protects the eggs from cracking and keeps the eggs from absorbing odors from other foods.

And, according to the American Egg Board, "fresh shell eggs can be stored in their carton in the refrigerator for four to five weeks beyond the date on the carton with insignificant quality loss." In other words, they are still okay to eat several weeks after that date, as opposed to the day you buy them.

Get eggs unstuck. When eggs get stuck in the carton, it's usually because one of the eggs has cracked and leaked.

The easiest way to remove the other intact eggs is to soak the carton in water. When the carton is soaked, you should be able to carefully lift out the whole egg or eggs. Place the rest of the eggs in an extra egg carton or in a bowl in the fridge. A word of caution: *Do not* use any eggs that are cracked or broken because of contamination and possible food poisoning.

Store flour handily. Use a plastic spice shaker (or an emptied spice shaker with sprinkle holes in the top) to store some all-purpose flour. When you have to flour a cake pan or need just a little flour in a recipe, it's easy to just shake some out instead of having to take out your flour canister.

Don't use waxed paper. Use thin, bendable paper plates instead of waxed paper when sifting flour. Keep two or three of these paper plates and the flour sifter in a 13-by-15-inch plastic bag, all ready for the next time you need them. You can use the plates over and over. Goodbye to waxed paper and a messy counter.

Keep flour close at hand. Reuse coffee creamer containers. A large canister of flour can be unmanageable at times, especially if you need just a little bit, to make gravy or thicken a sauce. You can store some flour in an empty, clean coffee creamer container, and just flip open the lid and shake what you need from the smaller container.

Just be sure to label the container—no one wants flour in his or her coffee!

Keep flour flowing. It can be difficult to pour dry ingredients such as flour into a narrow-necked container. They will clog a standard funnel. If you take an uncooked piece of spaghetti, and slide it gently up and down the neck of the funnel whenever the dry ingredients stop flowing, the flow will begin again.

Store greens. To store greens like lettuce and spinach in the crisper, wash and spin them dry. Then place them in cotton bags that you have made from dish towels. Finally, put the individual bags together in a plastic bag and place it in the crisper.

Use peel-off labels on herbs and spices. Make up large and small mailing labels on the computer with the following items on them, followed by lines to be filled in by hand before putting the items away. They are:

D.O.P.—Date of purchase. Handy to know when there is an undecipherable code date on the item.

Use by—The actual expiration date. If you are unable to find the date, you can consult one of the many Web sites that list the shelf life of most common grocery items.

From—Where it was purchased. Handy to know, especially when it is a new item.

Fill out the labels as you are putting away the groceries. This is similar to the freezer labels that we use.

Stockpile ice cubes. If you do not have an icemaker and want to stockpile ice cubes for a party, place the stored cubes in a brown paper sack rather than a plastic bag. The cubes will never stick together.

Give jelly a squeeze. Transfer jelly to a small, plastic squeeze bottle—no more messy, sticky jars or knives. Squeeze bottles also work well for homemade salad dressings.

Store fresh lemon juice. When you have an extra supply of lemons, or they are plentiful and cheap and you would like to conserve the juice, just squeeze, pour into ice-cube trays, and freeze for future use.

Place the frozen cubes in plastic freezer bags. Just remove as much as you need for a recipe. No more need for bottles and cans.

Label lemons. When you slice a lemon to have on hand for tea, peel the little sticker off the lemon and stick it on the container that holds the lemon slices instead of writing on a piece of freezer tape. In fact, you can label all leftovers so you don't have to wonder what's in a bowl in the fridge.

Squeeze the lemons and limes. Whenever you cook and use lemons or limes for their juice, keep the squeezed ones in a plastic bag in the refrigerator. When you use the sink disposal, or just to give the kitchen a nice citrus smell, throw one of the little pieces of lemon or lime down the disposal.

Reuse little plastic lemons. If you like to use the little plastic lemons filled with juice, keep a quart jar of lemon juice on hand to refill them

when they are empty, instead of buying another one.

First, run hot water over the empty container to soften it, squeeze the air out, then put it upside down into a custard cup full of juice from the quart jar. The container sucks all the juice from the custard cup, and you've saved a trip to the store. If the small container doesn't fill out again, run some warm water over it, and it will pop back into shape

Freeze leftover milk. When you are leaving on a trip, pour leftover milk into ice-cube trays and freeze. When you return, you'll have fresh milk for coffee.

Freeze onions. When you buy a bag of onions, you can peel and quarter them, then put them in a zippered freezer bag in the freezer. When you need onions for cooking, just reach in and take what you need.

CHECK FOR REFRIGERATOR RELICS

What's in your refrigerator, and how long has it been there? We decided to check here in Heloise Central, and I found a jar of jelly in my fridge that said "best when purchased by November 2001"! Needless to say, it must have gotten pushed back on a shelf and forgotten. It's now in the trash!

Take a look in your fridge. What is the oldest item? This might be a good excuse to give that fridge a good once-over. Ours in the office is spotless now!

The onions are easier to chop when they're frozen, and they also last as long as you need them instead of going bad.

But keep in mind that frozen onions will have a different texture when defrosted. So, they are best used for soups, stews, and cooked food.

Sort out packets. If you've got lots of packages of mixes such as chili, spaghetti sauce, taco seasonings, and onion soup in your kitchen, here's a handy way to store them.

Buy a shoe bag with clear pockets, hang it on your pantry door, and put the mixes in the pockets. All those packets will be organized, and when it is time to go shopping, you can see at a glance what you need.

Store natural peanut butter. If you

TASTY TIDBIT

Let's test your Heloise hint IQ. Ready? What is the refrigerator shelf life of margarine?

a) 2 to 3 months

b) 4 to 6 months

c) 8 to 12 months

If you chose "a," you get to go to the front of the class! Margarine has a refrigerator shelf life of 2 to 3 months. There is usually a "use by" date on the margarine, so check it out, too. Margarine and butter also can be frozen for 6 to 8 months for longer storage.

use natural peanut butter, after initially mixing it, store the jar upside down in the refrigerator or on the pantry shelf. Since the oil rises to the top, when the jar is turned right side up, the peanut mixture will not be so oily and will be ready to use.

Use popcorn buckets. Here's a hint for using those popcorn buckets you get from the theater: Use them to store your potatoes under the sink or in the basement. Use one for potatoes and one for onions (they should never be stored together). Always remove potatoes from the plastic bag you buy them in—they'll keep longer. And don't store them in the refrigerator, either.

Keep salad fresh longer. Prepared salad in a bag is convenient, but the leftovers spoil quickly. If you use a plastic container with a cover for leftovers instead of the plastic bag, the salad will last longer in the refrigerator.

Easy flip top. If your salad dressing hasn't got a flip-top cap, reuse a ketchup-bottle top for the dressing.

Make sandwiches to go. When you go out fishing or on a day trip, take along your sandwich fixings. One way to keep the bread fresh and in its original shape is to put it into a large cooler used for transporting liquid. It fits the loaf perfectly, and the screw-on lid keeps out dirt and water. The container protects the bread from getting crushed.

TOOLS AND APPLIANCES

Measure with a bottle. If your measuring cups don't have ounces on them, purchase a couple of baby bottles. When your recipe calls for a couple of ounces of milk or water, you've got an easy way to measure them.

Bake peppers in a Bundt pan. When making stuffed peppers, which vary in size and shape, you need a pan that is tall enough to hold them upright. Try a Bundt pan! It holds up the odd-shaped peppers in its indentions and is definitely deep enough to hold the tomato sauce without it running over.

Pack gifts in canning jars. It's fun to give homemade gifts from your kitchen as tokens of appreciation. However, pretty glass containers can get pricey if you've got a long list of recipients (teachers, coaches, school-bus drivers). It's no secret that glass canning jars topped with a bit of pretty fabric are economical, attractive, and traditional.

Buy those jars at the peak of canning season (which is summer through the first frost) for the best selection of shapes and sizes.

Keep recipes at eye level. When you're baking and not using your cooktop, use a strong magnet to hold your recipe on your vent hood. It's at eye level, and you won't drop, drip, or splash stuff on it.

When you need hot water, use your coffeemaker. When a recipe calls for a cup or two of hot water, run the water through the coffeemaker.

Cut cheese with floss. Have you ever tried to cut even slices of cheese from a big block? It's not an easy thing to do. But use a piece of unflavored dental floss to cut the cheese and you will get nice, even slices without a lot of work.

Dental floss is a great helper around

Store Pimentos

Here's another old hint from my mother (the original Heloise, who started writing the Heloise column more than 45 years ago). After opening a jar of pimentos, pour white vinegar on top of the pimentos to prevent molding. Be sure to rinse them off with water before using.

the kitchen. Did you know that it is also a great way to cut cheesecake slices and bread dough? Slip under, wrap around, and cross over at the top. It cuts the dough without squashing it down.

Use a cupcake tree for other things. Cupcake trees look so pretty to take to a party or for special occasions at home, but you can use them for other things, too. When tomatoes are coming in faster than you can eat them or give them away, use the cupcake tree as a tomato tree. Any fruit or vegetable would work, and it sure brightens up the kitchen.

Use an egg slicer. An egg slicer can be used for more than just slicing eggs:

- Use to cut uniform slices of mushrooms. Turn the mushrooms upside down for best results.

- Use to slice large, pitted olives.

- Use to slice bananas or strawberries.

Make a quick funnel. Need a funnel in a hurry? Cut the bottom off a gallon milk jug and use the top part as a funnel.

It has a handle, and most things will pour through the spout. If not, you can always make the spout bigger. This is quick for an emergency funnel, but you might want to keep one in your kitchen all the time.

PICK YOUR PAPER—PARCHMENT OR WAXED?

Can you substitute waxed paper for parchment paper? In a word: no. Parchment paper and waxed paper are similar, but different. It's a little confusing. Parchment paper costs a little more, is coated with silicone, and is used to line pans when you are baking foods that are gooey or sticky so they won't stick to the pan. It's also used to cook and serve foods like chicken or fish in a parchment-paper wrapper—this cannot be done with waxed paper.

Waxed paper is coated with paraffin wax so that it's moisture-resistant, and even though it could be substituted in some instances, it cannot in baking if it's not completely covered by the food (for example, you can use it to line the bottom of a cake pan, but not a cookie sheet). Waxed paper will smoke if it's exposed to direct heat. Parchment paper is recommended in recipes for this reason.

You can use either for baking cakes because the batter covers the entire surface. Look for parchment paper in specialty cooking stores and some larger supermarkets. It's available in a roll or sheets and is sold where plastic wrap and aluminum foil are stocked.

Use a grater. Use a cheese grater to grate the boiled eggs when making egg salad, instead of chopping them up.

Use a pizza cutter. Need to cut through soft bread or dough before cooking? Use a large pizza cutter. The pizza cutter makes a quick and easy job of slicing up sausage rolls and lots of other things.

Cut more than pizza. A pizza cutter can serve a dual purpose when used to cut flat sheet cakes or rolls. It makes the cutting easier and keeps the cake or roll from crumbling. The pizza cutter is also quite handy for cutting up food for a small child (like waffles, French toast, cheese, chicken, eggs, fish, and vegetables) and to cut fudge.

Pizza cutters are also very useful for people who have the use of only one hand. Use a pizza wheel to cut meats, sandwiches, and pastries if you can't use a knife and fork anymore.

Use old pizza pans. Old pizza pans that look rather ugly after much use are good to put under pies in the oven to catch drips and keep the oven clean.

Use a potato ricer. Use a potato ricer to rice hard-cooked eggs for egg salad.

Utility shears are versatile. Utility shears are a wonderful invention—you can use them for something different every day. Dice fruits, vegetables, and meat with them instead of a sharp knife, or sterilize a pair and use to cut up pizza for lunch.

Forget the spoon rest. Instead of buying spoon rests, take a saucer out of the cupboard and use that. When done cooking, just put it in the dishwasher.

Use a serrated spoon. Here's an easy way to clean out pumpkin pulp: use a serrated grapefruit spoon with your thumb in the bowl of the spoon and start scraping the inside walls. The serrated spoon makes quick work of a nasty job. It also works well for acorn squash and other winter squashes.

Use a grapefruit spoon. You can use a grapefruit spoon to clean out the interiors of peppers, and use an ice-cream scoop to remove the seeds from melons.

Whisk your flour. When you are baking, to get pre-sifted flour to feel sifted and stirred, stir the flour with the whisk before measuring. It only takes a second, and it works well.

Make smooth gravy. It's easy to make smooth gravy. The magic trick is to use a whisk. It's great for all kinds of things, including cake mixes.

Rub veggies clean. Keep a pair of exfoliating skin/body gloves from the beauty section of a drugstore in your kitchen, and use them instead of a veggie brush to clean the dirt from potatoes and mushrooms. Just put both gloves on and gently roll the veggies in your hands, loosening the dirt, rough "eyes," and skin.

Also use them to rub down carrots to get off any lingering root threads. They get tossed right into the washing machine with my kitchen towels. They cover a larger area than those dainty, cute little brushes and are much cheaper. They save on prep time in cooking, too.

Open jars with a glove. As we get older, opening twist-off lids on glass jars gets harder and harder, even with previously opened ones that have been in the fridge.

To open a jar, grab a rubber glove (don't even bother to put it on), place the cuff over the lid, and twist away. The glove gives enough traction to get even stubborn lids off, but when a new jar is exceptionally hard to open, take the other glove and wrap it around the jar itself. Twisting the top part counterclockwise and the bottom clockwise usually does the trick.

Open a lid. Unless you have a strong grip you may have to use vise grips to open juice bottles and, sometimes, soda-bottle caps. Glass jars of pickles, jellies, and jams are the most difficult. Another method is to use a regular bottle opener. Very gently insert the

---

Unlimited Uses for . . . a Pastry Blender

Here are some ways that a pastry blender is handy around the kitchen. You can use it to:

- Blend avocados for guacamole
- Chop up hard-cooked eggs
- Crush strawberries for strawberry shortcake
- Mix meatloaf
- Break up hamburger meat as it cooks

bottle opener under the cap and press up, then repeat all around the cap. When you reach the point where you started, the cap will come loose.

Open jar lids with ease. Jars with twist-off lids are all vacuum-packed, so by releasing the vacuum, you can easily open the jar. The way to do this is to take the back of a table knife and slip it under the edge of the lid where there is a ridge and pry up on it. This releases the vacuum, making opening easy. There are also gadgets resembling a plastic bottle opener that release the vacuum, much like opening a bottle of beer, and these work well, too.

Get a better grip. Here's an alternative to the thin rubber pads used to open stubborn jar lids. Cut a 6-inch square of rubberized carpet-backing mesh. It conforms perfectly to any lid,
and the irregular surface lets you get a better grip.

Strengthen your grip. Arthritis can make it difficult for people to open the lids of salad dressing and other small bottles. The wide rubber bands that hold broccoli stems together will fit around the lids and enhance your grip.

Handle can lids with care. When opening a can of food, place the lid in the can after the can is empty to prevent cuts on fingers or hands.

Keep ice cubes unstuck. Here's how to keep ice cubes from sticking to the bottom of an automatic ice maker bin.

First, clean the ice cube dispenser with mild liquid detergent and baking soda. After the bin is dried, place a piece of waxed paper inside the tray. The waxed paper prevents the first ice cubes from sticking to the bottom of

---

Unlimited Uses for . . . a Potato Masher

A potato masher sure comes in handy in the kitchen. Here are a few things you can do with it:

- Stir up eggs to scramble.
- Mix up meatloaf.
- Quickly crumble ground beef.
- Crush up crackers.

- Stamp grill-pattern designs on peanut-butter cookies.
- Crumble up feta cheese.
- Chop eggs for egg salad.
- Break up juice concentrate.
- Mix up guacamole.

the tray, and using waxed paper helps give a fresh, clean smell to the ice-cube tray.

Make great meringue. Here's a terrific use for a hand-held submersion blender that has a wire whisk attachment. When you're making a meringue, instead of getting the big mixer out, use the wire whisk on the submersion blender to whip the egg whites.

Use coffee filters. When you have extra coffee filters that don't fit your new coffeepot, don't toss them out. Salvage them and use them as little bowls for the vegetables you chop for use in stir-fries, omelets, or tacos and then toss them away without a cleanup mess.

Find a serving platter in the microwave. Do you need a glass platter in a hurry? It may be as close as your microwave. The carousel from the microwave oven makes a handy platter for sandwiches at a gathering.

Travel safely. Transporting a sharp paring knife to a picnic or other event is a concern. Purchase a plastic toothbrush travel container, about 8½ inches long, to transport a knife safely.

Make quick cornbread. Use your waffle iron to cook cornbread. It doesn't heat the kitchen and works very nicely.

Make a replacement gasket. If you can't find a new gasket for your old blender, cut the lip off a regular-size Mason jar rubber ring, and it may work perfectly.

Chop nuts with a grinder. Do you hate to chop nuts? Try looking at garage sales for an inexpensive coffee-bean grinder. It works perfectly for nuts! Unless you want them crushed, hit the button just a couple of times. A coffee grinder will also chop hard-candy pieces to use for decorating cookies.

Of course, you can also use the grinder for coffee beans, but be sure to wash thoroughly between ingredients.

For microwave cooks. Microwave instructions often call for wrapping frozen food in a paper towel to defrost and heat it. Many things, like frozen

TASTY TIDBIT

Let's test your grilling knowledge. People use different kinds of grills to cook their favorite foods. Which type of grill—electric, gas, or charcoal—is the most commonly used? The answer is . . . ta-da, a gas grill.

We did take a poll in Heloise Central, based in Texas, and most everyone uses a charcoal grill. Nothing is better than meat or fish grilled over our "famous" mesquite wood. It's great for grilling or smoking meat or fish, but as a "scrub brush tree," mesquite soaks up water like a dry sponge.

breakfast sandwiches, can be put on a plate and covered with a coffee filter. It's cheaper and gets the job done, and sometimes you can get multiple uses out of one filter.

Save a waffle iron. Here's how to restore a waffle iron that is dirty from lack of use and has lost its nonstick quality. Clean the inside of the waffle iron with a drop of dish soap and hot water, using a scrub brush or nonabrasive scrubbie. Rinse well and dry, then re-season it. Coat a slice of bread (one for each waffle section) with unsalted shortening, put the bread in the iron, then close the lid. Turn on, and once the bread is browned, remove it. The iron should be ready for use.

Note: Don't use cooking sprays when the iron is hot, only when it is cool. Lecithin, an ingredient found in many cooking sprays, burns when it comes into contact with a hot surface and can cause a gummy residue. Read the label and you'll see this caution on the can.

Something's cooking. When you're cooking something on the stove, always turn on the light above to remind yourself that a burner is on.

Save oven energy. When preparing food that requires baking in the oven, delay turning on the heat until preparation is finished instead of turning it on before. If you turn on the oven when you begin preparation, the oven could be on for 30 minutes before the food is ready to go in. Such a waste of energy in a time when we are being urged to conserve!

Protect burners. Put foil pie tins upside down over stove burners to keep unused burners clear of spatters when frying something.

Clean a bread machine. After baking, the kneading paddle on the bottom of the pan often sticks and seems impossible to remove for cleaning. Take a piece of thick string or twine about 12 to 18 inches long and slide the middle portion under the paddle. Grasp both ends of the string and pull. The paddle will pop off.

Add an island to your kitchen. Set up your ironing board in the middle of your kitchen. Make sure it's locked securely into position and use it as a temporary island when cooking.

You can also cover it with a long tablecloth in the dining room to use as a buffet.

Turn on the slow cooker. When you use a slow cooker with a stoneware liner, you can prepare the food the night before and then place the liner in the fridge.

In the morning, take out the liner

and turn on the slow cooker before you leave for work. Usually, when you return home, you'll have a delicious dinner all ready to go.

So you don't forget to turn on the slow cooker, put your purse or car keys next to the pot so you'll always remember to get dinner started before you leave.

COOKING TECHNIQUES

Chop nuts. When you chop pecans with a knife, they fly all over the place. Put them in a zipper-top plastic bag and chop. You can see what you are doing through the bag, and the nuts stay put.

Clean up with citrus. To remove a fishy smell or onion smell from your fingers, use lemon or lime juice. Squeeze the juice on your hands and rub them together well, then rinse and dry.

Get rid of foul food odors. Has this happened to you? You're making corned beef and cabbage, the guests will be arriving soon, and you notice that your cooking has caused quite a stink in the house! How could this have been avoided? Very easily—just by adding about a tablespoon of vine-gar to the boiling water. This works for other odor-causing foods as well.

Say goodbye to onion odor. When you are cutting up onions, just light a candle and set it close to you. The flame eats the "gas" the onion gives off when you cut, and you get no tears.

To get rid of nasty onion smell on hands after cutting, rub your hands on something made of stainless steel while washing your hands, and the smell simply disappears.

Wear gloves to mix or knead. Wear rubber or plastic gloves when you're mixing meatloaf, salad, or crabcakes or kneading dough. They'll keep your hands and rings clean, and protect your nails, too. Simply wash the gloves when done, or wear disposable gloves.

Grill with wood chips. If warmer weather is visiting your part of the country or is about to, grilling out might come to mind. Wood-chip grilling isn't only for charcoal grills—if you own a gas grill, you can use wood chips, too!

Here's how:

- First, soak the wood chips of your choice in water or beer for about an hour. This will help the wood burn slowly, giving off a nice, light smoke.

- Loosely wrap the wood chips in a foil pouch, then punch several small pinholes in the foil.

- Put the pouch on the grill near the heat source.

- Turn on the grill until you see smoke. Next, lower the heat . . . and then bring on the meat.

- Remember the grilling mantra: low and slow. As you grill, the smoking chips will give whatever you're cookin' up a wonderful smoky flavor.

While you have the grill hot, think about cooking extra beef or chicken to freeze for a quick main dish on a busy night.

Heat up charcoal. To get charcoal up to full heat in an outdoor barbecue, get the fireplace bellows and use it on the charcoal. You'll have it up to full heat in no time.

Drain a can in one step. When opening a can whose liquid will be discarded, only open the can halfway. With your hand-crank opener still on the can, turn and drain. After the liquid has drained, simply continue opening the rest of the can.

Crush crumbs right in the bag. When you need to make cornflake crumbs, don't crush them in waxed paper. Instead, save the inside bags that any cereal comes in. Put the cornflakes inside the bag and keep on a-rolling. No more mess, because it's all in the bag!

Make bread crumbs from crusts. If you've got a child who likes sandwiches without the crust, when you trim the crusts, put them in a freezer bag in the freezer. When you have a full bag, take out your blender and blend the frozen crusts into a fine bread crumb. Put the crumbs in a small container and keep frozen until you need them. Use your homemade crumbs to bread chicken and pork chops, and in homemade meatballs.

Make your own bread crumbs. When you need fine, dry bread crumbs for a recipe and don't have any on hand, make your own.

Toast two slices of bread twice. After the second trip through the toaster, the bread slices will be very dry and easily crushed into fine crumbs.

Make breading easy. When you bread things like cutlets or eggplant, use a piece of aluminum foil so you can just fold it up and toss it away for easy cleanup. Because it tends to slide around on the countertop, you can spray a little bit of water on the counter first and then place the foil on top. No more sliding around!

Grab an overhead pan. When you can't reach a pan in an overhead cabinet, instead of getting out a stepladder, take out your barbecue tongs and grab the pan with them.

Measure exactly. To measure an exact amount of water for a recipe, place the measuring cup on the counter next to your sink, then use the sprayer attachment on the sink to fill the cup to the required level.

Transport food with no spills. When taking food that has been prepared at your home to a friend's house, place the cooked dish in a cardboard tray. Pick up the trays left on shelves in grocery stores.

Grease a pan with a bag. To grease baking pans with solid shortening without making a mess, use a small plastic sandwich bag to "grab" a little shortening to grease a pan. When you are finished, leave the bag in the shortening can for the next time.

Don't put a hot dish on a cold plate. When you're preparing a hot dish, don't serve it on a cold plate. Place the dinner plate(s) on top of your toaster oven, timing it for a minute or two before serving time.

Measure onto paper plates. When measuring dry ingredients for baking, such as flour, sugar, brown sugar, or nuts, place the measuring cup on a cheap paper plate. If the cup overflows, fold the plate and pour the excess into the original container. Pour the flour, salt, and other dry ingredients onto a paper plate, and it is very easy to pour into the mixing bowl without spilling. You can also use paper plates when breading meat and fish for frying. The plates are easily used and thrown away.

Spray a pan where cleanup is easy. When using a cooking spray on a pan, place the pan on the open door of your dishwasher. Any spray that shoots over the edge will easily be washed off with the next load of dishes.

Shell walnuts in a bag. If you need to shell nuts but can't find a cracker, put the nuts in a plastic zipper-top bag and crack them with a hammer so the shells will not fly around.

Transport a cake. To transport a cake without a cake carrier and still keep the frosting intact, cover the cake with plastic wrap and spray nonstick vegetable spray on the wrap before covering.

RECIPES AND COOKBOOKS

Put ingredients into recipe directions. To save time when copying recipes for yourself, leave off the list of ingredients at the top and just copy the directions, inserting the amounts of each ingredient as you go and underlining each ingredient as it is used.

Just read the underlined parts to get your list of needed ingredients for the recipe.

Cook a little extra. Cook extra food from your low-fat or diet cookbook. After you make the recipe, write in the cookbook a rating number from 1 to 10 so you will know whether to cook it again. Freeze the leftover food and put the rating, calories, and fat content on the label for the low-fat meal.

Make a recipe book. Store recipes that you clip out of magazines and print off the Internet in a three-ring binder inside sheet protectors. You can take them out of the book when cooking without fear of spills. It's easy to photocopy recipes for those who want copies. You can also separate sections with divider tabs. This is a much easier way to store recipes than transferring everything to index cards or having them on a lot of loose papers

Make your own cookbook. When you're reading a cooking magazine, put sticky tabs on the pages that have a recipe you want to keep. When you're all through with the magazine, copy the pages you want using your computer's scanner, print them, and put them in a three-ring binder with plastic sleeves, by category. This also keeps the pages clean when you are cooking.

Keep recipe cards clean. When you use recipes that are on 3-by-5-inch file cards, put the one you're using in a plastic snack-size bag to protect it from spills and splatters.

Sortin' recipes. If you collect lots of recipes, first sort them into 9-by-12-inch envelopes. The recipes that you and your family like make it into a recipe binder. The recipes that make the binder are tried, tested, and proved delicious by family and friends. So, when you want to try a new recipe, choose from the envelopes—if it's a keeper, it goes in the binder.

Make a recipe index. Do you have a large cookbook collection? Here's a way to find your favorite recipes. Whenever you use a recipe out of one of your cookbooks that is a keeper, write the name of the recipe at the top of an index card. Then put the name of the cookbook on the card, and the page number. File the card in your recipe box, and the recipe will be easily located.

Cookbook organization. When you have many cookbooks, trying to remember the location of a special recipe can be frustrating at times. The solution is an alphabetical telephone file; just make sections as you do for your card file. Print the title of the recipe and name of the cookbook or location (as in a notebook or card file) and the page or section. The only recipes in the file are those tested and loved by your family. You can make notations as to seasons, occasions, and menu suggestions on the card.

Scan your recipes. Are you tired of searching for favorite recipes pasted in loose-leaf binders or card files where you have kept recipes for years? It's time to get organized. Go through all the binders, cut out your favorites, leave the "maybes" in the binder, and throw away the ones that you have passed over hundreds of times. Then, scan all your favorite recipes into your computer, putting several on a page. Start a new indexed

binder labeled "favorites." You'll save a lot of time for yourself, and you will also save all those precious handwritten recipes that were deteriorating from age.

Work from a copy. When planning an event with lots of recipes involved, to keep from having a stack of recipe books cluttering up the kitchen, make copies of all the recipes for use in the kitchen. You can recycle the backs of the papers to use when you make your grocery list, and the copy can be handy in case anyone asks for the recipe.

Color-code recipes. Use colored paper when you are printing out recipes from the computer. Do main dishes, vegetables, appetizers, and desserts each on a different color paper. At a glance you will know which folder to look in to find a favorite recipe.

Bring recipe cards. Whenever you make a covered dish for a get-together,

TASTY TIDBIT

Here's a hint when you are trying a new recipe: Always read through the ingredients and instructions at least twice so you know exactly what items you need and how to make the dish. It will save you from making a mistake or missing an ingredient.

write the recipe on index cards in case someone likes the dish. Also, place one of the cards in front of the dish so folks can see the ingredients. This way, they can tell if they're allergic to any of the ingredients and will know not to try any.

Keep a TV recipe notebook. Whenever you watch cooking shows on TV and see a new recipe you like, instead of copying it onto a small piece of paper, keep a small notebook in front of the TV and write it down in the notebook.

Keep a cookbook clean. When trying a new recipe from a cookbook, put a clear pie plate over the recipe page to avoid accidentally splattering the book.

Keep a cookbook clean another way. Tear off a large piece of plastic wrap to cover an open cookbook on your kitchen counter. It keeps splatters and stains off your nice cookbooks while you are cooking. Close the book with the wrap enclosed, and it'll be there the next time you use that book.

Make a cookbook of Mom's recipes. Here's an idea for teenagers learning to cook. It seems that there are always things that only your mother can cook right, so how about making

your own cookbook of your favorite dishes? Take a notebook and divide it into equal sections labeled main dishes, cakes and cookies, breads, meats, and whatever other categories you need.

Whenever your mother cooks something that you really enjoy, copy down the recipe in your notebook. Do it right away, not later when you might forget it.

When you leave home to go to college or off on your own, you will have your own tried-and-true cookbook full of Mom's recipes. You will have all of her little secrets and can then start adding your own.

Make a family cookbook. To hand down your recipes to children or grandchildren, make cookbooks for all of them. Purchase photo albums at a discount or dollar store, write your favorite recipes on index cards, and slip the cards into the plastic pockets. Index each section—desserts, entries, salads, and so forth. The books will be a one-of-a-kind gift.

Annotate cookbooks. If you have a collection of cookbooks, when you try a new recipe, write a notation on it. It might say what the occasion was for making the dish, which grandchild helped with it, the weather condition that day, or the date you first tried the recipe. You can also grade the recipe "A" through "F." The books will be fun reading for your children when they inherit them.

Make a cookbook stand. When you're short on counter space and have no place to put a cookbook holder, if you've got a musician in the family you have a ready solution. Retrieve a music stand and place your cookbook on it. Secure the pages with either a large clip (like a chip-bag clip) or with rubber bands.

Even your largest cookbooks fit on the stand, and you can easily move the stand to the counter, stove, or wherever you need it. The height of the stand can be adjusted to use while sitting at a table. And precious counter space is saved.

If you don't have a music stand, you might be able to pick one up at a garage sale, flea market, or secondhand shop.

———•———

Chapter 9

Living at Home

This chapter is full of hints for enjoying yourself at home. There are sections on parties and entertaining, decorating, holidays and gift-giving, crafts, and sewing and needlecrafts. They'll help you make your home a happy, fun, creative place to be!

PARTIES AND ENTERTAINING

Party for a "super" good cause. Lots of people have parties for the Super Bowl. If each and every person who was going to be present at a Super Bowl

PLAN A PARTY

Starting to think about having a party can seem overwhelming, but being organized and making lists can really help. I'd like to share five questions you can answer to help "shape" a great party:

Who are you inviting? Write down the guest list and do a head count.

What kind of a party is it? A casual patio barbecue, a formal sit-down affair, or a potluck dinner? What will you be serving—just cocktails and appetizers, brunch, or dinner?

When are you having this gathering? Set the date and time.

Where are you hosting this party? At home or in a restaurant? Make sure you have room at home, or if you're having it elsewhere, make arrangements and reservations far in advance. Also, consider parking—is there ample room?

How are you going to invite guests? By e-mail, handwritten invitations, or over the phone? That may depend on the type of party you have decided on. For the more formal ones, you should send invitations way in advance. An invitation to an impromptu bash can be offered over the telephone.

party (or any other party, or a local athletic event) would bring one can of nonperishable food, think of the results! The food could be donated to a local food pantry. Place a box near the front door to collect the items. After the party, deliver the goods.

 Ponytail a napkin. Use small ponytail holders as napkin rings for a party. They work very well, keeping the plastic tableware and paper napkin in place. Stand them upright in a basket, and they will be easy to handle. They are colorful, can be bought inexpensively at a local dollar or discount store, and will look nice on the table.

Separate coffee from milk and sugar. When using a coffee urn to serve a large group of people, place spoons, sweeteners, and creamers on a table or counter apart from the urn. The coffee line can move along, and those people who drink their coffee "black" can get their coffee and get out of the way, to the benefit of all concerned.

NEW LOOK FOR PARTY DECORATIONS

Here are some fun and unusual decorating ideas for your next party or backyard barbecue. Try some of these other uses for ordinary items:

- Use an old punch bowl to hold a large salad.
- Use a wooden bread basket for holding silverware and napkins on the buffet table.
- Use an ice bucket to keep cut-up veggies cool and crisp. It also makes a great serving container at a picnic.
- Buy a terra-cotta planter for keeping a selection of wines chilled. Just put a cork in the drain hole. If you want to use the planter permanently for this reason, use an aquarium sealant around the cork to ensure a permanent seal.
- Use backyard greenery for a wonderful centerpiece. Wild or garden flowers, berries, and ivy can be used with fruit or peppers for an eye-catching arrangement.
- Cut small holes out of the tops of different-color bell peppers, apples, or other fruits, and use them as colorful candleholders.
- A really fun idea for place cards is to use an instant or digital camera to take a photo of each guest as he or she arrives, then use the photo as a place card on the table.
- Make a name or photo cardholder by using apples and wire. Cut wire to desired height, wrap one end around a pencil two or three times, then remove the pencil. Stick the straight end into the top of the apple and carefully separate the looped end just enough to slide in a place card or photo.

Decorate with balloons for less. To add festive décor to any party, shower, or other event, instead of using helium-filled balloons, use regular ones and tie curling ribbon to the stem. Then use double-sided tape, or loop a piece of tape over itself so that it is sticky on both sides, and attach to the top of the balloon. Stick the balloons up on the ceiling. It gives the look of helium balloons without the expense.

Reuse foil balloons. You can save foil balloons to reuse on special occasions. When the helium goes down, use a straw to remove all of the helium. When you have an occasion to use the balloon again, just go to the store and pay about 75 cents to refill the balloon. It saves money and recycles the balloon.

Reinflate a balloon. Foil-type balloons can be reinflated by inserting a drinking straw in the end of the balloon. Blow into the straw, then remove it and tie up the balloon.

Blow up some balloons. When blowing balloons for parties, use a (soccer or basketball) hand pump. Just

FIND THE PERFECT CATERER

Are you planning a party and need to hire a caterer? Here are some helpful hints to find the perfect caterer for your big bash:

- Check with friends, family, and coworkers for recommendations. Meet with the caterer(s) and sample the food before making a decision.
- Take notes on the details about food and beverages. Ask how they will be presented and served.
- Determine the per-person price. Know exactly what that includes, such as open bar, wine, or desserts.
- Establish a date for you to give the final head count. Set a cutoff date for last-minute guests. Find out if you will be billed for those who don't show up even though they sent an R.S.V.P.
- Who provides tableware, table linens, trays, serving utensils, and centerpieces? Who purchases disposable plates, cups, and napkins?
- What cleanup does the caterer do? Find out who gets the leftovers.
- Get a written contract that covers everything you've discussed.

Now, send out the invitations, put together the perfect outfit, and prepare to enjoy your upcoming party!

remove the needle and place the neck of the balloon over the hole and pump away. It not only spares your throat and cheeks, but it also gives you a good arm workout!

Decorate a special cake. If your hobby is cake decorating, you're probably always looking for inexpensive cake plates that you can give away with the cake.

Here's a hint: Discarded turntable platters from broken microwave ovens make wonderful cake plates. Put a paper doily on them, and they look great! And, you're recycling at least a small piece of a discarded microwave.

Have a Willy Wonka party. For a fan of the movie *Charlie and the Chocolate Factory*, here's how to throw a candy-making birthday party.

Make invitations that look like golden tickets and put them in chocolate bars, then have the birthday kid pass them out to friends. They'll be very excited when they discover the invitations in the candy bars.

Go to a craft store and purchase chocolate pieces and colored candy to melt, and some candy molds.

Buy some things to add to the melted candy, such as peanuts, coconut, and raisins, and caramels and strawberries for dipping. Dry the candy on wax paper, and at the end of the party, put the candy you made into paper cupcake holders so they can be kept separate. Everyone takes candy home.

Make favors for a kids' party. To make party favors for children, save empty cardboard toilet-paper rolls so that you have one for each guest. Cover each tube with brightly colored tissue paper and fill it with candy and small toys. Tie the ends with a couple of pieces of bright ribbon to match the paper. The kids will love them!

Pre-dip ice cream. When you have to serve ice cream and cake to lots of children at a party, dip out the ice cream the day before and put it in paper baking cups. You can store the individual servings in cupcake pans covered with plastic wrap in the freezer. It sure saves time and confusion the day of the party.

Make party cones. For a child's party, make cute mini-cakes in individual flat-bottomed ice cream cones. When the cakes cool, frost them and then sprinkle toasted coconut on the top, make a little indentation, and fill it with small jelly beans. They look just like little birds' nests.

Make a creative party invitation. For a children's birthday party for twins, instead of sending out regular invitations, get a large poster board and write in large letters where and when the party will be held. Dress the twins in matching outfits and have them sit on the poster board.

Take several digital photos of the twins "on" the invitation. Choose the one you like best and take it to a photo processing lab in a large discount store, which can run off the number of prints you need. The photos are affordable. You could also run the copies on your home computer printer, depending on how many you need and the cost of printing supplies.

If you're into scrapbooking, this photo invitation will make a cute page.

Do wedding favors for charity. Instead of trying to find favors for a wedding reception, some couples are giving to worthy causes. Instead of giving the guests favors at their tables, set each place with a rolled-up paper tied with a ribbon, explaining that the bride and groom gave a special donation to the American Cancer Society, or another good cause.

Roll picnic utensils. Whenever your family goes to a picnic or you have a party at your house, instead of having all the tableware separate, roll the utensils into a napkin for each person and tie it with a pretty ribbon.

Have fun at your party. Do you

POTLUCK POINTERS

Don't you just love potlucks where everyone brings dishes to share? But sometimes it's not easy at the end of the party to get back that plate or casserole dish you brought. Here are some ways to make it easier:

- Label the dish by writing your name on masking tape or sticking an address label on the bottom.
- Use heavy-duty paper plates or sturdy cardboard and cover them with several thicknesses of foil. Great for carrying cookies.
- Go to garage sales and buy cheap plates, casseroles, and serving dishes that you are happy to pass along. Many are attractive, and after a good wash, they will be just right for any party.
- Get an inexpensive, 12-inch-square floor tile and cover it with foil, so it can be used for transporting cakes.
- If the party is at a friend's house, purchase a dish that matches something she has. It will make a perfect hostess gift, too.

Enjoy the party!

want to have fun at your own party? It's possible if you do a little planning ahead of time.

- If you have small children, try to hire a babysitter to entertain them either in your home or at the home of one of your guests.

- School-age children can sleep over at friends' houses, and you can return the favor when their parents have a party.

- Make a list of everything you'll be serving and keep it posted on the refrigerator, so you can refer to it as you prepare for the evening.

- Make dishes that you know your friends like and that were a hit at other parties.

- Always serve nonalcoholic drinks when you're serving alcoholic ones so that everyone has an option!

WEDDING HINTS

Do you want to go back in time a decade or so and learn a hint or two that may help you? Well, here's your chance. This column was originally printed June 8, 1997. Take a stroll through the Heloise archives.

Here are some great wedding hints from one of my books, *Heloise's Hints for All Occasions*. (You can find it on the Internet or in a local used bookstore.)

- If you will have many out-of-town guests, call local hotels, motels, guesthouses, and bed-and-breakfast facilities to see if you can get a group rate or discount. To transport the guests, rent a car from a car-rental agency or a limousine company, which will also furnish a driver.

- Some people like to throw birdseed to wish the "lovebirds" happiness as they leave for their honeymoon. Get prior permission to do this. Some churches and party locations discourage the practice because uneaten birdseed sprouts weeds in the lawn and flower beds.

- I've had this request from many brides and grooms. Please tape the card to the gift and write on the back of the card a description of the gift. Too often the gifts get separated from the cards.

- Follow these simple directions to make cute wedding favors: Buy white plastic spoons and place two chocolate-kiss candies in the bowl portion of the spoon and cover with your favorite color nylon net, which is very inexpensive, or tulle, which is finer and costs a little more, at fabric stores. Tie with ribbon and attach a small poem with the name of the bride and groom.

- To avoid possible messes, pretest the capacity of serving bowls by filling them with water measured according to the anticipated recipe amount.

- Lastly, enjoy yourself; if someone offers help in cleaning up, accept it!

Make a party ice ring. Make ice rings using tube pans or bundt pans. Put orange and lemon slices and cherries in the water. They are really pretty and usually last the entire evening.

Set out pretty condiment dishes. Lovely small crystal dishes for individual servings of jam, cream cheese, and salsa can be made with crystal votive candleholders from a store that sells things for a dollar.

Count the silverware. After entertaining and cleanup, but before you discard the refuse, count your silverware to make sure none was accidentally discarded. Spoons and forks can easily be tossed out with paper plates or napkins, so check.

WELCOMING GUESTS

Spend a night in your guest room. Here's a good hostess hint: Before guests stay in your guest bedroom, you should spend a night there! This way you can take care of anything that doesn't work—a lamp, a noisy clock, window-shade issues, or uncomfortable pillows. You might be surprised what you discover.

Donate travel shampoo. The small containers of lotions, shampoos, and other grooming aids in hotel rooms are handy for houseguests, and are often appreciated by shelters for homeless women and victims of domestic violence. Check with a shelter in your area to see if they accept such donations.

DECORATING

Recreate a wallpaper border. To replace a damaged section of a wallpaper border, if you can't find more of the border for sale, take a picture of the border with your digital camera and print it on the computer. You may have to print it several times to get the correct size.

Match the paint. When you paint a room, paint a sample of the color on a small white paper plate and keep it in your car. When shopping for accessories, there will be no second-guessing for a match. You can also keep the lids from the paint cans for the coded color mixture printed on top in case you need to buy more for touch-ups.

Mark hanging holes. So that you do not "lose" the holes where blinds or shelf brackets were hung when repainting the wall surface (or accidentally spackling over them), put toothpicks into the holes so the paint won't fill them in.

When the paint dries, remove the toothpicks and it will be easy to reinstall the blinds and shelf without having to remeasure or search for studs. This method could also be used for any artwork that is going to go back up on the wall.

If you are using more than one coat of paint, be sure to remove and replace the toothpicks after each coat so they don't get painted in.

Get hold of a nail. Before hanging any size picture on the wall, grab a small comb and place the small or long nail between the threads of the comb. When the nail is balanced on the comb, you can then hammer the nail into the wall without having the nail fall and having to spend time finding it. The technique will help you get hold of the nail correctly.

Hit the nail on the head. Here's a picture-hanging hint: If you have to put a hanger on the back of the picture frame, and the nails are too tiny to hold while you hammer them in, hold the nail with a pair of tweezers till the

WELCOME GUESTS WITH A BASKET

Make your houseguests feel right at home with a bag or basket filled with travel goodies. When people stay at your home, it might be awkward for them to have to ask for things they forgot to pack. So make it easy on your houseguests and have a supply of toiletries and other goodies—and here are some ideas:

- You can put together a special welcome basket with all the little things your guests might need during their visit. Include a toothbrush, travel-size toothpaste, shampoo, dental floss, baby powder, sunscreen, and soap.
- A disposable razor and a plastic comb are also nice ideas.
- If you travel a lot, you can also stock up on hotel freebies like shower caps, lotions, shampoos, and bath gels.
- Decorate with a pretty ribbon, add some fresh flowers and fruit, and don't forget to include a note welcoming your guests.

This welcoming touch will really make your houseguests feel at home.

nail gets settled in. This will work for any nail or screw that is too tiny to hold with your fingers.

Hold nails on a magnet. When you are hanging pictures, place all the nails on a magnet until you're ready to use them (sure beats holding them between your lips).

Hang crosses straight. When hanging an arrangement of crosses, if you find that some hang lopsided, fix the problem by sticking a straight pin in the drywall on the leaning side (under the cross "arm") to keep it in line. It's a quick fix, and the tiny pinhead isn't noticeable.

Cover a table with a sheet. A twin-size top sheet can fit a large table beautifully, and makes a unique, pretty, and practical tablecloth.

Recycle place mats. Use old vinyl place mats as tabletop protectors for small craft projects.

Preserve embroidered pillowcases. To enjoy hand-embroidered pillowcases without the risk of damaging them, use them as dresser scarves. They look very pretty and are fully displayed.

Make cabinet liner decorative. Use a pair of decorative scissors to cut the edge of a nonslippery, nonabrasive liner placed on a cabinet shelf. It will give the inside of your kitchen cabinets an antique-style look.

Use liquid potpourri instead of a candle. Some folks find that the liquid potpourri concentrates work better in the votive-size electric candle warmers than wax candles do. If you get tired of one fragrance and want to use another, the liquid scents are easier to change.

Add green to floral arrangements. Here are some suggestions for greenery to use around fresh-cut flowers when you create arrangements. Stick a little spider plant into a bud vase, then add a rose; the spider plant will survive in just water, and the effect is very nice.

Use those trailing philodendron bits to surround other fresh-cut flowers. Even when they have roots, the philodendron stems look good.

Recycle packing peanuts. To create a lightweight flower arrangement in a tin "wall bucket" (it holds flowers) that you want to hang, fill the container with foam packing peanuts, arrange the flowers, and hang the bucket on the wall.

Display a plant. Here is a way to display a cascading plant so that it can continue to grow and cascade down. If the plant itself is in a medium-sized terra-cotta pot, place a larger terra-cotta pot upside down and set the plant on it. Use poster putty to keep the pots secured to each other (they can still be separated if necessary).

Find nice art for little money. Want to know how you can get expensive-looking framed art for practically nothing? Before you toss out last year's calendar, take a quick look inside. There may be some beautiful pictures perfect for framing.

Check your favorite discount store or bookstore for an even greater selection after the New Year, when calendars are marked down for quick sale.

For a child's room, look for animal prints or photos with sport themes or flowers.

For a living room or entry hall, look for photos of classic paintings from your favorite artists.

Select one or a series you can hang together.

Once you have a picture selected, framing is easy. Find a ready-made mat and a frame to fit at a craft store or let the store frame it for you.

Then hang it up in your own home or give as a gift to a friend, coworker, or nearby nursing home. Nothing brightens a room like beautiful artwork. You'll love the results and the price.

I have several cut-out photos of hummingbirds taped inside my computer cabinet . . . it makes me smile when I look in there!

Decorate the shower walls. Deco-

HOW TO STORE A WREATH

Many people like to switch decorative door wreaths to coordinate with the season, but finding a place to store them without inflicting damage can be a challenge. Here are a few helpful hints:

- When taking a wreath down, clean it thoroughly so that it is ready to use the next time. Use the furniture attachment on the vacuum to remove dust.

- Remove delicate decorations that could get knocked off or smashed. You can wrap them in tissue or newspaper and tuck them into a zipper-top bag. Be sure to label it so you know what's inside. If possible, store the wreath in the box it came in or one similar in size.

- You can also wrap each wreath in a dry-cleaner bag and hang them side by side on a garage or basement wall. That'll add extra cheer to the area and make the wreaths easier to find the next time you want to display one.

rate your bathtub shower walls with window clings that can be bought inexpensively (the ones with a clear background look best).

You can go for a fun effect (fish, for instance) or just make a border along the top. With all the clings out there, there is a wide variety of decorations! They are fairly easy to maintain, although one must take heed of what products to use when cleaning the shower. Use mild soap (shampoo) to clean them in the shower periodically, and when the shower needs a good cleaning, the clings are easy to remove and replace.

HOLIDAYS

Decorate with holiday photos. For Halloween decorations, take photos of your children in their costumes and frame them. Keep the photos with your other Halloween decorations and take them out each year to enjoy in the appropriate season.

When the holiday is over, pack them up with everything else. You can do this with Easter, Christmas, and Fourth of July pictures, too.

Light a Halloween pumpkin. After you carve a Halloween pumpkin, put a solar-powered light inside instead of a candle. The pumpkin may last longer because it will not rot as fast as it would with heat from a candle.

Find a use for kids'-meal toys. If your kids love kids' meals from fast-food restaurants, it's hard to figure out what to do with all those toys. Keep them in a container in the pantry until Halloween, then dress up and give them to trick-or-treaters. You can do the same with the prizes in cereal boxes.

Make wedding gown angels. Here's an idea for mothers who hoped to hand down their wedding gown but had sons and no daughters. Turn your gown into special gifts for your family. Make Christmas angels out of the gown by using purchased angels found at finer decorating stores, stripping them down, and re-dressing them in pieces of your gown. Use the pearls on the bodices, the lace as wings, the satin for the gown, and the toile for trains. Make an angel for your tree and one for each of your sons.

If you like, buy or make a stand for your angel and let it spend the rest of the year in a glass curio cabinet. Take the remainder of the fabric and trims and make a number of smaller angels to use as ornaments. Save these for your grandchildren's first Christmases.

You will not only enjoy the dress all year, but you'll be passing down a little bit of history and legacy as well.

Make Santa's footprints. Here's a great Christmas-morning hint for creating Santa's footsteps from the fireplace (or front door if you don't have a fireplace) to the Christmas tree.

Make a stencil of a boot print by tracing a boot on a piece of cardboard, then cut out the drawn image and discard it.

Place the cardboard on the floor, starting at the fireplace, and sprinkle baking soda in the cutout portion.

Carefully lift the cardboard and brush the excess baking soda into a container. Now, turn the cardboard over and repeat to make the opposite footstep.

Children or grandchildren will be surprised Christmas morning to see that Santa really did come in the night to deliver presents!

Just vacuum up the baking soda at the end of the day—by then it has also helped deodorize your carpet!

Make decorations from alphabet blocks. You can use alphabet blocks that nobody plays with anymore to make Christmas decorations. Glue blocks together (use wood glue) to form words like "Season's Greetings," "Love," and "Peace."

Remember how to decorate. When your house is decorated just perfectly for the holidays, take a close-up picture of each spot that was decorated and put the pictures in a small album.

Pack away the album with the Christmas decorations after the holidays and bring it out the following year to refresh your memory. Then follow the pictures and decorate accordingly.

Display ornaments. When decorating for the holidays, you can display ornaments with rounded bottoms on flat tabletops. To keep them from rolling, take a pipe cleaner in a matching color, cut it in half, and make a circle-doughnut shape with it. Put it on the table and rest the ornaments on the pipe cleaner. Add a little angel hair or tinsel and ta-da.

Make a keepsake ornament. Here's a reader-favorite ornament hint: Save baby rattles, blocks, and other small toys and make them into keepsake ornaments by adding a cord or fishing line to hang them. Not only are they memorable, but they are also one-of-a-kind.

Make family Christmas ornaments. Start a special tradition by making Christmas ornaments for the tree and embroidering or lettering the name of each member of your family—from grandparents to newborns—on an ornament. (You can also make one for each of your pets.)

Grandchildren can have the privilege of placing their immediate family members' ornaments on the tree. When family members pass away, keep hanging their ornaments on the tree. It will bring up conversations about loved ones no longer with you, and it will become a treasured tradition through the years.

GIVING AND GETTING GIFTS

Give a gift made of memories. Here's a special gift idea for a parent. Get together with your siblings and make a list of all the things that you remember about your mom or dad. Some things will be funny, some sweet, and others just special memories that only she or he would know. You can make the list to reflect her or his age. For instance, if she is 50, the list would consist of 50 things. Give your list a title (such as "All the things we love about . . .").

Get the grandkids involved, too, and have them add to the list. Type up the list on a computer, print it, then have it framed.

Make a gift of photos. Create a wonderful gift by going through your pictures to find ones relating to a friend or family member who has lost all of his or her photos in a flood, fire, or other disaster. Make copies and put them in an album. Perhaps you could collaborate with other friends and relatives.

Make a memory book. At the start of each year, purchase two inexpensive, small photo albums and keep them in a convenient place. Throughout the year, add pictures of your family, children, and grandchildren. Also add a slip of paper for each photo with caption or date.

Give a book to your mother and mother-in-law at Christmas—a "brag book" of events from the previous year.

This is a great way to have photos handy. It's easy to take along on travels, and it provides a photo history of events through the years. It takes only a few minutes to add a picture or two.

Decorate a photo frame. When you don't know what to get for someone's birthday, make a special picture frame. Buy a plain frame and decorate it with buttons. It will be perfect for a family photo.

Give lots of little gifts. Here's a gift idea for a child who is hospitalized or ill for a long time. Instead of giving one gift, cover a box with brightly colored paper and fill it with small, wrapped gifts—little "surprises."

Make the gifts all things that the child can use and enjoy in bed. A lot of little gifts over a period of time sure beats a box of candy.

A paper anniversary gift. Make a special first-anniversary gift for a special couple. The first year is supposed to be paper, so collect party decorations for every holiday during the year.

Beginning with whatever holiday is closest to the wedding day, start buying themed paper plates, napkins, tablecloths, and other decorations for each holiday—Easter, Memorial Day, Fourth of July, Halloween—and continue collecting them for the rest of the holidays. Your gift will be a year of parties.

Since you have a whole year to collect the items, it is possible to catch them when they are on sale after the holidays.

Give a plant. A plant in a decorative pot makes a lovely gift, especially if you give plants that can be transplanted easily. A month or so before a birthday, buy a pretty pot and start a cutting in it so that when the day arrives, the plant will be thriving and lovely.

Give a dollar. When you host a birthday party for an elderly family member in an assisted-living or senior community, whose needs are well taken care of, what can you suggest to those who want gift ideas? You could suggest that they just place a dollar bill in the card.

A few dollars here and there would help give the person a feeling of independence so he or she could shop at the gift shop in the building for little things such as cards, candy, or mints.

You could also check with the gift shop to see if it offers gift cards or a credit account that the guests might be able to contribute to.

Give a gift of freedom. Here's a thoughtful gift idea for an older person who can no longer drive. Get in touch with a local taxi company where the person lives, and, for a gift, purchase 20 trips within the town. It will give the person freedom to get around without asking for a ride.

Give a special gift. Here's an idea for a special birthday gift for an elderly relative or friend in a nursing home. Purchase some nice vases and request that everyone bring one flower to create a special bouquet for her. Your loved one will enjoy the flowers, and everyone will feel included.

Keep the receipt for a resident. When buying gifts for people in nursing homes, please save the receipts and enclose them with the gift. This is especially helpful when you are giving clothing to residents who do not have family or relatives who can exchange the items or obtain refunds, if necessary. They may have to rely on the staff to exchange an item for them.

As you know, most stores will not make adjustments without receipts, so it is very important to enclose them with the gifts.

Give a thoughtful gift. For someone who has everything and doesn't need any more "stuff," contact the local utility company and arrange to have the utility bills paid for 6 weeks.

Make a special video. For your relatives who have everything, make a video on the computer of some old and new pictures of the family, set to music. This is a terrific gift for a special wedding anniversary. If you can, burn the video to a DVD so the recipients can watch it on TV. If you don't know how to do this, find someone

GIFTS FOR ONE WHO HAS IT ALL

Do you have to get a gift for that "hard to buy for" person? When it comes to finding the right gift for the person who has everything, don't panic—one of the following suggestions just might help you:

1. A roll or book of stamps makes a great and practical gift. A sheet of collectible stamps is also a nice idea! Package the stamps with some lovely stationery and pens.

2. A gift certificate to a favorite restaurant has double the pleasure—when it's received and when the time comes to enjoy the meal.

3. For the person who travels a lot or just has to make a lot of long-distance phone calls, how about a prepaid phone card?

4. For a thoughtful gift, how about certificates for help from you, like housework, yard work, or running errands?

5. If your state has scratch-off lottery tickets, buy a bunch of them for a gift. They're lots of fun to get, and who knows? Your gift could turn out to be worth millions!

knowledgeable and have that person make it for you.

Give a joke. Cut some of the funnies out of the newspaper and put them in a 4-by-6-inch photo album to give to friends to perk them up, or send them

A Gift for the Groom

Heloise Central was doing some research on wedding gifts and came across the following hint that was originally printed in my mother's (the late Heloise) column in 1967. She thought it was a good hint then, and we still think it is! Read on:

"Dear Heloise: You once suggested a truly inspired gift for the bride . . . a sort of housekeeping starter kit (dust cloths, scouring rags, light bulbs, etc.).

"While excellent for the bride, it occurred to me, after some experience involving harassed trips to the hardware store, banging nails with shoe heels, prying open gift cartons with new kitchen utensils, etc., that—like his bride—the groom also could well use a kit.

"In each newly established household, there are innumerable tasks:

"Curtain rods to hang, appliances to assemble, hooks to install, clothing poles to place, and many others.

"As it usually falls to the husband, apprentice or veteran, to handle these 'honey-do' chores, I submit the following absolutely basic kit for the groom as a needed companion to that suggested for the bride:

- A medium-weight claw hammer
- A pair of pliers
- A medium-size screwdriver, straight slot
- A small, versatile saw, e.g., a keyhole saw
- A good variety of screws, bolts, nails, brads, and tacks
- A variety of accessory hardware—hooks, hanging aids, etc.

"Naturally, this list could easily be expanded according to the experience and means of the giver, but, oh, how handy are just the above items for the new groom in the new household.

"And, thanks to you, John. And if a bride is smart (I wasn't!), she'll pretend she doesn't know how to use ANY of the above while those stars are still in the groom's eyes, eh?"

Don't you love my mother's comment? In fact, she could hang most anything, rewire a lamp, and fix a lot of things.

as a get-well card. It gives the recipients a good chuckle, and you'll enjoy finding the best ones to send.

Make a brag book of recipes. Keep your favorite recipe cards, including ones clipped from magazines, in the small "brag books" meant for 4-by-6-inch photos. The biggest plus with this system is that the recipe can stay clean in the book while you use it. Also, the 3-by-5-inch cards slip in and out easily. The recipes can be labeled to make them easier to find. These books also make a great shower gift for a bride-to-be, filled with all your tried-and-true recipes.

Give a gift to a patient. Here's a great suggestion when visiting someone in the hospital—take the patient earplugs and a sleep mask. The person will love you for a better night's sleep, as he or she can block out all the "hospital noise" and bright lights. Also, while you are visiting a female friend or relative, you could give her a manicure. She will feel pampered, and her nails will look great!

Make a gift for a far-away relative. Here's a great way to make a gift for a sick relative who lives far away from you. If you have a CD greeting-card program on your computer, transport a picture from the scanner to a page. Make a different card each week and put on it a picture of a family relative and note the name of the person. It's a nice way to keep in touch, and your relative can save the photos to put in a scrapbook.

It would also be a great collection of information for a genealogist.

Give a gift of picture magnets. Here's a hint for the free magnets that businesses give out. For magnets that are large enough, use your computer to print out pictures of your children and size them to fit the magnet. Glue the picture to the magnet and give the new "picture magnet" to your mother to hang on her refrigerator. She can enjoy the pictures of her grandchildren and not have to worry about frames taking up a lot of space.

A gift for a grad. Here's a gift idea for a special graduate who's moving away from home for the first time. Give one lasting present, perhaps an engraved letter opener. The rest of the gift can be geared toward life away from home. Purchase plastic storage containers to hold the rest of your gifts, which might include a crystal window dangle, a toolbox, an emergency kit, a hygiene kit, and a school box.

These are all inexpensive items, but they will give your friend a good start to her new life, plus a few items to remind her of her roots.

A box of odds and ends is the perfect gift for someone starting out or starting over.

Give a useful gift to a graduate. When your grandchild enters college, make up a small gift for each week of the first semester and date the gifts for every Thursday, figuring that, by then, a student needs encouragement to get through the rest of the week.

For early in the term, give office supplies such as a stapler or tape. Later gifts include mostly snacks like boxes of microwave popcorn or candies. Pack all the small gifts in one big box.

Life Hints 101 and the tools to accomplish them are some of the skills that college students need to learn. This hint is just the ticket to help them.

Creative baby shower gifts. Want to take a different kind of gift to a baby shower? If you want to give a special gift to a friend, here are a couple of homemade gifts from the heart:

- Make a baby basket. Buy a pretty wicker basket, line it with baby towels, and fill it with baby shampoo, baby cleaning lotion, baby oil, and towelettes. Add a sweater or blanket. And include several index cards with your favorite baby hints.

- Create your own gift certificates. They can include several hours of baby-sitting, cooking a meal, cleaning for several hours, or a manicure. New moms need pampering and time for themselves!

- One of my favorite certificates is for a mom's health day—at her home or yours. Someone takes care of the baby, while you take care of mom. Offer a long soak in a bubble bath, or a facial or foot massage. Prepare a nice lunch and give mom several prepared meals to take home—include heating instructions and decorative paper plates, so she doesn't have to worry about cleaning up.

Give a lasting baby gift. Books are great gifts for baby showers. Baby board books make the perfect gift. They're always the right size, won't need to be returned, will be used much longer than any outfit, and will enrich the baby's life far more than clothes could.

When the child has outgrown the books, just drop them off at a coin-operated laundry, and they'll continue to benefit other families.

Give a memory jar. To make a memory jar, write down in a notebook a memory for each one of your family members. Do 365 of them for an entire year. Each memory pertains to a particular family member and you. Then transfer those notes to colorful business-type cards. Fill jars with the cards and tie on a ribbon with a note that says, "Take one memory every morning to start your day."

This is a thoughtful act and doesn't cost a lot. It makes a great gift. A photo may be worth a thousand words, but a happy memory every day is priceless.

Give food and photos. Here's a gift idea that combines photography and baking. Each year, make homemade goodies for presents. Each little family in your ever-growing extended family gets a gift bag of cookies and candies.

Print out on your computer photos that you took of the family during the past year and tape the photos to the gift bags. This way, they not only get new photos but also know which bag of baked goods is theirs without searching for tiny gift tags.

Make a keepsake scrapbook. A special scrapbook will be a treasured gift for someone you love on a special birthday, anniversary, or other occasion. Here's how to make one.

Two months ahead of time, send a page from a scrapbook to family members and friends, asking them to create a memory page of events that they recall and pictures that relate to the gift-ee. Put the pages into a scrapbook with a beautiful cover.

At the end of the evening, present the scrapbook of all the pages you received. All the pages will be so different, yet so special, and the book will be full of wonderful memories.

Give a gift of potpourri. Add potpourri to a clean glass candle jar and tie a ribbon around it. Give filled jars to local senior citizens for bingo prizes or to local women's shelters.

Make birthday handkerchiefs. When grandpa is having a significant birthday, make him a special gift. Bring all the grandchildren together, and put them around a table with colored, permanent-ink pens and a stack of 100 percent cotton white men's handkerchiefs.

Have each grandchild decorate a handkerchief and sign it.

You can also sew all the handkerchiefs together to make a throw. Now that would be a unique gift, don't you think?

Make a T-shirt blanket. If your kids have loads of T-shirts from tournaments, sports camps, and numerous basketball and soccer teams, sew them together to make a T-shirt blanket.

Cut up an irregular twin-size flannel sheet (which you can buy inexpensively at a discount store) to sew on as backing. Another (uncut) twin-size flannel sheet can be used as a covering for the reverse side.

A memory blanket is a treasured keepsake that will surely bring smiles and fond memories for many years. There are many variations of this idea, using T-shirts, flannel shirts, men's ties, and even grandmother's aprons.

Give yourself a little present, too. When you buy a gift that feels more like an obligation, buy a little present for yourself as well. Buy a nice set of towels or a new sheet, a new pot holder, or dish towel to give yourself a big psychological boost.

Get a gift receipt. Returning unwanted gift items or trying to exchange them without a receipt can prove extremely difficult these days. Many stores are not allowing any types of returns without a receipt to reduce "shrinkage" or fraud.

It is so important to include a gift receipt with a gift that you give. You can ask for such a receipt when you purchase your gift, which, in most cases, shows the purchase information without the price or payment method included.

Don't toss your typewriter correction fluid. When you're giving a gift, use typewriter correction fluid to cover the price. Leave the tag attached in case the recipient needs to return or exchange the gift.

Use different gift wraps. Wrap presents for grandchildren in different wrapping papers. This way the labels do not get lost, and they cannot figure out who gets what until Christmas morning.

Keep gift wrap from unrolling. Cut an empty wrapping-paper tube into thirds, then cut through the middle so you can slip it over other rolls of paper to keep them from unrolling.

Use a glue stick for wrapping. Try using a glue stick or a leftover bottle of hobby glue instead of tape to seal gift wrap. You may find these tools handy and a good replacement for tape.

Speed up wrapping. Using a glue gun instead of tape speeds up wrapping multiple presents. It also hides the seam better, and you can attach bows faster and more securely. You can even attach the tag with the glue, and it keeps sliding ribbon in place.

Put a paper shredder to another use. Use your paper shredder on odds and ends of colorful gift wrap to make colorful material to put in gift bags or boxes to cushion those special gifts. You might think the shredded gift wrap looks even more festive than regular tissue paper.

And, as an added bonus, instead of those pesky plastic "peanuts," shred your junk mail and use it to pack boxes for mailing. It's good for the environment and a great way for children to learn about recycling.

Make tissue paper like new. Since gift bags are used so much instead of regular gift wrap, a lot of tissue paper is also used. You can iron used tissue with a steam iron and use it again. It comes out like new, thus you can recycle the gift bags and also the tissue paper that comes with them.

Cushion a CD. If you want to mail a CD as a gift, sandwich it between two bags of unpopped microwave popcorn. You not only protect the CD, but you also give a gift of popcorn!

Sign a gift card. Write your name and address on the back of gift cards for wedding or shower gifts. This way, if the card gets separated from the gift, the receiver can figure out whom to thank for that bag full of goodies. You can also do this when sending flowers for funerals.

Decorate a gift box. Have a gift box to wrap but no wrapping paper? You don't need it! Decorate the box with sequins, glitter, paints, markers, stickers, buttons, or crayons. No gift box? Recycle brown lunch bags in a similar way.

Make a matching gift tag. When wrapping a gift for a baby shower, cut out one of the cute little bears or bunnies or other animals from the gift wrap and glue it to a piece of card stock, then cut out the animal again. You'll have a clever card without any added expense.

Attach the card to the gift. If you're taking a gift directly to a wedding reception or party, a good idea is to securely tape the card to the item before you wrap it. That way, the card won't get separated from the gift and put the recipient in a quandary as to whom to thank for that particular present.

Make the wrap part of the gift. Instead of using wrapping paper, wrap a gift in a brand-new dish towel and finish it off with some festive ribbon. You'll be giving an extra gift and not wasting paper.

Make a gift basket. Weave a pretty ribbon through a plastic strawberry basket and use it as a candy gift basket.

Wrap a gift with fabric. Wrap a wedding gift in a pretty piece of lace fabric, and for the ribbon use pretty beaded trim. If you sew, you might find both in your fabric stash. The fabric and trim can then be used again, maybe to cover a scrapbook or to make a small keepsake.

Many things already come in nice boxes and really only need a ribbon and a small tag to dress them up.

Fabric scraps can also easily be made into drawstring gift bags for reuse.

Wrap a really big gift. When you purchase a gift that is large, heavy, or just plain hard to wrap, use wallpaper for wrapping paper. It handles odd shapes and heavy weights without tearing.

Another way to wrap a big gift. When wrapping big boxes and gifts, use paper or plastic tablecloths. Then dip cookie cutters into food coloring and dab designs onto the tablecloth. You can also use stenciling with a small cloth or a small paint roller.

That's a wrap. Here's a unique way of wrapping a gift: If you come across shiny, never-used paint cans at a yard sale or a paint store going out of business, buy some. Seal gifts that will fit inside a 1-gallon can and either make a paper label out of gift wrap or design your own.

Wrap gifts creatively. Come up with a special "wrap" to personalize a gift. You can use Chinese takeout boxes, toolboxes, and imported coffee sacks to hold gifts. As far as wrapping paper goes, the sky is the limit! Foreign newspapers (Asian ones look really sharp), old blueprints, movie posters, menus, and Sunday comics are all perfectly good for wrapping gifts.

Be creative with gift "wrap." When you choose a large gift for a shower or wedding—say, two large pillows for the bed—you may look high and low for a gift bag or box to accommodate them without finding anything large enough.

Instead of wrapping the gift, put it in a large plastic tote with a lid. Just add a big bow!

Find alternative gift wrap. When you need to gift-wrap a large object, such as a pillow, how about using the kind of large plastic bag that's made for compacting clothes. To use these bags, you suck out the air before putting the bag full of clothes in a suitcase or storage area so they take up less space.

This will work only for gifts without sharp edges. But the bag can be reused, so it's really two gifts in one.

Use cosmetic bags for gifts. Instead of saving and storing all of those promotional cosmetic and tote bags you receive with a purchase, use them as gift bags, in lieu of store-bought paper bags. It's a different and useful way of wrapping. Your friends may like them as much as the gift inside.

Make a gift box. Here is a hint for making a gift box. Take an old shoebox and wrap it with white or colored paper. Make the paper fit as if it were the original permanent covering.

Then you can write on it and decorate it however you like. You can even write your message on the box, so you don't have to buy a card, either.

Last-minute wraps. Need to wrap a present in a hurry? What can you do? You may already have everything you need, and the perfect solution is right at your fingertips. In a pinch, try:

- Wrapping the gift in aluminum foil, shiny side out, covered by a sheet of colored plastic wrap if you have it handy. Then add a ribbon or flower.

- You can wrap a going-away present in a road map.

- Wrap a baby present in a receiving blanket or cloth diaper with a rattle or toy attached with diaper pins.

- A child's gift looks great wrapped in comics or a kids' movie poster.

- Foil-type helium balloons make terrific wrapping paper.

- Use a curling iron to iron crumpled bows—it makes them look like new in seconds.

And please remember it's the gift . . . not just the wrapping!

Store ribbon. Here's a helpful use for those clear, cylinder-shaped containers for uncooked spaghetti: store spools of ribbon in them. They fit perfectly, and you can categorize each one by color or season—put Christmas ribbons in one, springtime colors in another, and wedding/baby colors in another. You can easily see which ribbon you need instead of sorting through boxes.

Say thanks with a photo. A great thank-you for a baby gift is to take a picture with the gift. If clothing was given, take a photo of the baby dressed in the clothing. Givers will appreciate the photo and the personalized thank-you.

When you receive flowers or a plant as a gift from someone from out of town, include a picture of the plant or flowers with your thank-you note so the giver can see just what was sent.

When a family member dies, take a photo of each flower arrangement and plant that is sent, and enclose it in the thank-you cards you send to the givers. That way, they can see what they sent and have a little something to remember the services.

Customize thank-you cards. If you like using computer card-making and scrapbooking software, make our own thank-you cards. Using a digital camera, take a picture of the bouquet you received. Then use the image as the design on the face of the card (half-sheet size), leaving the inside blank so you can write a thank-

THE ART OF WRITING THANK-YOU NOTES

Here are some helpful hints for writing thank-you notes. Really, it's an easy gesture that means so much to the person who receives it! But too often, thank-you notes are considered a chore, when the truth is that you don't have to write a novel—just a few simple thoughts tucked neatly in an envelope is all you need. Here are a few hints to get you started:

- First, greet the recipient: "Dear Aunt Martha."
- Then express your gratitude: "Thanks for the beautiful scarf."
- Follow with letting "Aunt Martha" know how you plan to us the gift. For instance, say "It'll come in handy during the cold-weather days ahead."
- It's also good to include a personal line to show interest in how the person is doing, such as "I hope your new job in Washington is going well."
- Last but not least, say thanks again and sign your name.

That's all there is to it. The next time you receive a gift or someone has done something special for you, take a minute and write a quick thank-you to show how much you appreciate the person!

you note. People love getting these custom cards and seeing their gift pictured on the front. Print out extras to send to others who are under the weather or need a pick-me-up note for the day.

Write a note that's easy to read. It can be hard to write a thank-you note to an older friend who has macular degeneration, since the person may need to have someone come over to read the mail to them.

Instead of sending a handwritten note, use one of the largest fonts on the computer, with a good amount of space between the lines. You can also "bold" the print to make it even more legible.

CRAFTS AND HOBBIES

Multiply picture frames. A great way to frame pictures when you want a double or triple frame is to buy cheaper plastic frames and tape them together with masking tape.

Put the fronts together and put masking tape along the sides to be joined. For triple frames, put the fronts of the second and third frames together and tape the joint.

Make pine-cone picture holders.

Don't know what to do with all those nice pictures (mostly school pictures of the kids) that came in Christmas cards from friends and family? Take a tray, fill it with pine cones (on their sides facing out from the middle) and insert the bottom of a photo in each pine cone. Or, you can display the pine cones and photos on a mantel. It sure is better than stashing the pictures back in the cards and in a drawer.

Use panoramic-view photos. Panoramic-view photos are nice for capturing scenery, but they do not fit in albums or regular frames. Here's a way to use them: Fold them in two and use them as note cards. Identify where the photo was taken for a personal touch. These folded notes fit into regular-size envelopes.

Make some music. When kids do a lot of banging around trying to make music, simply get an empty oatmeal box, decorate it, and they will have a drum!

Make a marble bag. When you have an old pair of slipper socks, sew up the holes in one of them, run some ribbon through the top, and make a marble bag. You can also put a small doll in one to use as a sleeping bag for her.

Make a place mat. An arts-and-crafts idea for a scout troop or other group is to make place mats. It is easy to do.

First, tear out 25 to 30 colorful magazine pages and, using a straw, roll them from corner to corner very tightly. Use transparent tape to keep the roll in place so it doesn't come unraveled. Now, tape or tie them together to make place mats. You can cut them off so that they are all the same size.

Apply shellac to seal the place mats so they will be waterproof, too.

Make photo place mats. One way to use extra photographs is to make place mats with them.

They are easy to make and wipe clean with a damp cloth. Glue photos accompanied by captions to a large piece of thin cardboard (the size you want for a place mat) and take it to a copy store for lamination.

Turn cards into place mats. When you get greeting cards that are too nice to throw away, make them into place mats to be used during the holidays. Buy paper in different colors, tear off the front of the cards, lay them out, and glue them down on the paper. Then have them laminated at a local store or printshop.

Turn cards into bookmarks. Cut pretty greeting cards into strips and make bookmarks. Leave them in the books when you pass them on to your friends. They can pass them to their friends, and on and on.

Reuse greeting cards creatively. Here are some ways to reuse the fronts of greeting cards:

- Cut into gift tags.

- Make into a postcard.

- Write recipes on the back.

- Decorate a box or an appointment-book cover.

- Use to decorate a CD case.

- Cut out scenes and glue to poster board with family photos to make a collage.

- Use the blank side for a shopping list.

No one likes to think about those pretty greeting cards winding up in a landfill, so check with your town to see if it recycles cards with other paper goods.

Make a glue board, protect a desk. Tape a piece of waxed paper to a large piece of cardboard to use when gluing, painting small objects, or doing other messy crafts. It keeps the desk neat;

just pull the waxed paper off when it's full of glue and replace it with another piece.

Make pickup easy. When you accidentally spill small beads or any other small objects—which are difficult for any of us to pick up, let alone for those with arthritis or problems with fine-motor skills—simply use a kitchen tool.

A metal pancake flipper will slide under the dropped items, and you can cup your other hand around or over the items and simply drop them back into the container. If necessary, place a small funnel in the container first. Saves a lot of time.

Iron doll clothes. Here's a hint for doll collectors who often get vintage outfits for them. When the clothing is wrinkled and too small for your regular iron, use a hair-curling iron. It's a bit slow, but it's worth the effort if you care how the doll clothes look.

Make a postcard collage. Here's a great use for postcards: make collages. If you hate to dispose of postcards you've received from family and friends, and don't want to stash them in a shoe box, make collages with them so you can continue to enjoy them.

Buy an inexpensive, 24-by-36-inch plastic-glass frame, and mount the cards with as many place names showing as possible.

Make a memorial wreath. When a family member dies, you can take flowers from the floral arrangements

On the Light Side
Things to Do with Leaves

Many readers have sent in hints about receiving fall leaves as a gift through the mail. Here are some of them:

• Peg of New York says: "I send leaves to my out-of-state family. I dip them in warm, melted paraffin, lay them on waxed paper to dry, and then send them."

• Ann of Missouri, says: "My family moved to Texas. I sent them a box of 'maple helicopters,' and they had fun with neighbor kids throwing them in the air to spin."

• E.M.J. of Texas, says: "Reading the letter about the maple leaves brought back memories. In 1948, my mother would place fresh orange blossoms in the wax sleeve of a cereal box and send the box to me in Texas. Just the memory of how wonderful they smelled is such a treasure."

• Judy of Minnesota, says: "When my mother-in-law was sick, I drove around our beautiful town and took pictures of the most vibrant trees. I picked up leaves of every shape and color, came home, and pressed the leaves in between clear sealing paper. I sent them and the pictures to my sister-in-law, who was caring for my mother-in-law. She hung them up around the room and really brightened it up. It also brought back some wonderful 'fall in Minnesota' memories."

that are sent and hang them upside down in the attic to dry.

Make one or more dried flower wreaths to keep as special reminders of your loved one.

Dress up a wastebasket and inspire using it. Want to get your kids to use wastebaskets more often? Let them decorate some on a rainy, boring day. Get some plastic trash cans or wastebaskets from a dollar or discount store. Let the kids glue all sorts of things on them like beads, marbles, paper cutouts, magazine pictures, and anything else they can find around the house. They'll have fun, and they might even think about throwing things away more often.

Make a magazine scrapbook. Old magazines make wonderful scrapbooks for young children and grandchildren.

This is a nice way to recycle and make something useful. A joint-effort scrapbook would be a good rainy-day project.

Make art. Want to make a special artwork project? All you need to do is get a piece of heavy cardboard, some white school glue, and some shavings from your favorite crayons.

An easy way to get the crayon shaving is to sharpen all your crayons and just save the shavings. Drizzle some of the white school glue all over the cardboard (in a design or not) and then drop the shavings onto it.

JEWELRY MAKING 101

Homemade jewelry is popular. Here are some hints for the jeweler in your family:

- Shop garage sales for beads. Buy necklaces, bracelets, and other pieces, and take them apart. Be sure to check carefully because some beads are glued onto strings and they can't be reused.

- Ask friends and family for jewelry bits and pieces that you can reuse. I think many people have a necklace or bracelet that they don't wear anymore and would be willing to donate to the cause. Why not make them thank-you pieces of jewelry?

- Use ice-cube trays or egg cartons to hold organized and separated beads.

- Buy one of those rolling chests with drawers and keep all your jewelry supplies inside it. This way, when you feel in the mood to create, you can just roll your supplies to where you want to work.

- Try to buy supplies in bulk, and watch for sales where craft supplies are sold.

Let dry and you have a great one-of-a-kind art picture.

Make paper dolls. Little girls love playing with paper dolls, but buying them can be expensive. Here's how to make some that don't cost anything.

Cut pictures of people out of magazines, then cut some cardboard to make them sturdy.

Make a plant holder. You will need three plastic foam cups, a stapler, six flat sticks (you can use Popsicle sticks), glue, heavy string, some soil, seeds, and a marker.

Draw a picture on each cup and staple the cups to one another at the top. Glue the sticks together to form a triangle that will fit around the rims of all three cups. Cut three pieces of string and tie pieces of string to each corner of the triangle, and tie the three pieces together at the top. Fill the cups with soil and plant some seeds in each.

BEADING 101

Beading is a popular activity for many of my readers. We thought we would share some helpful hints:

- Fishing tackle boxes are perfect for keeping beads separated by color or project, and they hold a lot of beads. You can also buy the clear-sectioned boxes sold for fishing lures to use for beads, too.

- Check home-improvement stores for other organizers. They have ones made to store nuts and bolts that are perfect for beading supplies.

- Save the plastic lids from margarine or yogurt containers. Pour beads onto the lids when you are working, and when you're done, the beads can easily be poured back into the containers.

- If you are going to bead, spend the money for the correct tools. In the long run, they will last longer and make your beading easier.

- Beaded projects make great gifts!

- When working with tiny beads, stick a length of double-sided tape to your non-beading hand. Press the double-sided tape into the tiny beads and you'll avoid all the rolling-around challenges.

- Check to make sure all of your beads will fit on your stringing wire before you start your design. You may need to change to a finer gauge wire or to a nylon fishing line if the bead holes are small.

Put the cups inside the triangle and hang it in a window.

Protect your hands from paint. Have you ever spray-painted something only to have your hands covered with paint? Protect your hands with small plastic bags.

Make sachets. Used fabric-softener sheets may still smell good when they come out of the dryer, and it's a shame to just throw them away. So, use them to make sachets. Cut some fabric into squares with a pair of pinking shears. Then sew all the way around them and gather each square into a ball. Stuff them with fabric-softener sheets and put them in dresser drawers and the towel cabinet.

Dry roses for decoration. When a bouquet of roses begins to wilt, pour off the water and leave the roses upright in the vase until they're dry. Then pop the heads off and you have beautiful dried roses to fill a coffee-table dish for decoration. This method works only for those roses whose petals don't fall off.

Noodle a necklace. Are you looking for a fun craft to make with the kids? Use your noodles! What's colorful, fun to make, and fun to wear? A noodle necklace, of course! It's a project guar-

anteed to keep the kids happy, and it's sooo easy.

Start with a bag of long tube noodles, some rubbing alcohol, and some food coloring for the dye.

Put the noodles on the bottom of a large container that you don't mind getting stained. Add enough alcohol to cover them and squirt in a few drops of food coloring. Mix to blend, making sure the pasta is completely covered.

For multicolored necklaces, make a separate batch for each color. The longer the noodles soak, the brighter the colors will be. Once they're dyed, place the noodles on some paper towels to dry.

Then let the kids string together the noodles for a fun necklace, or glue them onto construction paper and create a beautiful collage.

Use a paper plate palette. If you like to paint and use paint that comes in tubes, squeeze a little bit of paint onto a paper plate and mix it up, and you'll contain any mess right there on the plate. Try to use the plates a couple of times before you throw them away.

Scrapbooking hints. Here are a couple of scrapbooking hints from Heloise Central.

- Keep an eye on mail, stationery, and even magazines. Many times there are great borders and symbols that would work on a scrapbook page. The best part is that they are free!

- Keep pieces of ribbons, buttons, movie-ticket stubs, and other mementos, and add them to pages. They are special, personal, and one-of-a-kind!

Store scrapbooking supplies. Here's an inexpensive way to store scrapbooking supplies. Most of us do not have a spare room to devote to this craft.

Craft stores carry a variety of totes, but the big-wheeled items are too bulky and hard to fit into a closet. They also are very expensive, running as much as $150 or more. So, go to a thrift store and buy the largest suitcase you can find. It holds all of the smaller craft organizers for stamps and pads, scissors, punches, notebooks for ideas, and stickers. Plus the paper will go into the case or in pockets on the outside.

Organize scrapbooking supplies. If you do a lot of scrapbooking, your stickers, letters, and embellishments may always be a mess. Plastic pages for 4-by-6-inch photos work great for organizing these supplies. A plastic page that has pockets for three 4-by-6-inch photos is perfect. Put the plastic pages in a three-ring binder and use the pockets to organize your supplies by subject (birthday, sports, travel). You will always know what you have and be able to find what you want quickly.

Hang craft supplies. When you see self-adhesive hooks at a local dollar or discount store, buy a couple of bags of them and use them to hang different arts and crafts supplies. The hooks hold spools of ribbon, scissors, threads, small hardware accessories, glue, and other supplies.

Organize in an egg carton. Here's a

On the Light Side
An Oldie but Goodie

Here is a flashback hint from 20 years ago. "Dear Heloise: I found a great way to make a beautiful decoration for my room. All you need is a half an egg carton, Popsicle sticks, and construction paper. Cut the construction paper into shapes of flowers. Glue them on the Popsicle sticks and punch them in the bottom of the egg carton. There you have it—pretty flower garden."

This is still a fun project today.

handy way to reuse a clean, foam egg carton: Use it to separate craft items like beads or sequins.

Bag your craft supplies. These days, almost all bed linens and curtains come in thick plastic bags with zippers or snaps on them. Some even have pockets containing information about the product inside. These bags are handy for storing craft projects because they are clear, reclosable, and, best of all, free!

Use prescription bottles for storage. Use empty, transparent prescription bottles that you've washed, dried, and removed the labels from for storing small beads and sequins for craft projects. Using a funnel to fill the containers makes it easy, with few spills.

Stash craft supplies. Store small craft supplies in a clean yogurt container with a snap-on lid (the ones with foil covers don't work as well).

Use rope-handled bags. Don't you love the small bags with rope or plastic handles that come with a purchase at certain stores? These bags have a multitude of uses. They make it easy to grab and hold everything you need. They can also be recycled as gift bags. The larger ones are handy to keep craft projects in. When you want to work on a project, everything is contained in one bag.

Store paintbrushes. If you love to paint, you might have hundreds of brushes. To store them, buy clear-plastic food-storage containers in appropriate heights to use with small and tall brushes. To hold the containers upright, fill them with small, pea-size river rocks and then put in the brushes. They stand up, the brush size shows, and it's easy to grab the size you need at a glance.

Separate sequins. When you are using sequins for various purposes, put them in a small muffin tin. Each color sequin is put into the separate compartments, making the color selection fast and easy.

SEWING AND NEEDLECRAFTS

Join pieces with bobby pins. When you make a sweater or anything that has to be joined together, instead of straight or safety pins use large bobby pins, which never move. Straight pins can get lost in the material.

Thread a needle more easily. To make needle threading easier, touch the end of the thread to a nail-polish brush and roll the end of the thread. The end will be stiff enough to pass easily through the small hole of the needle.

Thread a needle another way. As we get older, it is harder to see to thread a needle. Something that helps is to use the bright-yellow lid of a butter tub. Hold the lid as background, and it makes the eye of the needle easier to see.

Thread a needle. Here's a hint for older ladies who sew and have trouble threading a sewing-machine needle or a sewing needle: If you cut a small square of white paper and place it behind the sewing-machine needle, it makes the hole in the needle look twice as big, thus making it really easy to thread the needle.

Cut your square from a card that buttons come on because it is thicker and easier to pick up than paper.

Check for lost needles. A hint for those who sew: Don't throw out that old pincushion until you remove all the needles that might be hiding inside. Instead, remove the pincushion's cover, empty the sawdust into a bowl, and use a magnet to collect any needles that have gotten buried inside the pincushion.

Store straight pins. A paper clip holder from an office-supply store is perfect for storing straight pins.

Store sewing needles. The little plastic containers in which mechanical pencil lead comes work fantastically for storing sewing needles. They're just the right size for standard needles.

Find a needle threader. Needle threaders are very useful, but they are so small and hard to find and hold on to. Solve the problem by gluing on a "handle" about 2 inches long, made from a doubled strip of seam binding. Pin the handle where you keep your needles; it's easy to see.

Find a thimble substitute. When you need a thimble and can't find one, here's a substitute. Find a hairspray bottle with a small cap. Take off the cap and push the sewing needle with it.

Make a sewing board. Store spools of thread and full bobbins on nails driven in at an angle into a board. The board should be a size that can hang above your sewing machine or in another easy-to-reach place.

Sort thread by color. Have you ever been frustrated by looking through a bucketful of spools for just the right color thread? Sort your thread according to general colors. Put each group of greens, blues, reds, yellows, or other colors into plastic bags. Keep the bags in a tall metal can for easy access whenever you have a sewing task that doesn't call for a new spool.

Sew with dental floss. Here's a hint for sewing by hand. When you sew, only use dental floss. No matter what you sew, if the floss is showing after finishing, you can just get that color of permanent marker and color the floss. It will never come undone.

Take a load off when sewing. When you are sewing drapes, coats, or any other fabric that's difficult to handle, push your sewing machine against your dining table, extending the cover of the machine over the table. It allows you to rest the fabric on the table while you sew. The table carries the heavy load of the material and makes sewing easier.

Plan out a pattern. When you start a new sewing project, you can buy patterns and study them at home before buying the material and notions. Instead of taking a pattern back to the store with you, scan it on your computer, reduce the size, and print it out. Then write what you need on the printed sheet. Either glue the picture in a small notebook or place it in a small photo album. Then take that along when you go shopping. It's a lot easier to shop with than the actual pattern.

Preserve patterns. Patterns these days are very pricey, yet still made of flimsy tissue paper. Here is a way to preserve patterns and make them sturdy.

Using quilt basting spray and a roll of paper, separate the pattern pieces, lightly spray the paper, and "float" each pattern piece down on top of the paper. The spray is forgiving—you can gently lift the paper to remove a crease or bubble. Then, working from the center to the outside, smooth the tissue a little at a time. Put the pieces aside for about a half hour as you work your way through all the pattern pieces. Keep some inexpensive self-sealing bags to place all the pieces, directions, and envelope into, because the pattern does gain bulkiness when done.

Mark the slot on the spool. Are all the ends of thread hanging from the spools because you can't find the original slot on the spool? Take a waterproof, felt-tipped pen and put a dot at the end of the slot—works every time.

Make a portable sewing-machine cover. A pillowcase, with a few adjustments, makes a suitable cover for a portable sewing machine.

Use your ironing board as a sewing table. If your sewing machine is kept in a spare room without a table in it, use your ironing board set down as low as it will go. The entire surface works as a pincushion, so instead of trying to place pins in a small container, you can keep your eyes on the seam you're sewing.

Prevent sewing mess. Sewing projects can create a mess to clean up afterward. To make cleanup a snap, attach a kitchen trash bag to the end of your sewing table. As you sew and have scraps, threads, and other debris, simply push them right into the bag. Your sewing room will always be neat.

Keep a lint roller in the sewing room. Use a sticky lint roller that has a long handle attached (like a mop or broom) in your sewing room. In just a minute or two, the thread and fuzz that come from sewing and serging are stuck to it and not the vacuum-cleaner roller. It saves the vacuum roller from tangles and saves you the time it takes to cut them away from the roller. The used sticky pad easily tears away, revealing a new sticky pad.

Make a photo blanket. Here's a unique gift for a family member. If you have one-of-a-kind photos of ancestors, perhaps from working on a genealogical project, use them to make a blanket. Pick about six of your favorite photos, take them to a photo shop,

and have them copied onto pieces of material.

Sew the squares together, add a flannel backing, and you'll have a very special blanket to give to someone you love.

If you would like to do this but can't sew, check your newspaper's classifieds for seamstresses or a fabric store for a recommendation. This would be a wonderful idea for those hard-to-buy-for relatives. Or, use photos of pets to make a blanket for a pet lover.

Display a quilt. A quilter always has a quilt or two she or he wants to display, but finding good display racks is difficult and often expensive.

CD storage racks make good substitutes. They are usually made of wood, and the shelf or rack part is made of three dowel rods set at angles. You can easily display one to three quilts on these rods. Since the rack is made of wood, it can be refinished in any color desired or painted. You can also use a CD rack in your sewing room to hold the fabric after you press it or to hold the cut pieces. This way you can see all the pieces at once, and they don't get creased as they do when folded.

You can usually find CD racks at thrift stores, some for as little as $5.

Turn a dress into a keepsake. If you

belonged to Camp Fire Girls or Girl Scouts and still have your old uniform stored away, bring back the happy memories. Remove all the beads, patches, pins, and buttons that were sewn on the uniform and make pillows with them. You will always have a reminder of the good old days when you participated in Camp Fire or Scouting activities.

Make pillows from favorite shirts. After a husband, father, or grandfather dies, keep some of his favorite shirts. Cut them into different shapes and pieces and make pillows for all the children and grandchildren.

Also, please don't be in a hurry to clean out, clear out, toss out, or give away things when someone dies. Later on you may regret that you didn't keep an item.

You can also use children's sport and school T-shirts to make pillows or blankets. And, a bonus is to put school or activity pins on the finished item to make it into a memory quilt or pillow.

Re-cover pot holders. When pot holders become unsightly, it takes just minutes to cut out some fabric and sew it up to re-cover an ugly one.

Buy used clothes for the fabrics. When shopping at garage sales, consider buying the clothing there in order to purchase the fabric. Garments in good condition—velvet, silk, or even pure wool—can contain enough material to complete a craft or a pillow and can be purchased at a fraction of the cost of fabric off the bolt.

Make a yarn dispenser. Wind a tennis-ball-size yarn ball and put it in a reclosable sandwich bag. Seal the top, but leave enough of it unsealed to pull the yarn out as needed. This is a good system to use when you're working on a project that uses different colors in the same row.

Store yarn. If you like to crochet with the new crazy/fancy yarns, you may find that the leftovers have a tendency to unwind and get tangled up with everything. To keep them contained, put each one in a separate nude-color half-stocking—the stockings are very inexpensive. The yarn stays neat and you'll be able to see what is inside each stocking.

For another handy storage container for balls of yarn, take a large coffee can and spray-paint it a solid color. Paint a scene on it, front and back, to dress it up. It's a pretty can that prevents crochet balls from rolling around the floor when you're crocheting.

More yarn storage. Take a 5-quart ice-cream container, make a hole in the center of the lid, thread the end of a ball of yarn through the hole, drop the ball of yarn into the container, and replace the lid. Now you are ready to crochet or whatever without your yarn rolling all over the floor.

For easy storage and easy access, cover each container with construction paper for the corresponding color of yarn inside. The containers can be easily stacked in your "craft room" and identified when you need a certain color.

Corral crochet hooks. Do you have an extra soft-eyeglass case with nothing to put in it? Don't fret—try using it to organize and keep crochet hooks in one place.

Make afghan assembly easier. If you love to crochet afghans, you generally make granny squares and then sew them together to form a design. Sometimes the patterns are very small and hard to follow.

To make assembling the afghan a little easier, copy the pattern on a copy machine and then highlight the rows as you put them together.

You won't have to "find your place" every time you want to work on the afghan.

Make an afghan for the grandmother who taught you how. A grandmother who crochets may teach her daughters and granddaughters to crochet, too. She has probably made all of them hats, scarves, and afghans. To do something special for this special grandma, make her an afghan from all of you. Have each person crochet five granny squares, or whatever number you need (using the same type yarn), and when you are done, sew them together.

The afghan will always remind your grandmother of the love that went into making it.

Keep track of knitting or cross-stitch. When doing a graph pattern, such as knitting or cross-stitch, where

Unlimited Uses for . . . Leftover Yarn

Here are four handy ways to reuse leftover yarn:

- Make a pretty afghan out of your scraps.
- Use as a ribbon to tie around a gift.
- Give to a school to use in its art classes.
- Braid and use as a zipper extender.

you have to keep track of each row, put your pattern inside a clear photo page. Then use a permanent marker to keep track of the rows you have done. You'll be able to keep the original pattern intact with no marks on it, and can use it over again. You can buy photo pages at an office-supply store.

Copy a pattern. To keep an original graph pattern fresh, try copying the pattern on a copy machine. Then take a light-colored highlighting pen and color the copy as you cross-stitch, crochet, or knit.

Make two copies for cross-stitching—one for the cross-stitching and one for backstitching. You can also cut and throw away the completed sections, keeping only the part of the pattern that isn't finished.

Preserve cross-stitch. To preserve handmade cross-stitch pieces, dust with a soft paintbrush. It's easy, and it works.

Match colors. Embroidery projects such as tablecloths are often worked on over several or more years, and many times are left for another generation to finish. It is often difficult to match brands and colors of threads on unfinished projects.

One solution: take the label with the brand and color number and loosely sew it to the project using the colored thread from the skein. You could also sew the entire skein to the project if you intend to set the item aside, using the label to attach the skein. You will no longer have to spend frustrating hours taking the article to the store and trying to color-match threads on old projects.

Bag embroidery thread. Put different colors of embroidery thread in little plastic snack bags, along with a threaded needle. Needles are cheap, and it is so easy to pull the threaded needle from a little piece of cardboard every time you have to change colors. Keep all the bags in an unused hanging file box, making it easy to start sewing.

Copy a knitting pattern. Instead of placing a knitting pattern in a sheer paper protector, make a copy of the pattern on a copy machine. You can mark up the copy and keep the original pattern clean.

Speed up knitting and crocheting projects. For all the knitters and crocheters out there, here's a simple solution to make your projects go faster and easier: Simply place your needles and hooks in a plastic bag, pour in some talcum powder, shake gently and voilà! See and feel the difference as your proceed.

Keep knitting needles in place. In knitting, use soft, orange earplugs (available inexpensively at drugstores) on the tips of needles to prevent stitches from sliding off when you set the work aside. It also protects the needle tips and your knitting bag. Just center the wide end of an earplug on the point of the needle and pull it down. Don't let the needle poke through.

Organize a needlepoint project. To make your needlepoint projects a little easier, separate the different colors and thread a needle with each one. Put the needles in a pincushion, and they are ready for use.

Make a picture hanger. If you need a picture hanger for a piece of needlepoint or other light-weight artwork, the pop top from a soda can will work fine.

Chapter 10

—•———————————•—

Taking Care of Yourself

This chapter is all about you—there are hints for staying healthy, managing your health care, and caring for others who are ill or disabled. You'll also find beauty advice, and some ideas for soothing spa treatments you can enjoy at home. Plus, there are some tips on being safe as you go about your life and activities. So read, relax, and enjoy!

MAKING LIFESTYLE CHANGES

If you're working on a lifestyle change—for example, losing weight, quitting smoking, or exercising more—there are things you can do to improve your chances of success.

Let's face it: Changing even minor things about ourselves can be difficult. So, making a big change can sometimes seem impossible. But here are a few things you can do to boost your confidence and help you attain your objective:

- Set several small goals instead of a big one. For instance, if you plan to stop smoking, focus on just getting through today without a cigarette . . . and gradually challenge yourself to take another step each day.

- Reward yourself for reaching your daily goals! Treat yourself to a manicure, a movie, or simply a relaxing bath.

- Don't expect perfection—if you slip up, don't be too hard on yourself. Stay positive and vow to have stronger willpower the next time!

- Surround yourself with positive reinforcements. Ask loved ones to help keep you on track, or consider a support group. It's always easier when someone else is there to cheer you on.

Shopping with a walker. Here's a hint from a former world-class shopper for the elderly or disabled:

When someone takes you to the mall, you probably use a walker. The baskets or bags made for walkers are often inadequate, so put several heavy plastic shower-curtain rings on the arms of the walker. When you make a purchase, slip the bag handle (as long as the bag is not heavy) onto the ring and snap the ring closed. It's surprising how much you can carry.

Clean a nebulizer. For allergy sufferers who use a nebulizer for breathing treatments, you can sanitize it with white vinegar. Naturally, check your instruction manual first. However, here's what many experts suggest: To help sanitize equipment, soak at least once a week in a solution of 1 part white distilled vinegar to 2 parts water for up to 30 minutes, then rinse well and dry.

Use empty tissue boxes for disposal. Instead of throwing away those empty tissue boxes, save them for the day a family member has a cold, and put one next to his or her box of tissues. When the person uses a tissue, it can be pushed into the empty tissue box. Germs and viruses are contained, and no one has to touch the soiled tissues.

In a public restroom, give your purse a seat. When using a public restroom that does not have a hook for your purse, use a seat liner. Place the liner on the floor and put your purse on top of it. When you're done, the liner can be easily disposed of.

Also, keep a package of hand wipes in your purse for a quick wipe-down of a sticky grocery cart handle or of leftover sticky spots at a restaurant.

Be careful with perfume strips. If you like to use scented strips from magazines as bookmarks, please do not use them in library books. The scent will transfer to the books and make them unusable to folks with allergies.

Do embroidery despite carpal tunnel. If you suffer from carpal tunnel syndrome in both wrists, you need to wear braces when you use the computer or do a hobby like embroidery.

The problem is that the braces' self-

On the Light Side

How to Tell You're Getting Older

One reader sent me the following:

"Here's how I can tell I'm getting older: It used to be that on my bedside table you could find nail cream, lotion, and lip balm. Now I have antihistamines, antacid, and cream for sore muscles! I had to laugh when I realized this!"

gripping fabric tape catches the delicate needlework. Here's how to fix it: Cut off the toe of a pair of old socks, and stick your hand in the sock, brace and all, so that your fingers stick out of the toe. Then cut a hole for your thumb.

The tape will no longer stick to your needlework, and you can wear the braces around the house without getting them dirty. Just strip off your "gauntlets" and throw them in the washer.

DEALING WITH DOCTORS

Fax your doctor. If you have trouble with your doctor's office not returning your calls, you can try faxing your questions to the office. You may get a speedier reply. Just make sure the doctor is receptive to this.

Fax a nursing home. If you have a friend or family member in a nursing home or assisted-living facility and you can't get by for a visit, take a few minutes to fax a note to let the person know that you are thinking of him or her.

Make it easier to fill out medical forms. Here's some advice from readers on filling out medical forms:

- Ask if your doctor's office would give all patients a copy of the last form they filled out and a red pen to make any changes. That would make it easier for the staff to make any corrections of information to be transferred to permanent records and also would cut down on the amount of writing a patient has to do.

- Most doctor's offices will gladly supply the forms in advance so you can fill them out at home. You can have them mailed to you, or stop by to pick them up.

- Keep a file in your computer of all significant medical problems and surgeries you have had, along with the dates of each. Also have a file with all current medications and dosages you are taking, including over-the-counter products such as vitamins. Print a copy of each and carry it with you anytime you are going for a doctor's appointment. Normally, with this in hand, all you have to do is fill in your name and address and say "see attached" for the other information.

Ask for help to fill out forms. When you make an appointment to see a doctor, tell the staff if you have difficulty filling out forms because of tremors or another disability, and ask them to provide help when you arrive. Perhaps you could use a desk if that would help, or maybe you need someone to assist you. But ask if someone can help you.

Don't put off your doctor's visit for this reason! Go, and when you are handed that dreaded clipboard, simply say, "I have difficulty filling this out— is it necessary, or just an update?"

Keep a medical notebook. To keep up with all of the medical appointments for an elderly parent, keep a notebook with the doctors in indexed files. Write all appointments down by date, time, and place, and keep track of bills and payments by Medicare and insurance. Take notes on what the doctor says.

Have a page with all of your parent's information to give to each new doctor, or an update if requested. Also, put a copy of the Medicare card and insurance supplement on the page and list all operations and serious illnesses, with dates.

This book will save you lots of frustration in filling out forms in doctors' offices. If they will not accept the form, at least you will have all the information you need to fill out their forms correctly.

Schedule an appointment when you won't forget it. Start making important appointments on days you won't forget. Schedule that checkup or mammogram on your birthday, Valentine's Day, or another holiday or important personal day. You could use April Fools' Day or Mayday, which fall on the same day every year. And if you haven't gotten a checkup or a mammogram in a few years, give yourself a gift and schedule one today.

Make a medical appointment calendar. For ready reference, keep a medical appointment calendar separate from other calendars, with the business cards of doctors, clinics, hospitals, and other important people or numbers attached.

Find a new doctor. If you move or your doctor retires, you might be suddenly faced with having to find a new physician. It's important to select one before you have an emergency. Take these steps:

- Ask friends, relatives, or business associates for references.

- Call your local medical association for a list of doctors trained in the specialty you are looking for.

- Check the physician's educational background and whether he or she is board-certified in the area you need.

- Inquire about the doctor's patient scheduling. Is there enough time for your visit? What are the office policies? Can you get a first appointment or a last-minute one? Write down the questions you have so you can ask the doctor and also take notes on his or her answers.

- Does the doctor have privileges in a surgical center or hospital near you?

- If you have preferences for your medical care, find a doctor who will work with you.

Thanking hospital staff. Hospital patients often buy chocolate for the nursing staff as a thank-you. Here's another gift suggestion: Medical personnel wash their hands constantly, so a gift of lotion would be practical, thoughtful, and meaningful.

CAREGIVING

Keep the sheet in place. Here's a way to keep the bedsheet from slipping down for a wheelchair or bed-confined patient. Sew two twin-fitted sheets together on three sides to make a large pillowcase, then slip it over the mattress, with the open part at the bottom. When the patient moves around, the top will not slip down or off, and it makes the bed more comfortable to lie on without the sheet bunching under him or her.

Make it easier to get into a seat. Putting a plastic tablecloth or any type of plastic on a tub or shower chair, or on cloth car seats, makes it easier for a person with limited mobility to slide around into position. Also, don't forget to tilt the shower or tub seat so that water is going down into the tub.

Put an alarm on a walker. While assisting someone in recovery from knee surgery, attach colorful bells to his or her walker. That way you will be able to hear when the person is up and about, and you will be able to come quickly if the bells make a sudden noise to indicate that he or she is in need. Place the walker at the bedside at night, and it'll be easy for the person to shake the walker to summon you.

Light the way. For someone with limited eyesight who must use a walker, it's very important that she have enough light when trying to get around. Add an inexpensive bicycle light to the handlebar of her walker. Whenever she needs extra light, she can just turn on the bike light.

Secure portable oxygen tanks. A patient who requires portable oxygen tanks when away from home may have many of them lying on the floor in his or her apartment. The heavy tanks tend to roll and may present a tripping hazard. To prevent this, secure the tanks in a wooden wine rack. Full tanks can be separated from empty tanks, and all are easily reachable when the patient changes his or her tank supply.

Cover up a catheter. For a post-surgical patient who needs a catheter for a time, the sight of the bag can be unpleasant for the patient and also for the family. Hide the device in a large, pretty gift bag.

Use swimming pool "noodles." Here's a new use for those "noodles" that are used in a swimming pool: Make a bed bumper. Cut one noodle lengthwise halfway down with an electric knife and place it on a trundle bed frame to keep a guest from scraping his leg should he bump up next to it, especially on the corner. It's an effective bumper.

Organize medical supplies. A shallow box with medicines, another with bathing supplies, and a third with a catheter or other supplies saves invaluable steps for caregivers. Also, when visitors come, as they do, the house is less cluttered, since the boxes may be placed in a corner or under the bed.

Prop up a leg comfortably. When a patient has to prop his or her legs up high because they are swollen, prop them up on something soft but sturdy. Place a large package of toilet paper rolls into a pillowcase. It will squash the rolls, but will support the swollen legs.

Monitor a patient. When someone is confined to an upstairs bedroom following surgery, use a baby monitor to keep in touch. Once put in place, the monitor allows you the freedom to work in the rest of the house, and the patient in bed can still call you if necessary.

Use a battery-operated doorbell. To enable an invalid to call for you when he needs help, buy a battery-operated doorbell. Attach the ringer button to a piece of fabric that you pin to the patient's clothes, or leave it on a bedside table. If the range of the bell is 100 feet, you could be anywhere in the house, garage, or yard with the chime and still hear the call.

Occasionally, there may be a false alarm when the patient rolls over on the button, but it is a small price to pay for the peace of mind that it will give you.

The doorbell can work for older family members, too. When your parents are elderly and still living in their own home, purchase two battery-operated doorbells. Give each of your parents a bell button and ask their kind neighbors on either side to keep a ringer. If they are willing, they can check on your parents if the bell rings, and call a relative who lives a few miles away.

Ring bells. Place inexpensive bells at different locations in the house where a handicapped or an ill person may sit during the day, so she can ring when she needs assistance. You could use the kind of bells that fishermen use on their lines.

Put a liner in a commode. When you are caring for someone who has to use a bedside commode, lining the bucket with a plastic trash bag is a most helpful thing.

Slide away from the table. If a relative or friend has a difficult time pushing into or out from the table, purchase an inexpensive, lightweight computer chair on wheels.

Visit the ill. If someone you love is very ill, don't be afraid to call or stop

by because you think she might not be up to a visit. She will cherish your visit and will let you know if she needs to rest. And when she does rest, hold her hand until she goes to sleep.

Just remember that not everyone is the same. It's important to learn from the person or caretaker if "drop-ins" are welcome. Many people want notice before receiving visitors.

MANAGING MEDICATIONS AND SUPPLEMENTS

Get directions you can understand. A medical doctor in South Carolina offers these hints:

Asking your pharmacist to type the purpose of each of your medications on the label not only is good for your own information; it also makes it easier for you and your doctor. For example, the doctor could say something like, "Cut your blood pressure medicine in half," rather than "Cut your hydrochlorothiazide in half." My what?! (Note that state laws vary—your pharmacist may or may not be able to add anything to the label.)

You can ask your doctor to do the same: When he or she writes out the prescription, it can read "Take once a day for diabetes," for example. In a computerized office, it is then there for every refill.

It never hurts, either, to question each prescription. Often we visit the doctor for specific complaints and don't think about the whole picture. If you ask aloud what a medicine is for, it gives you both a chance to reflect on its usefulness.

You may be continuing with medicines from past doctors that never seem to come off your list and that may no longer be necessary. Less can be better. Just be sure to discuss it with your doctor. Bring all your prescriptions with you (or a complete list) to every health care professional you visit.

Label new medications. When you get a new medication, write what it is to be used for in large, dark print on the label. This way, you will know you are taking the right medication for your symptoms.

Label the dosage. Here is a hint for those who take over-the-counter vitamins and supplements. The dosage for each one is usually different. Without your glasses on or your contacts in, it is hard to read the fine print on the bottles. So, take a fine-tip permanent black marking pen and write the dosage in larger numbers on the front of each bottle. This way, you will always take the right amount and won't have to struggle to read the fine print or take more than you need.

I.D. prescription bottles. This hint is not just for senior citizens. The print on prescription bottles is small, and the pills or capsules inside are sometimes similar. To avoid grabbing the wrong bottle, place a large first initial of the medicine on the label. You can also write the name of the medicine in large letters on the shoulder of the bottle. Do this on two sides, to make it easier to reach into the medicine cabinet and get what you need.

Use a red marker or nail polish to make it easily visible.

Another way to label medicines. When you have a number of prescriptions in bottles that look alike, it is hard to read the name of the medicine on the outside of the bottle without glasses. When you get your prescriptions, take a black marker pen and write quite large on the side of the label what the medication is for (e.g. pain, diabetes, blood pressure). You'll be able to read the label easily without having to put your glasses on.

Label bottles clearly. Prescription

medicines often come in a large white bottle with small black print. To read them easily, use a permanent red marker and label the lids. If you take different medications that come packaged in the same type of bottle, mark one of them so you can easily tell them apart. Label both the lid and the bottle with red nail polish so that you won't grab the wrong one by mistake.

Count your pills. Count your pills! One reader was given a prescription for one pill three times daily for 7 days for a short illness. That's 21 pills. They were $10 each, for a whopping $210! He started taking them the morning he got the prescription. When he got to the sixth day, he realized there were only five pills left. The pharmacist gave him only 20, one short. So, count your pills.

Keep track of pills. One way to keep track of the pills you need to take is to use a 7-day pillbox. Keep a thick rubber band around the box to make sure the lid stays closed. When you are ready to take your pills, put the rubber band on the table and drop the pills from the holder into the center of the rubber-band circle. That way you can make sure none of the pills roll off or are lost as you are taking them. You also can easily count them to

make sure you have all the ones you need.

Having two sets of these pillboxes and filling them 2 weeks at a time gives you a 2-week warning when it is time to refill any medication or supplement.

Manage medication. For someone who needs to take many medications, here is a system to help keep track of them. Those 7-day, four-time-slot boxes are handy, but they take a long time to fill correctly.

Try this: Type out a spreadsheet, color-coded to the colors on the compartment lids, with the medication name and dosage. Then take colored smiley-face stickers matching the color code on the spreadsheet and the compartment covers and place them on the medicine-bottle lids. If the patient takes the medication twice a day, she (or you, if you are doing it for her) can cut the stickers in half so both colors show on the lid. Now, instead of constantly checking the bottles to find the correct one, you can simply sort the bottles by their colored stickers and use the spreadsheet to verify the correct dosage.

You will be able to fill the patient's medicine box in only a few minutes with very little problem—before it was probably very time-consuming and stressful because you were constantly checking the labels because all the bottles look alike. When the prescription has to be refilled, simply take off the old cap with the sticker and put it on the new bottle.

Sort pills more easily. If you receive prescriptions by mail (they often come in 3-month allotments), write on the lids, with a permanent marker, whether one or two is taken before meals, and whether the time is a.m. or p.m. When the new supply comes, just transfer the lids, and then you can easily refill your 7-day dispensers once a week.

Remind yourself to take medicine. If you have a medical condition that requires you to take medicine every day at specific times, here's a way to never forget. What item do you take with you everywhere? Your cell phone! Simply program a reminder alert or an alarm into your phone so it will beep 10 minutes before you need to take the medicine. The 10 minutes ensures that you have time to get something to drink.

Put a reminder note on a pill bottle. When you're not sure you will remember the last time you took a pill, attach a large sticky note to the bottle, with the date and time you took the pill.

Remember bedtime medication. If you have to take a pill at bedtime and often forget to do it, put the pill bottle on your pillow. That way, it is there and you will never forget. Just please make sure no children or pets can get hold of this medication.

Remember your medication. When you have a medication that must be taken 1 hour before any other medication and not with any others, keep the prescription bottle on your nightstand (if you have no small children at home) and take the medication first thing when you wake up.

To remember whether you have taken it, turn the bottle upside down before going to sleep and place it right side up on the nightstand when you have taken it the next morning.

Take your vitamin. Do you forget to take your vitamin after breakfast and before you leave for work? Put the vitamin bottle in the cupboard with the cereal bowls. When you get out a bowl for your cereal in the morning, you will see the vitamin bottle and be reminded to take it.

Keep track of pills taken. If you have to take a pill every day for a certain number of days (say, an antibiotic), cut a small piece of paper and list the days down the left side. Roll it up and put it in the pill bottle (or tape it to the side of the bottle). Whenever you take your pill, check off the date and put the paper back in the bottle.

Dispense pills easily. For a patient on several medications who struggles with severe tremors, it is difficult to take pills without dropping them. Save the little plastic cups from sugar-free lemonade mixes and use them as pill dispensers. This makes it much easier to take the medication.

Sort pills with tweezers. If you take various prescription drugs and other supplements, count them out into daily containers every 2 weeks. Keep a pair of tweezers with your pills so that when you get one in the wrong slot (noon instead of morning, for instance), you can quickly and easily put it in the right place.

End medication confusion. An independent community pharmacy may be willing to blister- or bubble-pack medications for patients for a very nominal fee.

This consists of placing medications in bubble cards that are marked for each day, time of day, and dose (such as one for a.m. and one for p.m.). It makes it less confusing for patients and caregivers. And there is never the question of "Did I take or give that medication?" because if you did, the bubble has had the medicine pushed

out for the day and time. Most people do not realize that this service is easily accessed in their community. It really cuts down on medication errors and takes away a lot of stress involved with medication schedules.

If this is of interest to you, you might have to make several calls until you find a pharmacy that provides this service.

Change a patch. If you wear a medication patch that is changed weekly, it's easy to forget when the current patch was applied. Write the date on the patch so you know when a new one needs to be applied.

If you have trouble writing on your particular patch, write the date on a piece of medical tape or a bandage and put that on the patch.

Take a picture of your meds. Use the camera before a doctor visit. Line up all your medications on the counter and take a close-up digital picture of them. Print this picture on plain paper and give it to the doctor. It's much quicker and more thorough than writing the medications down.

Highlight expiration dates. When going through the medicine cabinet to check the expiration dates on over-the-counter medicine, take a marker and highlight the dates so you know when to throw the medicines out.

Remove labels from pill bottles. If you have a problem removing the labels from prescription bottles when you dispose of them, try using an emery board. Use it or a nail file to rub over your name, phone numbers, and doctor names. It will remove that information without your having to remove the label. It takes only seconds, and makes it very simple to dispose of the bottles without the worry of someone finding the data on the tossed containers.

FIRST AID, INJURIES, AND PAIN RELIEF

Fix a boo-boo. Keep a red washcloth in the freezer. When a child gets a cut, the washcloth not only soothes the cut and stops the bleeding, but the child won't get upset because blood won't show up on the red washcloth as it would on a white one.

Remove a bandage painlessly. To remove an adhesive bandage painlessly, rub cream or lotion on the bandage, and it will come right off.

Make tiny ice packs. Use the little packets of ketchup, mustard, or duck sauce that you receive when ordering takeout food as little ice packs. Just throw them in the freezer. They are great for small burns and cuts in the kitchen, and they're reusable, too. This also works for the somewhat larger packets of salad dressing you get with takeout.

Keep a bandage dry. If you have a bandaged injury and must keep the area dry for several weeks, here's a way to keep it dry when you shower.

Wrap a long piece of sealable plastic wrap, which sticks to itself, around the bandage and press it down so it seals to the edges, thus keeping the wounded area completely dry and safe while you shower.

Make a mini first-aid kit. Keep a metal bandage tin in your purse as a mini first-aid kit. It holds several small containers of pills, nail clippers, and bandages. Very easy to find when needed.

Fix a bandage without tape. For someone with an allergy to adhesive bandages, you may be able to use a knee-high stocking over a leg bandage to hold it in place. The stocking is lightweight and stretchy and should work well.

Remove a splinter another way. When you get a splinter that's not too deep, reach for transparent tape before resorting to tweezers or a needle. Simply put the tape over the splinter and then pull it off.

Remove a splinter with duct tape. One more way to use duct tape is for removing splinters, and thorns from cactus plants. Just place the tape over the thorns and pull.

Keep a cast clean and dry. Wrap an injured arm or leg in sealing wrap so the patient will not miss out on the fun and can still keep the cast free of sand and grit.

Treat a foot injury. When you sprain your ankle, it's hard to make ice stay on the ankle. Try using a bag of frozen veggies as an ice pack. It will fit perfectly.

Make a soothing heating pad. Having fibromyalgia or any other muscle or joint ache can be a real pain. One thoughtful young lady made heating pads for her family members for Christmas a few years ago. Here's how to make your own: Using polar fleece and a stretch stitch, make a 2-foot-by-6-inch tube and fill it one-half to two-thirds full with uncooked white rice (not instant).

You may choose to make any shape, but this one is for your neck and shoulders.

After sewing the end closed, place the bag in the microwave for only 3 minutes on low to warm the rice. The resulting warmth lasts more than half an hour, and the heating pad can be reheated and reused many times.

It isn't always easy to use an electric heating pad because it doesn't mold well to the body, but the rice certainly does.

The heating pad may help wonderfully with the joint and muscle pain associated with fibromyalgia. The cost is nominal, and well worth it.

I.Q. Test: Remove a Splinter Easily

It's time to test your first-aid I.Q. What do you have around the house that makes removing a splinter a snap?

a) baking soda
b) petroleum jelly
c) white school glue

The answer is "c"—white school glue! Just apply a thin layer around the splinter, let dry, and carefully peel off the glue in the direction you want the splinter to come out.

EYE AND VISION CARE

Protect your eyesight. The good people at EyeCare America have provided five healthy hints for the aging eye, especially important for people over 65.

EyeCare America's five hints are:

1. Always wear protective goggles when working with machinery and while engaging in athletic activities.

2. Find out your family history of eye disease. In many cases, having a family member with an eye disease, such as glaucoma, greatly increases your chance of getting the disease.

3. Vitamin A is great for your eyes and will help you maintain healthy vision. Foods rich in vitamin A include carrots, yams, and dark, leafy greens.

4. Protect your eyes from the sun. Overexposure to the sun's rays can lead to cataracts. Your sunglasses should have UVA and UVB protection.

5. If you or a friend is 65 or older, call EyeCare America's Seniors EyeCare Program to see if you qualify for a free eye exam—the number is (800) 222-EYES (3937) and operates all day, every day, year-round! Or, visit www.eye careamerica.org.

FYI: EyeCare America, the largest program of its kind in American medicine, helps people who live in medically underserved communities (and people who might be at risk for eye disease) with free eye exams and eye health information. Give EyeCare America a call today!

More info on eye exams. Seniors can maintain their independence with a free medical eye exam. In addition to making it possible to enjoy things such as reading, gardening, and golfing, good eye health influences many other aspects of life, including the ability to live independently as one ages.

A recent study conducted at the University of Texas Medical Branch in Galveston even found that impaired vision may speed older adults' mental decline. While the exact reason for this link is unclear, researchers believe that it has to do with the fact that poor close-range vision might limit older adults' activities and hence contribute to cognitive decline.

By age 65, one in three Americans has some form of vision-impairing eye disease. Many people assume that poor sight is a natural part of growing older. While certain eye problems are associated with growing older, failing sight doesn't have to be. Most eye diseases are treatable, especially if caught early. That's why annual dilated-eye exams are so important in helping seniors preserve their sight. Cataracts, glaucoma, and age-related macular degeneration are the most common eye diseases for those 65 and older.

I.D. contact lenses. Place a dot of bright nail polish on one lid of your contact-lens case. Always mark the left lid (or the right one, if you prefer) so that even with blurry vision (before putting your contacts in) you are able to tell which side of the case is for which eye.

Carry a contact-lens case. Here's a great way to recycle contact-lens cases. Use them to store pills that you have to take to work with you. With the screw-on lids, you won't have to worry about the pills getting lost in your purse.

Store eyeglasses handily. If you like to read in bed and tend to fall asleep with your glasses on, store them close by. Take an old eyeglass case and hot-glue it to the back of the headboard, or on a bedrail, where no one can see it.

Get your own style of glasses. When people reach that certain age (and you know what age I mean), it might become necessary to bite the bullet and get reading glasses to read books, menus, newspapers, and other printed material. If you live with someone who also needs reading glasses and the prescriptions are different, buy frames that look different. Otherwise, you may mistakenly pick up your husband's glasses, and he yours. This won't happen if the glasses look different.

Repair eyeglasses on the spot. If the little screw has fallen out of your eyeglass arm that connects it to the frame, insert a safety pin to hold it together until you can fix it permanently. You could also use a straight pin, twisting it in a circular fashion with needle-nose pliers. The head of the pin will hold the arm in place, and the twisting will keep the pin from scratching your skin.

These are only temporary fixes, so pick up an eyeglass repair kit, found at most drugstores and retail stores. You can also buy a cheap pair of glasses and use the screw from them to repair your good glasses.

Don't use toothpicks to fix glasses. An optician wrote in to say that for a temporary fix to missing screws on frames, safety pins, dental floss, and paper clips are okay, but please do *not* use wooden toothpicks. What happens is that the toothpick will swell inside the hole and become almost impossible to remove. Sometimes opticians have to drill them out. So please, don't use toothpicks for this kind of fix.

Fix an eyeglass earpiece. When one of the earpieces on your eyeglasses breaks, getting it replaced can be expensive.

Try going to a dollar store that sells reading glasses. Match your eyeglasses up with ones that will fit and purchase a set of jewelry screwdrivers to fit the small screws (also a dollar). Replace both earpieces so they will match. The screwdriver set will also come in handy for other items with tiny screws.

Flag important dates on the calendar. For someone with vision problems who can still see but has trouble reading some things, use fluorescent stickers on the calendar to make him or her aware that there is something happening on a particular day. He or she can then ask you to read the sticker when you are in the room.

Keep track of eye-drop applications. If you must use eye drops twice a day for glaucoma control, to make sure you have done your drops in the a.m. and p.m., make up an index card that lists the days of the week and notes "a.m." and "p.m." beside each day. Keep the card with the drops; when you use your drops, cross out the appropriate a.m. or p.m. You can fit 8

weeks on one side of an index card and then turn it over and use the other side. It is very important not to miss drops, and this system will make sure you don't forget to use them.

Mark the sprayer. If you need glasses for close work, here's how to solve one problem you may have— your spray perfume bottle. Without your glasses, you may always be catching yourself in the eye, ear, or other places. Take a marker and color the spray hole, and you will know where you're spraying.

Outwit macular degeneration. Here's a way to help someone with macular degeneration whose sight is very limited. Her phone can be programmed so she has to punch only one number, but today's phones have so many buttons that it can be difficult, even with the programming. Mark the button with a small, raised stick-on designed for handicrafts and sold in crafts stores. They have an adhesive back, and the smallest ones are perfect for the buttons on the phone. Others are a fit for a TV remote, microwave oven, answering machine, and other appliances.

Cool your eye drops. If you have to use eye drops for dry eyes, you might find them refreshing if you keep them in your refrigerator. But please give your doctor or pharmacist a quick call to make sure this is okay before you try it.

EARS AND HEARING

Compensate for hearing loss. Here are some "low-tech" tips from an audiologist that can further enhance the improvements that newer digital hearing aids provide:

- Listening in noisy environments is difficult. Move closer, and turn off the TV or radio before talking. (Hearing in noisy environments is the number one complaint of those with hearing loss/hearing aids.)

- Get attention. Make sure your face is visible, and avoid talking from another room.

- Practice clear speech. Speak in a natural way, pronouncing each syllable. This automatically slows your speech and gives the listener more time to process your information.

- Avoid cross-talk when in a group. In a restaurant, request that background music be turned down or off.

- Teach children to use their "big girl/ boy" voices. Lower-pitched voices are easier to hear.

Let's all be more considerate of those with hearing loss/hearing aides.

Send a fax or an email if you're hearing impaired. If your hearing is impaired, fax or e-mail your doctors when you need an appointment or have a question.

Have a family member call everyone you do business with, and then, if you need a plumber, you can fax or e-mail him or her with the problem; if the washer breaks down, you can fax or e-mail for a repair person. You can fax or e-mail your banker, investment broker, the drugstore, the hair dresser who does your hair—even the newspaper and TV offices.

Some companies also will fax or e-mail you about when to expect them, which means you don't have to worry about missing them.

DENTAL CARE

Keep the toothbrush fresh. After you brush your teeth, swish the brush in a capful of mouthwash—it keeps the brush fresher than just rinsing it in water.

Brush your teeth before seeing the dentist. From a dental professional, here are a few hints to consider before going to a dental appointment.

Whether for a cleaning, tooth pain, or just a checkup, it would be considerate if patients would brush their teeth right before their appointment. It's nice to see (and smell) someone with fresh breath and clean teeth in their chair. Also, state regulations require a rigorous and thorough cleaning and preparation between each patient. So help your dentist: Be on time or even a little early, and use the restroom, brush your teeth, or make that cell phone call before you are called into an examining room.

I.D. a toothbrush. To enable someone with poor eyesight to tell which toothbrush is his, wrap a rubber band around the handle of the person's toothbrush so he or she can identify it. The rubber band works well, and it doesn't matter if it gets wet.

Get out the last toothpaste. For that last dab of toothpaste in the (usually bent) tube, just hold the tube under the hot water faucet and squeeze . . . every last bit of paste will come out easily.

Another way to get all the toothpaste out. A plastic tube of toothpaste or makeup is still half-full when no more can be squeezed out. To get it all, just cut off the bottom and get twice as much for your money.

Keep mouthwash handy. Have your own recycled 12-ounce sport water bottle that you keep filled with mouthwash. No need for extra cups—just a squirt in the mouth for no-muss, no-fuss rinsing.

SKIN CARE

Soften hands with vinegar. Vinegar works wonders on overworked hands and is also great on your hair. Rinse your hands with vinegar after using harsh cleaners or after a day of yard work. It really makes a difference.

Soap film and hair-product residue can linger on hair and make it dull and lifeless, but rinsing with a tablespoon

On the Light Side
Vinegar Can't Help a Loose Tooth!

A reader reported the following: "I often tell members of my family different hints for using vinegar that I have heard. Recently, one of my grandsons had a loose tooth and was having quite a time getting it out. I asked him if he wanted me to help. Through his tears he said, 'I am not going to use vinegar!' "

of white vinegar added to 1 cup of warm water can make it fluffy and shiny again. Vinegar will help clean hairbrushes, too (except for wooden ones), if you simply soak them overnight in a 50/50 mixture of household vinegar and water.

Warm up your lotion. On cold mornings, place the bottle of body lotion a safe distance from your heater while you're in the shower. By the time you are ready to use it, the lotion is warm and feels wonderful!

Get the most from your lotion bottle. The pump on a bottle of body lotion often won't dispense the last ounce or so. Try to find a flip-top lid that fits the bottle. The lid is flat, so you can stand the bottle upside down in a corner of your vanity. The lotion drains down and dispenses without any shaking or mess. Save the cap after you completely empty all of the lotion from the bottle so you can clean it and use it again.

Get all the lotion. Try to get the last bit of lotion out of the plastic tubes they come in. When no more will come out, cut the tube in half. You would be surprised how much more lotion you can find in each half. Keep them in an airtight bag so the lotion does not dry up.

Tone down a scent. When the scent of a body lotion is too strong, mix it with unscented lotion in a separate container. The scent becomes more tolerable, and the scented lotion is used up more slowly.

Understand glycerin soap. Soap that has a high glycerin content is very moisturizing, but you may notice that there are beads of moisture that accumulate on the bar. Don't worry, the soap is not losing its moisture.

Here's the dish on soap: Glycerin is a humectant. This means that when soap has a high glycerin content, it will develop those beads because it absorbs water from the air. A soap that is high in glycerin softens the skin, as it attracts moisture to the skin. This also means that the soap will dissolve more quickly in water.

Smooth rough skin. Scrub elbows and heels with baking soda to soften rough skin.

Prevent an allergic reaction. An allergy to nickel can cause a skin rash that sometimes needs to be treated with an antibiotic. One of the things that may cause a sensitive person to break out is the snaps found on most pants. A solution is to buy iron-on patches, then cut a piece that's a bit bigger than the snap and sew it on that area of the pants that touches the skin. Put the patch on the inside of the pants so it doesn't show.

Cover poison ivy. If you get a bad case of poison ivy on your arm, use an old sock with the toe end cut off to cover it. First wash the area on your arm well, apply topical medication and let it dry a little, then pull the cutoff sock over your arm. The sock will prevent you from scratching in the middle of the night, and it also allows your spouse to stay "poison-ivy free" in case you bump him or her in your sleep.

Humidify your air. The dry, cold winter can take a toll on our skin. Heating systems dry out the air and can make our skin feel dry and tight. So, what can we do to help moisturize our skin?

Try the following hints to help put moisture back into the air in your home:

- Simmer a large pot of water on the stove for several hours. Drop in some spices like cinnamon or allspice to create a pleasant fragrance, too.
- Place several bowls of water in various rooms in your home.
- Add living plants because they help rehydrate the air—ferns, begonias,

coleus, and zebra plants like moisture and grow fast. Place pots in a shallow tray filled with pebbles and water to keep moisture in the air.

- Don't overheat your home. Set the thermostat cooler to save money and energy, and to prevent the air from becoming too dry.
- Allow dishes to air-dry in the dishwasher. Stop it after the final rinse and open the door. The steam will escape into the air.

Store cotton balls in a box. Do you use cotton balls to clean your face each night, but hate the bag they are in because when you grab it, cotton balls fly everywhere? Try this: When you use the last tissue in a cube tissue box, store the cotton balls in the box. It's handy, too, because you can just leave it on the bathroom counter.

BATHING AND GROOMING

Soften skin and clean the tub, too. Add a cup of apple-cider vinegar to a tubful of water. Not only will your skin feel wonderful, but cleaning the tub will be a lot easier.

Release the grease. Try using your husband's aerosol can of shaving cream to remove grease from your hands. It leaves a nice smell, too. Just rinse with warm water and that's it.

Make a post-surgery shower easier. When taking a shower after surgery, make sure you have a hand-held shower head, a bathtub stool, and a long-handled, soft-bristled back brush. Have your soap and lotions within reach when sitting down. The back brush can be used to wash your legs and feet with a minimum of reaching and bending. Grab bars would be a good safety feature. If possible, it's a good idea to have another person nearby when you get in and out of the tub.

Organize shower supplies. Here's a helpful idea for your shower. If your eyesight is terrible without your glasses and you can't tell shampoo from conditioner, buy a four-tier shower corner shelf. Shelf one is for shampoo; shelf two, conditioner; three, facial cleaners; and four, body washes.

Time family showers. Have your family plan on different times for each shower. Too many showers in a row will use up all the hot water. This time plan assures that everyone will have hot water.

Use leftover shampoo. At some time, most of us have bought a bottle of shampoo that didn't work for us. That leftover shampoo makes excellent bubble bath. The foaming agent makes a nice tub of suds with only a

---

THE RECIPE FOR BATH SALTS

This is one of my favorites, one of the Heloise "recipes" most often asked for. It's easy to do and makes a pretty homemade gift!

You will need:
- 1 tablespoon glycerin (found at the drugstore)
- Perfume, cologne, or essential oil, like lavender
- Food coloring
- 3 cups Epsom salts

Mix the glycerin, fragrance, and several drops of food coloring in a large glass or metal bowl (don't use plastic, as it might stain). Next, add the Epsom salts a little at a time, mixing constantly until the color is evenly distributed.

You can add a little more perfume and color if the salts aren't fragrant or colorful enough. Store in a pretty jar with a tight-fitting lid. To use, add about ½ cup to your bathwater.

tablespoon or so. You might even want to buy one brand of shampoo specifically for this purpose. Happy soaking!

Avoid the shampoo slip. Shampoo bottles get big, get small, and get big again whenever the economy changes. Many of the large-size economy bottles are slippery to handle when you're in the shower. Consider buying and installing one of the wall-mounted shampoo dispensers you'll find in catalogs and from online retailers. The dispensers often have separate compartments for shampoos, body washes, and conditioners, and let you portion out exactly what you need.

Make bath powder. If you have a favorite perfume, you can use some to make your own scented powder instead of buying the expensive brand-name powder. Pour some cornstarch into a container with a tight-fitting lid, then give the powder a few squirts of the perfume. You will have your own perfumed powder.

You will have to refresh the perfume every once in a while because the perfume does evaporate after time. In the meantime, you are saving a bunch of money.

You also might consider buying one container of the name-brand powder and stretching it with the cornstarch.

You may get more of a perfumed powder that way.

Stretch face-washing cloths. Some face-washing cloths come in a package of 30. They are really too big for just one washing, so when you get the package you can cut all the cloths in half, which doubles your money.

If you wash your face at night with these cloths, in the morning you can use the used dry cloth to wipe out the tub after your morning shower. One side of the cloth is a little abrasive, so it will work as a scrubbing cloth on the tub and shower.

Use small bits of soap. If you travel quite often and bring home small bars of soap from motel rooms, and you also have small leftover bars from home that are hard to hold when showering, don't waste them.

Put all these small pieces of soap together in the toe of a pantyhose or nylon knee-high and tie a knot to secure them. This makes using them easy and also gives you a variety of scents. The pantyhose soap also makes a soft "scrubby."

Use leftover shower gel. If you do not use all the liquid shower gel that you've received as a gift, put it into the liquid soap dispenser by the bathroom sink.

Keep cool in the bathroom. If you live in a humid climate, keep a small fan in the bathroom. Not only does it cool you after a warm shower, but it also keeps you cool while you apply makeup. It also circulates the air and is helpful in getting the shower to dry quickly, preventing mildew and mold from forming.

Clean up whiskers. Here's a hint for men who have a beard and mustache. When it comes time to trim, open a section of the newspaper over the sink, covering everything, including the counter. Trim your whiskers, then just refold the newspaper shut and chuck it and the offending whiskers into the recycling.

Shave with liquid soap. Many of the liquid soaps in bath-and-body shops contain silicone or glycerin. So, use a scant amount of one of them to shave your legs. You won't need to moisturize after the bath.

Shave with hair conditioner. When you run out of shaving cream, use your hair conditioner to shave your legs. It's a lot cheaper than shaving cream and leaves your legs really smooth. It's also a great way to use a conditioner that you bought but didn't like when you tried it on your hair.

HAIR CARE

Clean those hairbrushes. To clean hairbrushes or combs, all you need to do is fill a container—a glass canning jar works well—with some warm water and add a couple of tablespoons of baking soda, then stir the mixture well. Or, put 4 tablespoons of baking soda in 1 quart of water to accommodate more than one brush or comb. (Do not use this method on wooden brushes.) Clean any hair out of the brush's bristles and then add the brush or comb—make sure the solution completely covers the teeth or bristles. Allow the comb or brush to soak for an hour or so, then rinse well in hot water, and all the "gunk" should come right off. If you need to use the comb or brush right away, use your hair dryer to quickly dry the comb or brush.

Heavier residue might require a little scrubbing, and an old toothbrush works great for this. Routinely clean your brushes and combs so that buildup from hair products doesn't get too bad.

Clean hairbrushes with ammonia. Put a few tablespoons of sudsy ammonia in a jar containing 10 to 16 ounces of water. After 2 to 3 minutes of soaking in that mixture, brushes and combs are spotless. One caveat: Don't hold the jar under your nose!

Clean hairbrushes in the dishwasher. Remove all of the hair from your hairbrushes and then place them on the top rack of your dishwasher along with other household items that could use a good wash—for instance, hair clips and any washable hair things, and knickknacks. Try using the dishwasher on, for instance, a candleholder minus the candle, a cotton-swab holder minus the cotton swabs, and the toothbrush holder minus the toothbrushes and toothpaste.

Or, use the washing machine. To clean a hairbrush, just throw it in the washing machine with a load of laundry. It will come out looking brand-new. But you probably shouldn't use this method to clean wooden brushes because it could damage them. Also, be sure to add towels or other items to absorb the "clunking" of the brushes.

Clean hair-styling tools. With my busy speaking schedule, my hot rollers have been getting a real workout. When hair products and grime build up, I remove the rollers and loosen the dirt on the base with a soft, dry toothbrush, wiping away the crud with a water-dampened microfiber cloth. Next I tackle the rollers using the same toothbrush dipped in water (taking care to

CLEAN YOUR HAIRBRUSH

You probably use a hairbrush every day, but how often do you clean it? Hair gel, mousse, hair spray, even plain old dirt—all of it builds up over time in a hairbrush. But when was the last time you gave yours a really good cleaning? I'll help you brush up on cleaning it:

- To keep your brush clean and in good condition, you really should "dry" clean it every day, which simply means removing any accumulated hair from the bristles.
- About once a month or more often, you should "wet" clean it. Fill a bathroom sink with warm—not hot—water and about a teaspoon of shampoo. No harsh chemicals, just shampoo. Don't immerse the entire brush, especially if it's wood. Instead, dip only the bristles into the sudsy solution for about 30 seconds, scrub with a comb or other brush, then rinse with lukewarm water and let air-dry.
- If you use a lot of hair products in your hair, your brush might need a deep cleansing every 2 weeks.

keep liquid from dripping into the center heating elements), and then wipe and dry them with a soft, absorbent cloth. Finally, I give the cord a wipe with the damp microfiber cloth.

As for ratty hairbrushes, I first run a comb through the bristles to lift out hair. (Hint: A seam ripper is an even faster way to cut through thick hair tangles.) Next I hold the comb and brush under hot running water for a moment, squirt on shampoo, and scrub them with another hairbrush. After rinsing, I shake off excess water and place them on a towel with bristles facing down to air-dry. To quick-clean brushes: Comb out as much hair as you can, then pour a bit of rubbing alcohol on a smaller hairbrush and use it to rake out the rest. The alcohol sanitizes and dries in a few seconds.

Keep a hair dryer lint-free. It's important to keep the mesh screen on a hair dryer free of dust and lint to prevent overheating and your dryer from possibly quitting. An old toothbrush makes it very easy to clean out the lint.

Make shampoo and conditioner easy to see. Shampoo and conditioner manufacturers should put a very large "S" and "C" on their bottles so we who wear glasses can see which to use in the shower. Until they start, you can use a permanent marker and mark them yourself.

I.D. shampoo another way. Since shampoo and conditioner usually come in identical containers, slip a rubber band around the conditioner. You will no longer mistakenly shampoo your hair using conditioner, nor will you need to open your eyes to identify which tube you have in hand.

Try different shampoos. It's fun to try different shampoos. When you get one that you don't like, rather than throwing it away, use it in the shower as a body wash.

Tame flyaway hair. Do you get dry, flyaway hair frequently? It seems when you're out and about and brush your hair, it sticks up all over and can be embarrassing. So, keep an unscented dryer sheet in your purse or car, and when this happens you just take the sheet and lightly rub it on your hair to make your hair go back down instantly. It also takes away the static for the rest of the day; if you use an unscented sheet, it won't smell.

Get rid of hair static from a cap. To prevent static electricity in your hair when you take your cap off, place a dryer sheet inside the cap.

Don't muss your hairdo. Keep a

shower cap in your dresser drawer to put on when you are dressing so you don't muss your hair when you have something to pull over your head.

Spray your hair in the shower. Use the step-in shower for applying hair spray. Clean and squeegee the shower with each use, and the rest of the bathroom stays spray-free and unsticky.

Tame hair with water. Here's a hint from a 4½-year-old: If some of your hair sticks up in the morning, spray a little water on your hair and brush it.

Get rid of hair-spray buildup. To remove stubborn hair-spray buildup, add 1 tablespoon of baking soda to your shampoo. The baking soda removes leftover buildup that most shampoos leave behind. Do this once a week to maintain a clean and healthy scalp!

Banish hair-product buildup. Here's a variation on using baking soda to get hair-spray buildup off your hair: About once a month, mix a couple of teaspoons of baking soda with a couple of tablespoons of shampoo and wash your hair with that, then rinse well. Follow with a regular lather and again rinse well. This really gets all the buildup off, so use a deep conditioner when you're done.

Color-code hair clips. If you can't find hair clips in the colors you like,

take nail polish, and buy a card of plain silver clips in various sizes. Polish the clips while they are still snapped on the card and let them dry. Yes, hair spray ruins the polish, but you probably have plenty more polish where that came from!

Clean off hair color. When dyeing your hair, if some dye gets on your ears, face, or neck, rub the stained area with toothpaste to take off the dye.

Some toothpastes have a bleaching agent (such as hydrogen peroxide), so a white, nongel toothpaste should do the trick.

Keep gray hair from yellowing. For all those silver- or light-haired folks out there who use shampoos with blue or violet additives for removing the unwanted yellow tinge, here's a hint just for you. Mix the "bluing" shampoo with regular shampoo (start with half and half) and add a little water to thin the shampoo. This lets you use the "Heloise blue shampoo" without overdoing the bluing effect, or worse. It also saves money.

For removing product buildup that might cause your hair to yellow, you can also try using a solution of 4 tablespoons baking soda to 1 quart warm water. Mix well, pour on your hair, and massage it in, and be sure to bring it out to the ends. Then rinse, shampoo, and condition as usual.

Reuse hair color accessories. If your home hair-color kit includes two sets of plastic gloves in little plastic containers (like a film canister), reuse the canisters. These containers are perfect for quarters or quarter-size dollar coins.

Save an old T-shirt. When you have an old T-shirt that can't be worn anymore, save it to use when you color your hair. No matter how careful you are, you may manage to drip some of the color on your shirt. Then, you can either toss the shirt or save it for the next time.

COSMETICS

Use a shower cap outside the shower. Placing a shower cap over your face will protect your clothing from makeup. If you have fine hair, the cap will also help eliminate static cling when you pull on a sweater.

Be careful with that shower cap. It can be a good idea for a grownup to use a shower cap to protect pullover tops from getting soiled from makeup. But make sure young children are not in the room when you place a shower cap over your face. Even though a shower cap is easily pulled off, a small child could panic if he or she imitates you and the cap cuts off the air supply.

Mark a favorite makeup brush. When you're putting on makeup, do you need a special brush and can't find it in the collection of brushes? Just mark either the handle or the metal part near the bristles with red nail polish and you can find it easily. Also, to keep brushes in the best condition, be sure to store them with bristles up.

Clean makeup brushes. Soaking a makeup brush in water to clean it can cause the glue attaching the hairs to the base to come loose and ruin the brush. Instead, spray well with a makeup-brush cleaner and then rub vigorously over a thick terry towel. The makeup comes off on the towel, which can be laundered in the washing machine. You can make your own cleaner by mixing a drop or two of shampoo with equal parts of hydrogen peroxide and water in a very small spray bottle—it lasts a long time and saves money, too.

Clean makeup off phones. Cut facial cleaning cloths in half and keep them handy in a zipper-top bag to clean the makeup off your telephones. The cloths are treated to remove makeup and work on the phones as well as on your face.

Stash makeup in an eyeglass case. Do you have an extra soft-eyeglass case with nothing to put in it? Don't fret—try using it to hold makeup items, such as a tube of mascara and lipstick, small blusher and brush.

Protect your makeup with a scarf. Use a scarf over your head to protect your makeup and your hairdo.

Open a makeup case and save a fingernail. Here is a handy way to open small makeup cases containing eye shadows, blush, or other cosmetics without breaking fingernails. Use a penny to pry open the top, and the lid will simply lift up.

Make your own lipstick blotters. When the toilet tissue gets down near the end (maybe 15 to 20 squares left), change to a new roll and put the other roll in a handy spot on your bathroom sink near where you stand each morning and put on your makeup.

When you need to blot your lipstick, wipe off a makeup smear, or smooth your eyebrows, just tear off one square of toilet tissue, blot, and go.

A roll of toilet tissue lasts a long time and is flushable, while facial tissue should not be flushed, especially if you have a septic system.

Toss rancid lipstick. Once lipstick starts to smell bad, it is past its prime and really shouldn't be used. When lipstick changes color, texture, or smell, this is a sign that its shelf life has expired.

You will need to replace the lipstick. Take the old one to the store with you to compare shades.

Use all your lipstick. Every tube of lipstick that we throw away has at least ¼ inch of lipstick remaining in the tube. This lipstick is easily applied with a lip brush. You wouldn't want to carry this tube of lipstick in your purse, but you can easily do this at home.

Try clear mascara. In humid weather, mascara can smear around your eyes and make you look like a raccoon. A final coat of clear mascara will seal in the color and prevent that look.

Don't reuse dry mascara. Here's a perfect case of an old hint no longer being true. More than 35 years ago, I wrote in my mother's newspaper column that if your mascara is dry, you can put it in warm water to soften so you can use it a few more times. But today it's definitely a no-no. The Good Housekeeping Institute says:

"Don't try to prolong the life of mascara in any way! It's wise to throw out your mascara after three months' use. Never add anything to it, or heat it, as this will compromise the product's safety and effectiveness. Mascara is vulnerable to contamination due to frequent exposure to microorganisms (found on eyelids, lashes, and hands). If your mascara, at any time, has an off odor or becomes thick—toss it!"

So, there you have it. *Don't* put mascara in warm water to use it longer. I don't think that it is worth taking a chance of getting an eye infection just to save a few pennies.

Save broken blush. When your expensive powder blush cracks, put it in a small, plastic container and pulverize it with the end of a blush brush and you'll now have a few more weeks of use. You can easily keep this in your bathroom vanity with other makeup.

Prevent makeup meltdown. To keep lipstick and other makeup from melting in hot summer weather, buy a water-filled infant teether that you can freeze and keep in your cosmetic bag. Each evening, put the teether in the freezer overnight. In the morning, put it back in your purse. The teether may thaw, but the water stays cool enough to keep lipsticks from melting.

Remove makeup at night. You know why women in the 1950s and '60s used cold cream to remove their makeup? They were always so sleepy at night and didn't want to wash their face and lose that wonderful "ready to fall asleep" feeling.

If you have the same problem, purchase a baby-wipe warmer and fill it with lavender-scented baby wipes. Also put your eye-makeup-remover pads in the warmer. Your makeup removal will be warm and thorough. Afterward, just apply nighttime moisturizer, warmed in your hands first, and to sleep you will go.

You can create your own scents by applying a few drops of your favorite essential oil.

You can do the same by putting a little sweet oil or castor oil (no taste or odor) in the palm of your hand, rubbing it to warm it, and applying it to your face. Then use a hand/facial wipe to remove your makeup.

One note on essential oils: Most should *not* be put directly on the skin, so make sure you dilute the oil with a carrier oil like almond, sweet almond, castor, or olive oil.

Pack makeup remover for travel. Baby oil is an inexpensive makeup remover that also keeps skin soft. When traveling, rather than taking an entire bottle of baby oil along (and to avoid potential leaking messes), saturate several cotton balls with baby oil and place them in a zipper-top plastic bag.

NAIL CARE

Use nail polish for lots of things. Nail polish comes in handy for lots of things around the house. Use it to mark temperatures on the stove knobs, hot water on the clothes washer, and certain buttons (on/off or volume) on the remote control of the stereo/VCR unit.

Strengthen weak fingernails. A daily application of white (decolorized) iodine on your fingernails for 1 week will help strengthen them. After the first week, use it *only* once a week. This is not a case of more is better—*do not* continue to use white iodine on your fingernails every day, or they will become too brittle. It might take several weeks to see any improvement if your nails are paper-thin from using a primer on them (for acrylics) or from being roughed up so nail products would adhere better.

White iodine is available at some pharmacies, or the pharmacist can order it for you. It may be easier to find in local pharmacies rather than the big chains. Since it is relatively inexpensive and easy to use, it's the perfect "help" for soft, damaged fingernails. Clean an old fingernail-polish brush with polish remover, and use this to easily apply the iodine to your nails.

Note: Avoid using hydrogen peroxide (or anything containing it) while using white iodine—these two products "don't get along" and can cause your fingernails to turn orange.

Prevent nail-polish spills. To avoid nail-polish spills, cut off a small section of a cardboard egg carton (or use a six-egg carton) and stick your nail-polish bottle in a hole. No matter the size of the bottle, it always fits perfectly and never spills a drop. Just keep the section of egg carton with your nail-polishing kit; it will last a long time before ever needing a change.

Keep your nails healthy.

Here are some great nail hints:

- Moisturize cuticles and nails often.
- Try to keep nails out of water and harsh chemicals.
- Don't pick or peel off nail polish.
- Massage the cuticles to stimulate good bloodflow.

If you are past a certain age (!), ask your doctor about taking biotin, an over-the-counter B vitamin that seems to help with nail strength, which might decrease as we age. I am *not* a physician, and I don't play one on TV, but this is what I have learned recently.

Quit biting your nails. If you have tried to stop biting your fingernails but nothing seems to work, polish them. When you go to bite them and then see how pretty they look, you will stop.

Hold on to nail clippers. Do you have trouble keeping nail clippers in your hand? Cut a piece of self-gripping fabric tape to fit the clippers where your fingers hold the tool. Then peel off the sticky side and place it on the clippers.

Soak your cuticles. Are your cuticles a mess? Here is a way to get them back into shape. First, soak your hands in a solution of mild soap and water, and submerge your cuticles completely for just a few minutes. Remove them from the solution and dry completely. Then put some pure glycerin all around your cuticle area. Use an orange stick to gently push cuticles back.

Treat your nails while you walk. Every morning when you take a walk, break open a vitamin E capsule as you start and massage the oil into your nails and cuticles. By the time you get home, the oil will be absorbed, and you will have given yourself an inex-

KEEP YOUR NAILS CLEAN

Here are some helpful hints to keep your fingernails clean when the work you have to do is downright dirty. It's amazing how dirty your hands can get doing things around the house, the garage, or the garden. Even a good scrubbing won't always get the grime out from under your fingernails!

- When possible, wear gloves while you work. There are all types of gloves, from thick gardening gloves to thin, disposable ones that can be worn without getting in the way of many projects.

- If you'll be working with something that can get grit under nails—like dirt, oil, or clay— before you start, dig your nails into a bar of soap. The soap will get underneath your nails so that the grime can't. Then, you just have to wash your hands when the project is done.

- When painting with oil-based paint, try olive, vegetable, or baby oil as a gentle paint remover. Just rub a small amount in your hands (a dash of salt or sugar acts like an abrasive), and the paint should come off without much scrubbing.

pensive beauty treatment. Ragged cuticles will become more pliable, and you won't have to maintain them as often.

Remove a stuck lid. To get the top off a nail-polish bottle, saturate a cotton ball with nail-polish remover and wipe it around the lid. Then, holding the bottle upside down, let some of the remover drip in between the bottle and cap. After a few minutes the lid will come right off.

Keep essential oils away from nails. When using essential oils, the directions say to avoid contact with eyes, skin, lips, plastic surfaces, and painted furniture. But essential oils can damage a manicure as well. If you get some oil on your fingers, you may find that the polish has disappeared . . . but at least the room will smell nice.

HOME SPA TREATMENTS AND STRESS RELIEF

Take a soothing bath. You can melt away tension from a hard day by adding ½ cup baking soda to your bathwater along with a few drops of sweet or castor oil (odorless and tasteless) and a relaxing fragrance of your choice.

Make a salt scrub. Body scrubs can be made easily at home with just a few basic ingredients.

Get silken skin with a wonderfully scented salt scrub that has only two basic ingredients, Epsom salts and almond oil or any other aromatherapy oil, such as lavender or bergamot. To make 1 cup, measure 1 cup Epsom salts to use as the base, and slowly mix in the almond or other aromatherapy oil until the mixture is wet but not watery. Store in a margarine tub or glass container (clearly marked) in the refrigerator.

When you are ready to use it, jump in a hot shower and swirl a large dollop on your body and let the silkening magic begin. This mixture will help exfoliate dead skin, leaving silky, happy skin.

Make an aromatherapy salt scrub. Aromatherapy means using essential oils as a beauty or healing component. The oils come in a variety of scents— some of my favorites are lavender, rosemary, geranium, peppermint, cinnamon, bergamot, and eucalyptus. Essential oils can be found in many food stores and drugstores, as well as health-food and aromatherapy stores. You also can find them on the Internet, or call your pharmacist to see if they can be ordered.

Look for pure essential oils in brown or amber glass bottles—the dark glass protects the oils from heat and light, which can rob the oil of its scent.

Usually only a few drops are needed at a time, and a small bottle will last for quite a while, so buy the best quality you can.

To make an Epsom-salt-and-essential-oil scrub: Mix together 1 cup of Epsom salts and ½ cup of a carrier oil like almond, then add a few drops of an essential oil of your choice until the consistency is thick enough to work as a scrub. Put the mixture in a pretty container (clearly marked) or even disposable plasticware. Use while taking a hot shower or as a wonderful foot scrub, and say goodbye to dull skin!

Make a facial scrub. I learned this beauty hint years ago from a sweet Russian grandmother. She took mild face soap and made a lather in her hands and mixed a little (1 teaspoon) baking soda or table sugar for a mild facial scrub.

If you rub the sugar in your hands, it will dissolve and be less abrasive.

This is a great way to slough off dry skin. If you let the sugar and soap mixture set on your face, it makes a mask. Rinse with cool or warm water. Be sure to follow this with a moisturizer.

This scrub is also good for elbows, knees, and heels.

Facial scrub for sensitive skin. If you have very sensitive skin and facial scrubs make you break out, try this one. Put a little baking soda in the palm of your hand, wet it a little, and gently rub your face with your fingertips.

NATURAL BEAUTY TREATMENTS

Many of us are trying to do our part to help the environment by using fewer chemicals, recycling when we can, and reducing our dependency on plastic and plastic packaging. One area that many people might not consider is beauty products.

Instead of buying expensive eye treatments to perk up tired eyes, go natural by placing sliced, cold cucumbers over your closed eyes. Leave on for 5 minutes or until the cucumbers are no longer cold. And for a skin moisturizer, mix a little sweet oil (which is odorless and can be found in the pharmacy) or olive oil and some mashed-up ripe banana into a smooth paste and apply to your face. Let it sit for 5 to 10 minutes, then rinse with cool water.

For a facial scrub, mix three parts baking soda and one part water to make a paste. Wash your face, then apply the paste and scrub lightly. Rinse thoroughly and pat dry.

Don't use a washcloth or rub too hard. It's an excellent exfoliant, and there's no allergic reaction. It's cheap, too.

Soothe eyes with tea bags. After you brew a cup of tea, put the used bag in a container in the refrigerator, and save them up. In the morning, set aside 10 minutes to grab two of the tea bags and put them on your eyelids. Very soothing. These are also great for quick soothing of minor burns or bug bites.

Make a soothing foot scrub. Baking soda is just perfect for a soothing bath and foot scrub. Add a teaspoon of salt to a handful of baking soda, plus a drop of baby, olive, or other oil. Then scrub away dead skin. Who needs to buy expensive scrubs?

Relieve your feet. To relieve aching feet, sit on the edge of the bathtub and alternate running cold and hot water over your feet a couple of times. You can even do this with your pantyhose on when you're in a hotel and must zip between meetings. Towel-dry, then blast them with the hair dryer.

Cool tired feet. Here is an idea for

USING ESSENTIAL OILS

Essential oils can be found at many health-food stores, some grocery stores, aromatherapy stores, and on the Internet.

When buying pure essential oils (these have not been cut with a carrier oil), there are several things to keep in mind:

- A true essential oil should be sold in an amber or a brown glass bottle, or other dark glass. Light and heat are the nemeses of essential oils.
- Buy the best quality you can and the smallest bottle, since you usually use only a few drops at a time. One small bottle will last a long time!
- Most essential oils should not be put directly on your skin. They should be blended with a carrier oil such as sweet almond oil or olive oil.

My favorite? Lavender, because it's calming and relaxing. I even travel with a small bottle I mixed, with several drops of lavender added to a few tablespoons of castor oil. Don't grimace! Look for castor oil (at your drugstore or pharmacy) that is odorless and tasteless. I love this mixture because the castor oil is thicker than many other oils, and it seems to soak in and stay on longer, even through a shower. This is especially good for really dry, flaky skin. Just be sure *not* to use it on your lips!

There are numerous good books on using essential oils. Do yourself a favor and get one if you want to learn more.

an inexpensive "spa" treatment for hot, tired feet. Massage them with medicated face-cleansing cream and rinse. A generic store brand works just as well as a name brand. It makes your feet feel cool and smooth.

Relieve aching feet. When your feet ache, roll them over a bottle or tennis ball. A frozen can also gives great relief to aching feet. Use it the same way as a bottle or tennis ball, and it adds a nice, cool sensation, especially after long days on your feet.

Make a soothing thermal wrap. Fill a clean athletic sock with very coarse sea salt scented with essential oils, then warm it in a microwave for a soothing thermal neck wrap.

Take a deep breath to relieve stress. When something goes awry, one reader suggests you just sit down or stand still, take a deep breath, and say out loud: "What would Heloise do?" She says that it puts the problem in perspective. If you can seriously ask yourself this question, then your mind can

TREAT YOUR TOOTSIES WELL

Sandals and bare feet are everywhere in summer, but so are blisters and athlete's foot. Don't despair! I have the hints to help.

I don't know about you, but when my feet are "happy," so am I. That's why it's important to take care of your tootsies during warm summer months. To keep blisters away:

- Avoid shoes that rub or don't fit.
- If you have areas that tend to blister easily, treat them before the blisters happen.
- When a blister pops up, ease the pain with over-the-counter moleskin or blister pads.

To prevent athlete's foot:

- Keep your feet dry and clean.
- Wear socks made with an acrylic fiber to help wick away moisture, and change your socks at least once a day.
- If your feet sweat a lot, cover with antiperspirant. The active ingredients will help keep your feet from sweating.
- Don't wear the same shoes every day. Shoes need about 24 hours to completely dry out.
- Baking soda is a great deodorizer—just sprinkle a little in tennis shoes to keep them from smelling.

focus on a solution, not just on feeling sorry for yourself that something went wrong. You might not come up with the best solution, but at least your mind will "try" to figure it out.

I even "stop, breathe, and try to access," then ask myself, "What's the upside, downside, and outcome if I take these steps?"

Reward yourself. After you have done a particularly unpleasant chore, like heavy gardening or cleaning up the house, be sure to treat yourself.

Some simple and cheap possibilities for a treat might be a long, leisurely bubble bath, or eating lunch out somewhere. Even if you are on a strict budget, there are always inexpensive ways to enjoy yourself. Write a note to a friend. Go to the library and borrow a

USE SCENTS TO FEEL BETTER

Did you know your sense of smell has a lot to do with how you feel every day? You can raise your spirits or calm your soul and psyche with just the scent of a few drops of fragrant essential oils around your home. Here are a few sweet-smelling suggestions to get you started:

- Put a drop of oil of peppermint or cinnamon on some used dryer sheets and tuck them into athletic shoes or work boots.
- Keep eucalyptus oil in your shower and add just a drop on top of the shower knob when you turn on the spray—it will smell like a spa.
- Keep a small bottle of essential oil of lemon by the kitchen sink. Put a drop on your sponge or dishcloth to wipe the sink and faucet after cleaning—lemony fresh!
- In a small spray bottle, add distilled water (your tap water might have fluoride, chlorine, or other additives) and about 10 drops of lavender or lemon essential oil. Shake well and use this to lightly mist your linens for a gently relaxing lavender scent or a cleansing and uplifting lemon aroma.
- Make a Heloise homemade air freshener: In a spray bottle, add several drops of orange or lemon essential oil (depends on how strong you want the scent) to 16 ounces of cheap rubbing alcohol. Shake to mix, then mist the air—don't spray directly on fabric. The alcohol pretty much dissipates, leaving behind a nice smell. Label the bottle and keep the air freshener away from children.

Don't be afraid to experiment with essential oils. Most essential oils cost only pennies per drop, and you'll notice the savings as soon as you cut back on those commercially made "fresheners."

book you've been wanting to read. Rent a favorite old movie or call a dear friend. It doesn't have to be expensive to be a treat.

DIET AND EXERCISE

Measure your mug. If you are conscientious about your weight and always wondering if you are getting an 8-ounce serving of juice, a measuring cup can become your "health mug."

When you pour your juice, skim milk, or water, you will know exactly what 1 cup is and how many calories you've consumed.

You could also measure the 8 ounces in a measuring cup, pour it into another favorite glass, and then just mark the spot with a permanent marker for future reference.

Check your scale. To find out if your bathroom scale is registering correctly, simply lay a 5 or 10 pound bag of sugar on it.

Keep track of water. When you're dieting and trying really hard to drink eight glasses of water a day, you may find that you lose count after a few glasses.

So, buy eight fancy swizzle sticks to help you keep count. As you drink a glass of water, place a stick in an empty cup.

Get active. As you get older, don't be sad and sit in a recliner. Instead, get active. Join a gym, and take exercise classes or water aerobics. You'll be happier, and you will feel so much better!

Time your exercise routine. When you exercise at home, it gets tedious counting the repetitions of the exercises (such as lifting dumbbells or touching your toes). Counting is annoying while you are also trying to watch a TV program or listen to music. It's easy to lose track while counting your reps.

An easier and much less annoying way to keep track is to use a digital timer to determine when your exercises should end. Use a stopwatch to determine how much time your exercises take, to the nearest minute. Then record the times on a piece of paper. Now when you are exercising, you will be able to concentrate on the music or the TV program and let the timer beep you when it's time to stop.

SAFETY AND SECURITY

Keep "ice" in your cell phone. In your cell-phone address book or contact list, type the "Ice" contact. "Ice" stands for "in case of emergency." If, for example, you put in the name "Cherrie Ice" and her phone numbers, it will show up in your cell phone's address book as "Ice, Cherrie (803) 555-1234." Emergency personnel can look up "Ice" in your cell phone's directory and know the number and name of whom to call if you cannot tell them. Be sure to include your area code in the event that this is needed for an out-of-town number.

Carry a cell phone when walking. While you are out walking alone, pretend to be talking on a cell phone so a would-be wrongdoer would think you have a direct line to help. So many people carry mobile phones now that it is quite common to be chatting (or pretending to chat) most anywhere.

Do your walking indoors. If you are concerned about walking alone outdoors or you don't have an area that's walkable nearby, get your exercise by walking in a large grocery store, or a shopping mall—you could pick up an item or two while there and save yourself an errand later on.

Take care at night. Walking alone at night is definitely not a good idea for anyone of any age. But if you choose to, please be sure to wear some-

thing reflective, carry a cell phone, be aware of your surroundings, and let someone know your route and how long you'll be gone. If you feel unsafe, go home or call for help.

Carry an emergency calling list. Make your own "in an emergency" I.D. card to carry with you in case of emergency. You might fall while walking the dog, or have a sudden dizzy spell while shopping. List the names and phone numbers of your doctor (emergency and office) and two family members (cell and home numbers), daily medicines and dosages, and allergies.

If it's a computer document, it will be easy to update. Printed in a column and folded so there's a front and back, it's still credit-card size even with a lot of data, and you can cover it with clear packing tape to keep it weatherproof and sturdy.

Make several copies—one for your pocket whenever you're out walking, one for your wallet, and ones for easy reference for the family members listed, to have if they get "the call."

It is important to have some type of I.D. on you whenever you leave home, even if it's only for a stroll around the neighborhood. Also, if walking in the evening, a flashlight is a good idea.

Lock the door right away. Here are

On the Light Side
Lipstick, with Love!

If you want a family member to see your note, especially an "I Love You" note, write on the bathroom mirror with lipstick or lip pencil. The writing will wipe off easily with a tissue.

two safety hints that are especially important for the elderly and for single people.

First, every time you come inside, immediately lock the door. If you have a security screen door, whether the front door is closed or open you will have the locked screen door between you and any stranger who knocks. Keep all your other doors locked, too.

Second, when getting into your car, immediately lock the doors, even before starting the motor.

Hit the panic button. If you're staying alone with no burglar alarm, put your car keys/car door opener next to your bed and press the panic button if you feel threatened or think someone is breaking in. The car horn may frighten someone away.

FIRE SAFETY 101

What should you do it there's a fire in your home? Fires can break out in your home at any time! It's important that you and family members know exactly what to do and what not to do.

- Check your smoke and carbon-monoxide detectors every month! A few seconds doing this just might save lives.
- Have fire drills several times a year. Because fire can spread rapidly, do not spend more than 30 seconds fighting a fire!
- The heat and smoke can be more dangerous than the flames. Gases might make you sleepy. Asphyxiation is the leading cause of fire deaths—more than burns!
- If the fire is small, use an extinguisher to put it out. If you can't get the flames under control in under 30 seconds, get everyone out of the house fast.
- If your clothes catch fire, drop to the ground immediately and roll until the fire is out.
- If you see smoke, crawl on the floor—under the smoke—because smoke and poisonous gases initially rise to the ceiling.
- When everyone is out, use your cell phone to call 911.

—■—————————————————■—

Chapter 11

Family Activities

This chapter has hints for things to do with the family—playing games, working puzzles, reading books, taking and sharing photos, scrapbooking and hobbies, taking vacation trips, and keeping in touch with faraway family members. You'll be sure to find some fun things to enjoy!

Write a story from pictures. When you are really bored, get a magazine and cut some pictures from it. Then write a story to go along with the pictures. When you are finished, read the story to someone.

Draw your own outline. Here's an idea for a bunch of kids who get bored. They can lie down on the driveway or sidewalk and take turns using chalk to draw outlines around their bodies. Then color clothes on them and even draw faces. Take some photos, then get the hose and wash off the driveway.

Play house with cereal boxes. When you are done with cereal boxes, save them. Kids love to use them when they play house or market. They're free, too.

Bring a deck of cards wherever you go. Always bring a deck of cards wherever you go! There are a lot of games to play, whether you are by yourself or with friends. Card games—like rummy, spoons, and solitaire—are great for camping and vacation trips, rainy days, and for older kids in after-school care.

It's a wonderful way to make time go by faster.

GAMES, PUZZLES, AND HOBBIES

Make a treasure hunt. Here's a game to play when your kids are bored and don't have anything to do. Find something in the house for each letter of the alphabet. Then draw a map showing where each thing is located. It's fun and keeps the kids busy.

Go on a photo scavenger hunt. Here's how to have a fun, photo-taking scavenger hunt. First, divide the group into teams of two each. The goal is to take photos of a number of particular things in specific locations. The clues can be the scrambled name of the object to be photographed or a hint about its location. Give each team a few pages of directions. The first thing they have to do is unscramble the hint so that they know where to go. Here's an example: hsmrpi obta— shrimp boat. They have to find a shrimp boat, take a photo of it, and go on to the next hint. The first team that gets back to the house with all their photos wins.

One note: Give each group the same directions, but mix up all the items so that everyone doesn't go to the shrimp boat first.

This is a fun game for a family reunion or girls' weekend at a friend's house.

Make a puzzle portable. When you want to put a puzzle together, place the pieces on poster board so that the puzzle can be moved if you need the table before you can finish the puzzle. Also, arrange the pieces on several old cookie sheets so that they can be stored away easily until you have time to work on the puzzle again. You can even slide the puzzle under the bed to get it out of sight, if need be.

You can also use the cardboard "flats" that a case of beer or soda comes in to keep the puzzle pieces contained. Cut one edge of the box so the pieces are easily accessible.

Store puzzles in less space. Tired of taping the boxes of kids' puzzles and having them take up a lot of storage room? Cut the picture off the front of the box and put that and the pieces in a gallon-size, zipper-top bag. The slide makes sure little fingers get the bag

 More Ping, Less Pong

To take dents out of Ping-Pong balls, drop them into boiling water, turn them occasionally, and in a few minutes they will be as good as new.

closed every time. This way the puzzles take up very little room to store.

Transfer puzzle pieces. Do you love to do jigsaw puzzles? Sometimes pieces are put together outside of the puzzle frame. So, to transfer the put-together pieces, use a cookie spatula—it's thin and flexible, and works great!

Take a pic of a puzzle. When you run out of space to store completed jigsaw puzzles, take a photo of the finished puzzle and then take it apart. Keep the photos of your finished works in a scrapbook. Then donate the puzzle to a local nursing home. You've enjoyed it, and now someone else can.

This method also keeps you from buying duplicate puzzles.

Quench a golfer. Avid golfers in areas where summers are long and hot can carry a small container of sport-drink powder in a golf bag. At the water stops along the course, mix a little powder into a cup of cold water for a much-needed refresher. This is much healthier—and cheaper—than buying the drinks offered for sale.

A few soda/water/sports drinks a day can add up to big bucks over a short time.

Make your own fishing lures. If you like to fish, you can make popping bugs (lures) from wine-bottle corks. All you need is a sharp knife, some sandpaper, glue, paint, and an appropriately sized hook. Be creative with colors, sizes, and attachments, such as feathers, rubber band legs, and small buttons for eyes. You will have lures for actual use next time you go fishing.

Make cooler ice. If you take a cooler to keep the fish you catch, here's how to keep the fish cold. Paying for bags of ice gets expensive, and freezing all those cubes is tedious for those of us without ice makers. Far better is to fill one 2-liter soda bottle with water (leaving a little space for expansion) and freeze it solid. This will keep a moderate-size cooler chilled all day. On cooler days, the bottle will still be partly frozen at the end of the day, so just wash it off and place it back in the freezer for the next time.

ENTERTAINMENT

Watch HDTV on the right channel. If you subscribe to high-definition TV through your cable company, make sure you are watching on the specific high-definition channel. Otherwise, the picture may look distorted and the people seem stretched.

Organize DVDs. If you buy DVDs of TV shows, type up separate sheets for each so you can keep track of which episodes you have watched. It's just like a library list of books read.

Make popcorn boxes. You can wash empty milk cartons and use them as popcorn boxes. Fill the cartons with popcorn and take them to drive-in movies or use them at home. Use half-gallon cartons for adults and pint or quart sizes for children. Just cut off the carton at the top until you have the proper size for each person.

After the movie, you can wash and save the containers to use another time.

Watch family movies and videotape yourself. We all have old home movies that we never get around to sorting out. And we all want to keep the family information that is stored in our parents' memories, but don't take the time to ask questions and make notes. Giving our elders the chance to reminisce while watching old family movies is one way to entertain them—and adding a video camera to record them describing what they are watching, as well as the movies on the screen, gives us a permanent record of "who that person at Grandma's house was."

Later, if we choose to go through the old movies, we will have information as well as firsthand memories that won't be lost with time.

If a video camera isn't available, a tape recorder or CD recorder will capture a verbal description. You don't usually get a second chance, so record these moments when you can.

Keep wires tangle free. Music players have wires that tangle with a mind of their own! To solve this tangling problem, take a plastic soda straw and carefully slit one side lengthwise with a sharp hobby knife. Place wires within the straw and tape with small pieces of cellophane tape at several places along its length. This will keep the wires under control.

CD scratches gone! Place a dab of plain white toothpaste on a clean cloth. Working on the CD's shiny side, apply the toothpaste, working from the inside to the outside like the spokes of a wheel (not back and forth), then wipe away the toothpaste with the same inside-to-outside method.

BOOKS AND READING

Hold a page open. Here's a "new" use for the clips used to close a bag of chips. If you like to read a book while you eat lunch, you may have trouble keeping it open to the page while you eat your sandwich. Try these clips on the top corners of the pages, clipping them to the hard back, to hold the book open.

Make your own bookmarks. Cut off large corners of used envelopes for bookmarks. Decorate the corners with a flower, swirl, butterfly, or other image. Put one over the corner of the page. It does not harm the page—it rides on top of it. You might prefer colored envelopes from greeting cards.

Make a bookmark, take 2. Another idea for a bookmark is to use an index card. Take an index card and write your name, address, and phone number on one side. When you want to use it, the written side faces the place where you stopped reading. More important, if you accidentally leave the book somewhere, there's a better chance of having it returned.

You can also use an index card to jot down notes and page numbers you want to refer to.

Share a book. A way to share a book and continue being entertained by

DINING OUT

For most of us, dining out is a real treat, so we want the experience to be a good one. Here are seven hints from my longtime friend Francois, a chef and restaurant owner, to help you get the most enjoyment from a dining-out experience:

- If you are unhappy with the food or service, tell the waitperson immediately so he or she can try to make it right.
- If you make a reservation during the holidays, call to cancel if you cannot make it.
- If you want a dish that is not on the menu, ask for it. The chef or owner should be the one to tell you "we cannot make it."
- If you order a steak cooked to a certain temperature, slice it in the center to check for doneness—not the edge.
- Don't be afraid to ask questions or give feedback. Most restaurants like to know what you think.
- If you order wine, order a label you know something about, or ask your waitperson for advice.
- If you have a problem, tell the person in a polite manner, not a tone that is huffy, loud, or rude. You'll get a better response.

its journey long after you have "released" it is described at www. bookcrossing.com.

The idea is to put a label with a BookCrossing I.D. number in the book and then leave it in a public place. You can download and print labels, or purchase preprinted labels. As the book passes through the hands of future readers, they are encouraged to go to the Web site, make a journal entry under that I.D. number, and once again leave the book in a public place for yet another reader.

The journal entries give reader comments and record the progress of the book as it passes from one reader to the next.

Make your own bookplates for borrowers. Make labels (called bookplates) for books you loan out. They say, "This book belongs to . . ." Put these on the front of each book so whoever borrows the book can see at a glance whose book it is.

For books with dust jackets, also put a label inside. It should reduce the number of books that don't get returned.

If you save the labels on your computer, they'll be easy to reprint when you need more.

Pass on books. Pass books you've read to friends and family, and track them. After someone has read a book, that person writes his or her name and the year on a blank page (usually in the very front of the book). If you don't want to write in the book, add a "sticky" note to the inside cover for people to write on. This helps as a reminder—"yes, I've read this book before."

Share paperbacks. Start a family round-robin with the paperbacks you purchase. After each person reads a book, put your initials inside the front cover.

That way you will know when to stop circulating them (it's also helpful to see your own initials if you can't remember whether you've already read the book).

Search for library books online. Libraries are such a treasure trove, it can be hard to remember all the fascinating books and authors you've been meaning to read. So, line up books before you go.

Your library system probably has a Web site with a catalog search option. Search for books online right after you've read an interesting book review in a magazine and place them on reserve.

The library then may send an e-mail notice when the books are ready for pickup, and you will be delighted with your "personalized" selections.

Remember renewals. Here's another method for remembering when to renew or return library books. If your library has a system for renewing books online, use the reminder application on your computer. Each day, when you log on to check e-mail, the note is right there on the desktop to remind you when the books are due.

PHOTOS

Capture the moment in pictures. Once a year, buy a 27-exposure disposable camera and keep it handy at all times on your counter. If something interesting comes along, such as a rainbow, blooming flowers, or any unexpected pleasure, you'll be right there to capture the moment.

When you develop the pictures, it's a surprise to see exactly what is on the prints. It can become a fun hobby.

Send a visual gift to someone far away. For a birthday gift for a loved one overseas or across the country, make a big poster with a message such as "Happy birthday, we love you!" Have family members and friends write messages to the recipient on the back of the poster.

Snap a picture of everyone holding the poster. Print the pictures out on your computer and mail the poster and pictures to your loved one.

Photograph events and I.D. the participants. If you photograph sporting events, especially amateur ones, and post selected pictures on a Web site, it may be hard to match names to the participants. Most of these events do not publish programs or entry lists, but most events post event lists with riders (or participants) and numbers so that participants know which event they are in. Take pictures of these event lists so you can easily match participant names with their numbers in the pictures.

Put a camera in a tackle box. Put a single-use (disposable) camera in your child's fishing-tackle box when you go fishing together. If you do lots of catch-and-release fishing, the child can get a picture of "the big one" before letting it go, and you don't have to worry about bringing (or forgetting) the camera every time you go.

I.D. your disposable camera. Some

grandparents like to give out disposable cameras at family gatherings. Cameras look alike, with the exception of limited colors, and can easily become mixed up.

To identify them, use leftover stick-on gift labels for each camera. Put the person's name and date of beginning of use on each camera label. You can use this system to label other "look-alike" items at family gatherings.

Make a photo wall. Here's another idea for photo use. You probably have boxes of photos and other family memorabilia just stored in your garage that no one ever gets to enjoy.

So, take butcher paper and staple or tack it to the wall in your game room. Starting with the large items (like maps used on family vacations and large, framed portraits and awards), glue, staple, or nail them to the wall, dividing the bigger pieces throughout the room. Next, glue or staple on the medium-size photos to make a collage. Add a table to hold old yearbooks and scrapbooks.

It will take quite a few days to finish, but it'll be everyone's favorite room in the house. And if you ever move, you can take down the butcher paper and take your memories along.

Another way to decorate with photos is to use extra photos as a wallpaper border in the living room.

Create family scrapbooks. Making scrapbooks for each member of your family creates lasting memories. Your grandkids can have their own book from birth to graduation. They are so much fun to make.

For all the extra photos that don't make it into the books, take the pictures and make a collage photo page, stacking them on top of each other. You can even cut out cute things about

---

Unlimited Uses for . . . a Disposable Camera

Here are some great ways to use a disposable camera:

- Give to a child for a field trip.
- Put on tables at a wedding reception for guests to take photos.
- Take to a birthday party.
- Bring along to a special event for one-of-a-kind photos.
- Keep on hand for special family visits.

the picture and insert them into the page. If your scrapbook size is a 12-by-12-inch page, you can cut lots of faces to fill the page. You could even make a wall picture for someone in a framed 16-by-20-inch page.

Organize wallet photos. A good way to organize wallet-size pictures of family and friends is to put them in the vinyl sheets with individual pockets that are sold as baseball-card holders.

Place the sheets in a three-ring binder.

Repurpose a compact-disk case. Plastic compact-disk cases make inexpensive but nice photo frames. Remove the holder part and trim the photo to fit. Place on a plate easel display.

Use clear photo frames. Here are some other uses for clear, acrylic photo frames that stand alone:

- Use to hold recipes in clear view—also keeps them clean.
- Post frequently called numbers in a frame near the phone.
- Print a list of passwords, put it in a frame, and keep it next to your home computer.
- An 8-by-10-inch or larger frame can be used to hold copy at your desk—just add a binder clip.
- Slip project directions inside so both hands are free.

Archive holiday photos. Here's an easy idea to I.D. holiday photos and greeting cards for your photo albums.

PHOTO ALBUM DO-OVER

How do you remove photographs and newspaper articles from the adhesive backing in old-style photo albums?

First, do no harm! If the snapshot or album itself is precious, consult a professional photo restorer before you attempt to remove anything. Otherwise, try these steps:

- Put the page (if detachable) or the album into a large plastic storage bag, and place the bag in the freezer, unsealed. Leave it for a day or so to dry out the adhesive.
- Then use a putty knife or the dull edge of a table knife to pry one corner of the picture or clipping and remove.
- If the item still won't budge, cut it out of the page with scissors or a single-edge razor; scan or photocopy it as a backup.

Keep the picture and the greeting card together, and then when you have time to put the pictures in photo albums, cut out the family's name, place it beside the photo, and print the year.

You'll be glad you included names someday when your memory begins to fade.

Use extra photos. Do not discard that extra set of photo prints. Use the photos as postcards. Just divide the back for address and message. It saves postage, too.

This is a lovely way to use extra photos. Something to keep in mind is that if your pictures exceed the postcard size of 4¼ inches high by 6 inches long, you will be charged the first-class-mail letter rate, rather than the lower postcard rate.

VISITS AND VACATIONS

Pack for a picnic. Pleasant weather makes us think about picnics. Here are three good picnic hints:

- If you're transporting breakable glasses to drink from, slip a clean sock over each. It will keep them from rattling around, and will absorb the perspiration from the glass later.

- An umbrella with no handle is the ideal thing to rest over the picnic-table goodies to keep the bugs away.

- For transporting a long-pronged fork when traveling to picnics and barbecues, take a toilet-paper or paper-towel tube and flatten it. Tape one end shut and use the flat tube as a "sheath" for the fork. You can do this with hot-dog tongs, too.

- Keep a list with the supplies of all the things you brought so when you pack up for the return, you won't leave something behind.

Re-close picnic snacks. For picnicking or snacking away from home, put a rubber band around the new packages that are taken on picnics so that they can be closed after they are opened.

Be safe at amusement parks. When you take a young child to an amusement park, a county fair, or any crowded place, take a digital photo of her, what she is wearing, and one close-up.

If the child should get lost, you'll have an I.D. to give searchers. Later, the photos can go into her memory book.

Store camping supplies in small containers. Empty pill bottles and film containers can come in quite handy if you're going camping. They can be used to keep all sorts of camping supplies clean and dry:

- Store cotton balls. You can use cotton to remove burrs from your clothing; or tuck a cotton ball in each ear to cut out the cold or the wind. Cotton is also great kindling for a fire (by the way, so is lint from your dryer).

- Store wooden matches. For an easy striking surface, wrap a small piece of fine-grit sandpaper around the bottle and glue or tape it in place.

- Use to hold all sorts of other small items, like safety pins, sewing needles, and even bandages.

To identify each one at quick glance, label each container with first-aid tape and write the contents in permanent marker.

Use a bedspread when camping. If you clean out a closet and find a couple of old bedspreads, don't dispose of them. Instead, keep them with the camping gear. These spreads are great to place on the ground or on a cot, and serve as a little extra insulation.

Clean beach sand off the kids. Always keep baby powder in the car for when the kids have spent the day in the wet sand at the beach. Liberally sprinkle powder directly on the sandy areas, and the sand comes right off. It does leave them powdery white, but the sand in all the nooks and crannies is gone, so toddlers and babies will be comfortable for the ride home. Also, the sand on their feet will stay at the beach and not in the car.

Keep beach sand off car seats. On a seashore vacation, use a shower curtain on the seats of your car to keep the seats from getting wet and sandy. Just shake out the curtain after use.

Pack outfits together. When you go on vacation, pack complete outfits (slacks, tops, belts, scarves) on hangers in a garment bag. This is easier to move to a motel closet and choose from without rummaging through a suitcase.

On long car trips, a laundry bag and a small, plastic clothes basket for coin-operated laundry facilities are useful.

Save space when packing. When you go on vacation, pack all your clothes (even coats) in jumbo, self-sealing bags and squeeze all the air out. They take up less room, you can pack more in a suitcase, and, if they search your bags at the airport, it is easier to get everything back in. Plus, you then have bags for dirty laundry on the return trip, and you can pack more in a smaller bag.

Pack earrings for travel. When you travel, put pairs of small earrings in a pill container that has sections for the seven days of the week. They are easy to keep track of, and you will not have to search through your jewelry case for unmatched earrings. Use your jewelry case for larger items.

Preaddress postcards. Here is a timesaving idea: Before leaving for a trip, purchase some blank, self-adhesive address labels. While you are on a long flight, fill out the address labels (or preprint labels on your computer) for people you want to send postcards to. When you get to your destination, all you will have to do is buy the postcards, write a quick note, and attach the label. You won't have to dig out your address book for every postcard, and you can make sure you don't forget anyone.

Secure the luggage without a lock. When you travel by plane you may not feel comfortable without your luggage being locked because of theft, but for security reasons at the airports, it might need to be checked when you aren't around with the key. Put a metal key ring through the two zippers on the suitcase—hopefully it would take too much time for a would-be thief to bother with.

Mark your black suitcase. So many people these days travel with a black rolling suitcase that it is difficult to recognize your own. Whenever you receive a bouquet of flowers with a pretty ribbon or have a short amount of gift-wrap ribbon left over, tie it onto one of your black suitcases. That way, you can quickly identify your bag when it comes down the baggage-claim conveyor belt.

I.D. your luggage with paint. Ribbons you place on luggage to identify it can come off or be removed by the time the luggage gets to the baggage-claim area. Instead, use artists' acrylic paints and paint a bright design—perhaps yellow and green flowers—on all six surfaces of your bags. You'll be able to spot them immediately on the conveyor belt, trolley, or wherever they end up.

Another way to I.D. your luggage. Purchase brightly colored luggage straps and use them on all pieces of luggage, even your carry-ons. Not only does this make them easy to find, but the straps also keep the luggage closed in case the latches should happen to come open.

Organize travel documents. When you go on a car trip, put all your travel documents and maps in one folder. Take along a small spiral notebook that fits in a shirt pocket. On sequential pages, write the directions for the motel where you are staying, the address, the phone number, the date the reservation was made, and the confirmation number. Do the same for car rentals. This saves shuffling through papers to find the correct information when checking in, the directions if a map is lost, or the phone number in case of a delay.

Leave your contact info. Before you go on vacation, leave a list of phone numbers for a neighbor who is going to be watching your home and taking care of the pets. If he needs to get in touch with you, he will know where you are each day. This is important if you travel to remote areas that don't have cell phone reception.

Cell phones are handy, but there are times that a land-line phone and contact information are important to have.

Carry I.D. wherever you go. Always carry information with next of kin or someone to be called in case of an accident.

How to never forget your cell phone. Here's a travel hint from a flight attendant: If you are prone to forgetting you cell phone (while it is recharging) in your hotel room when you check out, try this.

Take the shoes you will be wearing and place one shoe right in front of the door, blocking it. Then place the other shoe with the cell phone and battery charger wherever they are plugged in.

You might leave your room without your keys, sunglasses, wallet, or coat, but you won't leave without your shoes!

Don't let your passport expire. Keep your passport up-to-date if you have relatives living—or just traveling— abroad. If your mother has an accident overseas, you can go get her if your passport is up-to-date.

Nowadays, it's probably more important to keep all official identification (passport and driver's license) current.

Copy your passport. Whenever you travel outside the United States, make photocopies of your passport and give one or more to close friends in the event that your original is lost or stolen when you're traveling abroad.

Also keep a photocopy somewhere in your luggage for the same reason. Obtaining a reissued passport in a foreign country (or at home, for that matter) can be greatly facilitated if you can show proof of a valid one that has disappeared by whatever means.

Scan travel documents. When traveling, especially abroad, scan all documents that you might need in case of an emergency, like passport pages, visa pages, hotel vouchers, plane receipts, birth/death/marriage certificates, and also an "in case of emergency" document, and save all the info on a flash drive. You can purchase a flash drive almost anywhere now for a small cost, and it is an easy way to carry this information without having to go through tons of paper.

If you forget your flashlight. Here's a hint for those who travel, stay in hotels, and forget their night-light or flashlight. Before going to sleep, turn on your TV, turn the volume to the lowest setting, then turn it off and leave the controls on your nightstand. Turn on the TV if you need to get up in the middle of the night, and there'll be just enough illumination.

Remember your charger. Many people travel with computers, cell phones, DVD players, and other electronic devices these days. They need recharging, and too often the chargers are left in the hotel-room sockets.

Here's a simple solution so you don't forget your charger. With a permanent marker, write "battery charger" on a zipper-top bag. When you use the charger, place the bag on top of the contents of your suitcase, as a visual reminder to pack the charger when leaving.

Here's my hint: I put bright-red nail polish on the charger (plus a business address sticker) as a visual reminder, and I try to put it in the bathroom outlet so it's hard to miss. I also write a note and place it with the room key.

Take your medications. If you are going on a trip, please be sure to take all your medications with you on your person. Never take a small supply along with you on a trip—always take the full bottle.

This is good advice, particularly for people who are on "must have" medications. If you're traveling far from home, you should carry the medications in original bottles or have all of the prescription numbers and your pharmacy's telephone number handy.

Make a bed from cushions. When you need a quick guest bed for a visiting child, use cushions from outdoor furniture. Bring in two cushions (check for insects and spiders first!), lay them side by side, and cover them with a heavy quilt to keep them in place. Put a sheet and blanket on top, or let your visitor sleep in a sleeping bag on top of the pillows.

Keep memories of departed loved ones alive. To keep memories of departed loved ones alive, you might enjoy sharing your memories of them at a family reunion. Some people release helium balloons inscribed with mes-sages for the departed, and the senti-ments and gestures are lovely.

However, we now know that when the balloons return to the earth, they can be mistaken for food by animals that are harmed when they ingest pieces of the balloons.

Another suggestion is to plant a tree or give a donation to a charity in remembrance of somebody.

Organize travel in an album. If you travel extensively or serve as a tour guide for friends and family who come to visit, it helps to be orga-nized.

Buy an inexpensive photo album that holds about 50 4-by-6-inch photos, and

---

WORLD TRAVELING

If you are planning a trip out of the country, being prepared can make a world of difference. Since traveling abroad requires a little more planning than domestic travel, here are some hints to help you:

- Locate your passport now and make sure it hasn't expired. It can take anywhere from 2 to 6 weeks to renew and sometimes longer to request a new passport.
- Do your homework and check on any travel warnings for the countries you plan to visit.
- Take the time to read up on the laws of that country—remember, when in Rome, do as the Romans do!
- Be sure to leave your itinerary and hotel information with friends or family so that they know how to reach you in case of an emergency.
- If possible, leave your expensive jewelry and clothing at home, and be discreet when handling money. Don't draw unnecessary attention to yourself.
- If you find yourself in any trouble you cannot handle, contact the closest U.S. Embassy.

Bon voyage!

fill the pages with your itinerary, maps, train schedules, hotel confirmation numbers, and other useful info. Use your computer to reduce or enlarge the information to fit the pages.

Use index cards to jot down interesting facts and tips, and include simple language phrases and translations for menu items when you are eating out.

Make a trip notebook. Whenever you start to plan a family trip—vacation, amusement park, family reunion—get a notebook and label it with the trip name. Put all the reservation information, sites to visit, activities, contacts, and other relevant info in this notebook. When you have a question or need to check something, simply pull out the book, and all the information is right at hand. Upon return, put receipts in it so that you can check them against your credit-card statements.

Keep track of reward numbers. If your occupation involves traveling quite a bit, you've amassed, of course, quite a few hotel, airline, and car-rental award memberships.

There's no need to carry all the award cards in order to present your account number to the appropriate party. All you need are the appropriate account numbers. So, write down on a 3-by-5-inch card (which, when folded, fits in your wallet) all your award companies and account numbers.

But remember that many cards have the number on the magnetic strip so the card can just be swiped.

Plan for plant care while on vacation. If you are going to be away for a short time, you need to make plans to care for your houseplants before you go. Here are some helpful hints I'd like to share to keep the plants happy while you're away:

- Give them a good watering (but don't drown them) right before you leave. During the summer or winter, do not turn your air conditioning or heating completely off. Instead, set it at a temperature where your plants survive.

- If there's a natural light source like a window or skylight in your bathroom, put plants in the bathtub with several inches of water and cover each plant with a clear, plastic dry-cleaning bag to create a greenhouse or terrarium effect.

- If you have rare or costly plants that require TLC, it might be better to have a neighbor or friend water and look in on them every couple of days.

- For outdoor potted plants, place a couple in a large, plastic garbage bag and fill the bottom with water, to keep them watered for up to a week. If you have a child's wading pool, put a larger group of plants in it and add enough water to keep everyone well hydrated.

A few convenient travel tips.

- Always carry a can of disinfectant or antibacterial spray to spray down the bathroom, remote control, doorknobs, and other surfaces.

- Rubber flip-flops worn in the shower can prevent athlete's foot.

- Bring your own small alarm clock—many of us can never figure out how the hotel-room alarm clock works.

Turn down the volume. When you go away on vacation, turn the volume down on your phone and the answering machine so an unanswered ringing

KEEP YOUR HOME SAFE WHEN YOU GO ON VACATION

Home-safety experts say that when you will be leaving your home for a trip, it's important to make sure the place doesn't look empty—sometimes easier said than done! Here are some hints to help protect your home while you are away and to give it that "lived in" look:

- Set automatic timers in several rooms that turn lights on and off at various times. These timers also can be used for radios.

- Park a car halfway up the driveway to prevent an unauthorized vehicle from being parked there, which would give a thief the means to unload the contents of your home and drive off virtually unnoticed.

- Have someone pick up mail, fliers, newspapers, or other deliveries. Don't let anything accumulate that would indicate you are away. If you don't have anyone to do this, visit www.usps.com to have mail stopped during your absence. Your newspaper should have a similar service.

- Make sure the trash is taken out and the lawn is maintained as well. Set sprinkler systems or use a specially designed timer to turn on movable sprinklers once or twice during your absence.

- Turn off your automatic garage-door opener. Someone just might be on the same frequency.

phone will not be heard from outside your house.

Program travel numbers into your cell phone. Before your vacation, program all your hotel telephone numbers and the confirmation numbers into your cell phone. You will have the information you need at your fingertips in an instant.

Double-check your hotel reservation. When traveling, and checking into a hotel where there are several of the same chain in the city, make sure you have the correct street address and phone numbers. You may want to double-check your reservation before leaving home to ensure that you arrive at the correct hotel.

Pack travel essentials. Here are a few things to bring on vacation to make life on the road more convenient:

- A small bag of pinch clothespins—can keep drapes closed, can be used to hang up towels, and can hold snack bags closed.

- A small bottle of fabric freshener—can be used to freshen up a "smoking" room when it is the only one available, as well as freshen linens.

- A laundry pretreatment stick—on an extensive road trip, once clothes are too dirty to be worn, they can be placed in a hotel laundry bag and kept in the car. On the night before returning home, take out only the things you will need in the morning, and sort through all the laundry at one time, separating it by load and pretreating it. Then pack the clothes by load in the suitcases, and use one suitcase for all of your toiletries. Upon returning home, you're halfway to getting the laundry done, and it is so much easier to transition back into your daily routine.

Make a compact travel kit. When you travel, carry a small shaving kit (available at many stores). In it place a variety of items: very small sewing kit, small containers of shaving lotion and cream, toothpaste, toothbrush, spare screws for eyeglasses, medication, antacids, and many other little things that might be needed. Replenish the kit after each trip, and keep it packed on a permanent basis.

Essential travel advice. Here is a travel hint I received from Bob Weiss while I was in Hawaii a while back doing a speech: "Carry a small flashlight in a toiletries kit, and always leave the hotel key on the floor by the door. You won't leave the room without it."

Keep hotel curtains closed all the way. When you close the curtains in your hotel room, you may find that they don't close completely. To make matters worse, the air conditioner may cause them to billow.

Take one of the hotel's wooden pants hangers and clip the curtains together in two places, which will secure them closed. The weight of the wooden hanger will keep them from billowing out. Problem solved.

Get lint off your clothes without a lint brush. Here's how to get dog hair or lint off of black clothing when you're on vacation and don't have a lint brush with you. Take the luggage tags off your suitcase (the ones the airlines stick on to show your destination). The sticky stuff on the back of them makes a terrific lint-picker-upper!

When you fly, try these hints. Here are a couple of hints for air travelers:

Since you should not lock your luggage when checking it anymore, use the kind of plastic ties that lock when pushed through the opposite end of the tie. That way, your luggage won't come open, and the ties can be cut off easily for inspection. Also keep a small bundle in an inside pocket of the suitcase. You can get them at hardware stores and some dollar stores.

Also, put your underwear and shoes in plastic, self-closing bags, which inspectors can see through; they won't have to scatter the items all over.

Lighten your luggage. With the increase in airline screening for overweight bags at check-in, here are two simple hints that can save you time and embarrassment:

First, have the clerk weigh your heaviest bag. If it is overweight, you can take out some items and put them in your other bags that might be lighter. Too often I have seen people weigh their biggest bag last and then wish that they could retrieve their lighter bags that already went down the conveyor belt into the depths of the airport.

Second, carry an empty fold-up bag in your luggage. Not only is it helpful at the end of your trip if you have bought more souvenirs than your initial luggage can hold, but also at the departure counter you can take items from your heavy bag and check them in a lighter-weight second or third bag. This is an easy way to avoid hefty extra-weight fees.

Many airlines limit the weight per bag—some 50 pounds per checked and about 40 per carry-on. So, don't try to carry on those dumbbells! Check the airline Web site or call to see what the guidelines are.

Keep luggage from getting lost. Here's one way to keep from losing your luggage when you fly. On plain paper, print the date, your name, the airport, departing flight, connecting flight, and destination city. Use clear packing tape and entirely cover the information paper. Also, type up directions for your return trip and slip it inside your suitcase with a small roll of packing tape.

Try these travel tips. A seasoned business traveler shares these travel tips:

- Compartmentalize packing. When you're living out of your suitcase, with little time to pack or unpack, separate your clothes and put them in large plastic bags: shirts in one, pants in another, undies in another. The bags minimize the time you spend rummaging around and make it a breeze to find things quickly and put everything back.

NO LOST LUGGAGE

Here are a few hints to make sure your luggage arrives when you do:

- The best way to avoid losing luggage at the airport is to travel with only a carry-on bag—there's no checked luggage, and most worries will be gone.

- To keep from drawing unwanted attention, don't use noticeable expensive luggage.

- If you do check luggage, make sure all old travel tags are removed before the correct tag is put on each item. Also, check to confirm that you are given the corresponding claim tickets.

- Go directly to the baggage-claim area to pick up your luggage. Don't get a bite to eat or lounge around—luggage that stays on the conveyor belt too long is usually removed and set aside, where it can be lost or, worse, stolen.

- Never, under any circumstances, leave luggage unattended—when traveling, your luggage should go everywhere you do!

Hopefully these "travel smart" hints will keep you and your luggage on the same path!

- Take a night-light. Plug it into the bathroom socket and you will always be able to find your way around the room in the middle of the night.

- Bring a small flashlight, alarm clock, and earplugs in the "bed bag"—the one that goes by the bed.

Roll clothes to save space. Rolling your clothes when packing not only helps decrease wrinkles but also allows you to pack more in the suitcase. This is an old hint, but a very valuable one.

Give a traveler a great travel bag. Buy a friend who loves to travel and is getting married a travel bag filled with necessities like bandages, a sewing kit, lip balm, lotion, and a sponge.

Send film for developing on the road. Even though digital cameras are all the rage now, plenty of us still prefer to use a camera with film. When you go on vacation, bring along several of the film envelopes that are from the developing company you use. When you take a whole roll of film, fill out the envelope and mail it from wherever you are. By the time you

CAR RENTAL KNOW-HOW

If you are going to rent a car, here are a few hints that could save you some time and a lot of headaches!

It seems like everyone is in a hurry and no one wants to waste time if it can be avoided. Here are several hints from people in the car-rental business that will help you have better and faster service. So, before you make that call or check online to rent a vehicle, get ready to make a list of important information you'll need to know:

- The specific location. Large cities have several sites, so know which one you'll need. If you are flying in, you might want the location closest to the airport.

- Your identification number if you are a frequent renter.

- Dates and times for picking up and dropping off the vehicle.

- What size car you want and whether you want one that is "no smoking."

- Any association, auto-club, or senior-citizen discount, as well as frequent-flier memberships or coupons. If in doubt, it doesn't hurt to ask—it could save you some bucks! Also, make sure you take any card, coupon, or code that has been used for your rental with you when you pick up the car.

- Have a credit card ready. Most car-rental agencies don't accept debit cards or cash.

arrive home, the photos will be there waiting for you.

Unstick a suitcase zipper. What can you do to make a sticky zipper on a suitcase slide smoothly again? Try rubbing a No. 2 lead pencil or a candle over the zipper's teeth. But first check the zipper carefully to see if the lining or any bits of fabric might be stuck in it. Use tweezers to pull out stray threads. Adding a stronger pull may also help. If the suitcase is old, how-

---

On the Light Side

Welcome to Hotel Hostility

Here are some reader complaints about hotel rooms:

• Jean of New York says: "Facial tissues, if provided, are the worst available. Garbage pickup is too early in the morning, and, worst of all, people who stay there are not considerate of others—they slam doors or let them slam, talk outside of windows or in halls at times when others are trying to sleep, and beep horns at others in parking lots."

• Dianne of New York says: "Having just spent a weekend at a hotel in a large city, I have a pet peeve to add to those mentioned in your newspaper column. Since two people often share a room, when the first person is done showering, the second person follows. The bathroom is then occupied (and steamy), and it is necessary to apply makeup and style hair with electric appliances in the bedroom area. Alas, there is no mirror there, and not only is the lighting poor, but the only electrical outlet is wedged between the desk and the TV cabinet, a hard-to-reach spot. Grrr!"

• Lorraine of Arizona says: "Window coverings do not close tightly. Light comes in from the center of the drapery. Another complaint is the ice buckets that sweat and leave water whenever they are put down."

• William of Colorado says: "Shower heads that are too low. You have to duck your head under to wet or rinse and risk bumping your head when you straighten up."

• Lisa, via e-mail, says: "I have one gripe about some hotel rooms that have doors inside so that you can walk from one room into another person's room, and you can lock the door on one side but not the other. That was one sleepless night we had on our anniversary."

• R. Thomas, via e-mail, says: "Bed-sheets that are laundered in bleach and scented laundry soaps, then dried with scented fabric softener. I have severe allergies and have started bringing along my own bed linens."

• Sibylle of Kansas had this to day: "I am delighted to report that my hotel experience was completely different from that of your readers. I was offered a discount, there was plenty of free space in the room, all promotional material was in a cubbyhole, there was ample room in the bathroom and plenty of fresh towels."

My complaint? The lighting in many bathrooms is so bad that I need a flashlight to put on makeup.

ever, the zipper could just be worn out and may need to be replaced.

Dry your towels outside the bathroom. When your family travels on vacation, you might take two showers a day if you've been hiking, swimming, or sightseeing before going out to eat. After each shower, hang your towels up in the closet with the spring-clip hangers, and space them so that enough air can circulate so they dry out. Hanging towels up in the bathroom usually doesn't work because the humidity keeps them damp.

Recognize kids from a distance while camping. Here's a hint that eliminates campground arguments and makes each child recognizable, even at a distance. Pick a color for each child, and then make sure the camping gear for each child is that color. Say, for example, that the color is red. That child will have a red plate, cup, toothbrush, polo shirts, shorts, sweater, jacket, and hat; another will have a different color. Happy camping!

Travel with dollar bills. When traveling, take along a good supply of single dollar bills. They come in handy for tips and for using washing or vending machines.

Cool a curling iron. When travel-ing, if your curling iron is still hot and you're ready to pack, you can put it in an oven mitt.

Or, just unplug it and run it under cold water (just the iron part), wipe it off, and it's ready to be packed—no waiting for cooling down and no packing something hot or warm.

Take a break from driving. When your family travels by car, take a picnic lunch and stop at a "Welcome Center" on the interstate for a relaxing lunch at the picnic tables. You can get a break from riding, stretch your legs, and enjoy the fresh air while you eat your lunch. And you can pick up the new state maps and other information inside the center.

Make traveling comfortable. Here are some travel hints for your next vacation:

- Put an inch or two of water in the bottom of a disposable bathroom glass. You can now store your toothbrush in it, and the glass won't fall over.

- If the outside temperature permits, turn the heat/air conditioning in your hotel/motel room to "fresh air only." The compressor won't cycle on and off all night long and wake you up, and the white noise will block out noise from the street or hallway.

- Buy an inexpensive pair of slip-on "spa socks" or "lounge socks." Stuff them in your purse and wear them in the security line and then to keep your tootsies warm and relaxed on the plane.

Don't forget your shampoo. Have you ever forgotten your shampoo in the shower at the hotel/motel when you're on vacation? To solve the problem, when you unpack your toiletries, leave the cap for the shampoo bottle on the sink next to your toothbrush. That will remind you to check behind the shower curtain for your shampoo as you pack up to leave in the morning.

Send an e-mail to yourself. When you travel to Europe, scan into your computer copies of your passport, itinerary, driver's license, and any credit cards you are planning to take and e-mail them to yourself. Because they are saved in your e-mail, you can access them anywhere.

Stash a stroller. When traveling with a small child, it's helpful to bring along a lightweight stroller. However, it is

VACATION MEDICATIONS

Don't let what the doctor ordered go by the wayside when you go on vacation. If you are taking medications, keep them in mind when you make travel plans.

- Make a list of all the medications you're taking, including the dosage and trade and generic names.
- Bring enough of each medication to last the length of the trip and maybe a day or two longer, just in case.
- Pack your medications in their original containers instead of pill cases or other unlabeled bottles.
- Put your medications in your carry-on bag and always keep it with you. It's a good idea to check with the airlines regarding their policies related to carrying medications.
- If your medication requires refrigeration, talk to your pharmacist or doctor about what to do.
- If you'll be crossing through several time zones, you might need to adjust the times when you take your medication. Again, ask you doctor or pharmacist for advice.

difficult to deal with at the airport. To make this easier, put the stroller in the zippered bag from your collapsible chairs and check it at the baggage window. This makes a handy carrier in the airport and also on vacation—small children often like to walk, but then get tired.

Make a toilet seat cover and recycle, too. Keep plastic grocery bags to use as toilet seat covers in public bathrooms when you travel.

Smooth out the bags and cut a big "U" out of the center of both back and front, being careful not to cut the side folds and leaving about 5 inches at the bottom of the "U."

In a questionable bathroom, simply open the bag, holding the handles on either side of the seat, and slide the bag on to cover the seat. Best yet, to remove it and throw it in the trash, you need only touch the clean corners of the bag.

These bags are lightweight, and it's easy to pack bunches of them for large families or for longer trips. Just please be absolutely sure that the plastic bag is not flushed.

Something *not* to worry about on vacation. Many of us have been told that cards used for keys in some hotels and motels should be destroyed and not returned to the hotel or motel because they contain important information, including your address and credit-card numbers, with expiration dates. Anyone with a card reader, or an employee of the hotel, can access this personal information. According to two major hotel chains, this information is not true. The only information on the magnetic strip of a "key card" is that needed to access your room. The hotel key-card system is different from the billing system.

Take a shoe holder along on vacation. Hanging shoe holders with pockets come in handy in lots of ways, and you can take one along when your family travels.

There never seems to be enough counter or drawer space in hotels or motels. So, keep a shoe holder (the kind with the holders on the front and back, and a coat-hanger-style hook) with your luggage at all times.

When you get to the lodging, put shoes in the bottom pockets and shampoo, curling iron, and other toiletries in the top.

The shoe holder would also come in handy at home for those who share a bathroom and have a lot of things to use.

Pack undies in your shoes. Here is a

travel hint I received from David Sayre while in Hawaii a few years ago doing a speech for the Society of American Travel Writers:

"Pack your T-shirts/underwear in your shoes to give you more room in the suitcase and to protect your shoes from being crushed."

Choose an inside cabin on your first cruise. When you book a cruise, you might want to choose rooms that are at the water level and at midship, since these rooms usually have the best stability and the least rocking-and-rolling motion. Also, contact your doctor for medications if you are prone to motion sickness.

Make your own iced tea on the road. Here's a quick, easy, and inexpensive way to enjoy iced tea on the road without paying restaurant prices.

Purchase a 24-bottle case of individual-size house-brand water. Bring a variety of flavored tea bags with you. Each morning, open a new bottle, take a couple of swigs of water, insert a tea bag, then replace the top and place the bottle in the mini-fridge in your room. By the time you come back from a day of activities, you will have a chilled bottle of herbal iced tea awaiting you, with no deposit/no return on the bottles!

Don't buy new toothpaste. Instead of buying a new toothpaste tube in each city you travel to or having to bring and then return with a mostly full tube, just save the end of one of your tubes at home and take that tube with you. This will save you money, and you won't have to bring it home with you.

Make family car tips more comfortable. Here are a couple of things you can do to make car trips more comfortable:

- Take along a pillow and a blanket. No matter the time of year, this makes taking a little nap more comfortable. Put a bright-colored pillowcase on the pillow so that if you take it into a hotel room, you will remember to grab it when you are leaving.

- Also take along a small bag of some of your favorite goodies. These snacks keep your family from having to stop for sodas or snacks. You'll arrive at your destination sooner.

Recycle a comforter bag as a travel tote. When you buy new bed covering, often the packaging is a sturdy plastic cover with zipper or snap enclosures. Save these plastic bags and use them in your travels as a laundry bag. You can use the smaller ones for toiletries, shoes, note cards, and miscellaneous things.

The bags can stay in the suitcase, but are completely sealed. They are perfect for those quick day trips to the beach for wet towels and swimsuits.

Don't forget anything when you pack. If you travel a lot, you probably worry about forgetting important items for your trip. Here's a hint for you: Make a checklist of everything you will need: shoes, glasses, papers, ticket, and so on. Repeat out loud each item as you pack it, then go over the list just before leaving the house or hotel.

Pack entertainment for kids on the road. Traveling with kids can make trips challenging. Here are a couple of ideas to make a trip more memorable:

- If you have young children, have them each pack a bag with things they can do while riding in the car. Then make a kit for each of them. Include a map of the route you are taking, some waterproof markers, and printed papers of some of the interesting sights you will be passing by.

- As you pull away from your house, give your children the maps, mark-

FUN IN THE CAR

A long car trip can be exhausting for everyone! To make trips more enjoyable and seem to go quicker, here are some games that can be played by the young and not-so-young.

- Cut out of magazines pictures of things that you will see while traveling, like livestock, buses, fire trucks, bridges, and water towers. Tape or glue the pictures to index cards. Deal out the cards, and the first child to spot all of their cards is the winner.

- Before the trip, write down all 50 states on a sheet of paper and make several copies. During the trip, hand out these sheets and find out who can see the most license plates from different states. Kids can take turns calling out cars. The winner is the one who ends up with the most states marked off the list. The real challenge is to spot license plates from Alaska and Hawaii if you are driving the mainland states!

- Buy some maps or download maps from the Internet of where you will be traveling and give them to the kids. They can use the maps to follow along, and they can also bring up points of interest, etc. One of the winners could choose a place of interest to stop and visit. They can also keep track of mileage—how far you've gone and how far you will need to go.

ers, and papers. Tell them they can follow along on their maps and mark how far you go that day.

- The kids will be busy watching for signs of attractions and then finding them on their maps.

- Planning ahead and having toys, games, snacks, and other distractions really can make a car tip more bearable.

Hand out office supplies on car trips. Use office supplies to entertain kids on long trips.

Give each child a box of identical items that are safe for them and the car interior. The most interesting item may well be a package of self-sticking notes. There may be notes everywhere, but the children will be entertained.

Create a "Vacation Central" cabinet. Here's one solution to the "Mommy, where's the . . . ?"—you name it—scissors, insect repellent, vitamins, or whatever. These kinds of questions may drive you to insanity if you have several children, and trying to keep track of the many shared items in the car, hotel, or cabin is no vacation for mom!

First, make lists of shared items that you will pack (think of an "everything" drawer—desk items, first-aid kit, tools). Then purchase a plastic three-drawer chest (for less than $10). Load and label the drawers.

Nicknamed "Vacation Central,"

FUN AT THE BEACH

If you are planning a vacation at the beach with your kids, take along some items to let you create lasting memories, while leaving the sand behind. Remember, a day at the beach is a popular way to make everyone happy.

- Take extra plastic measuring cups or utensils for sandcastle making. The more shapes and sizes, the better.
- Plastic margarine, yogurt, or cottage-cheese tubs are great for holding shells and other beach finds. Make sure the shells are uninhabited before saving them.
- Be on the safe side and pack a "just in case" bag, too. Include a small container of meat tenderizer for jellyfish stings, extra sunblock, antibiotic cream, and adhesive bandages. You'll be prepared for most beach mishaps.
- Pack lots of water and fresh fruits. Keeping hydrated is important when out in the sun!

this cabinet is loaded into the back of your car or van so that it can be easily accessed whenever you stop en route.

Each year, you will be able to pull "Vacation Central" out of the attic. If you revised the packing lists as you drove home last year, the items will be in their respective drawers, ready to rescue another vacation.

Take along a rolling ice chest. When your children are young, think about using a rolling ice chest as one of your pieces of luggage. After you get to the hotel and unpack, go to the grocery store and purchase milk, yogurt, drinks, and snacks. Instead of having to go out to breakfast in the mornings, you can eat cereal, yogurt, and other healthy foods while you are getting ready in the mornings. You may be able to get to the theme parks before they open. Also take the ice chest with you on day trips.

Make a travel journal. If you take many trips, it's a good idea to make a journal for each trip as you travel. Thus, you can read the journal and enjoy the trips again. When you take pictures, mark the pictures as you take them and the name of the place where you were at the time.

Prevent a mess with plastic wrap.

Before traveling, unscrew or uncap toothpaste, hand lotion, shampoo, and other toiletries, put some plastic wrap over the opening, then re-cap. These items are then put in a plastic bag. No more messy surprises when the suitcase is opened. A square of plastic wrap can really prevent a mess. Also put some small garbage bags in the suitcase for dirty clothes.

Every drop counts. When your makeup cleanser is empty, slit the tube, use a cotton swab or Popsicle stick to get all of it out, and put it in a small plastic container. It's amazing how much product most people throw away! This also can be done with hand cream and toothpaste. Those dibs and dabs of products left in containers are usually just enough for a short trip.

Make an album with postcards. While on vacation, purchase doubles of all interesting postcards. These pictures are taken by experts during perfect weather conditions and are great for introducing or expanding on an area or a specific site. Lay out the postcards, back side (information side) down, on a copier and print. Cut out each individual "blurb," and you'll have a label ready to accompany the postcard in your album. Use the second set of cards for notecards.

Freshen a suitcase. To make suitcases smell fresh, spray fabric freshener in the suitcases before storing. Or, use fabric-softener sheets in your suitcases or anything that you want to store to make it smell fresh. You can cut fabric-softener sheets in half for small containers.

KEEPING IN TOUCH

Send mail every week. Everyone likes to get mail, so send elderly grandparents and great-grandparents a postcard every week, no matter where you are. If you are traveling, take along some preprinted labels and stamps to speed up the process.

Send news from home. Send care packages to your college students so they won't feel homesick. To make them seem ultra-homey, wrap the items you're sending in your local newspaper. It will help the student stay in touch with things going on at home.

We all love news from home. Almost all newspapers have Web sites, so it's easy to check what's going on. However, all of the paper might not be

KEEP TRACK OF FRIENDS

The friends in our lives are incredibly special. Sometimes our schedules are so hectic that we might forget special dates like birthdays or anniversaries. To prevent this from happening, here are some hints to help you stay in touch with the special people in your life:

- At the beginning of the year, write all the birthdays and other occasions you need to remember on a calendar. Then check the calendar on the first of each month.
- Purchase your greeting cards for the month at one time. Write a note or greeting, then address and stamp them so they are ready to go. No more last-minute rush.
- Buy greeting or blank cards you like whenever you see them. Store them in your desk drawer, so you'll have one for whatever event or celebration comes up.
- Get postcards in a pack and put them in the bag you carry around. Stamp them in advance. You can write short notes to friends while you are waiting at the salon or doctor's office.
- Call friends when you have a moment or two. Remember, the phone works both ways. Don't wait for them to call. Friends are too precious to ignore.

posted or stay up long. As far as I'm concerned, nothing beats turning the pages of a newspaper, waiting to discover that gem of a news story or delightful photo. So keep sending that newspaper!

Send mail to shut-ins. This is a hint for those who write to shut-ins or patients in hospitals or retirement homes. People living in an assisted-living facility look forward to mail and something to relieve boredom.

Write to them often, and always include a self-addressed, stamped envelope and notepaper to make it easy for them to write back to you. Writing notes and receiving them is important healthwise for anyone in this situation.

Help a loved one keep in touch. To help a loved one in a nursing home or care facility keep in touch with friends and family, when you go for a visit, leave two boxes of greeting cards. The first box includes birthday, anniversary, and other cards for the family. The envelopes have been addressed and stamped. The other box has cards that haven't been addressed yet, but have been stamped. You can even have some address labels printed up and put them on all the envelopes.

Give thanks before dinner. Children—and grownups, too—can forget to send thank-you notes. Here's a way to remember, and to teach your kids to write thank-you notes: Keep in the kitchen, where the mail is placed, a box of thank-you cards and some stamps. When a gift comes in the mail, pull a card out of the box, stick a stamp on the envelope, and set it and the gift at the dinner place of its owner. That way, the blank card is staring at the child, who doesn't eat until the card is written.

A thank-you note is a small gesture that carries a large dividend. Teaching your children to send thank-you notes is a lesson they will carry with them for the rest of their lives.

Print pictures for our troops. Send a photo and letter all in one to a service person you love. Print some pictures off the computer on one side of a piece of photo paper and write a letter on the other side. Your loved one will receive a picture or pictures *and* a letter. You can set up as many pictures as you can get on the paper.

Send video greetings. Our service men and women deployed overseas need to keep in touch with their children back home. Here's what one dad did to keep in touch with his children when he could not be there for Christmas or birthdays:

While he was gone, he asked a buddy to videotape him reading stories and wishing each child a happy birthday.

With all types of cameras available today, videos can be made whenever possible. It's never easy being away from family, but it is oh-so-much-better than the olden days.

Videos are great because they make it feel like the missing family member is right there in the living room sharing memories. In the old days, many military families would record audio cassettes (and way back, "reel-to-reel" letters), and it was wonderful for children to hear their daddy's voice.

Work on genealogy. At family get-togethers, addresses are often exchanged, but it's easy to forget the relationship once you are back home. So make a simple card to help out. The basic blank card can be purchased at many crafts stores. Card stock or plain paper is fine if your printer doesn't handle another kind. Even small index cards work.

On one side, include your name, address, and e-mail address. (Now you

TRACING THE FAMILY ROOTS

If you've ever been curious about your family roots, but you don't know how to start, here are some genealogy hints to help you:

- Talk to the oldest members of your family. They can give you a list of their older relatives who came before them. Try to tape or video-record their answers. You don't want to miss anything. Remember, once they're gone, so is all the information they have.

- Go to your library or favorite bookstore and get a book on tracing your family roots. There are many good ones available.

- Check courthouses, churches, cemeteries, and libraries for public records, like birth, marriage, death, baptism, probate, military, land purchases, and wills.

- Look for your same last name in telephone books and on Web sites. This works especially well for unusual surnames.

- The military may also provide a wealth of information for deceased members. The library can give you the addresses for the different branches so you can write and request records.

Good luck with your search, but be warned, it can be addictive.

know what to do with all those left-over address labels!) On the back, list two to three generations of your family's names, dates of birth, and countries and states of birth.

Have on hand some cards with blank lines indicating the above information to give to the long-lost cousins so they can fill out the information for you. Once you get home, you will know where they fit in the genealogy. If you're a really efficient person, store the cards in separate envelopes.

Every little bit of information helps. You never know how you may be able to link things together.

Share your anniversary. Share a special wedding anniversary (a 30th, 40th, or even 50th) with the members of your wedding party.

For instance, you might purchase round, stained-glass sun-catchers with flowers, birds, and butterflies on them and send them to the ladies who were your wedding attendants and flower girl at your wedding.

The children of the anniversary couple can compile an album of memories with letters and cards sent from friends or relatives you have known for many years.

OUR ANIMAL FRIENDS

Trick with a treat. If your pet won't take a pill, try disguising it with peanut butter. Most pets eagerly lick the peanut butter and never realize there's a pill going down the hatch.

Save a turtle with duct tape. If you see a turtle with a cracked shell, you may be able to offer first aid by taping the split shell with duct tape. Obviously, the turtle may have other injuries, but it may be worth a try.

Make pet beds from recycled materials. Use a zippered pillow cover to make pooch or kitty a new bed. Fill the pillow cover with wood shavings, then zip it closed. If your cat loves the crinkly sound of plastic bags, you can also stuff a pillow cover with them.

Stop the jingling of pet tags. Buy adhesive-backed felt and cover the wrong side of pet tags to muffle the clanging.

Clean pet bowls with salt. When pet bowls get crusty, pour on a good helping of salt and scrub with a sponge. It may take several tries to remove the mineral residue, but salt's abrasiveness will do the job.

Chapter 12

■———————————■

Life's Little Messies

Life presents us with challenges and problems—big and small—every day, and we just have to deal with them. I like to call them "life's little messies." This chapter has hints to help you deal with some of your little messies. There are hints on preparing and dealing with storms and natural disasters, helping others when you don't have a disaster of your own, maintaining your car and taking it on the road (and being safe when you do), and coping with travel emergencies.

HELPING OTHERS IN NEED

Donate food painlessly. To make it easy to donate to your local food bank, get one item for it each time you grocery shop. When the bag in your kitchen is full, deliver it.

Also keep a running list of prices of donated food for tax purposes.

Help the needy. Many churches help support food banks and other social service agencies. One way to donate is to buy the weekly grocery-store specials, keep what you need, and give the rest to the church. Also look for "buy one and get one free" specials, and donate one.

Donate nonperishables to a food bank. If you want to donate items to a food bank to help those in need, especially after a disaster, choose products that show up on your own shopping list week after week, especially nonperishable items. Canned items like vegetables, spaghetti, ravioli, meat, and tuna are good choices. So, pick up a few extra canned items when you're out shopping to pass along. This won't put a big dent in your budget, and if everyone pitches in, think of all the food that will be donated. Food banks and other organizations *don't* want exotic, partially consumed, expired, or homemade items. These cannot be used.

Give to Stamps for Children. The nonprofit organization Stamps for Children has shipped, conservatively, more than 19 million canceled stamps (about 4 tons) all over the country in their 21 years. A lot of kids have benefited from these stamps.

E-mail and electronic bill payments have certainly reduced the use of stamps, but there are still plenty out there.

Save all your canceled stamps and send them along to Stamps for Children. They are recycled and sent to children's organizations. Send the stamps to: Stamps for Children, Harold Effner, 117 Court Street, Suite A, Elkland, PA 16920.

Donate your old cell phone. One way donated cell phones are used is to benefit survivors of domestic violence. The phone is a lifeline for someone faced with an emergency situation. Refurbished cell phones can only call "911" and other nonemergency help numbers, such as a domestic violence shelter.

Here's how to help: First, deactivate your phone service and erase all personal information. Go to www.wirelessfoundation.org/CallToProtect, where you'll find detailed directions for removing personal information from a cell phone by entering the manufacturer and model number. Then, mail the phone to Call to Protect, 2555 Bishop Circle West, Dexter, MI 48130. Be sure to include the battery and charger, if possible. The phone and mailing expenses are tax-deductible, so be sure to print off a tax receipt from the Web site.

Also, start a collection box in your office or neighborhood. When you have several phones to donate, mail them in—it's that easy!

This would be a perfect project for a service group. Folks, clean out that drawer of "old" cell phones, batteries, and chargers.

Donate extra books and DVDs. Take books and extra movies to your local American Legion post to be sent to our soldiers. They can watch the movies on laptop computers.

Be sure to call the posts first to see what is needed. Why not include a note of support to let our service members around the world know we care about them?

Donate old glasses. Lions Clubs

International collects old eyeglasses to redistribute them to the needy. They usually have drop boxes at restaurants and other public places. To find a box in your area, call the Lions Club, which should be happy to help you.

They also accept lenses (preferably in pairs). So, take a few minutes and look through your home to gather old glasses and drop them off.

But keep a spare pair of glasses. When you get ready to donate your old eyeglasses to the Lions Club, keep the most recent old pair you have in case you break your current pair. Always carry an extra pair of glasses every time you go out of town, just in case.

Donate disposable silverware. Save prepackaged plastic flatware from takeout restaurants instead of throwing them out. After saving a couple of bagfuls, take them to the local food shelter.

Make thrift stores work better. Educating the public about what not to drop off would be helpful to thrift stores and to those of us wanting to donate items. For instance, don't just drop off the leftovers after a garage sale. Throw away dirty, broken items. If you wouldn't use or wear them, don't donate them.

Perhaps thrift stores and trash companies should work together. A trash company could donate trash service to the store (as an outreach to the community), and thrift stores might be able to handle the donations more easily.

If your thrift shop is short on volunteers, write up a form letter and ask for help from your local high schools and churches (explain what's needed—sorting, folding, hanging clothes—and let them know it's easy enough that anyone could do it!). You might be amazed at the response.

Should you donate in the name of others? When we printed a letter from a reader about a friend who made charity donations in the reader's name but made them to her own favorite charity and asked readers for input, we got a *lot* of responses. Here are some of the comments:

- Don from Texas says: "Next time, tell your friend that you very much appreciate the idea of a charitable donation and that you in fact have a dear favorite charity that you enjoy donating to. Then tell her about your favorite charity and the good that it does."

- Barb of Minnesota says: "Maybe, when someone receives a notice that a gift has been given to a charity in his or her name, the person should make a note of it and, on the next gift-giving opportunity, give a gift to her favorite organization. That way, both organizations will receive needed funds."

- Jennifer of Arkansas says: "If someone is donating to a charity in your name and you want that person to donate to your charity, perhaps a little role reversal would do the trick. Donate in that person's honor at least once and ask him or her which charity he or she would prefer. Maybe the person would get the hint and do the same for you."

- Suzie in Texas says: "I volunteer many hours a month for my charity, but would be thrilled if my family chose a charity and donated to it in my name instead of giving me funny house slippers or fruitcake."

- Charlene, via e-mail, says: "I have had the same thing done to me. A present to someone is a thoughtful personal touch that gives a feeling of being loved. There are many ways to make a person feel loved through gifting, and this isn't it."

END OF LIFE

Record funeral arrangements. Use your digital camera to take two pictures of each flower arrangement at a loved one's funeral—the spray itself and the card at close range to read the sentiment and signature. Using the sign-in book and florist cards, it should be possible to send thank-you cards and a lovely photo to the kind people who remembered your relative.

Help out. Instead of taking food to a family following a death, take ground coffee, tea (instant or bags), and soft drinks, disposable plates and cups, napkins and paper towels, utensils, toilet tissue, or a bag of ice. All of these things are really needed.

Leave your address in the guest book. When you attend a funeral or memorial service, be sure to leave your address—not just your name—in the guest book. The family may want to acknowledge your attendance at this difficult time, but won't be able to unless you let them know how to get in touch with you.

COPING WITH STORMS AND OTHER DISASTERS

Plan fire strategy. Before a home fire happens, have a family meeting to determine a safe meeting place for the entire household—members and pets—to gather after they have evacuated the home. Consider it a check-in point.

This could help prevent a child

being in the backyard and safe while the parent is worried in the front yard or thinking the child is still in a burning home.

This "little" drill could save many lives, including those of firefighters who risk their lives to save yours and your family's.

Prepare for emergency evacuation. If you have school-age children, place a copy of their last report card and a copy of their immunization records in your emergency preparedness kit that you will take with you in case you must evacuate your home in an emergency.

Get a cell-phone charger for your

HOME OFFICE CONCERNS

Here are some disaster preparation considerations for people who work from home:

• Do you have enough paper for your printer(s)? How about ink and toner cartridges for copiers and laser printers?

• Is all your work backed up on the computer? Could you get to the backup copies quickly if you had to?

• Do you own several battery-operated radios that can get weather forecasts? They could be a lifesaver in a storm or if the power goes out. Change batteries several times a year. Battery-powered wall clocks are good—they keep running through a power outage.

• Is your vehicle fully serviced and ready to go? Change the timing belt in the engine. If it breaks, you are in for expensive repairs—maybe a new engine.

• Usually, cell phones will work. But most cordless-phone manufacturers recommend having at least one wired (noncordless) phone in the house. Remember, cordless phones will not work without electricity.

car. A useful hint for cell-phone users who may lose electricity at home once in a while: Have a car charger handy so you can still use the cell phone by charging it in your car.

Put together an evacuation kit. Hurricane, flood, fire—any of these disasters could happen suddenly, and you might have to evacuate quickly from your home. What would you take? An evacuation kit should include such things as water, food, a first-aid kit, and important papers. And don't forget about any prescriptions you will need.

Assemble these things and put the majority of them in a suitcase, which you keep in your car. Have gallon jugs of water and a box of nonperishable foods stored in the garage, and have sleeping bags nearby. We all think that a disaster is not going to happen to us, but if one does, will you be ready?

Keep some cash on hand. There are many things people will say and do to be prepared for a hurricane, but most will forget this: Get a lot of cash! People do not think about the fact that without electricity, businesses cannot cash checks or run credit cards for purchases. That means no food or supplies. Even if you are well outside your home area, you might not be able to use your debit card if your bank within the area of destruction is down and it does not have a backup server.

Use solar lights after storms. When power is lost after a significant weather event, it can take days to restore. But the sun shines soon after a storm and recharges the solar lights. Put them around the house to light your way during the night. They are safer than candles. These solar lights can hold their charge for two to three nights.

Reset the clocks. If you need the exact time to reset clocks after a power outage, just look at your cell phone.

MAINTAINING YOUR VEHICLE

Clean your car without chemicals—for just a few pennies. Here's a hint for people who like their cars sparkling clean, and you'll save on buying expensive car care products. If you don't want to put all those chemicals on your driveway, get a bucket of water, then put a few squirts of mild hair shampoo in the bucket. Then mix it around with a piece of towel. After that, quickly scrub the sudsy water on the car and then rinse it off with a hose. The car will look like it's been through a carwash. and there is no mess left on the driveway.

Wax with shoulder pads. Keep old shoulder pads from clothing. They are excellent for applying wax to vehicles!

Don't get gas when the truck is there. When buying gasoline, do not stop when the tanker truck is unloading. The gas all goes to the bottom by way of a pipe that stirs up all the dirt on the bottom of the tank. You do not want that in your vehicle's tank.

Remove tar with peanut butter. If you have splatters of tar on your car's surface, rub some peanut butter on the tar and then remove it easily with an old towel. It's the oil in the peanut butter that does the trick. Just be sure it's creamy, not crunchy!

Keep your windshield frost-free. Vinegar can help keep your windshield free of frost if you leave your car out overnight in the winter. Use a solution of three parts white or cider vinegar to one part water, and brush it onto your windshield when you park the car for the night.

Keep a heat pack in your car. During cold weather, a simple addition to the emergency items for your car should be chemical heat packs. These can be bought at a medical-supply company or a store that sells hunting and camping gear. They will provide heat in an emergency, which could mean time for help to arrive.

Keep a sunshade in place. In a mini-van with a rather large windshield, it

CAR CARE

Keeping your car's exterior and finish looking good seems to be a never-ending battle. If you don't want to go to the carwash, here are some do-it-yourself car-cleaning hints:

- To protect the finish, wash it with products specifically made for that purpose.
- Be aware that regular household detergents might be too harsh and can dull paint finishes. Wash your car with cleaners that are labeled "zero pH," and rinse with cold to lukewarm water.
- Don't wash or wax your car in direct sunlight, and never use alcohol-based cleaners or polishes. Avoid abrasive or chemical cleaning solvents on the plastic parts of the car.
- Remove bird droppings, splattered insects, tree sap, and gasoline ASAP—before they harden or dry on the paint.
- After washing and rinsing the car, wipe it down with an old towel or a chamois.

is hard to keep a silver folding sunshade upright in the window. If your sun visor hooks into place, you can align the sunshade with the place where visors hook in. Mark the sunshade, then use a needle and some string and make a loop on each side.

You'll be able to unhook the visor, hang the loop over the hook, and latch the visor back into place. Your sunshade will stay in place.

Get motor oil off your hands. Here's an inexpensive way to get motor oil off your hands: Lather liquid soap on dry hands, sprinkle on some baking soda, and work it into the soap lather. Rinse with water.

Freshen your car. Leave an open box of dryer sheets under your car seat—they make an excellent air freshener for the car. It saves on those costly air fresheners that lose their scent in a week's time. When the scent does begin to fade after several weeks, just use the sheets as you normally do.

Refresh your car's air. A little baking soda may be all you'll need to freshen the stale or stinky air in your car.

If the interior carpet and seat are fabric (not leather), sprinkle them with a generous coat of baking soda. Brush or rub it in, leave it on overnight, then vacuum it up. This works great for trunk odors, too.

Find a good repair shop. One way to find a good auto mechanic is to ask local tow-truck drivers. Seasoned tow-truck drivers know what's going on in town.

Keep your keys. Whenever you take your car to a garage or repair shop, remove the house keys from the key ring.

It's easy for anybody to imprint your house keys if he has access to them, and you know what that means—burglary, assault, or even worse!

Keep stuff from sliding around in your trunk. When you buy a new car, the carpet in the trunk may allow

Keep a Shade in Your Car

Always keep a discarded window shade in the trunk of your auto. If you have to get out and change a tire or have any kind of trouble, you can unroll the shade on the ground; it will help keep your clothes clean while you work on the car.

sacks and boxes to slide around. Buy two rolls of mesh shelf liner and spread them across the floor of the trunk to keep things in place.

Check car locks. Check your car door locks. If you rely on your remote door entry every time you park your car, you feel secure that the doors are locked because the driver door and the passenger door are locked. But a mechanical malfunction can cause the rear doors and cargo door to fail to lock. The security alarm can be armed, but the vehicle can be unlocked. Periodically verify that your remote entry does in fact lack all doors.

Check your spare. When you check the air pressure in your tires, take a few extra minutes to check the pressure in your spare also. It could save you from a bigger problem.

Clean the windshield. When the bugs are really bad on the windshield, and you aren't near a service station, use hand wipes that you keep in the car all the time to clean them off. If the wipes start to dry up, just add some more water and alcohol to them.

Teach vehicular knowledge. When your children become of age to drive, make it a point to show them the workings of their cars, how to do routine maintenance (like checking the oil), jump-start a battery, and change a flat tire. Also make emergency kits for them with gloves, a few simple tools, and a roll of duct tape.

Do your own oil change. If you like to change the oil in your vehicles, rather than use the old drip pan and let it sit around, place an empty one-gallon, wide-mouth plastic juice container underneath and collect it that way. When the bottle is full, take it to a local gas station or municipal trash facility, where they recycle it.

Recycling used motor oil is good for the environment and easy on the purse strings when you do it yourself. And the lid helps make saving and transporting the used oil a little less messy.

Secure a handicapped emblem. Here's a hint for using the heavyweight rubber bands that come on vegetables—keep your handicap emblem safe and handy in the car. Place several rubber bands around the sun visor. While driving, slip the handicap emblem (the kind you hang from the rearview mirror) under the rubber bands. In your state it may be illegal to drive with the emblem hanging from the mirror. This keeps the emblem handy and safe so it isn't damaged or lost.

Cover your car mats. In winter and on rainy days, put an old towel down over your car mats. It keeps the car cleaner.

Remove window tinting. It might be possible for you to remove window tinting yourself, but it's going to require some work. There are usually two layers to the film. One is tint, and the other is adhesive. The tint layer is usually easy to remove, while the adhesive is stubborn and can be very hard to remove.

The only way to remove the adhesive is to scrape it off with a razor blade. It's best to use a razor blade attached to a handle (available at hardware stores).

Get a free car wash. When you're gassing up on a rainy day, use the sponge side of the station's windshield squeegee to wipe down the whole car. The rain will rinse it clean.

ON THE ROAD— PREVENTING AND DEALING WITH TRAVEL EMERGENCIES

Hide a spare key. If you need to hide a key on your car (in case you lock your keys in the car), put it in a place that is seldom looked at, and use one of those magnetic key devices. Don't tape a spare key behind the license plate, where thieves can easily find it.

Shield your hands to pump gas. Here's a use for the plastic sleeves your newspaper comes in. Fold them and put them in the pocket of your car door. When you stop for gas, slip the plastic sleeve over your hand and up your arm as far as it will go. Then use that hand to touch everything at the pump. When you're done, it comes off easily, and you can throw it away. You will no longer smell like the gas you've been pumping.

Take your gas receipts. When you purchase gasoline at "pay at the pump" stations, be sure to take your gas receipt from the pump. Vital information is contained on these slips of paper.

Be safe when getting gas. Here is a safety hint for women traveling alone: When you pull into a service station— or anywhere, for that matter—don't turn off the car and get out right away. Instead, casually look around and take note of the surroundings and other people at the fuel pumps. Then get out and go about your business, but don't let your guard down. It sounds a bit paranoid, but the times we live in require caution.

Lock that car, no matter who you are. It is extremely important to lock your vehicle at the gas-station pump, even for a few seconds. You can have everything stolen out of your car during an "unplanned" trip to the gas-station attendant for a receipt because the pump did not give one. Everything can be taken from your vehicle in about 60 seconds.

If your electronic organizer, cell phone, pager, and purse are taken, you will have to replace everything. You'll also have to get credit-card charges made by the thieves canceled. It only takes one time, one minute, to be cleaned out. Now you know better.

If you walk with the aid of a cane, you could never run from someone or run after someone. But everyone, physically challenged or not, should heed this advice.

Get the gas cap off easily. If you have small hands and arthritis, you probably have a really hard time getting your car's locking gas cap off, especially in the winter. A rubbery jar-lid gripper works wonderfully to loosen a gas cap, so carry one in your car.

Keep duct tape in your car. When you have a minor accident—a fender bender—duct tape can save the day.

You may be able to duct-tape a damaged bumper, or a rear corner of a travel trailer, back together until you can get to the repair shop.

Keep info on the front seat. If you drive long distances alone, when you leave, have your itinerary on the front seat, attached to a copy of your living will. In case of an accident, also have contacts on the bottom of the itinerary.

When traveling to visit relatives, write the name of the person you are going to visit on an index card, along with the name of another contact person, and tape the cards to your dash.

If you are in an accident, there will be no time lost by emergency personnel trying to figure out how to contact a family member to assist in your care when time might be of the essence.

Keep info on family cars. It's a good idea to keep a file with info on the makes, models, colors, and license plate numbers of the cars your family—and extended family—members drive. When family members travel, having this information is crucial to help in locating them in case of an on-the-road emergency or delay.

Keep emergency contacts in the car. Keep a list of emergency contact numbers in the glove compartment with your motor-vehicle registration. List family, friends, a pastor, or someone who should be contacted in case of a serious injury in an accident.

Keep a disposable camera in your car. Keep a disposable camera in your car in the glove compartment. If you have an accident, you can take pictures right away for your insurance company. Replace the camera at Christmas and the Fourth of July.

Document an accident. If you are involved in an auto accident, being able to document it with photos can be invaluable. Take every angle necessary to show any damage to your car or any other car involved. Be sure to get license plates, too.

If you have a cell phone that has a camera, great! If not, a disposable camera will do the trick. It will be very helpful when dealing with the insurance claims. Just keep one in your purse or briefcase.

Here's more on using a camera in case you have an accident:

- Take a picture of the other drivers and their companions.

- Get the road surface, and snap their license plate and driver's license.

- If there is a street sign nearby, get it. If possible, include a clock or watch in the photograph. Later, when the accident report is filled out, you will need much information.

Refresh your skills. Check with your neighborhood community center about defensive driving classes. They are inexpensive, provide a lot of valuable information, and save you money on car insurance. For everyone, young and old, a driving "refresher" course is valuable in several ways.

Keep emergency numbers with you. It's important to keep emergency contact numbers listed in the glove compartment of your automobile when you travel. It is also important to list them in your cell phone. Put them under "Ice" (in case of emergency) in your contact list. First-responders will also look in the cell phone for your contacts under this listing.

How to stick together on a dark road. You know how hard it is to follow another car in the dark—all cars look alike. If you have to follow a family member or friend on a long trip at night through some traffic and on the freeway, here's a way to keep track of each other. Put a dome-shaped "push" light in your car. (This type of light uses batteries—you just push on the dome and it stays lit until you push it again.) Put one in each of the cars that are traveling together; even when you get separated, you will know which car you are looking for.

Record rental car info. Here's a hint for all of us who rent cars: Take a picture of the dashboard, including the mileage and fuel gauge, with your cell phone or camera when returning the vehicle. This will confirm the mileage and that the fuel tank was full when returned, thus eliminating any possible future disagreements.

One more consideration for renting a car. When renting a car, make sure that the renter has a valid driver's license. If you try to rent a car and your license has expired, you will be stranded at the airport.

Remember where you parked. To remember where you parked your car at work, the mall, or a concert or other event, use your cell-phone's camera to take a photo of where the car is parked. When you head back to the car, simply look at your photo.

Copy CDs in case of theft. A car break-in can result in the loss of an entire CD collection. Instead of carry-

ing CDs in your car, burn all of your collection onto the computer and only put CD copies in your car.

Take your belongings out of the car. Never, never, never leave all your belongings in your car while taking in just what will be needed for that night in a hotel or motel. If your car is stolen from the motel parking lot, the car and your belongings may never be recovered. Your homeowners insurance may cover a maximum of $1,000 on contents, which wouldn't begin to pay for all that was lost. Either don't take as much luggage with you when you travel, or plan to take it inside.

Take I.D. photos. When you go on a family vacation, take digital pictures of your kids in the clothes they will be wearing on the days of air travel. Print out the pictures with names and emergency contact numbers just in case you get separated. Give the children a copy of them in their carry-on travel bags, and the adults, too.

Share your itinerary. Whenever you travel, e-mail a copy of your itinerary to everyone you are planning on seeing during your trip. Include not only the flight plans but also the names and phone numbers of those you plan to see, including the street addresses and (when possible) the approximate dates when you hope to visit them. Also send a copy to your own e-mail account so you can quickly look up the addresses to find a map to their homes or call to get directions.

Have an emergency contact. If you and your spouse normally drive or fly together when you travel, designate an adult child as an emergency contact should there be an accident and both of you are incapacitated. Give your designee a medical power of attorney.

Travel with binder clips. Keep a binder clip or two (from an office supply store) in your travel bag. You can use them to hold hotel-room drapes shut or for holding the rolled-up end of a partially used toothpaste tube. They also make great chip clips and bookmarks. You will find many uses for them if you have an RV, so keep a supply of different-sized clips in it.

Travel comfortably with a bad back. If you have a bad back and need a cushion when you travel by car or sit someplace for a while, take a cushion with you in a tote bag. It is easy to carry and easy to use without having to take the cushion out of the bag. Just grab your bag and you are ready to go.

An inflatable bath pillow or something similar can also travel with you easily. This is good to know when you are flying, too, as many airlines no longer supply pillows or have only a few on board.

Give yourself a spritz when feeling hot or stressed. Carry a small mister bottle filled with water in your purse when you're on the road. When you're hot and uncomfortable, or feeling stressed, give yourself a small spritz. It's quite refreshing. You can add a drop or two of lavender essential oil to the water for a calming effect, especially at night in your hotel room.

Keep a travel bag ready. Keep a travel bag packed at all times, stocked with small plastic bags with your "doctor stuff." When you travel with your family, designate someone to pack the medical items someone might need on a trip (often this is Mom). Keeping the travel bag replenished after every trip saves a lot of time and money when you're getting ready to travel.

Also make a copy of your travel schedule (where you are going and times, dates, airlines, for both ways) and put it in your bags in the event that a bag does get lost—the airline can send it where it should be. Put it in one of the front zipper compartments.

Keep an emergency bag packed. When you take family trips, the chief packer is usually so concerned that everyone else has what he or she needs that you always leave something out of your bag that you desperately need.

So, learn to keep you own bag mostly ready to go. Load your overnight bag with a small container of everything you need (deodorant, lotion, facial soap, makeup remover). Also have an extra pair of undies, nightgown, swimsuit, flip-flops, socks, and little things that could easily be forgotten. Keep a list attached to the bag of the things that you can't keep packed, like your makeup, phone and charger, and contact-lens solution.

This bag can be a lifesaver if you become suddenly ill and your doctor sends you immediately to the hospital—with no trip home to pack a bag. The bag will make it easy for someone to go home and get the things you need, with a bag that is mostly packed.

Make an I.D. for your suitcase. If you frequently travel out of the country, make an 8½-by-11-inch I.D. for each of your suitcases. Print these on

Be Safe While Traveling: Don't Open That Door!

Here is a very instructive hint from a reader:

"On a car trip back from Florida recently, my husband and I, along with our faithful Lab, stopped in the late afternoon at a well-known motor court for the night. We were assigned a room away from the main office in the second section. Only two other cars had checked in at a distance from our room.

"Shortly after dark, a loud and demanding knock came at our door. The dog barked furiously as my husband said, 'Don't open the door!' Insistent banging on the door continued as I slightly pulled back a corner of the window curtain to see a young man insisting in a hurried voice that we should come out and see what is going on.

"So we phoned the office, and the person said someone would be down immediately with a security guard. A few minutes later she phoned to say that as soon as they got there, three men jumped in a van and sped away. They were unable to get a license-plate number but stressed that we did the right thing by not opening the door.

"People should be warned to never open a door unless you know the person on the other side. I felt this warning worthy of passing on."

Never open a motel or hotel door for anyone unless you are expecting the person. When in doubt, call the front desk. It doesn't matter if it's 10 a.m. or 10 p.m.—don't become a victim.

the computer, place each one in a plastic sheet protector, and place either on top of your clothing or in the mesh pocket on the inside of your suitcase.

The first telephone number could be that of a friend in your hometown who knows where you are in case of emergency, and the second number is the home or hotel where you are staying.

When you travel abroad. Here are some hints for world travelers:

- Notify your credit-card company. Before you travel abroad, call your credit-card company/companies for the cards you plan to use. Let them know the countries and the dates on which you plan to be gone. The companies may give you a number to call while you are away in case there are any problems using the cards. Also call them when you get back.

- Cell phones that work in the United States might not work in European or other foreign countries. You might consider getting a special cell phone or an international plan to use. Another option is to purchase a prepaid international telephone card that you can use to make international calls. Call the toll-free number on the back of the card to find out the local access number for the countries you go to.

- It is nice to save a small amount of foreign currency from one trip until the next so that you are prepared to make telephone calls, take a cab, or purchase a soft drink while in transit.

- If you are concerned about pickpockets, take along some large safety pins. Use one to pin paper money to the inside of your pocket, and another to pin the pocket closed. This makes for a bit of fumbling when you need to pay for something, but you definitely are more secure. Don't carry a lot of cash or valuables, and keep your passport and travel documents in a safety pouch (around your neck, inside your clothing, or in a money belt).

- Make photocopies of passports, tickets, and credit cards to leave with a trusted person in case these are stolen.

Avoid illness while traveling. If you will be traveling to another country, consult an infectious-disease doctor or your primary-care physician several months before you go. Many foreign destinations require one or more vaccinations, and this is best done many months in advance.

Travel with a smoke detector. Always take a portable smoke detector along when you travel (it just hooks over the top of any door). You can pack it when you visit friends and relatives, too—you'd hope everyone checks his or her detectors regularly, but you never know.

Friends and colleagues may think you're a little odd, but the alarming number of house fires that happen because there is no smoke detector or the battery is dead is staggering. Play it safe!

I.D. your laptop. When you are traveling with a laptop, place an address sticker label on the inside edge of your computer. It will save your laptop from being taken by someone else who had the exact same laptop while going through the security checkpoint. You will be able to quickly and efficiently identify your computer.

PRACTICE FLIGHT SAFETY

When you are flying, it's important to pay attention to safety instructions from flight attendants or videos because the information can save your life if there's a crash. Here are some hints that you should know from the Federal Aviation Administration:

- When you board the plane and sit down, make a mental note of where the exits are. Count the rows from your seat to an exit. If there is an emergency, the plane could be dark and smoky. Knowing how far away you are from the exit could be vital. You won't get confused about where to get out.

- Follow emergency instructions; assume the crash position by putting your head in your hands, and lean on the seat ahead of you to brace yourself.

- Try to stay low, and don't panic. There could be lots of fire and smoke, so breathe slowly.

- Exit the plane as quickly as you can. Leave your luggage or property behind. Head to the exits or to the evacuation slide ASAP.

The chances are infinitesimal that a crash could happen, but a few seconds of "safety school" could save your life.

Index

Underscored page references indicate boxed text.

Index

C

Index

Index

Index

Index

Ironing clothing, 158–59, _158_
IRS forms, sealing, 208
Isopropyl alcohol for cleaning, 104

J

Jam, 305–6, _312_, 330
Jars
  canning, 333
  cleaning out, 38, 237, 311–12
  label removal from, 20, 68–69
  for leftover food, 325
  memory, 365
  opening, 325, 336–37
  recycling, _21_
Jeans
  fading, preventing, _62_, 141
  hems, preventing roll-up of, 141
  identifying personal, 114
  laundering, _62_, 141, _142_
Jelly, 305–6, _312_, 330
Jewelry. _See also specific type_
  cleaning, 122, 163
  downsizing, 4
  making, _374_
  packing for travel, 436
  shopping for, _123_, _125_
  storing, 122–25, 163
  unknotting, 122–23
Juice cubes, making, 301–3
Junk mail, 209

K

Keeping in touch with people, 210, 454–57, _454_
Keyboards, cleaning/stabilizing computer, 112, 193–94
Keys, personal, 48–49, 465
Kidney beans, _268_
Kitchen
  appliances, 103
  cleaning, 61–80
  decluttering, _5_
  fires, avoiding, 237–38
  flowerpot in, for storage, 24
  island in, adding, 339
  pliers in, 20
Kitchen towels. _See_ Dish towels
Knitting, keeping track of, 383–84
Knitting needles, organizing, 385

Knit tops, 155
Knives, 17, 37

L

Labels
  for appliance cords, 192–93
  for checkbooks, 222
  on clothing, 133–35
  for coins, wrapped, 213
  for favorite household products, 58
  for freezer bags, 324–25
  for Halloween treats, 213
  for herbs, 330
  for iced tea, 304
  for leftover food, 320
  for lemons, 331
  for linens, 131
  making, 22
  for medications, 393–94
  for moving, 227
  for packages, 36
  for phone books, 208
  removing, 20, 68–69
  for spices, 330
Ladder safety, _187_
Laminate floors, caring for, 173–74
Lampshades, cleaning, 108
Lasagna, 252–54
Latex gloves, loosening stuck and using, 84, 106
Laundering clothing. _See also specific item_
  basics, 139–44
  bleach for, _146_
  day of week for, _134_
  delicates, 142, 144
  family involvement in, _134_, 136–37
  jean fade prevention, _62_, 141
  labels on clothing and, 133–35
  organizing, 136–39
  prewash spray for, homemade, _145_
  quiz, _143_
  sorting, 136–39
  stain removal, 149–53, _150_, _152_
  symbols and, laundry, 139
  water temperature and, _135_, 136
Laundry detergent, 139, 143
Laundry symbols, 139
Leather furniture, cleaning/caring for, 160
Leaves, uses for fall, _373_
Leftover food, 319–23, _320_, _322_, _323_

Index

Index

Index

Index

Index

About the Author

Heloise is an internationally syndicated newspaper columnist. Her column "Heloise to the Rescue" is featured monthly in *Good Housekeeping*, where she is a contributing editor. As a speaker, she travels the country sharing her wisdom with college students, charity organizations, and business and civic groups.

Heloise is the author of a dozen best-selling books with more than 7 million copies in print. She is a frequent guest on national and local radio and television shows, including *The View* and the *Today* show. She lives in San Antonio, in her home state of Texas, with her husband, David, and their miniature schnauzer, Cabbie.

Heloise Central, located in her home, is a beehive of activity. She records in her Heloise Studio and stays busy researching and testing hints with her many assistants. Please visit her Web site at www.heloise.com.